The Unsettled Land
State-Making & the Politics of Land in Zimbabwe
1893–2003

D1457331

Books on Southern Africa
published by James Currey, Weaver Press
& Ohio University Press

Jocelyn Alexander
The Unsettled Land
State-making &
the Politics of Land
in Zimbabwe
1893–2003

David Maxwell
African Gifts
of the Spirit
Pentecostalism
& the Rise of a Zimbabwean
Transnational Religious Movement

Patrick Harries
Butterflies, Barbarians
& Swiss Missionaries
in South-East Africa

The Unsettled Land
State-Making & the Politics of Land
in Zimbabwe
1893–2003

JOCELYN ALEXANDER

Lecturer in Commonwealth Studies
University of Oxford

James Currey
OXFORD

Weaver Press
HARARE

Ohio University Press
ATHENS

James Currey
73 Botley Road
Oxford OX2 0BS

Weaver Press
P.O. Box A1922
Avondale
Harare

Ohio University Press
19 Circle Drive, The Ridges
Athens, Ohio 45701

British Library Cataloguing in Publication Data

Alexander, Jocelyn
   The unsettled land: state-making and the politics of land in Zimbabwe, 1893–2003
   1. Land Tenure - Zimbabwe - History. 2. Nation-Building - Zimbabwe
   3. Zimbabwe - Politics and government
   I. Title
   968.9'1

ISBN 10: 0-85255-893-7 (James Currey cloth)
ISBN 13: 978-0-85255-893-5 (James Currey cloth)
ISBN 10: 0-85255-892-9 (James Currey paper)
ISBN 13: 978-085255-892-8 (James Currey paper)

ISBN 10: 1-77922-055-3 (Weaver Press paper)
ISBN 13: 978-1-77922-055-4 (Weaver Press paper)

Library of Congress Cataloguing-in-Publication Data
available on request

ISBN 10: 0-8214-1735-5 (Ohio University Press cloth)
ISBN 13: 978-0-8214-1735-5 (Ohio University Press cloth)
ISBN 10: 0-8214-1736-3 (Ohio University Press paper)
ISBN 13: 978-0-8214-1736-2 (Ohio University Press paper)

Typeset in 10.5/11.5 pt Monotype Ehrhardt
by Frances Marks, Harare
Printed in Great Britain
by Woolnough, Irthlingborough

Contents

Contents

List of Maps

Acknowledgements

In the course of a project that has taken as long as this one, the range of debts incurred is bound to be enormous. I cannot hope to mention all of those who have helped me in one way or another, and so I restrict my thanks here to a select group. Terence Ranger and JoAnn McGregor must take responsibility for much of my understanding of Zimbabwe, and for the great pleasure I've taken in coming to that understanding, however flawed. They make up a central part of a peripatetic community of scholars, most often encountered in Oxford, who have listened to my seminar papers, read my chapters, and given me forthright criticism over many years. David Maxwell, Gavin Williams, Robin Palmer, Marieke Clarke, Diana Jeater, William Beinart, Richard Werbner and Ken Wilson deserve many thanks. The book was revived while on generous leave from the University of Bristol. My colleagues there, especially Kirsty Reid and Robert Bickers, were never short of good humoured support.

In Zimbabwe, I must thank the many people who spent their days explaining and debating history and politics and policy with me in Chimanimani and Insiza, Harare and Bulawayo. Lancelot Moyo sadly died before the completion of this book. He was one of my most incisive and insightful guides. Chamunorwa Manyoni Ndlovu and Marvin Phiri accompanied me on my district interviews, and helped me with much more than the interpretation of language. The University of Zimbabwe offered me an intellectual home. I owe many thanks to Pius Nyambara, Eira Kramer, and Joe Mtisi for the hospitality of recent years, and to Sam Moyo and Brian Raftopoulos who have, in their different ways, done so much to shape my views on Zimbabwean politics, agrarian change and the 'crisis' since 2000. Were it not for the harmony and efficiency of the National Archives of Zimbabwe I could not have written this book. I must also thank a number of people who made papers in their possession available to me: Phillip Warhurst allowed me access to his copious notes from the Rhodesian Criminal Investigation Department, Marshall Murphree made his copies of delineation reports available to me, Bill Kinsey gave me access to hard-to-come-by papers and documents on agrarian policy. I am, in addition, indebted to Nigel James for his generous advice on map-making.

Dori Kimel's tolerance has been tested more than once, but he has remained an unstinting source of peace, love and understanding.

List of Acronyms & Abbreviations

ADA	Agricultural Development Authority
Agritex	Department of Agricultural and Technical Services
ANC	African National Congress
ARDA	Agricultural and Rural Development Authority
BSAC	British South Africa Company
BSAP	British South Africa Police
CFU	Commercial Farmers' Union
CID	Criminal Investigation Department
CIO	Central Intelligence Organization
CNC	Chief Native Commissioner
CSC	Cold Storage Commission
DA	District Administrator
DC	District Commissioner
DERUDE	Department of Rural Development
GAPWUZ	General Agricultural and Plantation Workers' Union of Zimbabwe
ICFU	Indigenous Commercial Farmers' Union
LAA	Land Apportionment Act
LGPO	Local Government Promotional Officer
MDC	Movement for Democratic Change
MIA	Ministry of Internal Affairs
NAD	Native Affairs Department
NC	Native Commissioner
NDP	National Democratic Party
NLHA	Native Land Husbandry Act
PA	Provincial Administrator
PC	Provincial Commissioner
PNC	Provincial Native Commissioner
TLA	Tribal Land Authority
TTL	Tribal Trust Land
Vidco	Village Development Committee
Zanla	Zimbabwe African National Liberation Army
Zanu	Zimbabwe African National Union
Zanu(PF)	Zimbabwe African National Union (Patriotic Front)
Zapu	Zimbabwe African People's Union
ZCTU	Zimbabwe Congress of Trade Unions
ZFU	Zimbabwe Farmers' Union
Zipra	Zimbabwe Peoples' Revolutionary Army

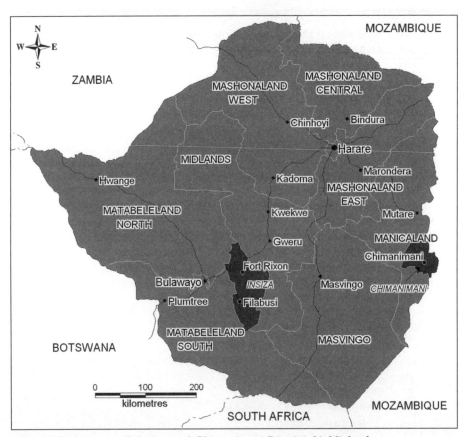

Map 1 Zimbabwe, with Insiza and Chimanimani Districts highlighted
Source: Map derived from mapping © Collins Bartholomew (2000), reproduced by kind permission of
Harper Collins Publishers

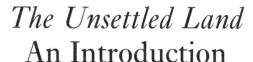

The Unsettled Land
An Introduction

The 'unsettled land' is a metaphor with manifold meanings in Zimbabwean history. It conjures settler fantasies of an empty, unproductive land, ripe for exploitation. It encompasses the harsh disruptions of colonial conquest, eviction and agrarian intervention. In the territory that was to become Southern Rhodesia, the violence of military subjugation was followed by the displacements of territorial segregation. Africans faced eviction, sometimes several times over, from their homes and farms. Half of the country's agricultural land, and much of the most fertile, was designated for European occupation, while Africans were forced into reserves. Once there, policies of agricultural and social 'development' ensured that they had to move and move again, to settle in straight lines or on a particular category of land. In the 1950s, many were denied land in the reserves altogether, a measure that vastly expanded the burgeoning ranks of African nationalism. Land was central once again in provoking the brutal conflict of the liberation war, and in ultimately bringing about the demise of the settler state.

The 'unsettled land' equally refers to the ambitions of post-independence agrarian reform. Settlement patterns in the former reserves remained subject to state efforts to order and reorder the use of the land. At the same time, the state oversaw a tightly regulated process of resettling the vast farms once exclusively owned by whites with black smallholders. Great tracts of 'white' land nonetheless remained very visibly untouched twenty years after independence. In 2000, they became the subject of a hotly contested process of land occupation, led by veterans of Zimbabwe's liberation war and backed by official sanction. Zimbabwe's landscape was once again dramatically unsettled, as hundreds of thousands of black Zimbabweans moved onto 'white' land. The partisan violence, international isolation and economic collapse that accompanied these momentous movements underlined them as a crucial turning point in Zimbabwean history.

This book is not, however, just about the geography of displacement, expropriation, and re-appropriation: most broadly, the 'unsettled land' refers to the making and unmaking of authority over people and the land on which they lived and farmed. As Sara Berry writes, struggles over land in Africa are 'as much about power and the legitimacy of competing claims to authority, as about control of property per se.'[1] State interventions created and transformed the institutions that shaped access to

1

and the use of land, and they created and transformed the means by which access and use was justified and legitimised. In so doing, they were intended to fashion institutions of governance able to order, discipline, develop, and at times represent, the majority of Zimbabwe's people. Settling the land was fundamentally about building and legitimising the state, and its successes and failures profoundly shaped Zimbabwe's political allegiances, identities and social relations.

In focusing on the period from World War II to the 'crisis' of 2000, the book offers a fresh perspective on the forces that led to the extraordinary displacement of Zimbabwe's white farmers in the name of long-delayed revolution. In focusing on both the making of policy and its often tortuous implementation, the book explores the local state as a key locus for debate over the relationships between people and land, power and authority. This is a story in which questions of state-making and ideology, of resistance, coercion and consent, take centre stage. It is a story in which contested histories loom large.

Colonial States

The establishment of settler rule in Zimbabwe rested on violent dispossession. The wars of conquest fought under the auspices of Cecil Rhodes' British South Africa Company (BSAC) the 1890s paved the way for a rapacious period of 'speculation and violence' in which African cattle was looted, land alienated, and labour coerced.[2] One hundred years later, and twenty years after Zimbabwean independence, the division of land between black and white still indelibly marked the Zimbabwean landscape. Its return to political prominence in 2000 seemed to underline the centrality of dispossession to settler rule and to mark it as its most devastating legacy. Certainly, in the glare of international attention Zimbabwe has received since 2000, it is race and dispossession – of both black and white – that have grabbed the bulk of attention, as they have in much scholarly work on Zimbabwean history.[3]

A number of writers have, however, identified another legacy as the key inheritance of colonialism: the nature of the state. Mahmood Mamdani has argued that it is the mode of domination not the mode of accumulation that constituted the most lasting and destructive legacy of colonial rule in Africa as a whole.[4] He contends that colonial rule created a 'bifurcated state' that distinguished between citizens on the one hand and subjects on the other. Citizens – largely limited to the urban and European – enjoyed rights in the civil sphere; subjects languished under the 'despotism' of customary law, institutionalised through the indirect rule of chiefs in rural areas. Post-colonial states succeeded in de-racialising but not in democratising, instead reifying the authoritarian characteristics of indirect rule in a variety of ways, and so maintaining the colonial divisions between urban and rural, citizen and subject. This, Mamdani argues, not economic inequity, was colonialism's most dangerous legacy, and it stands as the key obstacle to democratisation, political stability and an accountable state.

In a very different vein, work on African environmental history and state agrarian intervention has focused on the authoritarian legacies of colonial policies implemented by centralised bureaucracies and legitimated by reference to scientific rationality.[5] James Scott has explored this theme in a broader context. His book *Seeing Like a State* emphasises the inherent conflict between agrarian communities and the grand plans of states imbued with 'high modernist' ideology. High modernism combines a utopian confidence in scientific and technical progress with a desire to expand production, master nature (both human and natural), and produce a rational design for social order. Such ambitions require the state to render the world 'legible', and so it gathers and orders knowledge as a basis for intervention. But high modernism always fails, according to Scott, because it can only produce simplifying, schematic plans incapable of capturing reality and unreceptive to the 'practical knowledge' of farmers.[6] It is nonetheless reincarnated time and again in states that are bureaucratic, ambitious and able to ignore civil opposition. The logic, and repetition, of such state strategies is a key theme in critiques of 'development' in their colonial and post-colonial guises.[7]

Michael Drinkwater's work on Zimbabwe is a particularly sophisticated effort to explain why it is that coercive agrarian policies were produced and reproduced within state bureaucracies despite their repeated failures. Like Mamdani, his emphasis is not on the economic and racial legacies of colonialism but on 'the transformation which occurred in the nature, role and power of the state'.[8] It is not the creation of subjects through indirect rule that interests him, however: chiefly rule and customary law warrant little consideration. Instead, like Scott, he argues that the colonial state took the form of a particular kind of centralised bureaucracy that functioned according to a particular kind of rationality, typical of the modern capitalist state. This state dominated society from on high. In the colonial as in the post-colonial context, it was unable to 'understand' the social and economic workings of African agriculture, instead seeking to impose technical solutions that failed in their own terms and met with repeated resistance. It was, in this view, the inheritance of centralised bureaucracies bound to technical solutions and their coercive implementation that prevented real democratisation and development.

These explorations of customary rule and technocratic bureaucracy have the merit of taking history, ideology and institutions seriously – which is far from always the case[9] – but they stress very different legacies for the state. Their arguments are so different because they tend to treat the colonial state as far more ideologically and bureaucratically homogenous and effective than it was, and to focus on one strand of intervention, one form of power, to the exclusion of others. Such work stands at odds with much recent literature on colonial states, and particularly on settler states, which has stressed the deep divisions among bureaucracies, the divided class and political purposes they sought to serve, and the ways state institutions were shaped by popular struggles, nowhere more so than in the field of 'native administration'.[10] As William Beinart and JoAnn McGregor write, 'the colonial state should not be seen simply as an instrument of intervention, but also as the bearer of complex and conflicting values, with internal tensions and disputes about the most appropriate way to rule.'[11] The colonial state's 'hegemony' was fragile, and there were real limits to its capacity to command, to shape consciousness and identity, and to direct change.[12] The 'customary' local state, so central in Mamdani's analysis, and the centralised, technocratic bureaucracies key to work on agrarian history and development, did not exist in separate worlds: both impinged on the land and on the exercise of authority over it in mutually constitutive ways, and both did so in ideologically mixed and institutionally delicate contexts.

3

The diverse forces at work in colonial states, and the fragility of colonial authority, meant that the state had to make contradictory alliances in order to exercise power. Crucial in this was the role played by missionaries, with their varied ideas of civilisation and individual progress. Such ideas sat uncomfortably alongside the customary and communal appeals of chiefly rule. As Karen Fields writes, missions served the colonial state: 'They aided it practically by mediating the spread of Western culture, and morally by helping to legitimize colonial rule.' But they were 'untidy tools', for they also undercut chiefly rule by attacking as '"heathenism" much that was customary.'[13] In Southern Rhodesia, missionaries' 'civilising mission' antagonised settlers by creating an educated and skilled class of African competitors and by defending African land claims. They undermined the administrative alliances between chiefs, male elders and Native Commissioners, by offering an alternative source of authority, and by challenging polygamous marriages and male control over women's mobility.[14] Nonetheless, their moral and practical utility meant they were not just tolerated, but actively subsidised. They formed a crucial part of the 'thin white line', bolstering the prestige and authority of the white community at large, and so the maintenance of colonial order – if not always in ways approved of by settlers and officials.[15]

Particularly in the inter-war years, missionaries in Southern Rhodesia engaged directly in policies of 'development', and here too they created contradictions.[16] Science and morality, bureaucracy and evangelical zeal, sat side by side, bringing missions into conflict with a jealous Native Affairs Department, and offering alternative visions of African society and authority to those on which administrators sought to build order.[17] The technocrats of the 1940s and 1950s were far more bureaucratic and professional than their inter-war predecessors. They were armed with all the confidence of the high modernist project, and exerted an overwhelming control over policy in these decades. Nonetheless, the practitioners of the sciences of development were neither always in agreement nor so confident as to be unwilling to question their assumptions. And they had to confront an African society with diverse notions of what constituted authority, and to rely on administrators and their hierarchy of appointed chiefs, headmen and village heads for the implementation of policy. Realising the ambitions of the 'technical imagination' was often beyond the state's reach in Southern Rhodesia as elsewhere.[18] Technocrats were brusquely sidelined in the 1960s and 1970s by a shift in emphasis, from the agricultural and economic to the human sciences. Faced with fierce resistance, the Native Affairs Department sought solace in building rule on the basis of assumed cultural differences, differences which handily explained African resistance to the reputed benefits of science. The African relationship to the land, African authority and African society were reconceived as traditional, spiritual, unready for the strict discipline and rationality of high modernism.

The colonial legacy for land and authority thus cannot be construed in terms of simply one or another dominant strand, either of scientific knowledge and bureaucratic practice or of customary rule. The local state is particularly revealing for the light it throws on the negotiated terms by which authority was constructed and power exercised.

The Local State: Negotiating Authority

The focus on institutions and ideology in much of the work discussed so far is important, and they form a central part of this study. But we need to consider the effects of the multiplicity of institutions and ideas at work, and to ask what happened when officials actually intervened in divided and fast-changing African communities. That is, the formulation of policies and promulgation of rules needs to be placed alongside the process of implementation, the process of engagement with colonial 'subjects', through which institutions were built, consent gained, and power given effect. It is in local struggles over power and authority that states must take root.

Mamdani's one-size-fits-all model for the local state tells us little about these struggles. He argues that 'everywhere' rural authority was organised on an ethnic basis, through the 'decentralised despotism' of indirect rule. Thus all colonial powers sought to transform pre-colonial institutions into units of administration, based on the 'tribe', in which chiefs appointed from the centre and answerable only to their administrative superiors exercised unprecedented power under the rubric of customary law.[19] The local colonial state was 'tribal', simply so many variations on the customary. While Mamdani acknowledges that the development of customary rule in settler states was 'informal and protracted', he nonetheless asserts that the delayed turn to indirect rule was simply a matter of formalising a system in which chiefs' duties and obligations were already crucial.[20] But in such cases and more widely this was a much more complex process in which the 'perpetual contest' over authority, labour and property that Berry so fascinatingly explores transformed policy and institutions.[21] Nor were chiefs merely the tools of officialdom: they were everywhere constrained by the diverse demands of their followers, and they had their own frustratingly unpredictable agendas.[22] Struggles within African societies eroded the effectiveness of colonial appointees: the state could determine who could speak, but not what they said; it could delineate and privilege custom and ethnicity, but it could not unilaterally give them meaning and authority.[23]

While Mamdani acknowledges the 'invented' nature of the customary, he is largely concerned to demonstrate its use as a top-down means of legitimising extractive and coercive laws and policies. Recent literature has, however, convincingly questioned the extent to which 'invention' worked as a top-down process. It has emphasised the degree to which law, ethnicity, land tenure and religion – cloaked as unchanging and primordial – were constantly re-shaped, often in ways colonial officials were helpless to control. Terence Ranger has criticised his own use of the term 'invention', preferring Benedict Anderson's 'imagination', so as to underline the extent to which Africans played a central role in what was an ongoing process.[24] Colonial 'inventions' did not so much determine the social order as provoke debates which themselves shaped struggles over authority and resources, remaking the state in the process.[25] The durability of custom, and the intense debates over it, derived from its role in mediating the influences of a changing political economy, of urban and workplace influences, of the new sources of wealth and division that characterised the colonial order. If the imagination of custom was in part a response to capitalism and colonial domination, its effects were often unanticipated by officials and its meanings were hotly contested among Africans.[26]

Custom is at any rate too narrow a seam to mine if we are to understand the production of authority within the local state. In Rhodesia, Drinkwater's rural Africans came face to face with a very different set of ideas, embedded in the arrogant insensitivities of science. Rather than finding common ground in the customary ideology of indirect rule he emphasises that, 'from the outset, white and black misunderstood each other.'[27] Officials and Africans lived in distinct worlds, each operating according to its own impenetrable logic. It was not the chief with his customary garb that stalked this countryside, but, from the 1920s, the technocrats of the Native Affairs Department – the agricultural and pasture officers, the demonstrators and land development officers, armed with the authority of western science, and an unshakeable belief that what they were doing was good for Africans, regardless of what Africans thought. Africans objected to the 'irrationality' of technical development and were met with coercion.

This is indisputably a central aspect of the interaction of officials and Africans in Rhodesia, notably in the 1940s and 1950s, and it played a crucial role in shaping authority over the land. But the focus on the alienating effects of technocratic bureaucracy, on 'misunderstanding' as the root of coercion, obscures the complexities of local state politics. As Sam Moyo has argued, the tendency to see the state as monolithic and alien – as at least implicitly opposed to a static set of rural African institutions that govern behaviour in relation to land use and governance – sorely underestimates the heterogeneous nature of the state and its negotiated involvement in administration and agriculture.[28] Technical officials worked with administrators, they interacted with Africans, and they were divided among themselves. There was certainly no shortage of scientific hubris as justification for coercion, but the coercive tendencies of technical officials were constantly undermined by compromises, as a result of African argument or resistance, as a result of technical officials' self-criticism, and as a result of administrators' concerns for order and even fair play.[29]

The Rhodesian state, though undoubtedly potent, faced tremendous difficulties in building effective means of rule. Like all colonial states, it had to make power productive, rather than simply relying on coercion, and so it had to engage with African agents. The Boards and Councils and hierarchies of chiefs, headmen and village heads that complemented administrative and agricultural bureaucracies proved singularly unreliable, but officials had to work with them. Rural rule was initially about finding effective aids to administration: elaborations of 'custom' and 'tribe' went undeveloped in practice. Customary land tenure, supposedly so crucial to chiefly authority, was much disputed among Native Affairs Department officials and anthropologists, as was the very existence of custom as a coherent set of rules attachable to a 'tribe'.[30] Boards and Councils, with their balance of 'progressives', i.e. educated and Christian Africans, and chiefs, marked an explicit recognition that African society and authority were not one-dimensional. It was possible, at one and the same time, to make claims as an ethnic subject and as a citizen.

The limits to and nature of state authority which made the application of custom such an ambiguous process also applied to technocratic interventions, as the logic of bureaucracy battled against other logics – tied to ideas of paternalism or means of legitimating order through custom, or missionary ideas of civilisation – and did not always win the day. Wary of the disordering effects of coercion, agricultural officials' engagement with rural society drew them into African logics of production and power. Witness, for example, the work of agricultural demonstrators, intended to act as purveyors of agricultural prescription but reinvented at times as aids to new means of accumulation or sources of status; witness the ways in which policies requiring the 'centralisation' of settlement were recast by headmen as a means to bring wayward evictees and migrants under their control, to reassert control over the young, or to expand their own fields.[31]

It is no accident that Drinkwater's treatment jumps from the 1940s and 1950s, the high point of settler technical development, to the modernising policies of 1980s' Zimbabwe, neglecting the two decades prior to independence when technical officials were sidelined in favour of an administrative ideology predicated on the legitimising capacities of custom and chiefly authority. But even in the post-World War II push for 'development', contradictory ideas about African society and capacities sat side by side: Africans were supposed to be modern 'economic men' but they were also still cast as tribesmen bound by custom, and the 'progressive' still had a narrow space within which to speak. The modernising discourse drew its strength from attacking the presumed 'traditional' nature of African society and production, a traditional nature which was at the same time central to administrative strategies of constituting authority. These were two sides of one coin that flipped back and forth. The dividing line between what was deemed 'traditional' and what was deemed 'modern' was a false one, but it was exceptionally useful in constituting and legitimising the state, even if it only did so in a highly unstable way. In the 1960s and 1970s, the legacies of technical development never went away, but were overlain by the newly created 'Tribal Land Authorities', intended to distance the state from its coercive role, counter the rise of nationalism, and legitimise land use as customary.[32] These ambiguities were played out most clearly in the contests over policy implementation, in the troubled process of creating authority over the land, and in the realm of rural politics and local state-making.

Rural Politics and the Problem of Chiefs

The 'modes of domination' central to Rhodesian rule, and which left such an influential legacy for independent Zimbabwe, were contradictory and often unsuccessful. Africans were well aware of the range of competing claims to legitimacy the state made, and drew on these in their interactions with officials. They were not trapped in an ethnic box, nor were they unable to engage with (and transform) the logic of technical development, and they had other sources of inspiration besides – ideas about progress and democracy and rights and nationalism which were combined in novel and subversive ways.

The battle over how to live and farm in the reserves was always politically explosive; it was never detached from the overarching processes of dispossession and exploitation, processes that posed a profound challenge to the state's legitimacy and so to its ability to build institutions of rule. Land alienation, racial segregation and order were central motives in the constitution of chiefly authority, just as they were a central force behind technical development. At its most basic level, chiefly rule was meant to underwrite the system of labour migration and reserves; technical development was seen as, among other things, a means of squeezing more Africans into reserves and denying their demands for land. At the same time, dispossession and discrimination made both difficult to implement. The constant movements of people and chiefs as they were evicted from farm to farm and into reserves, or worked under the 'domestic government' of white farmers,[33] or travelled to towns and mines in search of jobs, made the constitution of chiefly authority an ongoing challenge, and one that the Rhodesian government only truly grasped far too late in the day to allow the construction of 'tribal' rule. The interventions of technical development – all those policies of agricultural and economic improvement – likewise often foundered on the rocks of African anger over their dispossession. Promoting intensive farming, limiting cattle numbers and the size of fields – all were difficult to justify to people able to look over the boundaries of the reserves at the lush lands they had once farmed. Resistance was not so much the result of 'misunderstanding' the science of technical development, of seeing it as 'irrational', as understanding all too well that it was an integral part of the 'trickery' involved in ruling Africans and robbing them of resources.[34]

The technical and the customary came together nowhere more uncomfortably than in the state's efforts to gain the allegiance of chiefs. Chiefs were supposed to be the bearers of customary authority. They were also supposed to aid in the implementation of technical development. This placed them in an unenviable position. As Berry writes, chiefs too were farmers, and they were often as heatedly opposed to eviction and agricultural 'development' as their followers.[35] Moreover, they were engaged with a wider set of ideas, as the work of David Maxwell and others has so eloquently shown for Zimbabwe.[36] It is unsurprising that chiefs should go beyond the 'tribal' world in expressing their views. Zimbabwean chiefs were (and are) an extremely mixed lot: some were young and dynamic, some old and withdrawn; some were literate and Christian, proud of their brick houses and suits, while others eschewed any interaction with the mission world; some were wealthy entrepreneurs while others owned little at all. Some spent years working in mines and cities while others stayed at home; some joined protest movements and nationalist parties, while others threw their lot in with the state, or did both at different times. Some ruled over people of many different ethnic origins, and themselves came from families with no claim to pre-colonial power, while others could trace a lengthy royal history and intimate connection to their followers. This diversity was amplified by the range of alliances chiefs made within and beyond rural society, and by the variegated impact of the settler economy and state. Over the course of the colonial period, it is small wonder that chiefs drew on everything from technical to supernatural precepts, from firmly rooted local histories and moral economies negotiated with Native Commissioners and land owners, to ideas of ethnicity and Christian civilisation and nationalism, in their interactions with the state. As in Stephen Feierman's subtle treatment of African rural societies as an 'unbounded local', chiefs and their allies were able at once to draw on national and international ideas and to ground them in local concerns and traditions.[37]

For African rural politics generally, wearing many hats – teacher, farmer, chief, nationalist, Christian, traditionalist, worker – was the norm not the exception. Involvement in a wide range of associations and institutions was typical. Bierschenk and Olivier de Sardan have argued that a 'diversity of political institutions, cultures and logics' is characteristic of local politics in post-colonial Africa.[38] Such diversity also applies in the colonial period, though perhaps not, as they suggest, to the same extent. It nonetheless makes a mockery of notions of a single African political culture,[39] as well as of the strict divisions between the customary and the modern, so often reified in official discourse and in social analysis, and which find their echo in the characterisation of the state as technocratic and alien and rural society as bounded and traditional. It is also important to emphasise the challenge such diversity and boundary-crossing poses to the binary opposition between collaboration and resistance in which chiefs in the colonial context are straightforwardly cast as conservative and reactionary, if not simply as 'stooges'.[40]

As the chosen intermediaries of the state, chiefs inevitably worked closely with it, but they did so in the service of goals that were often at odds with official intentions. They sought negotiation and compromise, they and their followers dissimulated and drew on the whole grab-bag of what James Scott has called the 'weapons of the weak' when confrontation was deemed counterproductive. And many moved to overt resistance when pressed too hard. The 'weapons of the weak' figure prominently in African strategies of resistance, and the exploration of this field has been central to opening out a whole range of previously unseen action and ideas.[41] But the focus on class in Scott's analysis obscures a range of other solidarities, shaped by institutions, history and culture, that cut across communities, dividing and uniting in different ways.[42] Likewise, relations of domination did not exist solely between different classes, between the state or landlord and peasants or tenants, but also between chiefs and commoners, men and women, young and old.[43]

In their careful focus on the local and hidden, studies of the weapons of the weak obscure the ways in which African resistance linked such strategies to a concern with the institutions of the state and to organised politics. Where the state was ambitious, if not necessarily strong, local struggles engaged the state directly. In migrant labour societies, rural politics was closely linked to workplace and township associations and ideas. The relationship between formal and informal politics, between overt and covert resistance needs to be explored, and to be treated historically.[44] Mamdani's analysis has a similarly narrowing effect on the study of African politics, though for different reasons: he grants colonial ideology a tremendous success in creating 'tribal' institutions able to comprehensively shape the world of rural Africans, and in so doing denies rural people and resistance movements the capacity to understand the state in its totality. But one of the key epiphanies of nationalists was that the central state, not the local one, was the problem. The local state bore the brunt of rural nationalists' attack – how could it be otherwise? – but nationalists understood that this was simply a branch: the trunk also needed to be transformed.[45]

If we accept that chiefs were capable of thinking in other than ethnic and customary terms, and that they were in need of popular support to be effective, then we must also accept that chiefs would seek to build a wider range of alliances than those that could be contained within the social or geographical unit of the 'tribe', and that these alliances might range from the narrowly self-interested to the radical and populist, and use the weapons of the weak in tandem with other strategies explicitly targeted at institutions and forms of governance. Chiefs' state-sanctioned office may have been hemmed in by the language of custom, but their alliances, their politics, and even their state-sanctioned roles were not. Nationalists often recognised the chiefs' ambiguous position, and sought to make common cause with an elaboration of history and tradition in which chiefs played an important role.[46] It was only with the rise of the guerrilla war that the chiefs' position within the Rhodesian state, no matter how ambiguous, became unacceptable to the forces of opposition.

Land and Authority in Zimbabwe

The politics of Rhodesian state-making was centrally about land – how it should be used, who should gain access to it, how it should be settled, what sort of authority was to be exercised over it – just as the politics of land was centrally about state-making. It was, in the context of the settler state, a battle for legitimacy and power that intertwined in a highly contradictory manner ideas about custom and scientific agriculture, about civilisation and progress, each expressed in the architecture of institutions, in the disciplining of social relations, and in the definition of property rights.

The legacy for independent Zimbabwe was necessarily complex. Following Mamdani's model, there was a process of deracialisation; there was also a process of democratisation which, as he predicted, ran into trouble all too quickly. But it did not do so solely or even primarily because of the legacy of 'indirect rule', such as it was in Zimbabwe. The inheritance of technical development played a central role, as did the nature of nationalist ideology and the frustration of redistributive demands for land. The Zimbabwean state was subject to a diversity of economic and political pressures, just as the settler state had been, and behaved in contradictory ways. It retained the centralised, bureaucratic power and commitment to 'development' of its predecessor, it retained in part and eventually expanded the trappings of chiefly rule, and it treaded carefully in 'deracialising' the economy.

Building effective means of rural rule was no easier after independence, and was characterised by an even more diverse set of institutions, each with its own claims to legitimacy and each making its own uses of history. Thus the party committees that were a product of the nationalist struggle and liberation war sat alongside the elected development committees and councils established after independence, and the hierarchy of chiefs, headmen and village heads dating from much earlier, and sanctified still by appeals to state-sanctioned custom. Each made claims to authority over people and resources, and all were subject to the contradictory demands of an intrusive state, still intent on technical development but still unable to convince its citizens of its merits. As William Munro writes, 'To put its imprimatur on rural society, the state had to put its imprimatur on rural land rights', and to do this it had to 'devise the institutional and discursive means to convince rural dwellers that the state was not only the legitimate but indeed the appropriate agency to define and regulate rights of access to land'.[47] This was no easy task: contests over land remained hotly fought battles over authority and claims to office, determined not by legal rules and regulation but by negotiation and conflict.[48]

These three institutional groupings inter-penetrated each other and the state: some chiefs were nationalists, many nationalists sat on councils and village development committees, and so on. That the claims to authority made by each group should assert a distinct basis and history was more an ideological strategy, aimed at specific audiences, than a sign of firm division. The appeal particularly of the opposition between 'modernity' and 'tradition', so long a characteristic of the Rhodesian state (and the analysis thereof) lived on, both as a means of contesting and constructing authority, and of justifying the imposition of 'modernising' policies on people construed as traditional and thus resistant to 'development'.[49] In all this, chieftaincy and custom not only survived as a central locus of politics, but thrived.[50] However, the insertion of nationalism into the mix made for a newly trenchant and threatening set of claims with a particular purchase on Zimbabwe's new leaders. They had to 'demobilise' this powerful set of claims in order to assert the central state's authority. And so they quickly moved against demands for land as expressed through 'squatter' movements, and against the expression of an alternative nationalist loyalty embodied by the prime loser in Zimbabwe's first elections, Zapu. In the 1980s, the first was met with bureaucratic control, and the assertion of a developmental ethos that drew heavily on technocratic technique and ideology, the second with state violence so extreme that the liberation war paled by comparison.

The former reserves were also reshaped by economic change. Thus some regions boomed, while others stagnated; some sections of rural society prospered as they took advantage of new opportunities to market crops, better paying jobs, and improved infrastructure and services. The state delivered a great deal in the 1980s, offering the possibility of education and health care and agricultural prosperity – at least to some – that could only be dreamed of before. But it did so in a way that offered insufficient challenge to the territorial and economic divisions of the settler period, and which ran out of steam all too quickly. The economy was the arena in which race retained its force, and this legacy of settler rule would also play a central role in the post-independence politics of land. Resettlement was significant in scale, but one-third of the land, and much of the best, was still concentrated in the hands of the largely white and foreign-owned commercial sector in the 1990s. As the post-independence boom slowed, Zimbabwe signed on to its version of structural adjustment, heralding a period of economic stagnation and contraction that badly damaged the promise of 'development'. The racial division of land and wealth unsurprisingly came to the fore. At first, it was most overtly attacked by a frustrated black elite, both in and out of government, though the strategies of poaching, encroachment and squatting continued, largely out of view. In 2000, race and the unequal division of land became the central focus of the ruling party and a following mobilised on the basis of a redefined nationalism. This marked a dramatic shift, one long prefigured, but subsumed under first a developmental discourse and then the strictures of neo-liberal structural adjustment.

Zimbabwe's rulers enunciated a new vision of Zimbabwe, based on an aggressive assertion of sovereignty against the forces of global capitalism, neo-colonialism and the internationally mediated demands of good governance.[51] This was to be about realising the long-delayed goals of the revolution, with land standing centre stage.

It required a radical transformation of the state: as in earlier periods, the role of land, the institutional workings of the state and the political ideology of Zimbabwe's rulers shifted together. For the rural areas, this meant a dramatic reworking of power which built on the decades of conflict over land and authority, over 'development', and over custom and nationalism. It was not one legacy but the interaction of many that shaped the explosive crisis of 2000. It is only by understanding the inconclusive, conflict-ridden history of attempts to build authority over the land that the particular shape it has taken can be understood. This was, as Terence Ranger has written, a crisis dominated by competing interpretations of the history of political struggle and the role of land in it.[52]

Chapter Outline

The book begins by exploring some of the key developments leading up to World War II. In doing so, it underlines the complexities of pre-colonial polities, and the mixed agendas which shaped the foundation of the settler state. Its focus is on the ways in which rural authority was constituted and transformed, and land alienated and regulated. This was not a straightforward process of appointing and empowering chiefs, and it took place across a variegated landscape. Over time, state justifications for intervention and strategies of rule shifted, as did conceptualisations of African society's capacities and purpose. I introduce the two case-study districts whose history runs through the book as a means of rooting the analysis in the workings of the local state and African politics. They illustrate the great diversity in pre-colonial institutions and economies, in the impact of conquest, and in the development of African political associations and economic strategies in the face of settler rule. The chapter ends with the dramatic evictions from 'white' land of the post-war period.

The history of violent removal sets the scene for the subject of Chapter 2: the Native Land Husbandry Act (NLHA) of 1951. This was the most ambitious, and most disastrous, of the settler state's attempts at high modern social engineering, and it required a vast expansion of the state and its knowledge of its subjects. The NLHA rested on a conception of African society – economic men regulated by the market and science – that was at odds with the vaguely defined precepts of custom and chiefly authority. Chiefs were placed in an ultimately untenable position. The toppling of the NLHA was first and foremost an effect of African resistance, and the threat that such resistance posed to the state's authority.

Chapter 3 concerns the supposedly kinder and gentler replacement for the NLHA, the policy of community development promulgated in the 1960s. Africans were reconceived as unready for modernisation. It was not the fault of the technocrats that the NLHA had failed, but that of Africans. In the face of African nationalists' urgent demands for citizenship and rights, officials chose to interpret resistance as a consequence of the neglect of custom, the failure to recognise that Africans' relationship to the land was essentially different to that of Europeans. Once again, the state had to get to know its subjects, but now it deployed a decidedly different set of tools than those of technical development. This was to fail as a means of state-making just as dramatically as the NLHA's modernising promise. Though the settler state found itself unable to root authority effectively in the rocky soil of custom and community, the move to empower chiefs nonetheless had important consequences, as I explore in Chapter 4. Here, we see how decades of state intervention in and struggle over land rights and authority produced a hotly contested and contradictory set of claims that posed a direct threat to state authority.

Chapter 5 concerns the policies of the independent Zimbabwean government with regard to land and rural authority. The efforts to create new institutions of rule while at the same time attending to the redistributive promises of nationalism and reconstituting order proved difficult. Much of the new state's repertoire was drawn from its Rhodesian predecessor. Thus policies that had provoked a ferocious nationalism were retained, in the name of the state's duty to develop the nation's resources. Popular demands for land could only be met, in the official view, through a tightly and centrally controlled process, replete with the trappings of technical development. Rural institutions had to be subordinated to bureaucratic control; land use had ultimately to be the state's to shape. But the state could not constitute authority unilaterally, much less enforce policies that so clearly lacked moral purchase. So we see shifts in – and divisions over – policy and ideology as officials sought to come to grips with the complexity of power in the rural areas. Crucially, chiefs and custom retained their force, emerging as both a key focus of popular opposition and a crucial ally of the state.

Chapters 6 and 7 explore the rural experience of the new state, in the former reserves and in resettlement schemes. They trace the diverse means by which people were 'demobilised', either through violent repression or through removing control over resources and decision-making powers. This was not, of course, an uncontested process. Rural leaders negotiated with and challenged the state. The state's efforts to ground its authority in control of the land was contested by the demands of 'squatters', and the discourses of custom, technical development and nationalism, now put to new use. Chiefs, party committees and elected councils engaged in intense debates over authority and land, and their contestations once again posed a formidable challenge to state-making. Finally, Chapter 8 turns to the shifting politics of land in the 1990s, and the crisis of 2000. Land, for so long cast as a space in which the state rationally allocated productive potential, now took on a wholly different role amidst the violent politics and intolerant nationalism of Zimbabwe's ruling party.

Sources

I have sought to explore these questions through the use of a range of archival sources, government records, and interviews. The bulk of the research was carried out in 1988/89, and on two shorter trips in 1990 and 1991. Further archival and oral historical research was carried out in the mid-1990s, and in 2000 and 2002. The analysis of the settler state relies largely on the archival records of the Ministry of Native Affairs. I have traced officials' interactions with African leaders through using reports of political meetings, records of councils, and chiefs' and headmen's meetings, some of which are found within district Ministry of Local Government and council offices. Of great use in constructing post-independence debates among officials and local leaders were district records regarding chieftaincy and the minutes of council, district development committee, squatter control committee and other meetings. I also draw on press reports: high profile events such as the political conflict in Matabeleland, squatter evictions in the 1980s, and the land occupations since 2000 have received extensive coverage by a remarkably critical media.

The book also draws on interviews carried out with officials of the Ministries of Local Government and Lands primarily, but also with other officials involved in rural development, from the national to district level. Within districts, I carried out multiple interviews over time and in informal contexts. The views of officials were extremely diverse between provinces and districts and among departments, a diversity that shaped processes of policy implementation significantly. Members of Rural Councils and of Intensive Conservation Areas, both representing the areas that used to be 'European' land, were also interviewed.

Most extensively, interviews were carried out with the leaders of three rural institutions in the former reserves of Insiza and Chimanimani districts: members of the village development committees and councils established after independence, chiefs, headmen and village heads, and party leaders. These interviews ranged over a wide variety of questions. They were loosely structured around attitudes to agrarian, judicial and local government policies and perceptions of constraints to agricultural production and development more widely. Where possible, I combined group interviews with individual interviews so as to be able to debate different views. Local leaders proved more than willing to speak critically of official policies and to describe practices on the borders of legality. It was an attitude born of anger over economic hardship and the perception of the government's failures to respond to rural demands that found ready voice in the opening of political space in the late 1980s, following the end of the Zanu(PF) government's brutal repression of Zapu. In 2000 and after, the rapidly deteriorating political climate placed new constraints on field research, and for this period I rely far more heavily on the press and on the reports of NGOs and human rights groups.

Notes

1 Berry, 2002, 639.
2 Phimister, 1988b, Chapter 1. See also Palmer, 1977b, Chapter 2.
3 See Moyana, 1984, and Palmer's classic account, 1977b.
4 Mamdani, 1996.
5 For seminal work, see Anderson and Grove, 1989. For more recent work see Beinart and McGregor, 2003b, and Beinart, 2000.
6 Scott, 1998.
7 See, for example, Castro, 1998, and Escobar, 1995.
8 Drinkwater, 1991, 29.
9 See Young, 2003 for a review of recent tendencies in particularly political science literature.
10 See, for example, Berman, 1990, Lonsdale and Berman, 1979, Berry, 1993, Beinart and Dubow, 1995, Manicom, 1992.
11 Beinart and McGregor, 2003a, 21.
12 See Ranger, 1993, 89-96, for a wide-ranging review.
13 Fields, 1997 [1985], 41.
14 For example, see Schmidt, 1992, 10-11 and passim.

15 Fields, 1997 [1985], 41-50. On the importance of prestige to authority in settler communities, see Cooper and Stoler, 1997.
16 On the nineteenth century roots of missionary ideas about 'development', see Comaroff and Comaroff, 1997.
17 See, for example, Summers, 2002, and Murray, 1970, chapter 9.
18 See Beinart, 1985.
19 Mamdani, 1996, 24, 54, and see chapters 4 and 5.
20 Ibid., 87-9.
21 Berry, 1993, 40.
22 Many decades have passed since Max Gluckman noted the strenuous demands on 'village headmen', at once answerable to the colonial administration and in need of the support of those they led. See Gluckman, 1949.
23 See especially discussions in Lonsdale, 1992, and Feierman, 1990.
24 See Ranger, 1993, 62-111.
25 On land, see Berry, 1993, 24; Berry, 2002, 644-5. On law, see Falk Moore, 1986, and Mann and Roberts, 1991.
26 Diana Jeater's work on Zimbabwe teases apart the unexpected effects of the elaboration of custom, and the debates among Africans over custom. See Jeater, 1992.
27 Drinkwater, 1991, 29.
28 Moyo, 1995, 69-70. Worby, 2001, 489, makes this point.
29 See, for example, Mackenzie, 2000.
30 See discussion in Cheater, 1990, 188-206; Worby, 1994, 380-85.
31 There are many such examples. See, for example, McGregor, 1995, 264; Summers, 2002, 130.
32 See discussion in Nyambara, 2001b.
33 Rutherford, 2001b.
34 McGregor, 1991, 105, makes this argument in an explicit criticism of Drinkwater. Drinkwater also emphasises that Africans saw technical development as a means of impoverishing them.
35 See Berry, 1993, 52-3.
36 See Maxwell, 1999, Summers, 2002, Ranger, 1999, and the classic study of Beinart and Bundy, 1987.
37 Feierman, 1990.
38 Biershenk and Olivier de Sardan, 2003, 148. Also see, for example, Lonsdale, 1986, Falk Moore, 1996, Hagberg, 1998, Helle-Valle, 2002, Boone, 1998, Manor, 1991, and work on post-colonial identity such as Werbner and Ranger, 1996.
39 See Englund, 2002.
40 On this tendency, see Rathbone, 2000, 3-4; Maxwell, 1999, 5.
41 See Scott, 1985, and 1976.
42 See Glassman, 1995, Kaarsholm and James, 2000.
43 Isaacman, 1996 and 1990.
44 See Yeros, 2002, 19.
45 This is a central argument of Alexander, McGregor and Ranger, 2000.
46 See especially Ranger, 1999.
47 Munro, 1995, 107-8.
48 See Andersson, 1999, and Nyambara, 2001b, 772.
49 See Robins, 1998.
50 The 'disconcerting tenacity' of chieftaincy, as Rathbone puts it, in post-colonial Africa is the subject of a growing literature. See, for example, Rathbone, 2000, Maxwell, 1999, Berry, 2001, Dusing, 2002, contributions to Van Rouveroy van Nieuwaal and Van Dijk, 1999, and to Van Rouveroy van Nieuwaal, 1987, Oomen, 2000, and Fisiy, 1995.
51 See Worby, 2003, and Raftopoulos, 2003.
52 Ranger, 2004.

1

Making the Settler State
Authority & the Land

Settler states faced a formidable task in seeking to balance the interests of their white and black constituencies. They were as a result complex institutions, shaped by internal divisions and shifting ideologies. Founded in violent conquest, they struggled to build and to legitimise effective institutions of rule. In Rhodesia, the quest for authority was rapidly rooted in the land. In what follows, I explore the process by which power over Africans and the land they lived on was constituted in the period up to the 1950s. This was in part a story of dispossession and repression, but it was also a story of contradiction and compromise in which the state's goals were far from easily realised. Neither a system of indirect rule nor a technocratic bureaucracy ruled the day: state-making drew on diverse notions of rural authority, which were constantly challenged and transformed by Africans. I focus on the districts of Insiza and Chimanimani to illustrate the wide variations in history, production and political ideology that shaped the making of authority over the land.

The Legacies of Conquest

The form that Rhodesia's settler state would take was rooted in the uneven ground of the nineteenth century. This was a time of upheaval in southern Africa: there was no fixed baseline of custom and identity, polity and economy. The territory that is now Zimbabwe was invaded repeatedly by both Africans and Europeans. Among others, the Ndebele settled in Zimbabwe's south-west in the 1840s, while the Gaza reached over what was to become its eastern border in the 1860s. They were followed by Cecil Rhodes' British South Africa Company (BSAC), which occupied what it called Mashonaland in 1890 and Matabeleland in 1893. The regions that were to become today's Insiza and Chimanimani districts – one located in the open grasslands of the Ndebele state in the west, the other on the mountainous margins of the Gaza Kingdom in the east – exemplified the turmoil of the nineteenth century, and the diverse consequences of conquest.[1]

Insiza fell under the rule of Mzilikazi Khumalo's Ndebele. It constituted part of a political system made up of people incorporated during the migration from South Africa's Natal region and those settled on the high veld surrounding modern

Bulawayo. In the settled Ndebele state, ties of allegiance were ritualised around the king, whose authority came to lie less in his status as a warrior than in his abilities as a rainmaker and provider. This was a multicultural and multilingual state: in incorporating others it adopted aspects of their agricultural methods and religious institutions, notably an adherence to the High God of the Mwali cult, based in the Matopos hills.[2] Relative to its counterparts in Mashonaland, the Ndebele state was certainly centralised and militarily formidable. Nonetheless, one of its key characteristics was the autonomy and civilian character of the *izinduna* (sing., *induna*), the men who came be to known as 'chiefs' after conquest, and who were the king's subordinates. These were less royal officials or military figures than hereditary leaders of 'mini-states'.[3]

The Godhlwayo 'regiment' under the Mafu family, later recognised by the BSAC as the 'Maduna' chieftaincy of Insiza district, is an instructive case. The Mafu *izinduna* had a marked propensity for rebellion against the king, but retained continuity in the father-to-son line of succession. They incorporated the mix of largely Rozwi, Sotho and Venda groups they encountered in Insiza, appointing men from their ranks as sub-chiefs.[4] These people herded Ndebele cattle, sent young men to the military, intermarried and adopted Ndebele cultural practices. Men engaged in herding, hunting and raiding, while women held primary responsibility for the cultivation of grains and other crops in scattered family groups along rivers. Leaders' wealth rested in their ability to command labour, partly through raiding, but primarily through the accumulation of cattle and its use in the payment of bridewealth for wives.[5]

The Ndebele state was established in a period of regional flux, and soon found itself disrupted by economic change, due to the expansion of the private cattle trade and young men's migration to the region's fast growing mines,[6] and to military challenge. In 1893, BSAC columns, in alliance with several 'Shona' dynasties, invaded, raiding for cattle, looting villages, and occupying the Ndebele capital. King Lobengula was driven north never to be seen again. The BSAC set about carving up the Ndebele heartland into ranches. Miners staked some 60,000 claims in the region. Cattle looting, forced labour conscription, and a series of devastating natural disasters followed. This was a period of violent expropriation, and it provoked violent rebellion.[7] In March 1896 Maduna Mafu and his brother launched the first attacks on Europeans. The Ndebele recorded dramatic early successes, but the tide soon turned. Chaos reigned as displaced people searched for food, led small raids, and died from disease and starvation. Central social institutions like the payment of bridewealth broke down.[8]

Military conquest left a number of legacies for this region. First, the loss of the Ndebele king provided a focus for national claims, and the promises made to rebels served as a basis for land demands. Second, the alienation of land was extreme. The whole of the vast Insiza district was allotted one tiny reserve. Even with the addition of two 'Native Purchase Areas' – areas where Africans could purchase small farms – in 1925, over 80 per cent of the district lay in white hands.[9] But extensive alienation did not at first lead to eviction. Much of the land was held by speculative land companies which relied on extracting rents from resident Africans. Spared immediate eviction, they remained closely linked to the markets and politics of the fast growing city of Bulawayo. Third, with the abolition of the monarchy, control over cattle, land, labour and settlement fell increasingly beyond the authority of political leaders.[10] All this went hand in hand with the expansion of missionary activity: new ideas percolated through the region, unfettered by the strict controls previously exercised by the king.

The processes that reshaped Insiza also applied to the dynasties of Chimanimani, but with important distinctions. These were smaller, less centralised polities, located on the margins of what came to be called the 'Shona' people, an anachronistic label applied to a diverse range of groups with no single cultural or political identity.[11] The founders of the chieftaincies to be found in Chimanimani today claim a common origin, but distinctions were drawn on the basis of political affiliation, geography, dialect and culture.[12] Political power was held by hereditary leaders who oversaw a number of subordinates, usually heads of families related to the royal lineage. These men circumscribed the chief's power, exercising control over the location of villages and fields, and settling disputes. Chiefs ruled with the advice, and consent, of a wide range of people: the heads of lineages, advisors, and sometimes a *svikiro* (spirit medium) possessed by a former chief. A key idiom of political conflict, and one which distinguished it from *izinduna*, was the succession dispute. Rather than father-to-son succession, large numbers of candidates competed for chiefly office, mobilising backing from religious and secular authorities within and outside the dynasty. These were intimate disputes that set 'cousin against cousin and brother against brother'.[13] Founding stories of conflict and migration served as a chieftaincy's (highly malleable) 'charter of legitimacy'.[14] Nineteenth-century political leaders were 'big men' with the capacity to trade, raid and amass labour through polygamy, the pledging of young girls in marriage, and the bride service of young men.[15]

As in Insiza, controlling rain and labour was crucial to political authority, but the Chimanimani economy differed in that it was less dependent on the long distance trade in cattle and ivory. Key to it was the local trade, driven by *shangwa* (drought and disaster), between the large villages of the mountains and the scattered lowland settlements.[16] As in the west, however, there was no static nineteenth-century base-line. Most significantly, the Gaza, part of the same set of movements that brought the Ndebele to the region, established themselves at the southern end of the eastern highlands in 1862. The name 'Ndau', which came to characterise the people of Chimanimani, was introduced by the Gaza, and subsequently taken up locally as missionaries created written versions of dialect and history. Subordination to the Gaza was short-lived: following their military defeat by the Portuguese, the territory of the Ndau chiefs was divided between the BSAC and the *Companhia de Moçambique*. The Portuguese side of the border hosted few white settlers and was ineffectively administered, leaving an important space for movement.[17]

Following the establishment of BSAC rule, it was not land speculators and miners that flooded in, as in Insiza, but impoverished Afrikaner farmers seeking to flee the agricultural depression in the Orange Free State, and drawn by promises of vast land allocations. The Martin and Steyn Treks arrived in the highlands between 1893 and 1898, deliberately selecting densely settled areas for their fertility and resident labour. Settlers' poverty and illiteracy were subjects of ridicule among the mainly English missionaries and officials. These were 'near destitute debtors' who 'lived in mud huts' and 'bartered for food with Africans'.[18] Though virtually all of the heavily populated highlands were alienated, few settlers put the land to use: many survived as transport riders and traders, or employed brutal labour practices to eke out a bare living. This was an isolated district: not until 1907 was a road opened to the town of Mutare, and even this remained impassable in the rainy season.[19]

The risings of 1896/97, so influential in Insiza, left a very different legacy here. Chimanimani remained largely peaceful. The Ndau dynasties were left in disarray by the withdrawal of the Gaza, and the whole area was cut off from the rising by a 'chain' of polities that sided with the BSAC. Africans responded to conquest not with arms but through moving from occupied land, non-cooperation, and labour migration.[20] Compared to the conquered people of Insiza, Chimanimani fared far better with regard to land demarcated for reserves. Concerned by the large settler presence, the Native Commissioner established three reserves prior to 1909. The 1925 Land Commission added two tiny Native Purchase Areas. Though all but one reserve fell in the drought-prone lowlands, they provided a haven from the demands of settlers. African polities were nonetheless dramatically transformed. Factions could no longer break away from established dynasties as the number of titles and access to land was limited, leading to more permanent divisions within and between chieftaincies, but certainly no end to conflict over titles. Chiefs were threatened by the administration's establishment of courts and taxation in reserves, and by resident white farmers' control over land and people, forces that impinged on many more here than in Insiza.

The remaking of authority over land and people in Chimanimani and Insiza took very different forms, but everywhere the uneasy peace that followed the risings was followed by movement. People spread out from hilltop fortifications; they fled from landlords; they sought to evade tax.[21] And everywhere they sought means of engaging with the settler economy on favourable terms. This involved 'self-peasantisation'[22] – taking advantage of the agricultural markets offered by mines and towns and settlers – and labour migration. The accumulation of wealth by house-holds and young men accelerated as more young men migrated, entrepreneurs used the plough to expand fields, and many made a living transporting produce to new markets.[23] Women attained new forms of independence (while losing others) by exploiting market opportunities and seeking alternative patrons in missions and the administration.[24] These strategies created tensions that challenged chiefs' authority. Controlling young men and their earnings, controlling labour through marriage, regulating settlement and access to land, now needed to draw on new constructions of authority. Chiefs had also to contend with the sometimes distant, sometimes all too intimate, demands of the new holders of power. Administrators, settlers, and missionaries demanded taxes and rents, interfered in social practices, and offered new sources of wealth and ideas about status. Everywhere they competed for authority over land and people.

State-making from on High

The issues of land and governance rapidly took pride of place in the BSAC's calculations, famously owing to the failure to discover a 'second Rand' comparable to the fabulous wealth of the Transvaal's gold mines, and to the costly – and highly embarrassing for the BSAC – risings of 1896/7. The focus on promoting settler agriculture was accompanied by a turn towards a policy of territorial segregation. Mooted after World War I, territorial segregation gained force with the transition from Company to settler rule in 1923. The policy was enshrined in the Land Apportionment Act of 1930, through which the division of land between freehold farms for whites and 'communal' reserves for Africans, was formalised. Dispossessing Africans of their land and supporting white producers required a complex process of state-making, as exemplified in the practices of the Native Affairs Department (NAD).

The NAD's origins lay in the period of conquest. The 1896/7 war and a widespread perception of BSAC misrule formed the backdrop to the employment of Native Commissioners (NCs). The source of their authority was not the BSAC but the Imperial Government, acting through a resident commissioner. This was the first step in creating a separate branch of administration concerned with African interests. It was to become a 'government within a government', with wide-ranging powers and autonomy. NCs developed a philosophy that combined authoritarianism and paternalism, reflecting the need to maintain order and to extract taxes and labour, as well as a sense of obligation to their wards.[25] They engaged in debates over morality, custom, and the merits of civilisation, as well as in conflicts with land owners, missionaries and other government departments.

NCs were from early on outspoken critics of state extraction, abusive landlords and extreme land alienation. They vociferously argued for more land for African occupation. In Chimanimani, their main concern was to defend existing reserves, and to acquire additional land in the highlands.[26] In Insiza, they warned repeatedly of the inadequacy of the tiny Insiza reserve, and the threat of unrest.[27] The NAD also objected to the imposition of rent on Africans living on unalienated land ('crown' land after 1918), calling it 'a most unwise and unfair proposition', and only halfheartedly collecting rents.[28] On alienated land, the extortionate excesses of absentee land companies' rent and fee extractions in districts like Insiza, and the violent efforts of settlers to extract labour in districts like Chimanimani led to intense lobbying from NCs, though their efforts more often than not ran aground on the political opposition of white farmers.[29]

The NAD's ambitions expanded over time. From the 1920s, it focused its energies on elaborating means of administering and 'developing' the reserves, with contradictory repercussions for authority over the land. Following the turn to territorial segregation, reserves were cast as the permanent homes of the majority of Africans. This marked a significant shift from visions of a 'detribalised', proletarian African population in which a reputed 'tribal communalism' would be replaced with the 'individualism of the European'. Such thinking had assumed that the reserves would die out along with chiefly rule.[30] Drawing on the South African Cape's example, NCs were particularly keen on introducing individual land tenure. The move to segregation was the outcome of intense debates between and among black and white constituencies, over civilisation and morality as well as over the shifting economic and political interests of settlers and Africans, and it was to have profound implications for the settler state and the place of Africans within it.[31]

Reserves underwrote a system of labour migration, acting to subsidise African wage labour by leaving workers' families to support themselves on the land. Africans were to be mere visitors in 'European' areas. NAD policy at first had been about usurping the role of chiefs, and moral debates had centred on 'emancipating' women in order to force what were cast as inherently lazy men to work, rather than rely on the labour of their wives. But labour migration required a different logic: women had to be kept on the land, and under the control of husbands and fathers whose claims to land, children, and labour were made through them. The legal definition of women as perpetual minors, the criminalisation of adultery, the toleration (against missionary objections) of polygamy all indicated a growing alliance between elder African men and the NAD, and set in train the development of new ideologies of kinship and custom.[32]

This alliance was, however, a far cry from a system of 'indirect rule' on the model propounded by Mahmood Mamdani. Chiefs and headmen were not mere salaried civil servants, but the 'customary' basis of their authority was only weakly buttressed. As Diana Jeater argues, the passage of laws such as the Native Marriages Ordinance of 1917 did involve the 'creation of customary law', but the ways in which it strengthened chiefs was often unintentional and unanticipated.[33] There were no customary courts. NCs in theory if not in practice heard all civil cases,[34] and criminal law applied to black and white with few exceptions. NCs, not chiefs, stood at the helm of local administration. Even as the NAD moved towards a more overt policy of relying on chiefs and headmen the imperatives of effective administration remained paramount. 'Tribal leadership' – the hierarchy of chiefs, headmen and 'kraal' or village heads, all subordinated to the NC – was only codified in the Native Affairs Act of 1927. The Act was intended to reinforce mechanisms for extracting tax and labour, duties that increasingly desk-bound NCs could no longer undertake in person.[35] But many NCs remained sceptical of the efficacy of chiefs and the morality of custom. They were unsure of whether a coherent set of customs could be attached to a 'tribe'. They could not agree on the nature of African land tenure or chiefs' role in it. Proposals were mooted for the appointment of selected Africans as 'government representatives' where hereditary chiefs were ineffective, and in practice many appointments were openly divorced from concerns for custom or 'tribe'. [36]

The ambiguity in official views on African authority and society was not solely due to NCs' attitudes, but also to the missionary project. Missionaries' influence on Premier H. U. Moffat's administration led to the creation of a Native Education Department (later the Native Development Department) outside NAD control in 1927. The department was headed by Harold Jowitt, a man much influenced by South African 'liberal' thinkers. Under his leadership, Jeanes teachers, Africans trained at the government industrial school and paid by Jowitt's department, but operating under mission control, were sent into the reserves. In alliance with missionaries, they promoted new ideas about status and authority, took over land, 'mobilised' labour, and challenged NCs in the name of a civilising project.[37] The institution of Native Boards in 1931 likewise drew on more than a customary model of authority. Boards formalised the existing meetings of chiefs, headmen and NCs, but broadened representation to include educated and Christian 'progressives', thus recognising that these men formed an influential part of African society.

Neither Jowitt's department nor Native Boards were popular with the NAD. NCs attacked the 'development and progress' promoted by missions as a source of disorder; Chief Native Commissioner (CNC) Jackson repeatedly denounced the 'dangerous duality of control' embodied in Jowitt's department.[38] NCs only invested in Native Boards where they had a particular commitment to 'progress' or where their authority was challenged by independent African associations. Most Boards collapsed during the depression. The depression in fact dealt a heavy blow to the missionary-inspired initiatives of the 1920s as a whole. In the 1933 elections, Godfrey Huggins' Rhodesia Party took up the question of African 'development', exploiting fears of black competition. Huggins' triumph saw the rapid transfer of all 'native' questions back to the NAD, firmly establishing the basis for 'separate development'. As M. C. Steele writes, 'Whereas Moffat had been a product of early Victorian missionary paternalism, Huggins' philosophical roots were embedded in the more recent soil of Social Darwinism. "It is purely a biological problem," he observed…. "There is no such thing as equality."'[39] Huggins was adamantly backed by CNC Colonel C. L. Carbutt, who saw no place for 'advanced natives' in Rhodesia, even proposing that they be despatched *en masse* to distant northern colonies.[40]

The move to separate development reinforced the tendency towards relying on chiefs as the 'stabilising agent in tribal society'. The authority granted to African pastors and teachers and Christians by missions and Jowitt's department came under heated attack. A Government Notice instructed teachers in 'kraal schools' to 'subject themselves to the tribal control of kraal heads'.[41] Judicial powers were gradually devolved to chiefs and, in 1937, the Native Law and Courts Act granted limited civil jurisdiction to 'customary' courts. Native Councils were established at the same time to act as advisory bodies. Their members were appointed by NCs, and contained the same mix of educated and chiefly members as the Boards, though now 'progressive' members were more often drawn from the advisors and relatives of chiefs.

The 1930s has been cast as a time in which 'customary authority' was 'restored', but the NAD's concern remained far more with authority than with the customary.[42] NCs deployed the dichotomy between the 'tribal' and the disruptively 'modern' where they sought to justify the repression of African associations or to deny that Africans had 'real' grievances. Thus they routinely detailed strings of complaints – discriminatory pricing, forced labour, taxation, evictions – and in the same breath described political opposition as the work of 'malcontents' and 'agitators', almost invariably of urban origin, who only managed to gain support due to the disruption of 'tribal life'. They sought a remedy in what was assumed, often mistakenly, to be the conservative influence of chiefs and headmen. NCs' practices nonetheless remained highly diverse. As one veteran of Native Administration explained: 'There was just no theory. Each person learnt from the District Commissioner he was with and, of course, there were various little exams, but there were no principles of administration.'[43] This was not a recipe for the construction of powerful 'native authorities': chiefs had no budgets, no trained staff, no criminal jurisdiction in their courts, no law-making authority.

The nature of NAD interventions is further complicated when we consider the policies that fell under the rubric of 'technical development'. From the late 1920s to the 1960s, technical development encompassed four main policies: demonstration, centralisation, destocking and, finally, the Native Land Husbandry Act. Each policy was justified in different ways, although, as Drinkwater writes, all were premised on a set of beliefs that assumed the superiority of western culture and science, and the laziness and irrational conservatism of Africans.[44] They drew on appeals to individual moral progress or science, or a vision of a wholly revolutionised African society of economic men. Custom was cast as an obstacle, not an ally, in this.

E. D. Alvord, an American missionary and agriculturalist, played the central role in initiating interventions in African agriculture. In 1926, he was appointed as the first Agriculturalist for the Instruction of Natives in the NAD. He initiated the demonstration policy at a time of official concern over African production methods but, as JoAnn McGregor explains, Alvord's motives were diverse. He saw agricultural change as part of a 'wider civilizing package' incorporating Christian conversion, and intended to lift 'those in the reserve out of their laziness and backwardness, out of the "sea of superstition and fear which engulfed them"'. Demonstration was to win 'converts' to 'modern scientific agriculture', defined as intensive permanent cultivation, crop rotation and the use of fertiliser and improved seeds. African demonstrators were sent into reserves where they farmed plots in the fields of 'cooperators' using Alvord's methods, in the hope that this would lead to their adoption. Based on individual appeal, demonstration had little time for the communal language of custom. The policy caused complaints from NCs, much as Jeanes teachers had. In some cases, chiefs and headmen were threatened by an individual's ability to 'cooperate' without their approval; in others, it was precisely chiefs and headmen who proved most able to adopt Alvord's advice due to their ability to mobilise labour and resources.[45]

Centralisation was a more ambitious policy requiring the reorganisation of settlements into linear villages, or 'lines', such that they would separate grazing areas from fields. Launched in 1929, the policy marked the first concerted state intervention into land tenure in the reserves. Chiefs' approval for the policy was sought, and the demarcation of fields was often done in tandem with headmen or village heads. In practice, the demarcation of lines was used in local disputes over land, and tended to grant new authority to village heads in the allocation of fields, practices at times incorporated into shifting ideas about custom. But for Alvord, centralisation, like demonstration, was part of a civilising agenda. An aesthetic concern for square, brick houses was placed on the same plane as agricultural change. There was also a concern for 'legibility': centralisation was praised as a means of making dispersed settlements more accessible and visible.[46]

As the depression took hold in the early 1930s, white opposition to assigning further land to reserves and to devoting resources to African 'development' gained force. Alongside an array of discriminatory legislation designed to undercut African competition and subsidise white production, notably the Maize Control and Cattle Levy Acts of 1931 and 1934, centralisation was recast as a conservation measure and means of 'squeezing' more Africans into the reserves, not as a means of 'development'.[47] Official criticism of African farming methods focused on the use of the plough, which had allowed vast expansions in arable acreages. Once seen as a positive sign of Africans' willingness to adopt new technology, it was now depicted as no more than a 'labour saving device', an aid to the environmentally destructive, congenitally lazy African.[48]

Demonstration and centralisation were far from successful. Even Alvord despaired of the possibility of 'conversion'.[49] In the early 1940s, his methods were superseded by a far more interventionist ethic, promoted by a rapidly expanding technical corps within the NAD. Fears of African competition were sidelined by dramatic shortfalls in food production and shortages in the supply of African labour, due to the expansion of secondary industry and white farmers' move into the lucrative tobacco market. At the same time, concern over the shortage of land for African occupation was heightened by massive evictions from 'European' land consequent on white immigration.[50] In this period, the passage of the Natural Resources Act and the Compulsory Native Labour Act, the establishment of the Natural Resources Board (NRB), and the Report of the Native Production and Trade (Godlonton) Commission, laid the foundation for a new regime.

The NRB focused its attention on 'overstocking' and, in 1943, compulsory destocking regulations were passed, not least as a convenient means of increasing wartime African beef sales.[51] More widely, in an effort to halt what was described as the 'wholesale rapid destruction [of the reserves] due to bad tillage and over-stocking', a bevy of soil conservation, agricultural, and livestock demonstrators, along with pasture officers, land development officers and lands inspectors, roamed the reserves armed with a growing array of coercive powers.[52] As one NC put it, these officials acted as 'virtual policemen', bent on prosecuting 'agricultural crimes'. African farming methods were, in effect, criminalised on the authority of science, a more unforgiving judge than the pieties of Alvord's evangelism.[53] The Godlonton Commission proposed even more ambitious plans for state intervention, presaging the Native Land Husbandry Act of 1951, the high point of the Rhodesian 'technical imagination', and placing direct emphasis on the state's duty to ensure African agricultural productivity. It called for 'compulsory planned production whereby a statutory body should be empowered to direct what crops, acreage and areas should be planted and what livestock should be kept, to enforce good husbandry conditions and to control the distribution and marketing of consequent products'.[54]

The policies promoted in this period were contradictory and technically flawed, based on an ideological construction of African farming methods as 'traditional', unproductive and destructive, as a vast literature has shown.[55] Drinkwater cites cases where NCs simultaneously backed technical officials' calls for destocking while praising the condition of cattle and veld.[56] McGregor shows how ecological damage caused by centralisation and contour ridges was noted but never used to criticise policies justified in terms of their conservation benefits.[57] The importance of holding to beliefs in the superiority of western science resulted in blatant contradictions in official reports, much as the ideological adherence to 'tribal rule' insisted on casting chiefs as 'conservative and stabilizing' regardless of their politics. Even if technical prescriptions had been sound, they would have remained impossible for many Africans to adopt, owing to shortages of labour, land, capital, stock or fertiliser – shortages that were, of course, exacerbated by destocking, labour on conservation works, evictions, and discriminatory pricing and marketing policy.

The scientific arguments used to justify intervention into the ways in which Africans lived and farmed constituted a powerful means of extending state control over African production and denying African demands for land. At the same time they undermined the state. Unsurprisingly, they provoked resistance. They also heightened a growing contradiction in ideologies of governance: technical development, 'tribal rule', and 'civilisation' were based on different views of African society and African capacities. Custom sat in destructive tension with technocracy. Both were complicated by missionaries' civilising mission, and all rode on the rocky ground of an increasingly differentiated society.

State-making in Practice

Just as ideas about authority and land were contested and contradictory within the state, they were the subject of struggle among African leaders, and between them and officials. In the inter-war years, the ways in which chiefs sought to retain authority were diverse. They had lost their military power, and their authority over women and young men was increasingly challenged. In response, some of them elaborated new ritual grounds for their claims on land and people.[58] Others sought to use schools and missions, actively demanding education, seeking to control its content, and making alliances with educated Africans.[59] Some sought to develop their role as patrons, through the lending of cattle or control over land. Many exploited their privileged access to the state.[60] Chiefs and others also turned to new African associations and ideas about rights or religion to challenge the state's authority.

African leaders' choices must be seen against the backdrop of conquest, the continual threat of evictions, and the coercive measures adopted to extract labour and tax. They must also be seen in the context of local histories, institutions and economies. These differed markedly between Insiza and Chimanimani. Let me start with a consideration of Insiza. As we have seen, in Matabeleland many Africans lived on 'European' land, and hence beyond the direct administration of NCs and often also chiefs. Their relationships with NCs and their frequently absentee landlords consisted in meeting a host of demands for rents, taxes and fees. They responded with selective labour migration and 'self-peasantisation'. Success depended on access to markets, the adoption of new technology like the plough, control over land and labour, and the accumulation of cattle. Africans deployed the 'weapons of the weak' in defense of their resources, and they also entered into new political associations with far-reaching ambitions.

The ownership of cattle was central to African autonomy in Insiza. In the 1920s, Africans greatly expanded their herds, and adopted a variety of tactics to protect their wealth. They evaded rents and dipping fees, refused to repay grain debts incurred in times of drought, migrated to more tolerable landlords, refused to sell cattle when prices were low, and at times resorted to burning the fields and pastures of unpopular landlords.[61] Their success allowed Insiza's young men to avoid the poor employment conditions on local mines: they could 'afford to sell cattle to satisfy their wants and the majority have to remain at home to husband their wealth'. Labour had to be imported from outside the district, while men from Insiza went to the better paying jobs in the nearby city of Bulawayo and in South Africa.[62] These strategies were, however, dealt a severe blow by the depression. The Maize Control Act effectively ended the sale of maize by Africans. The closure of mines cut off local markets, while drought and restrictions on cattle movements led to large-scale stock mortalities. A ban placed on labour migration to South Africa, though often evaded, limited access to lucrative jobs.[63] But no linear 'destruction' of African production followed.[64] Instead, cattle herds and sales recovered rapidly in the late 1930s, leading NCs to complain once again of the dearth of African labour.[65] Outside of drought years, NCs protested through most of the 1940s that cattle sales meant that 'the ordinary kraal-Native ... is normally not compelled to work continuously on mines and farms, it seems. This semi-independence is cherished by him'.[66]

Cattle were also important to chiefs' standing. Many chiefs had accumulated large herds following the 1896/97 war, and used them to buttress their authority by loaning cattle to clients and engaging in new markets.[67] Chiefs and elder men worked to re-establish control over young men and women by re-instituting the use of cattle for bridewealth, receiving the support of officials keen to bolster 'customary' social relations and so stability in their efforts.[68] Chiefs were central in the elaboration of new ideas of community, both ethnic and political, and some engaged in religious innovation, adapting the edicts of the Matopos rain shrines, or sending their sons to mission schools.[69] They also acted to limit the state's demands for labour and fees. Chief Maduna Mafu refused to aid in labour recruitment in the 1920s, much as he had in the 1890s, and in 1926 he organised a 'passive resistance movement against dip fees', in protest against what the NC termed the 'so-called difficulties' of falling cattle prices.[70]

The weapons of the weak were a central tool in Insiza, but politics was far from restricted to this sphere. Up to the mid-1930s, two political movements, the Matabele Home Society (MHS) and the Independent Industrial and Commercial Workers' Union (ICU), linked protest in town and country through chiefs, labour migrants, and mission-educated Africans. The key chief in Insiza was Maduna Mafu, one-time instigator of armed rebellion against the BSAC. He proved suspicious of the elite Ndebele nationalism propounded by the MHS, with its focus on the reinstatement of the monarchy and the establishment of an Ndebele homeland. It was the ICU, under the leadership of Masotsha Ndhlovu, which had the most dramatic impact. The ICU's concerns encompassed opposition to taxes and fees, demands for better schools and wages, a direct role in governance and, centrally, land. The aspirations of the ICU, and the role of chiefs in it, underlined the extent to which the administrative idea of 'tribal rule' failed to capture the alliances and ambitions of African politics. It also called into question the common depiction of chiefs as primarily concerned with their own status and wealth, or trapped within an ethnic sphere.[71]

In 1931, ICU committees were established in Insiza, and 'regular meetings' were held at the homes of Chief Maduna and headmen. The ICU played on the introduction of Native Boards, the dislocations of the depression, and the growing insecurity of Africans on alienated land and the Godhlwayo Native Purchase Area (NPA). The NPA, on which Chief Maduna and many others lived, was due to be 'sold at any time'.[72] ICU activists initially put their concerns to the Native Board. Maduna's delegates, notably a man educated in South Africa's prestigious Fort Hare college, heatedly criticised the land set aside for Africans, and then rejected the Board's authority entirely. Masotsha Ndhlovu was subsequently banned from the reserves, much to the NC's relief:

It is felt that if the progress of this Union's activities had not been stemmed, it would have disclosed that its aims were directed towards the ultimate government of the native people by themselves, responsible only to and under the guidance of the Minister of the Crown responsible to them.[73]

Chief Maduna continued to send representatives to ICU meetings in Bulawayo, however, and when the NC sought to revive the Board, ICU members objected, 'pointing out how the Native Boards in the Transkei had brought ruin on the Natives'. People insisted Masotsha be made Board chairman. Despite CNC Carbutt's personal intervention, further meetings failed to overcome 'antagonistic feeling'. The NC suggested that the 'democratic' ICU be countered by 'the fostering of the Ndebele caste system': 'A more pronounced tribal control would secure better administration than "Vox Populi" methods.'[74] He calculated that 'tribal control' could be 'revived' and that it was by definition conservative, despite the manifest evidence to the contrary. In the end, Maduna's obdurate non-cooperation was only softened by concessions on the central issue of land: CNC Carbutt promised that the Godhlwayo NPA would not be sold in his lifetime, an undertaking that was to haunt later NCs.[75]

Chief Mdala's Native Board fared little better. Mdala lived with his followers entirely on alienated land. He used early Board meetings to demand land, invoking broken promises made at the time of the 1896 rising, and eventually siding with the ICU.[76] He and his followers also petitioned the NAD for a school that taught English. Carol Summers sees this initiative as an effort both to lay claim to land through the construction of a government school, and to cement the bonds between young and old men by gaining for the young access to the kind of education that would see them prosper in formal employment. The Umchingwe school in the end collapsed due to its failure to offer the academic education demanded by its African sponsors.[77]

In 1933, Masotsha Ndhlovu was imprisoned for holding a meeting in Insiza. Chief Mafu Maduna, by then an old man, died shortly thereafter and ICU activity dwindled, victim to repression and the pressures of the depression and drought. The NC noted that the ICU's 'propaganda' had adversely affected payments of taxes and rents, and undermined the Native Boards and the Umchingwe school. Masotsha Ndhlovu had 'acquired a considerable following in the district and, to a certain extent, achieved his undoubted object, that of undermining the authority of the Government by a form of passive resistance and obstruction.'[78] The ICU established key characteristics of rural politics that would spread through the region in later years: the influence of ideas from Bulawayo and South Africa; alliances made between chiefs, educated activists, and urban movements; the centrality of land and the multiple strategies for making claims on it; and the combination of the weapons of the weak with attempts to remake the state.

In Chimanimani, the politics of land and state-making differed dramatically. The principal economic strategy employed here was overwhelmingly labour migration, a strategy that made full use of the porous border with Portuguese East Africa. The district's agricultural economy remained dominated by internal trade. It offered less opportunity for accumulation, but was also isolated from the discriminatory legislation of the 1930s which so devastated producers elsewhere, and the vagaries of national markets. White farmers' greatest challenge lay in controlling labour, not extracting rents as in Insiza, and to do this they had to keep Africans on their land. This was not easy: the burdens of tax and demands of farmers caused constant movement, into remote areas of the mountains, into reserves or across the border. The NC simply could not find people, due to 'the nature of divisions of the country, and … to the fact that the kraals as shown in the Tax Registers … are actually split into a number of small kraals, some of which are far remote from the titular head'.[79]

For the young men of Chimanimani, labour migration to South Africa assumed the status of a 'custom': 'at a certain age the young men must proceed to Johannesburg and remain away for at least twelve months failing which he becomes a subject of scorn by the others'.[80] In the 1920s, the NC estimated that one-third of tax-paying males worked outside the district. He described a three-tiered labour hierarchy: 'those who work on the farms within the district being, all of them, tenants of the farm-owners…; those who go to work on the mines or in the town-ships in other districts within the colony, and those, the best men, who seek the best wages where they may be earned, namely in the Transvaal'.[81] Migrants went to great lengths to defend their access to the best jobs. When attempts were made to ban migration to South Africa, they migrated illegally, using false names and Portuguese addresses. As the NC wryly noted, 'these men have learned that they must break the law to observe it, for they cannot by cultivating the soil earn the money for payment of the tax which the good tax gatherer has taught them is the prerequisite of all law'.[82]

Young men used their wages to pay taxes and fees and to invest in household goods and farming. Their earnings were also circulated through bridewealth (*lobola*) payments, cash and gold having replaced stock, grain, child-pledging or periods of labour as the principal means of payment.[83] Such payments constituted a key means by which parents gained access to the earnings of the young. Parents were also crucial in protecting migrants' claims to land at home, and in exercising control over women in their absence, in collusion with the state. Some young men earned bridewealth locally, from white farmers able to lend lump sums in exchange for labour, though most of the district's 60-odd farmers were too poor to do more than exchange access to their well-watered land for labour.[84]

Investment in better communications and in tea and tobacco estates in neigh-bouring Chipinge slowly integrated Chimanimani into a wider market in the late 1920s. But most European enterprises were entirely shut down by the depression. Africans' key mode of agricultural exchange remained the trade between the lowveld and the highlands. In the midst of drought and depression, the pressure on low-landers was such that *lobola* was once again paid in grain, and child-pledging in exchange for grain spread.[85] Food shortages sustained local grain prices at a time when they were bottoming out elsewhere and the Maize Control Act was cutting off grain markets for Africans. The Act was not implemented in Chimanimani until 1940, and even then highland Africans were able to sell their grain at 'remunerative prices' to missions, settlers and lowlanders.[86] Grain markets elicited little state interest, and served as a less important source of accumulation here than in Insiza. The same was true for cattle. Far from constituting a crucial means of self-peasantisation, a source of patronage, and the basis of bridewealth, cattle came to play a less and less significant role. Gold or currency served for *lobola* transactions; cattle-owners often chose to sell up rather than pay dip fees; marketing and husbandry were continually hampered by tsetse fly and foot-and-mouth disease restrictions. In many areas, cattle were not useful as draught animals owing to the rocky and mountainous coun tryside, a characteristic that also prevented the emergence of 'plough entrepreneurs' on a large scale. 'Overstocking' did not excite Chimanimani's NCs as it did their counterparts in Insiza.

Chimanimani's politics likewise elicited far less concern on the part of NCs. The early 1930s witnessed the establishment of Native Boards for a brief period, and the emergence of African associations. At Board meetings, chiefs and headmen complained about their low salaries and the burdens of tax collection. As in Insiza, they called for more and better schools, a reduction in crown land rents, famine relief and, most passionately, more land. Highland chiefs, who lived almost entirely on private land, passed a resolution requesting their own reserves so as not to be 'driven into Portuguese East Africa', a prospect that threatened their own authority as well as white farmers' access to labour. Crown land rent was in fact reduced in 1930 and then suspended in 1932 for fear of causing a cross-border exodus.[87]

The associations that did emerge in Chimanimani were decidedly different from those of Insiza. They also illustrated the variable views of NCs, who might be as concerned with civilisation as custom. The 'liberal' NC Peter Nielsen arrived in Chipinga in 1926. He encouraged the formation of the aptly named Native Self-Constructing Society, an 'improvement association' that incorporated chiefs, headmen, mission teachers and evangelists. The Society focused on the problems of elites: the desire for freehold land, a local institution of higher education, economic opportunity, and respect for missionaries. Hohoza Dube, brother of Chief Mapungwana and an ordained minister, proved adept at uniting chiefs and the mission educated – the NC considered that he had been influenced by South African nationalist Solomon Plaatje.[88] In marked contrast to the ICU, this Society received the NC's approval and did not broaden its base beyond a tiny elite, though it did reflect the emergence of new identities and alliances.

If the Native Self-Constructing Society largely expressed the concerns of the older, educated and respectable, the Zion Apostolic City movement of the early 1930s provided a voice for the young and poor. It challenged elders, NCs and missionaries, calling into question the legitimacy of both custom and mission Christianity, and thus the state's very claims to authority.[89] Migrant labourers imported the movement from South Africa in the midst of the depression. NC Nielsen attributed its appeal to 'economic dislocation' which caused people to 'look heavenwards for the change they desire from their earthly condition which they have come to believe has been unjustly imposed upon them by whites. At first, therefore, we hear only whis perings and prayers, later we may see open defiance and attempts at direct hostility.' Chief Mutema's nephew, Jeremiah Magodo, himself recently returned from Johannesburg, spoke in tongues and 'denounced all those who have not been baptized by immersion in the true Zion manner, among whom he has especially mentioned the local missionaries, the Native Commissioner and the Governor. These all carry, according to Jeremiah, the Mark of the Beast on their foreheads, and their lot is with the ungodly!'[90]

Jeremiah's movement challenged African healers by offering free treatment of disease and witchcraft eradication; it rejected elders' right to migrants' earnings through the payment of *lobola*, thus striking directly at a key source of their wealth and power. It served as 'an alternative source of authority to the illiterate or barely literate'.[91] The movement was resented and feared by chiefs and mission Christians who lodged their outraged complaints at Native Board meetings. NC Nielsen banned the movement's preachers, but one Johannes persisted, leading children away from a mission school in Chimanimani in 1933. Finally, four preachers were summoned to a Native Board meeting and warned to stop their activities. The movement subsequently died out following heavy-handed repression.[92]

Labour migrants returning from South Africa introduced very different ideas to Chimanimani's rural areas than those that moved through Insiza. Though far from the ICU's secular challenge, they nonetheless demonstrated a finely attuned understanding of the bases of the state's authority, as well as the fault lines within rural society. The alternative to Zionist zeal was the 'progressive' alliance between mission christians and chiefs. Fostered by an unusual NC, this alliance was able to negotiate concessions on specific issues – crown land rents, or the repression of the Zionist movement – when such actions were perceived to be in the interest of retaining labour, controlling the young, or defending a civilising agenda. In both districts, officials and African leaders grappled with the task of building authority over land and people in ways shaped by the weight of local history, the variable demands and opportunities of the settler economy, and the influence of ideas – official, religious and political – drawn from across the region. Their efforts would prove all too easily threatened by the harsh dislocations of post-war evictions and technical development.

Evictions and the Rise of Technical Development

The 1940s marked a crucial phase in the making of authority over the land. In this period, the coercive implementation of technical development policies was accompanied by an increasingly acute 'squeeze' on land, processes that were closely linked in official and African eyes. For NCs the link lay in the promise of fitting more Africans into reserves, and ordering them in a 'legible' way. For Africans, technical development was variably seen as a prelude to further land alienation, a route to accumulation, and a means of seeking secure tenure. 'Legibility' worked both ways: as a means for the state to 'see' its charges, and as a way for Africans to be 'seen', and so gain recognition for their claims to land.[93] In the context of dispossession and coercion, claims to land drew on the adoption of technical advice, as well as on narratives of progress and histories of settlement, on the promises of officials and on ideas of justice and rights.

LAND AND THE STATE IN INSIZA

In Insiza, technical development was concentrated in the tiny Insiza reserve and on Glassblock and Panasequa farms (later the Glassblock reserve, and referred to here as Glassblock). The vast majority of Africans were beyond the state's developmental reach because they resided on private land. Action within the reserve was deemed urgent. The NC worriedly noted that it could not absorb even half of those who would soon face eviction 'without proper land development and control'.[94] Development had not fared well in the 1930s. When restrictions were imposed in Glassblock, people had simply moved out.[95] In the reserve, people had greeted the first demonstrator with suspicion, fearing that 'the motive for the installation of the demonstrator was the Government's intention to limit the size of native lands'.[96] The demonstrator's advice was interpreted in the light of dispossession, not developmental intent, and it was at any rate only relevant to those with greater access to labour and cattle. Even then it was modified to suit local soils, and adopted in aid of accumulation rather than intensification. The NC concluded, 'If the soil is to be saved, then I am afraid persuasion and propaganda as to how the soil is to be used must give place to explicit direction.'[97]

In the mid-1940s, the NC's plea was heard: the reserve's lone agricultural demonstrator was joined by a land development officer, an agricultural supervisor, two more agricultural demonstrators, a lands inspector, and forestry, community and soil conservation demonstrators. A new era of intervention had arrived. Destocking began in 1944. Its effects in combination with drought left the Insiza reserve 'understocked' by 1947, cattle numbers having been almost halved.[98] Officials also devoted their energies to conservation works – drawing on poorly paid or forced labour – and centralisation. Chiefs and headmen were required to recruit labour, a task they bitterly resented; young men simply fled.[99] Centralisation was a hugely disruptive process in which people were moved into 'long lines' surrounding large blocks of land designated for arable use. The NC praised the 'successful results', though it would not be long before another band of experts condemned the lines and called for people to move again.[100]

The introduction of these measures coincided with attempts to establish a Native Council, the first local government initiative since the failure of the Boards. Conditions were not propitious. The council immediately faced opposition from its educated members and from Chief Jim Mafu Maduna, son and successor to Maduna Mafu and a wealthy entrepreneur who had, in 1948, become the district's first bus owner.[101] The NC was not a fan: 'The outlook of the senior Chief, a young man, leaves much to be desired.... He lacks personality and there is reason to believe that his general attitude is antagonistic to good administration, although he is careful to pretend otherwise.' He attributed Maduna's opposition to the council to his 'lack of common powers of understanding', but also noted that 'malcontents' were gaining a following throughout the district due to the 'burning question of land'.[102] A council was only reluctantly accepted in Insiza reserve and Glassblock in 1948. Councillors immediately asked that Glassblock be incorporated into the reserve, and 'recommended that the Department of Native Agriculture be asked to centralize [Glassblock] without delay so as to enable the residents to establish permanent kraals'.[103] The call for technical development lay fully in the recognition of peoples' precarious claims to land and in the desire to be legible in the state's eyes.

The council's concerns reflected the severe crisis facing central Matabeleland: the enforcement of the Land Apportionment Act, and thus the eviction of tens of thousands of Africans living on crown land or under rent agreements on private land. Piecemeal evictions took place in the early 1940s, but there were still 5,843 'excess families' in Insiza in 1947.[104] The most devastating evictions throughout the south west fell between 1948 and 1953. They ushered in a period of sustained political activism, led most importantly by the Bulawayo-based British African National Voice Association (the Voice), headed by lawyer and trade unionist Benjamin Burombo. The evictions did not, however, lead to violent resistance, an outcome that Ngwabi Bhebe attributes to the NAD's success in 'co-opting' chiefs.[105] But the reasons were more complex: resistance was divided by the varied threat that evictions posed over time and space, and by the uneven efficacy of people's claims to land. Strategies of resistance were intensely debated, and shaped by the fearsome might of the state. Chiefs were far from straightforwardly 'co-opted'. Rather, they in concert with others used strategies of confrontation and negotiation interchangeably over time towards the goal of secure tenure, a goal seen as increasingly within the state's gift.

African leaders in Insiza were acutely aware of the threat of evictions – to those such as Maduna and his followers on the Godhlwayo NPA, to those on Glassblock, and to the far larger communities on crown and alienated land. In 1948, councillors expressed concern for those 'unsettled' by the prospect of eviction. Linking once again secure tenure and technical development, they recommended that the NPA and Glassblock be 'declared a Native Reserve with an official guarantee of permanent occupation and that an agricultural staff be appointed to instruct the inhabitants'.[106] The NC was in fact feverishly lobbying for more land, but he refused the council's requests. The council subsequently collapsed, and the Voice came to the fore. Maduna and other chiefs began to attend Voice meetings in Bulawayo. In 1949, representatives of most of Insiza's chiefs and headmen attended the Voice congress in Salisbury; Maduna's delegate chaired the meeting.[107]

Parallel to growing Voice activism, the pressure for evictions increased. Residents on private farms, led by chiefs and the Voice, resolved that they would rather die than leave their homes.[108] When the NC tried to issue eviction orders to a meeting attended by Chief Maduna, headmen and 400 others, people became 'unruly and defiant', forcing the NC into a hasty retreat.[109] Deputations met with the NC to appeal against eviction on the grounds that it was 'against the law of Jesus' and 'contrary to British Justice'.[110] These appeals carried little weight, but legal recourse did, briefly, win the day. In 1951, 379 family heads were summoned under the Land Apportionment Act and there followed an historic legal victory for the Voice.[111] Sibuzana of Anglesea farm was the first to face charges. Under cross-examination, NC Holl admitted that Anglesea's owner lived in England and that 'it is quite possible' that Sibuzana had been born on the farm. He admitted that there would be no compensation for the loss of homes and that Lupane and Nkayi, to which people were to be moved, lacked services and carried severe health risks for both people and animals.

None of this was considered relevant; instead, Sibuzana was acquitted on a technicality – notice to quit was judged insufficient – and the rest of the families awaiting trial enjoyed a brief reprieve.[112] In response, the Land Apportionment Act was simply amended, following which the Voice's defense crumbled. In the interim, the 'political situation' deteriorated: 'The general feeling of unrest and bitterness prevails in all areas. Numerous native meetings continue to take place at various centres throughout the district, at which agitators and other malcontents denounce

Native Administration and Government policy regarding land'.[113] Conflict intensified over what tactics to adopt. Delegates from the crown lands asked the NC for permission to visit private farms in order to convince people there to move together with them.[114] Others held no such views about the value of moving as a community, or moving at all. Criminal Investigation Department (CID) reports noted talk of violence, chiefs refused to attend meetings, and farmers' stores were boycotted. Activists swore to resist, and threatened those willing to move.[115]

The state responded with overwhelming force, focusing first on Insiza's crown lands. According to the CID, a police column 'descended without warning on a number of kraals before the inhabitants could take any action. Resistance was negligible, the natives being somewhat overwhelmed by the force brought to evict them.'[116] This was a terrifying moment, as one evictee recalled: 'We waged a war of words with the whites for five years when they were trying to evict us. When the whites realized the situation was getting worse and worse, those whites sat and discussed and one day we woke in the morning – it was so bad, trucks all over and we were arrested and handcuffed.... It was an abnormal situation, it was war.'[117] The crown lands were effectively cleared, and a salutary message was sent to those still awaiting eviction. On the NPA, Chiefs Maduna and Ndube changed tack, seeking to exploit the forum of the newly instituted Chiefs' Assembly as well as the NC's desire to revive a council and to re-establish order. Maduna turned from the Voice's legal appeals to an historical argument, citing the promises of permanent occupation made by the CNC to his father 20 years earlier. Crucially, the PNC backed the claim, arguing for compromise on the grounds that Maduna's father 'was a power in the land and the name "Mafu" still carries great weight'. The strategy worked, and most of the NPA was turned over to communal occupation.[118]

While Maduna's negotiations paid off, those living on private land suffered a different fate. Africans living on these farms had often led a relatively unfettered existence; some did not even pay rent. They considered that 'they were given this land to live on long ago'.[119] African policemen reported 'considerable discontent' and numerous meetings.[120] In the end, however, evictions from private land were delayed less because of the militancy of opposition than due to the NAD's difficulties in finding land to which people could be moved. Eventually, the government simply decreed that it 'was not responsible for the moving of Natives on private lands'.[121] Insiza's NC protested against this 'bombshell', querying just where the hundreds of families with their thousands of cattle were to go. Eviction orders would not solve the problem: 'Supposing the Native obeys the order where does he go, he cannot sit on the main road, he can't be absorbed locally, he can't stay where he is, and I can't help him. He is surely entitled to ask me for help.'[122] The PNC underlined the sorry history of land in Insiza and, in the spirit of many members of the NAD before him, pronounced such treatment unjust.[123]

The previous crown land eviction crisis looked due to be repeated – but it was not. The prospect of eviction – literally to the road-side – at the hands of a police column led to a dramatic political shift among Fort Rixon tenants. They now said they would take their chances on any land, 'settle down, fend for themselves regarding water, and so forth and hope that development of the areas would follow'.[124] People who had once adamantly refused eviction now protested because they were not being helped to move. Eventually, the NAD negotiated a compromise, largely by invoking the threat of political unrest, and the evictees were moved at government expense.[125]

The preponderance of coercive power on the side of the state, and the vulnerability of a legal defence, left those facing eviction with neither the means of overcoming police raids, nor the possibility of sustaining courtroom victories. Voice activism delayed eviction, but it could not prevent the dispossession of Matabeleland's heartland. The legacies of the evictions shaped subsequent processes of state-making. Within Insiza, people cooperated with councils and technical development, while those evicted turned to a militant rejection of state intervention and support for nationalism.[126] Chief Maduna's 'co-optation' was in aid of a specific goal: by breaking with the Voice he had secured the biggest single concession on land in the district. But he had made no more than a temporary compromise, as would soon be apparent. Chiefs in alliance with urban and educated activists were crucial in shaping resistance and in linking urban and rural areas. In doing so, they drew on a range of ideologies and tactics, from offering a violent challenge to the justice of evictions to seeking legal redress, from invoking the historical promises of officials to seeking to defend land claims by appeal to the state's desire for technical development and the 'stabilising' force of customary authority. All would underlie the politics of land in Insiza in the coming decades.

LAND AND THE STATE IN CHIMANIMANI

In Chimanimani, the response to both technical development and evictions did not gain the militant edge demonstrated in Insiza. The principal intervention in the reserves was the introduction of heavily regulated irrigation schemes, and labour remained central to struggles with the state. Evictions occurred in a piecemeal way and a number of compromises were achieved, in part as a result of white farmers' need for tenant labour. Where whole communities faced eviction, they responded by petitioning the government, elaborating narratives of loyalty and progress, and invoking history and custom. Underlying their appeals was the threat of cross-border movement, and disorder in the absence of 'tribal' control.

The arrival of demonstrators in Chimanimani shortly preceded, and soon focused on, state-regulated irrigation schemes. In 1928, the first demonstrator found his advice only selectively accepted. Over time, he reported growing hostility, notably from the many women-headed households who objected to the labour demands of recommended methods.[127] Irrigation at any rate soon monopolised state resources. Africans had long undertaken irrigation: state interventions sought to regulate and expand irrigated production. The Mutambara and Umvumvumvu schemes predated the expansion of state intervention, while the Nyanyadzi scheme, initiated in 1935, was a product of it, and soon became the flagship of irrigation policy. Officials linked the schemes to the goals of moving Africans into reserves and bringing them 'under more satisfactory control'. In 1939, H. W. Guest took up the post of irrigation supervisor at Nyanyadzi, and a demonstrator was appointed at Umvumvumvu. At Mutambara, African authority came under attack. This was an unusual scheme in that it had been established under the auspices of the American Methodist Mission and Chief Mutambara, and had long served as a source of patronage and accumulation for the chief and his followers. The scheme was run by a plot-holder committee, chaired by the chief. But the push for state control led the NC to 'dissolve' this 'most unsatisfactory' committee.[128] Plot-holders bitterly resented state regulation: the scheme's placement under Guest's supervision in 1940 met with such resistance that plans for centralising the area were delayed for a full seven years.[129]

In the midst of these interventions, abortive attempts were made to establish Native Councils. The imperative to form councils had nothing of the urgency it had in Insiza due to the lack of links to African associations and NC's derisory view of the district's chiefs. The Assistant NC placed his hopes in younger, 'elected' councillors, usually relatives of chiefs, who were 'fairly well educated and of a progressive type'; chiefs and headmen he saw as 'poor in ability and initiative'. He planned to 'guide the activities of these Councils into channels which aim at better methods of agriculture, soil conservation, animal husbandry and veld management', but this proved a narrow basis for institution-building. The Mutambara Native Council was proclaimed in August 1939, but 'nothing further was done'. A similar lack of success was recorded elsewhere.[130]

In the 1940s, technical development picked up speed. A demonstrator worked in the highland Ngorima reserve, promoting fruit trees and coffee in one of the few success stories. In the lowland Muwushu and Mutambara reserves the focus remained on irrigation. Under the new regime, irrigators were 'obliged to attend lectures and to comply with the regulations governing cultivation, crop rotation and the harvesting of crops.'[131] People were 'encouraged' to move into village lines, all of which provoked widespread non-cooperation. The NC was forced to import irrigators from other districts and repeatedly noted that highlanders were 'loath' to move to the schemes due to their low altitude, onerous labour requirements, and large settlements which, they held, would spread disease. In the face of 'apathy and opposition' forced labour was introduced. The NC concluded that 'the only possible remedy' to all the 'supervision and chasing' was 'eviction of those plotholders who don't toe the line'.[132]

Other development work was similarly undermined by labour shortages and non-cooperation. When the Land Development Officer tried to peg grass strips in arable lands as a conservation measure, he found that the pegs 'were too easily knocked out in ploughing, usually accidentally on purpose'. With regard to labour, the NC complained, 'there are practically no male adults of workable age in the district. The few one sees from time to time can almost all produce leave passes from employers.' Resignedly, he concluded: 'It appears to be hopeless to plan soil conservation work, new road programmes, dam building, and development of water supplies having regard to the labour position.' The government wage of £1 per 'ticket' could not compete with the five to seven pounds migrants made in an equivalent period in South Africa. The situation was considerably worsened by young men's flight from forced labour and by the labour demands of Chimanimani's fast growing forestry industry.[133]

While Chimanimani certainly suffered under the glare of post-war 'development', its experience remained unusual. Stocking rates, a source of panic in other districts, evoked no calls for intervention. Conservation works proceeded slowly, victim to the lack of labour, while the alarm over deforestation elsewhere did not reach

Chimanimani. There was nothing akin to the massive land clearances of Matabeleland. Nonetheless, evictions did threaten people in the highlands due to the expansion of European farming and the timber industry. The African response was largely to migrate in family groups to the reserves, other districts, or Portuguese East Africa. Even where whole communities faced eviction, they rarely turned to confrontation, instead engaging with official and missionary discourse.

Chief Chikukwa and his people resided entirely on European land in Rhodesia, with the majority of followers in Portuguese East Africa. They had come under threat of eviction repeatedly. In 1941, the issue came to the fore when the Land and Agricultural Bank requested their removal from Dunblane farm.[134] Chief Chikukwa had lived on Dunblane since before European conquest. The NC gave him a rousing endorsement: his followers were 'a very useful source of labour supply' and the chief was 'a fine type of native'. He sought to find alternative land in Muwushu reserve but Chikukwa's followers stated that 'definitely they would move to Portuguese territory' rather than to the lowlands.[135]

Chief Chikukwa and 150 'tribal members' subsequently took the initiative, writing to the Governor to 'ask for your protection and paternal consideration of our troubles'.[136] The letter relied heavily on an appeal to the success of the European civilising mission, arguing that the latest proposal to move them into a remote border farm would send them into the barbarous past: 'We have inspected the land it is proposed to shift us to and find it totally unsuitable.... There is no land to plough and as we have been civilised by the Europeans to use ploughs and possess them we cannot make any use of them in the proposed area. Any land there may be will have to be worked with picks and we have traveled beyond such an unsatisfactory and primitive method of cultivation.' What would become of their stock, their furniture, their school? Even the NC deemed the land 'unsuitable for occupation by human beings'.[137] The petitioners could not 'understand why the rights we have had from time immemorial should now be disturbed. We have given our services to the Europeans and have had no trouble with them and they have found us handy and nearby when they wanted workmen.' The petitioners also played on the fear of 'tribal conflict': 'we are now going into the area of a strange chief.... This can only lead to dissatisfaction and may even have serious consequences in the way of tribal fights. We do not know ... by whom we are to be ruled.'

Although the Governor's response was largely circumspect in tone, it made one fatal slip. He assured Chikukwa that his people would be moved to land which was 'suitable and similar to the land on which they are now living',[138] thereby effectively ruling out all available land in the district. In the short term, Chikukwa was moved to a nearby private farm, from where he carried on protesting, writing letter after letter to an increasingly frustrated NC. The NC continued to lobby for a reserve, expressing concern over the dangers of breaking up the 'tribal unit' and undermining the chief's authority.[139] A temporary resolution was finally achieved when the government acquired the group of farms where Chikukwa's people lived and entered into labour agreements with them.[140] Land was thus finally secured through labour.

A second case concerned Headman Dzingire. Though affiliated to the lowveld Muwushu chieftaincy, Dzingire lived on the border of the highland Ngorima reserve. This prosperous community suddenly found itself faced with eviction from a 500-acre section of land, due to an error in the demarcation of the boundary with neighbouring Uitkyk farm. Uitkyk's new owner, one J. F. Conway, started to construct a boundary fence in 1949 which would cut off Dzingiri school and a large portion of what had been considered reserve land, evoking a protest from the Superintendent of nearby Rusitu Mission. Eviction threatened 228 people, all of whom were cooperators of the agricultural demonstrator. They constituted 'one of the most prosperous and progressive settlements in the Native Reserves of this District' and had 'a great number of fruit trees (citrus, peaches, mangoes, bananas etc.), a nice school with neat and tidy layout and a really good teacher's house'. They had 'received considerable encouragement from what they regard as the Government to better themselves'.[141]

The threatened landholders played heavily on these credentials. The headman and his sons, notably Dzawanda Dzingiri, an agricultural demonstrator based in the town of Mutare, led the campaign to stave off eviction, evoking a threatened narrative of progress much as Chikukwa had done. A committee, based on the headman's court, wrote to the NC: 'We were ignorant, living in darkness. You sent us Mr. Alvord to show us how to plough, to plant fruit and to keep our kraals clean.... We said our area was too small and was very steep. He said "It does not matter. Work, we shall adjust this matter later".' The letter mourned the impending loss of their 'great works' : 'Today we die Sirs.... We give thanks to your [sic] Sirs, who have uplifted us from bad ways.' The appeal moved the NC, who recommended the land be purchased so as to safeguard 'the progressive development of these people'.[142]

Conway, however, was unmoved. He only offered to sell at the extortionate rate of £12 per acre, an offer the NAD was obliged to refuse.[143] Conway's intransigence led the NC to make an extraordinary proposal. He asked whether the government could claim the land under the 'Law of Prescription' on the grounds that Africans had been in continuous occupation for decades. The idea that continuous occupation could be used to make a legal claim to land was, of course, in direct conflict with the policies for which the government stood. Needless to say, the Department of Justice refused to take up the case.[144]

Meanwhile, the 'Dzingire Tribal Community Committee' pressed on. Two of the headman's mission-educated sons raised money to send representatives to testify before the parliamentary committee charged with assigning land for 'native occupation', and requested an audience with the CNC.[145] The CNC declined, leading to a switch in tactics. Headman Dzingire and his sons broke ranks with the more widely defined community in an effort to safeguard their land claims, especially those of sons absent at work. Dzingire asked that the 'non-indigenous' people living in his 'tribal area' be removed. He cited the needs of his five sons, asserting his right as headman to make exclusive land claims for kin. But the NC rejected this appeal to custom, eventually settling the majority of the community inside the reserve or on labour agreements. Further appeals by Dzawanda Dzingire led to the award of over £428 as compensation for improvements in the disputed area. Dzawanda eventually bought a farm in a nearby NPA and, after his father's death, became the Dzingire Headman and an active nationalist.[146]

In Chimanimani, the question of overt resistance was rarely mooted and the idea of legal appeal was introduced by the NC, not the Voice as in Insiza. Claims to land lay in the progressiveness of its occupants, histories of occupation, loyalty and labour, and under pressure, the claims of 'tribe' and custom. Yet there were parallels to Insiza: chiefs and headmen allied with educated, often employed, younger men, usually relatives in the Chimanimani case, who were able to draft letters, aware of changes in the law, and familiar with the administrative hierarchy through which they had to appeal. This mix of tactics reflected the variegated nature of the settler state and of people's understandings of its claims to authority over people and land. By the end of the 1940s, however, a new dispensation was in the making, in which authority over the land was to be mediated by an increasingly uncompromising technocratic bureaucracy.

Conclusion

Fifty years of settler rule had dramatically transformed the land and authority over it, creating a racially based division between freehold 'European' land and the 'communal' reserves, each with distinct forms of governance. But this division was not so neat in practice. The NAD's efforts to fashion authority in the reserves on the basis of 'tribal rule' were constantly complicated by Africans' interaction with urban areas and work-places across the region, by the ideas of missionaries and religious and political movements, and by its own efforts at 'development'. The NAD recognised the diverse nature of African society in the mix of 'progressive' and customary leaders who sat on Boards and Councils. The customary was only partially elaborated, and it was undermined by efforts to make the reserves 'legible' and productive on the basis of an alternative, scientific authority over the land mediated by technical officials. Africans' defence of their livelihoods and autonomy in these decades drew on the diverse legacies of pre-colonial polities, on state and mission discourse, as well as on the radical politics of organisations like the ICU and Voice, and the religious fervour of the Zionist movement. It was onto this variegated landscape that the most ambitious of the settler state's efforts to transform the ways in which Africans lived and farmed was introduced: the Native Land Husbandry Act.

Notes

1 Insiza comprised two sub-districts, Fort Rixon in the north and Filabusi in the south. Chimanimani was originally a sub-district of Melsetter, later Chipinge, district. See Map 1, p. x.
2 See Bhebe, 1978, Ranger, 1979, chapters 1 and 2, and Ranger, 1999.
3 See Cobbing, 1976. Cobbing's thesis remains the key work on the Ndebele state.
4 See the delineation reports of the Ministry of Internal Affairs, 1963b, 1963c, for Chiefs Sibasa and Ndube, and Cobbing, 1976, 71-4.
5 On the Ndebele economy, see Cobbing, 1976, Chapter 5, and Palmer, 1977a, 224-5.
6 Cobbing, 1976, 207-19, 375-7, and Phimister, 1988b, 13-15.
7 See Ranger, 1979, 100-108; Cobbing, 1976, 372-82; Palmer, 1977b, 42-3.
8 See Cobbing, 1976, 347-460 on the campaigns and conclusion of the war; Iliffe, 1990, 13-30, on the aftermath of war; Jeater, 1993, 64-70, on bridewealth.
9 For a summary of the creation of Insiza's reserves, see Palmer, 1977b, 272-3.
10 See Phimister, 1988b, 24; Ranger, 1985b, 116; Palmer, 1977a, 229, 233; Cheater, 1990, 190-91.
11 See discussion in Maxwell, 1999, Chapter 1.

12 On these polities, the central work is Rennie, 1973.
13 Beach, 1991, 4.
14 Rennie, 1973, 83.
15 Maxwell, 1999, Chapter 1.
16 Palmer, 1977a, 224.
17 See Rennie, 1973, 139-70; Beach, 1991, 3, 27-30.
18 Rennie, 1973, 171-4. Also see Palmer, 1977b, 19-20, 41.
19 See the first hand account of Sinclair, 1971.
20 See Rennie, 1973, 177-8, 180-204; Palmer, 1977b, 41, 45; Beach, 1986, 70-71.
21 The 'spreading out' of people is everywhere recorded. See Drinkwater, 1991, 32; Maxwell, 1999, 40; Phimister, 1988b, 82-3.
22 The term is from Ranger, 1985.
23 Ranger, 1985, chapters 1 and 2; Phimister, 1988b, 24, 72.
24 Jeater, 1993; Schmidt, 1992.
25 Holleman, 1969, 15-18.
26 32.11.5F/35541, Internal Affairs, Land: Melsetter, correspondence.
27 32.11.5R/35539, Internal Affairs, Land: Fort Rixon and Filabusi, correspondence; Palmer, 1977b, 147.
28 Palmer, 1977b, 90; Steele, 1972, 425-7.
29 Rennie, 1973, 181-92; Palmer, 1977b, 90; Steele, 1972, 418-20.
30 Steele, 1972, 80-2.
31 See discussion in Gray, 1960, 3-31; Jeater, 1993, 49-63.
32 Schmidt, 1992, Chapter 4; Vail, 1989b.
33 Jeater, 1993, 212-14.
34 NCs simply could not adjudicate all disputes, and Africans had their own ideas of which sort of justice best suited them. See Steele, 1972, 82-6; Holleman, 1969, 92.
35 Holleman, 1969, 35-43; Steele, 1972, 80-6.
36 See Worby, 1994, 384; Cheater, 1990; Smith,1992b, 15; Ranger, 1999, Chapter 4.
37 See Summers, 2002, Chapter 4.
38 Steele, 1972, 314.
39 Steele, 1972, 33, and see 317-51.
40 Murray, 1970, 288-9.
41 *Ibid.*, 292, and see 294-9.
42 See Smith, 1992a, 5, and 1992b.
43 ORAL/HO 3, Henry Roger Howman, interviewed by M.C. Steele, 10, 26 August 1971.
44 See Drinkwater, 1991, Chapter 2.
45 See McGregor, 1991, 84-7.
46 McGregor, 1991, 87, 95-107. Also see Scott, 1998, on 'legibility' and the aestheticism of modernist planning.
47 Palmer, 1977b, 202; Steele, 1972, 417.
48 S235/509, Assistant NC's Annual Report for 1931, Fort Rixon; McGregor, 1991, 78-81.
49 Drinkwater, 1991, 57, 64.
50 Phimister, 1986.
51 See Samasuwo, 2003.
52 S1563, Annual Report of the Director of Native Agriculture for the Year 1945.
53 S1563, NC's Annual Report for 1947, Wedza. And see Wilson, 1986.
54 Government of Southern Rhodesia, 1944, 36.
55 See, for example, Scoones, 1990; Wilson, 1986, 1990; Beinart, 2000; Robins, 1998.
56 Drinkwater, 1991, 59-63.
57 McGregor, 1991, 108-10.
58 Maxwell, 1999, 40-2; Mukamuri, 1995.
59 Summers, 2002, Chapter 1.
60 Schmidt, 1992, especially Chapter 4.
61 Such tactics are regularly recorded in NCs' reports. See, for example, S235/501, NC's Annual Report for 1925, Filabusi; S235/505, NC's Annual Report for 1927, Fort Rixon; Palmer, 1977b, 147.
62 S235/506, NC's Annual Report for 1928, Fort Rixon; S235/503, NC's Annual Report for 1925, Fort Rixon.
63 S235/508-513, NC's and Assistant NC's Annual Reports for 1930 to 1935, Fort Rixon and Filabusi.
64 Ranger, 1978.
65 S235/516, NC's Annual Report for 1938, Filabusi.
66 S1051, NC's Annual Report for 1948, Filabusi, and see series S1563 for 1941-45 and 1947; S235/518 for 1946, Filabusi and Fort Rixon.

67 Phimister, 1988b, 72-8, and Ranger, 1970, 28-9.
68 See Ranger, 1999, 100-101, and 1985, 116-17.
69 Ranger, 1999, chapters 2-4.
70 S235/502, 504, NC's Annual Reports for 1924, 1926, Fort Rixon; Steele, 1972, 420.
71 Here I am arguing against the interpretations of Maduna's activities specifically in Phimister, 1988b, 200-202, and Steele, 1972, 181-91, and of chiefs more broadly in Mamdani, 1996.
72 Assistant NC, Filabusi, to NC, Fort Rixon, 13 March 1933, cited in Ranger, 1990b, 1-2; S235/509, NC's and Assistant NC's Annual Reports for 1931, Fort Rixon and Filabusi.
73 S235/510, Assistant NC's Annual Report for 1932, Filabusi.
74 Ranger, 1990b.
75 Palmer, 1977b, 216.
76 *Ibid.*, 64.
77 Summers, 2002, 61-9; S235/511, NC's Annual Report for 1933, Filabusi.
78 S235/511, NC's Annual Report for 1933, Filabusi.
79 S235/505, Assistant NC's Annual Report for 1927, Melsetter. More than a decade later, NCs often did not know how many people lived where, and confused reserve and crown lands. See 32.11.5F/35541, Land: Melsetter, Assistant NC, Melsetter, to NC, Chipinga, 14 March 1940 and 19 July 1940, for example.
80 S235/509, Assistant NC's Annual Report for 1931, Melsetter.
81 S235/504, NC's Annual Report for 1926, Chiping. Also see S235/505, Assistant NC's Annual Report for 1927, Melsetter.
82 S235/508, NC's Annual Report for 1930, Chipinga.
83 *Lobola* payments were roughly £25 in cash or gold, paid over several years. See S235/505, 509, Assistant NC's Annual Reports for 1927, 1931, Melsetter; S235/508, NC's Annual Report, 1930, Chipinga.
84 S235/506, NC's Annual Report for 1928, Chipinga; S235/505, Assistant NC's Annual Report for 1927, Melsetter. White farmers employed on average only three taxpayers each, some none at all.
85 S235/513, Assistant NC's Annual Report for 1935, Melsetter.
86 S1563, Assistant NC's Annual Report for 1942, Melsetter.
87 S1542/N2/B-D, Native Boards, 1931-1939, Minutes of Meetings of Chiefs and Headmen and Native Board, NC's Office, Chipinga, 12 June 1934, 28 February 1931; Rennie, 1973, 237-9.
88 Rennie, 1973, 547-8; S235/505, NC's Annual Report for 1927, Chipinga; Summers, 2002, 181-4.
89 See Fields, 1997 [1985]; Rennie, 1973, 481-9; Ranger, 1970, 199-222.
90 S235/510, NC's Annual Report for 1932, Chipinga.
91 Rennie, 1973, 486.
92 S235/511, NC's Annual Report for 1933, Chipinga; S1542/N2/B-D, Native Boards 1931-1939, Minutes of a Meeting of Chiefs and Headmen and Native Board held at the NC's Office, Chipinga, 12 June 1934.
93 Chaumba, Scoones and Wolmer, 2003, make this point with regard to post-2000 land politics.
94 S1563, Assistant NC's and NC's Annual Reports for 1942, Fort Rixon and Filabusi.
95 S235/514-516, NC's Annual Reports for 1935, 1936, 1938, Filabusi.
96 S235/512, NC's Annual Report for 1934, Filabusi. Interventions with regard to forestry or improved cattle were greeted with similar fears of expropriation. See McGregor, 1991, 86-93; Steele, 1972, 353-74.
97 S1563, NC's Annual Report for 1944, Filabusi.
98 S1563, NC's Annual Report for 1947, Filabusi. The numbers are misleading to the extent that people were able to move their cattle to other sources of grazing during the drought, as they commonly did.
99 S1563, NC's Annual Reports for 1945 to 1947, Filabusi; Minutes of the Insiza Reserve and Glassblock and Panasequa Native Occupation Areas Native Council (hereafter the Insiza Council), Filabusi, 22 March 1949. Forced labour was common. See Johnson, 1992.
100 6.5.9R/842/3, Assessment Committee Report: Insiza District Native Areas, Filabusi, 14 May 1956; S1563, NC's Annual Report for 1947, Filabusi.
101 See Bhebe, 1989a, 126. Bhebe incorrectly implies that Maduna's wealth was owed to advantages accorded chiefs under the Native Land Husbandry Act of 1951. The Act had yet to be implemented.
102 S1563, NC's Annual Report for 1947, Filabusi.
103 Minutes of the Insiza Council, Filabusi, 9 September 1948.
104 See Filabusi and Fort Rixon Annual NC's Reports in the series S235/507-S235/517; S1563/1940-S1563/1947. In the country as a whole, there were 71,182 'excess families'. See 14.8.8F/69691, Native Land Position, Summary of Ad Hoc Reports, January 1947.
105 Bhebe, 1989a, 125-6. Also see Ranger, 1985, 130.
106 Minutes of the Insiza Council, Filabusi, 19 October 1948.
107 CID, Memo 35, British African National Voice Association, 16 March 1949; S482/517, Military Intelligence Reports, Criminal Investigation Department Report on a meeting held on 26-27 November

41

1949, Salisbury; Bhebe, 1989a, 35.

108 CID, Memo 50, Filabusi, 1950. Compare to Ranger, 1999, Chapter 6.

109 S2236, Criminal Cases, Filabusi, 1951-1954, Rex v. Sibuzana, 20 July 1951.

110 CID, Memo 53, Filabusi, February 1951; S2236, Criminal Cases, Filabusi, 1951-1954, Rex v. Sibuzana, 20 July 1951. See also Ranger, 1999, Chapter 6.

111 See S2236, Criminal Cases, Filabusi, 1951-1954, Rex v. Sibuzana, 20 July 1951. Also see Bhebe, 1989a, Chapter 7, on this and other Voice cases.

112 35569, P3623, Vol. 2, National Park, NC Matobo to PNC, 29 August 1951 and Attorney General's Memorandum, 5 September 1951; CID, Memo 56, Native Unrest, Filabusi, July 1951; CID, Memo 59, Native Unrest, Filabusi, August 1951.

113 NC's Annual Report for 1951, Filabusi.

114 32.11.5R/35539, Assistant NC, Fort Rixon, to PNC, Matabeleland, 8 May 1952.

115 CID, Memo 66, Filabusi, 30 May 1952; Memo 67, Filabusi, 27 June 1952.

116 CID, Memo 70, Native Affairs: Removals, Matabeleland, Hadane, Rhodesdale, 30 September 1952.

117 Interview with Paul Mapetshwana Moyo, Gampinya, Nkayi, 19 October 1995, in Alexander, McGregor and Ranger, 2000, 49.

118 See 35596, Assembly of Chiefs, Matabeleland, Matobo Assembly, 29 August 1952; PNC, Matabeleland, to Secretary of Native Affairs, 9 December 1952; Chief Land Officer to NC, Filabusi, 15 January 1953; Assembly of Chiefs, Matabeleland, Matobo Assembly, 4 August 1953

119 For example, see CID, Memo 64, Fort Rixon, Sampson and Montrose, 31 March 1952.

120 CID, Memo 65, Native Unrest, Filabusi, 29 April 1952.

121 32.11.5R/35539, Secretary of Native Affairs to PNC, Matabeleland, 9 December 1952; Assistant Secretary, Native Economic Development, to all PNCs and the Chief Land Officer, 25 September 1952; Assistant Secretary, Native Economic Development, H. F. Child, to CNC, 19 January 1953.

122 32.11.5R/35539, Assistant NC, Fort Rixon, to PNC, Matabeleland, 17 November 1952.

123 32.11.5R/35539, PNC, Matabeleland, to Secretary for Native Affairs, 27 January 1953.

124 32.11.5R/35539, PNC, Matabeleland, to Secretary for Native Affairs, 7 April 1953.

125 32.11.5R/35539, Assistant CNC to PNC, Matabeleland, 12 June 1953.

126 See Alexander, McGregor and Ranger, 2000.

127 S235/508, NC's Annual Report for 1928, Chipinga; S235/509, 512, Assistant NC's Annual Reports for 1931 and 1934, Melsetter.

128 S235/517, Assistant NC's Annual Report for 1939, Melsetter.

129 See S1563, S235/518, NC's Annual Reports for 1940, 1941 and 1946, Chipinga; 6.5.6R/84266, Assessment Committee, Mutambara Irrigation Project, 23 May 1956.

130 32.14.3R/35580, Assistant NC, Melsetter, to NC, Chipinga, 13 March 1939; 18 May 1939; 15 July 1939; 27 October 1939; NC R. Cashel, Melsetter, to PNC, Umtali, 10 March 1955.

131 S1563, NC's Annual Report for 1940, Chipinga.

132 S1563, NC's Annual Report for 1942, Chipinga; S1563, S235/518, S1051, NC's Annual Reports for 1945, 1946, 1947-48, Melsetter.

133 See S1563, S1051, NC's Annual Reports for 1947-48, Melsetter.

134 32.11.5F/35541, Acting Manager, Land and Agricultural Bank of Southern Rhodesia, to NC, Melsetter, 7 February 1941.

135 32.11.5F/35541, Assistant NC, Melsetter, to NC, Chipinga, 12 February 1941; 13 March 1941.

136 See 32.11.5F/35541, Chief J. Chikukwa to Sir Herbert Stanley, Governor of Southern Rhodesia, 15 July 1941.

137 32.11.5F/35541, Assistant NC, Melsetter, to NC, Chipinga, 12 August 1941.

138 32.11.5F/35541, His Excellency the Governor H. Stanley to the Prime Minister, 12 August 1941.

139 32.11.5F/35541, Assistant NC, Melsetter, to NC, Chipinga, 19 September 1943; Acting PNC, Umtali, to CNC, 7 October 1943.

140 32.11.5F/35541, NC, Melsetter, to PNC, Umtali, 15 October 1945; Conservator of Forests to CNC, 4 December 1945.

141 32.11.5F/35541, J. M. Watermeyer for Lands Inspector to PNC, Umtali, 25 November 1949; Assistant NC, Melsetter, to PNC, Manicaland, 14 December 1949.

142 See 32.11.5F/35541, Tinidzo Samson, Munyori we dare redu repa Dzingire, Secretary of our Committee (of people removed from Uitkyk), to NC, Melsetter, 26 November 1949; Assistant NC, Melsetter, to PNC, Umtali, 14 December 1949; PNC, Umtali, to CNC, 17 December 1949.

143 32.11.5F/35541, J. F. Conway to Secretary for Native Affairs, 17 January 1950; Secretary for Native Affairs to J. F. Conway, 11 February 1950.

144 See 32.11.5F/35541, Assistant NC, Melsetter, to PNC, Umtali, 24 February 1950; PNC, Umtali, to CNC,

27 February 1950; Secretary for Native Affairs to Secretary, Department of Justice, 1 August 1950; Secretary, Department of Justice, to Secretary for Native Affairs, 23 August 1950.

145 32.11.5F/35541, Dzingire Tribal Community Committee, Secretary K. David Dzingire, to Assistant NC, Melsetter, 4 January 1950; Dzawanda Dzingire to PNC, Umtali, 28 September 1950.

146 See 32.11.5F/35541, Headman Dzingire (written by K. David Dzingire) to Assistant NC, Melsetter, 31 September 1950; Dzingire Tribal Community Committee to Assistant NC, Melsetter, 14 September 1950; D. D. Dzingire to Assistant NC, Melsetter, NC, Umtali, and CNC, 16 October 1950; Assistant NC, Melsetter, to CNC, 18 October 1950; PNC, Umtali, to CNC, 20 October 1950; Acting Secretary for Native Affairs to Minister for Native Affairs, 18 April 1951.

2

Remaking the Reserves
The Native Land Husbandry Act

Throughout British colonial Africa, the late 1940s inaugurated what has been called the 'second colonial occupation'.[1] This was a period in which great faith was placed in 'high modernism', in the merits of state planning, and in the possibilities of increasing productivity through technical innovation. The expansion of state activity relied on the generation of new scientific practices and knowledge, and the institution of cadres of experts. It heralded unprecedented intervention into African lives, a new conceptualisation of Africans as workers and farmers,[2] and innovations in ideas about governance. In Southern Rhodesia, the high point of 'technical development' went hand-in-hand with a tentative move away from segregationist ideology marked by the policies of 'partnership', and with the creation of the Central African Federation (encompassing Southern and Northern Rhodesia and Nyasaland). The ambition and optimism of this period was at first buoyed by the booming post-war economy, but it did not last. It was the very centrepiece of Southern Rhodesia's modernising plans, the Native Land Husbandry Act (NLHA), that would in the end generate the greatest crisis of authority the settler state had faced since its foundation.

The NLHA and the State

The NLHA was promulgated, with World Bank support, in 1951. It was 'one of the most far-reaching land reform measures in Africa';[3] without a doubt, it provoked 'the most violent outbreaks of rural opposition since the First Chimurenga of 1896/97'.[4] The economic changes of the 1940s had set the stage for the Act. As we have seen, growth in secondary industry and a boom in white farmers' tobacco production had created severe labour shortages alongside shortfalls in food production, while massive evictions from 'European' land had increased pressures within the reserves, heightening official concerns over conservation and productivity. For many NAD officials, these developments confirmed the possibility – and the necessity – of a radical restructuring of the African role in both urban and rural economies.

The Godlonton Commission of 1944 had set out much of the thinking behind the NLHA. It presumed African farmers to be lazy and destructive, and it justified coercive intervention in the name of the state's duty to bring progress and increased productivity. The Commission was accompanied by a major revamping and expansion of the bureaucracies concerned with administering and developing the reserves. The 'specialist' branches – Education, Labour, Agriculture, Accountancy, Native Engineering, Native Marketing – were, with District Administration, cast into a single superstructure, the Division of Native Affairs. Arthur Pendered, previously secretary of the Godlonton Commission, secured the key post of Under Secretary of the Division.[5] The technical branches rapidly expanded and, as Michael Drinkwater writes, 'the belief in the superiority of formal scientific knowledge was institutionalized in dogmatic form'.[6] Administrative ideas about custom took a back seat. As J. F. Holleman explains, technical officials 'had gathered hard facts, were building up a vast organization of specially trained people, and were able to present concrete plans.... Against this elan the administrators could do little better than advise caution, and speak vaguely about the dangers of disturbing the social system'. NCs were no longer to be the 'principal custodians of tribal life', but the 'captains of its social and economic transition into the modern world'.[7] As the CNC commented: 'There is no stopping these agriculturalists and economists. We want economic improvement in the Reserves, and these chaps seem to have all the answers.'[8]

A number of innovations in African rural authority were proposed in this context, though none were pursued with great resolve. The Godlonton Commission had called for the appointment of younger chiefs and their education in 'progressive' attitudes and scientific agriculture, such that 'better discipline and greater sense of responsibility will develop'.[9] In this view, chiefs were to be aids to agricultural improvement. Administrators' concerns lay more in countering the post-war rise of nationalism, first through the Southern Rhodesian African National Congress (ANC) and then the National Democratic Party (NDP), and making order out of the chaos caused by evictions. In the year of the NLHA's promulgation, steps were taken to 'rationalise' chieftaincy, and to bolster chiefs' loyalty. Provincial Chiefs' Assemblies were established, chiefs' subsidies were increased, and titles were abolished where chiefs had lost followers. These steps were not wholly successful: rationalisation required people to transfer their allegiance arbitrarily from one chief to another, and caused such resentment that it was partially reversed six years later.[10] Many administrators at any rate remained more than a little sceptical of chiefs' utility. In 1953, the CNC wrote: 'A description of chiefs, particularly in Mashonaland, takes on the nature of a catalogue of the vices and virtues of an old men's home. So many are beer-ridden, old, blind, opposed to all new ideas, senile, swayed by an entourage of hangers-on, lethargic and chronic invalids that they are of little use administratively.'[11]

Belatedly, an effort was made to give the struggling Native Councils a new lease of life, with an eye both to containing nationalists and placating the British Colonial Office. The African Councils Act of 1957 was largely the work of Roger Howman, whose guiding principle was that a distinction needed to be made between local and national African representation. He argued, 'it would be foolhardy not to ensure that Local Government remains local and is not mixed up in any way with a structure that permits political ferment to seep down'.[12] Councils were to be 'insulated' from 'political activity'.[13] The new councils provided in theory for greater powers and a more flexible election of representatives, the idea being that 'progressives' would find an outlet for their political aspirations within a carefully demarcated local context.[14] Rural governance was explicitly conceived in terms of bridging the divide between the 'ancient duties' of chiefs in their 'traditional sphere', and the 'needs of a money economy and an educated, partly individualised society'.[15]

This shaky set of rural authorities was given the tall order of aiding in the implementation of an Act that had no concern for either the cares of custom or the ever more insistent demands of nationalism. On the one hand, the NLHA simply extended and enforced earlier policies with more punitive powers: the precepts of centralisation still shaped settlement patterns and the division of land between individually farmed arable fields and communal grazing areas; destocking and grazing schemes remained the primary means of stock management; physical conservation works and agricultural intensification on the Alvord model continued to dominate interventions in arable production. On the other hand, the NLHA was revolutionary: unlike previous policies, it was not intended to 'squeeze' more Africans into the reserves. The problem of the reserves was reconceived in terms of overpopulation, and so the answer could only lie in limiting the numbers of Africans with land rights.[16] To do this, a stop had to be put to labour migration between the reserves and urban areas. Further settlement in the reserves would be halted by issuing saleable land and stock rights to a permanently limited number of African farmers. The Act sought a transformation of African participation in the economy. As the CNC put it, by making a 'final allocation of land', 'the Native will either become a peasant farmer only' or 'an industrialised worker with his tentacles pulled out of the soil'.[17]

The NLHA called for a significant ideological shift: Africans were no longer to be thought of as communal tribespeople, but as rational individuals operating in an impersonal market in the idealised guise of the yeoman farmer and proletarian family.[18] Official justifications for the NLHA rested heavily on its promise of increased economic efficiency. As Arthur Pendered wrote,

> The time has now come when all indigenous natives can no longer continue to maintain a dual existence as part-time employment in the European areas and part-time farming in the Native Reserves for, apart from its impossibility, it does not conduce to efficiency in either area, nor can the economy of the colony afford to offer satisfactory conditions in both areas for the dual mode of life.[19]

Those excluded from land would provide a stable workforce for industry. In the reserves, limiting the number of farmers and giving them secure tenure would promote individual responsibility, investment and the adoption of recommended agricultural methods. Technical officials expected an 'almost immediate beneficial result' in productivity and conservation to follow from the change in tenure.[20] This logic captivated administrators too. 'The communal system and capitalism are incompatible and cannot flourish within the same economy', the CNC argued. 'The communal system of land tenure hangs as a dead weight upon the Native and frustrates all his endeavours to attain Western standards.... It retards his transition from a subsistence to a money economy, and is out of keeping with our declared purpose in Southern Rhodesia, which is to develop the resources of the country to the utmost.'[21] For many NCs, the idea of a 'final allocation of land' had the additional appeal of promising an end to the unceasing demands for land from Africans facing eviction.

The NLHA thus directly repudiated 'customary' and 'communal' rights to land in favour of individual right holders and 'secular state power',[22] i.e. the government officials (including chiefs) who monitored land use and land transfers. Yudelman argues that 'it was the intent of the act that the intricate network of social and tribal customs regarding land use and land transfer would give way to the marketplace.'[23] Official commitment to the 'marketplace' was, however, to be tempered by a host of restrictions. Only those who farmed and owned stock at the time of the Act's implementation were eligible for rights; land rights could not be used as collateral against a loan; the size of arable allocations and number of stock rights was limited in line with technical estimates of carrying capacities, while accumulation was limited to three times the 'standard holding' designated for each reserve. In addition, conservationist concerns were used to justify an array of punitive measures to enforce 'good husbandry' and provide labour for conservation works. African 'rights' to land were to be subordinated to the discipline of 'development'.[24]

The heavy regulation of the reserve 'marketplace' and African production reflected officials' belief in the need for close state direction of the process by which Africans' farming methods were to be transformed. To achieve the NLHA's ambitions, the state needed to 'become both far more knowledgeable and far more intrusive'. It needed to make the reserves 'legible', and so capable of manipulation.[25] What was needed was the collection and analysis of data by a huge corps of experts on an immense scale and at huge cost: £15 million was spent between 1950 and 1958, a large part of which was drawn from levies on marketed African produce.[26] Employing recent advances in aerial photography, an initial mapping and land classification process was to be undertaken in each reserve.[27] Land Development Officers with African staff were then to take a census of farmers, arable land and stock. Detailed land classification and conservation plans were to be drawn up by specialists and an Assessment Committee was then charged with setting standard field sizes and stocking rates. Destocking would follow, and farming and grazing rights would be registered. The registered holder was then legally responsible for the construction of conservation works within one year. After all this had taken place, a final plan for land use was to be made, agricultural extension resumed, and a second round of aerial photography undertaken.

These elaborate procedures left chiefs, headmen and NCs with much reduced authority and with little ideological purchase, at the same time as their enforcement duties were greatly expanded. As the NLHA was implemented, administrators began to worry over the position of chiefs: the 'onerous and unpleasant' duties they had to carry out, notably destocking, meant their loyalty was severely strained. As nationalism burgeoned, NCs called for further measures to bolster their authority. In 1957, the Minister of Native Affairs warned: 'With the spread of the African National Congress into the rural areas, it is more important now than ever to have the Chiefs and rural people working with us and not against us.' The ANC was 'sowing seeds of discord': 'it would appear that the exploitation of imaginary grievances, e.g. destocking and the allocation of land, is the method employed to win support.... We must obtain and maintain, through the Chiefs, administrative assistance and political stability.'[28] Losing the loyalty of chiefs promised chaos: 'If the Government fails to range the chiefs on its side then either the chiefs will surrender to the demogogues [*sic*], or the people, denied a strong lead by the chiefs, will be at the mercy of every soap box orator.'[29]

It was partly in response to this growing strain that a shift within the NAD began to take place. Initially, technical officials had exercised unprecedented control. With the help of a dire report on the state of conservation by the Natural Resources Board in 1954, they vastly increased the speed of the Land Husbandry Act's implementation.[30] But only a few years later, as growth in the national economy slowed and African nationalism boomed, the confidence and dominance of the technical branches waned. Technical officials themselves in fact led the critique of the NLHA.

The NLHA's flaws have been discussed at length, both in academic circles and by contemporary officials.[31] Here I touch on only a few of the problems relating to productivity and land shortage. The 1955 NLHA Five Year Plan had projected massive and rapid increases in productivity, but these goals went unrealised.[32] Agriculturalists' projections were based on the unrepresentative (and inaccurately calculated) yields supposedly achieved by the less than one per cent of farmers who were demonstration plot holders.[33] There were, in addition, serious constraints on establishing the 'economic unit' on which the yields were to be realised, as there was nowhere near enough land for all those eligible: the Quinton Report noted in 1960 that there was land available for only 235,000 of the eligible 346,000 farmers.[34] Officials at first sought to accommodate more farmers by reducing the size of the 'economic holding'. They then sought to reduce the numbers of right holders by speeding the pace of registration and placing new limits on eligible claimants, thus arbitrarily excluding many farmers.[35] These measures failed to solve the problem of land shortage, but they did greatly undermine, rather than increase, security of tenure – one of the key goals of the Act.[36]

These were not the only problems. Stock holdings were required to maintain fertility on arable land under the agriculturalists' model, but often farmers had too few or no stock, and this in areas that faced severe destocking in line with pasture officers' assessments of carrying capacity.[37] NCs' reaction to such 'imbalances' was often a straightforward call for the addition of more land to the reserves, but only piecemeal concessions were made, largely in an effort to ease the ongoing eviction of Africans from 'European' land.[38] In the second half of the 1950s it became clear that the industrial and white farming economy could not absorb those denied land. In the first half of the 1950s, population had grown by 16 per cent and employment by 15 per cent, but between 1956 and 1961, population growth stood at 18 per cent whereas employment growth registered just five per cent, thereby creating a massive category of 'landless unemployed'.[39] Moreover, wages, housing, and welfare provision in the urban areas were far from adequate to provide for the envisioned proletarian family, while the extent to which successful agricultural production in the reserves relied on migrant labour remittances proved to have been sorely underestimated.[40]

The state's 'technical imagination' was not only far off the mark regarding economic and agricultural realities, but it also outstripped its capacity. Agriculturalists complained that the Technical Block responsible for training field staff simply could not cope.[41] Extension work ground to a halt; Soil Conservation Officers were under 'considerable strain'.[42] In practice, shortcuts and compromises were the norm, and Africans took full advantage of state weaknesses. Where officials were thin on the ground, as they often were, chiefs and headmen were given far more latitude in implementing the Act than intended, and used their power to evade limitations on land and stock, bolster their own positions, and bribe or otherwise influence demonstrators.[43] NCs increased carrying capacities so as to reduce the level of destocking when they felt political stability or production to be threatened, provoking the ire of the uncompromising Natural Resources Board in the process.[44] NCs often simply could not enforce policies. In Buhera, for example, African stockowners hid cattle on neighbouring European farms prior to destocking, and then imitated the ear-marking the NC used to designate counted cattle. When the NC switched to marking cattle with branding fluid, stockowners simply purchased the fluid themselves.[45] It proved equally problematic to keep track of people. As the NLHA Standing Committee complained, 'it was very difficult to control or prevent infiltration into the reserves. In many areas the number of people without permits exceeded those with.'[46]

These pressures and problems were heatedly debated in the national forum of the NLHA Standing Committee, and led to clashes between administrators and technical officials. Destocking was perhaps most controversial. NCs argued that it was causing 'political restlessness', and undermining their relationships with chiefs and headmen. They asked for destocking to be carried out over longer periods, but were only able to extract minimal concessions. R. L. C. Cunliffe, Administrative Officer for the NLHA, simply urged the adoption of a Machiavellian strategy: 'Everything should be done to foster an intense feeling of rivalry between the graziers of different grazing areas', thus creating incentives to exclude others' cattle.[47]

Though the Director of Native Agriculture was willing to allow small changes in the timing and method of the Act's implementation, he was not willing to question its merits, and nor, despite the obvious discomfort of NCs, was CNC S. E. Morris.[48] But this did not mean, as Drinkwater argues, that 'throughout the technical development phase', officials 'remained confident and complacent about the presumed benefits of the policies they were enforcing'.[49] In fact, NAD economists began to admit that their understanding of African production systems was badly wrong in the mid-1950s. Pending, or as a result of, economic evaluations, the Act was suspended on irrigation schemes in 1956 and in high rainfall areas in 1957. In 1959, the efficiency and viability of the NLHA in low rainfall areas was called into question.[50] In an economic report on the country as a whole, Dr S. M. Makings summed up the pervasive doubts about the Act's most basic assumptions:

> The Act is based on the major principle of individual incentive and responsibility as the outcome of individual ownership and the latter is given status as perhaps the chief factor in forward development. But if in fact there is little prospect for individual economic holdings except in limited areas it is very important that forward planning should take full cognisance of this position. It would be better to found thriving communal systems in which there were necessary restraints in the common welfare rather than a patchwork of individual holdings forever battling with abject poverty as the price of independence.[51]

These profound doubts were underlined by the findings of the Central Statistical Office's *Sample Survey of African Agriculture*. Undertaken in 1959/60, the survey showed that the NLHA had had a negative effect on yields and crop diversity in most regions. Though the results were withheld from publication until 1962, they were circulated among officials.[52]

There were thus, from 1956, cutting critiques of the NLHA from within the technical branches which had so recently championed its promulgation. But the final blow to the Act was to come less from uncertainties over the authority of science than from the political crisis that the Act engendered. Ultimately, the Minister of Native Affairs' contention that, 'To a large extent the implementation of the Land Husbandry Act will stand or fall on the measure of cooperation and enthusiasm we can elicit from the people', proved correct.[53]

Rural Politics and the NLHA

The NLHA was unevenly implemented, and provoked a wide range of responses. It nonetheless created a diverse constituency for African nationalism. As Ian Phimister points out, the literature on the NLHA has long recognised the intensity of resistance but has shed little light on precisely who led and participated in it. He questions the leading role attributed to those denied land by the NLHA, arguing instead that 'reserve entrepreneurs', motivated by the desire to safeguard their disproportionate hold over land and cattle, were key in leading resistance and so in shaping nationalism.[54] While the role of rural elites was certainly important, the heterogeneity of their political views, and the cultural and social links that tied them to other social groups meant that resistance cut across class.[55] Strategies were also shaped by the history of interactions with the state, local ecologies and economies, and shifts in the constituency for resistance over time.

The response to the Act tended to go through several phases, creating a snowball effect. Broadly, chiefs, headmen and councillors who sat on Assessment Committees, and who were called upon to aid in the Act's implementation, voiced the first objections and tried to negotiate for better terms, sometimes with concern only for protecting their privileged hold on cattle and land.[56] Crucial to the resistance the Act provoked, however, was administrators' diminished capacity to make or maintain compromises: efforts by rural leaders to mitigate the effects of the Act were often brushed aside and previous compromises, made at no mean cost, came under threat. Where the Act proceeded, it tended to provoke resistance among a much wider group than simply those with larger than average land and stock holdings. If destocking was severe, the threat it posed extended to those with small herds as well as anyone hoping to own stock in future. Large herd owners often loaned cattle to those with no stock: destocking thus affected a wider community.[57] Land allocations likewise threatened not only large landholders but often also whole communities who were forced to move or were deprived of access to fertile lands. As labour migrants learned of their exclusion from land and as the economic slump forced many out of work in the later 1950s, they became increasingly outspoken. One Clifford Chigwedere, unemployed and denied land, angrily expressed his sense of injustice: 'Birds of the air have nests as their homes and foxes have caves, but I, a human being, have no home. How fair is the Land Husbandry Act?'[58] The Act threatened the link between migrant earnings and rural production, as well as rural elders' role as guarantors of migrants' access to land. The next generation of married couples as well as those returning to retire in the rural areas faced dispossession. The NLHA certainly did divide communities, but the methods of implementation and the broad threat it posed focused anger on the state.

Rural leaders used a wide range of arguments in their interactions with officials. Some sought to engage with the state's technical evaluations. Others invoked custom or religion or economics. NC Coleman's report on a meeting in Gwaai Reserve illustrated the interlinked range of objections.[59] People objected to the Act as an abrogation of moral economy; they condemned European science – represented by the beacons which marked their new lands – as an offence to the spiritual order:

> The Government is killing people with this Act. How does the Government expect people to live off 10 acres? It is not economic. How does the Government expect a man to cultivate if he has no cattle.... The Government and the European hate the African and are grinding him into the ground. Since beacons have been erected there has been nothing but starvation. The beacons and the Land Husbandry Act are the cause of it all. They have offended God.

Job seekers noted that 'promises of expansion of industry in the future are all very well but what of the immediate future?' Men requested that women and foreign Africans be barred from employment. Parents complained of the threat to their children: 'If they cannot live on the land then it becomes a complete break up of tribal life. Where are the children to go? To the nonexistent industries?' Youth had become 'insolent': 'They blame this on the lack of security of employment. They pointed out that the youth says "Why should I pay taxes – I have no land, I have no cattle and I have no employment".' The future of the old caused concern: 'As they see it these people are floating back to the Reserves where they are having to support them on say 10 acres and 3 head of cattle.' Commenting on the report, the PNC lamented that 'the Land Husbandry Act is the theme song at all meetings.... [E]ven the rural African is now becoming politically minded. He is now questioning Government Policy and he expects answers.'[60]

Africans saw this as a problem of the state, and their response was nationalism. They literally demanded that nationalist parties represent them. An angry F. Sibanda wrote to the *African Daily News* to complain that no one had ever been consulted about the NLHA, that 'the Native Commissioner is just telling people not to plough. I therefore want the N.D.P. to come here.' NDP leaders were the 'only people who can stand for us'.[61] Nationalist leaders fully recognised the opportunity provided by the Act, calling it their 'best recruiter'.[62] Though opposition to the NLHA certainly provided an impetus to rural nationalism, the spread of resistance and its conversion into nationalist demands for a transformed state took very different forms. Insiza and Chimanimani illustrate the range of responses to the Act, the diverse nature of the NLHA's effects on agrarian change and authority, and the impact of earlier histories of political activism, mediation with officials, and dispossession.

Insiza: Building and Breaking Rural Authority

The NLHA in Insiza was preceded by massive evictions, carried out with over-whelming force. The memory of the state's coercive power, and the fear of further evictions, powerfully shaped responses to the Act. As with previous agricultural interventions, the NLHA was interpreted as a means of gaining secure tenure, not because of the individual rights it offered but because of the protection from evic-tion that people felt cooperation with the state would provide. The period of cooperation was significant for the transformations it brought to settlement patterns and political authority: chiefs were shuffled around the district, the village 'lines' established by the NLHA created a new notion of community identity, and a council functioned throughout the district for the first time.

The strategy of cooperation was led by the same leaders, notably Chief Jim Mafu Maduna and his advisers, who had previously led opposition and who would turn to resistance once again in the 1960s. The cooperative stance held sway until the late 1950s in part because the administration believed Chief Maduna, as with a number of chiefs in Matabeleland, to be an influential leader who should be carefully courted: the NC considered that he 'had great power and influence, and no project whatsoever ... could hope to succeed unless he had given his blessing'.[63] Maduna had achieved the conversion of most of the Godhlwayo NPA to a reserve in 1953. In exchange, he supported the establishment of a council for the first time. He also reversed his views on the NLHA. In 1951, Maduna, along with Chiefs Ndube and Sibasa, had heatedly objected to the Act, arguing that 'cattle should not be destocked as this was the only means by which people can live', and that 'all grown-up children should be allowed to live and remain in the Reserves'. They had expressed 'displeasure at the idea of having lands allocated and reduced in size'.[64] But between 1953 and 1956, Maduna supported the Act's application in Godhlwayo.[65] As with the earlier implementation of centralisation, the Act served as a way both for the state to 'see' its charges and for them to become visible to the state, and so legitimise their claims to land.

In 1955, the NC optimistically commented on the 'feeling of enthusiastic progress and development':

> It is at times difficult to appreciate that this District was one of the worst black spots in the country a matter of three years ago when political strife was rife throughout the District.... Today the district is without any political problems.... The people are happy to leave its prob-lems to its chiefs, council and the administration.

Chiefs had been 'particularly helpful' in implementing the NLHA, playing a key role in 'vetting' applications for land. The NC considered it a 'tragedy' that chiefs' courts did not have criminal jurisdiction since the Act's implementation 'would be a far easier measure if one could deal with more powerful chiefs'.[66]

Maduna used this period to develop the resources of the new Godhlwayo Reserve. The main developments – school buildings, a clinic, cattle sale pens, a business centre with a butchery and shops and council buildings – were all located in the vicinity of Avoca, Chief Maduna's home. But all was not well. The focus of service development at Avoca was resented by people in other areas, and the collection of rates had been a sore point since the council's inception. Evasion was so severe that the council had to employ two 'police boys to chase tax defaulters'.[67] Other running complaints concerned the poor quality and expense of the district's missionary-run schools, low cattle prices, and the administration of cattle sales and dipping.[68] The grievances expressed by and about the council would not, however, cause its breakdown until the early 1960s.

In addition to the introduction of a council for the first time, rural authority was transformed by the NAD's 'rationalisation' of chieftaincy. The NC held that chiefs' areas had to be 'properly defined' in order for chiefs to carry out their duties with 'proper efficiency'.[69] This was an efficiency that had scant regard for customary ties. Maduna was moved from the small area still designated as Godhlwayo Purchase Area to the new Godhlwayo Reserve. Chief Ndube was moved, 'against his wishes and those of his tribe', from the south-east corner of Godhlwayo Reserve to the northern section of Chief Sibasa's jurisdiction in Glassblock. Sibasa's followers 'were required to acknowledge Ndube as Chief'. Chief Ndube's followers, with the exception of seven people who moved with him, were required to 'redirect their allegiance to Chief Maduna', via Headman Ngomondo who was transferred from Chief Sibasa's area into the area formerly under Chief Ndube. These moves tended to undermine other chiefs in relation to Maduna, who was the only one who neither lost followers nor found himself presiding largely over people previously loyal to another chief.[70]

The NLHA's settlement patterns introduced further changes in the organisation of local leadership when the Act was implemented in 1956. People in Insiza date the office of the sabhuku or 'village head' , literally the holder of the tax book, to the creation of 'lines' under the NLHA. Though there had been designated tax collectors prior to the lines, they established a firm identification of the sabhuku with a residential area. Male elders in a line developed the practice of appointing their own line representative, the position not being hereditary or having a formal connection to the office of chief or headman. In later debates over rights to land and the authority to allocate land, the sabhuku would not challenge chiefs and headmen with anything like the success of the parallel administrative position outside Matabeleland.

The establishment of the new 'villages' was hugely disruptive, and highlighted just how poorly planned the centralisation policy of ten years earlier had been. Insiza and Glassblock Reserves had to be 're-centralised'. Technical officers held that the long 'lines' established by centralisation suffered a range of weaknesses. They had trapped grazing land within areas designated as 'arable', rendering it inaccessible in the rainy season. Individual arable allocations had not been made, and so there was no control on field sizes. Grazing was concentrated along the village lines, and was thus very uneven.[71] Under the NLHA, the huge arable land blocks and long settlement lines were broken up, requiring some people to move and rebuild their homes. The heated complaint that followed led to the area's designation as a 'special project': labourers were imported at government expense to do the demanding physical conservation work and messengers and rangers subsequently maintained conservation works.[72]

Though the first stages of the NLHA's implementation were a cause of considerable hardship, cooperation was maintained. This was in part due to the concessions on land, conservation labour, and development resources, and peoples' perception that the NLHA would spare them from further evictions. It was in part due to the control allowed chiefs. The cooperation thus achieved was, however, soon to be broken by the enforcement of destocking. The only previous destocking in the district had taken place in Insiza Reserve in the mid-1940s. The effects then had been masked by the accompanying drought in which many animals had died and people had voluntarily sold stock. Moreover, the lack of controls on stock in neighbouring Godhlwayo and in the many then unoccupied 'European' ranches had allowed stock to be hidden or loaned out to those with access to more land. Now that Godhlwayo was to fall under the destocking programme, and now that many more ranches were occupied and fenced, the strategic movement of cattle was greatly inhibited.

The Assessment Committees which sat in 1956 recommended that Glassblock be destocked from 3,781 Animal Units to 3,200, and Insiza Reserve from 6,496 to 5,150. In these areas, chiefs and councillors engaged in a technical debate over the carrying capacities of different soil types, arguing they had been misjudged and undervalued while, in recently settled Glassblock, they argued people should not be destocked below the number to which they had been limited when they had first moved in. These arguments failed to persuade technical officers, and nor was the NC overly concerned to make concessions because of the relatively small margin of destocking. The real blow would come in Godhlwayo, where 19,689 Animal Units were to be reduced to 11,200, the second highest rate of destocking anywhere in the province.[73] Godhlwayo was unusual in comparison to Insiza's other reserves in that a significantly higher percentage of taxpayers owned stock, herds were larger, there was a lower rate of labour migration, and cattle sales were higher. In a survey of five lowveld areas, it was only in Godhlwayo that the value of cattle sales exceeded that of crops.[74] Destocking posed a devastating threat, and it worried the NC. He admonished councillors to get rid of cattle on loan from outside the district. Very few were disposed of as a result, indicating both the importance of these arrangements and the difficulty in identifying owners.[75] The NC, councillors and Chief Maduna successfully lobbied for an increase in Godhlwayo's carrying capacity from 11,200 to 14,000 in 1959 by agreeing to implement paddocking, a measure that was never carried out.[76] Such agreements typified the importance of concessions made by NCs to rural leaders, concessions that undercut technical officers' goals and cushioned the NLHA's impact. But in this case it was too little too late.

In 1960, destocking was enforced in the midst of a severe drought. By 1961 all areas were 'understocked'.[77] The drastic losses in Godhlwayo in particular were deeply resented; everywhere the failure to distribute food relief during the drought fueled people's outrage. Though the council survived until early 1964, this marked the breakdown of cooperation, the re-emergence of political links with Bulawayo, and an upsurge in nationalism, backed by Chief Maduna. Workers from Bulawayo arrived to lobby the council, and NDP meetings proliferated. Maduna had already started to turn away from the administration's ideology of development. In 1958, he had backed a revival of the Mwali cult and its alternative understanding of the environment. This meant supporting the shrine's messengers in enforcing Wednesday as the day of rest to assure good rains, a move which outraged the Christian entrepreneurs of Godhlwayo. Such moves were common in Matabeleland at this time, and were, as Terence Ranger and Mark Ncube argue, part of a shift in the ideology of resistance, away from Christian elites and towards a locally grounded cultural nationalism.[78]

In Insiza, the NLHA reshaped political authority and rights to land in enduring ways. It also struck a devastating blow to the agricultural economy and undermined rural institutions, leaving the door open to alternative ideas about authority and the land, both religious and political, that appealed to a broad constituency.

Chimanimani: Technical Failure and Non-Compliance

In Chimanimani, the politics of implementing the NLHA, and the Act's effects on production and settlement patterns, differed greatly from those of Insiza. The Act faced unusual technical obstacles due to the relative lack of previous interventions outside irrigation schemes, and the district's ecological and economic diversity. Chimanimani was divided into a total of eight 'zones': the highveld Ngorima Reserve, the three irrigation schemes, and the low and middle veld areas of the Mutambara and Muwushu Reserves. Each environment presented unique problems, requiring a massive production of technical data to make the land 'legible' and so allow intervention. Legibility in this case had, however, the opposite effect: in much of the district, technical officials simply judged the Act inappropriate.

Where implementation went ahead, politics did not focus on negotiation between chiefs, councillors and officials as in Insiza. Rural leaders relied on passive resistance to attempts to involve them in governing, and on non-compliance with policy. The Act's piecemeal implementation rarely threatened whole communities and thus did not provoke united resistance. Nor did Chimanimani's NCs place great stress on co-opting chiefs, considering their influence to be limited, or on instituting councils. Councils had never functioned in Chimanimani. Renewed attempts to establish a council in Mutambara in 1955 had little success. The NC's agenda indicated part of the reason: '1. Nomination of Councillors. 2. Imposition of Taxes. 3. Any other Business'.[79] In 1956, an auditor reported that the council, 'has no money or assets and that, to date, it has achieved nothing.'[80]

Resistance in Chimanimani consisted largely in evasion, non-compliance and sabotage by individual households, while the spread of nationalism played on dynamics largely divorced from the NLHA's implementation, though it drew on insecurity caused by the Act. Nationalist activity was concentrated in the dense settlements at irrigation schemes. The schemes were convenient sites for holding public meetings, and had long been a source of conflict over state intervention. Many irrigators were entrepreneurial adherents of the American Methodist missions in Chimanimani: they played an important role in nationalist mobilisation; Methodist missionaries were themselves considered suspect by the administration.[81] On the Nyanyadzi irrigation scheme, ANC rallies multiplied in the late 1950s. Following the ANC's banning in 1959 there were widespread detentions of ANC members, partic-ularly from the Nyanyadzi and Mutambara schemes. Nyanyadzi nationalists subsequently formed a branch of the NDP, sent delegates to the 1961 NDP congress, and organised the district to vote against the 1961 constitutional proposals.[82] While nationalism spread through the work of educated Christians, the fate of the NLHA was largely determined by its own inadequacies.

TECHNICAL FAILURES IN THE HIGHVELD AND IRRIGATION SCHEMES

Highveld Ngorima's dense population and unusual ecology confounded the NLHA's need to simplify and categorise. The area had never been centralized nor had conservation measures or destocking been implemented, though a demonstrator had successfully promoted fruit and coffee production.[83] Ngorima's altitude ranged between 1,500 and 5,000 feet. The area received an annual rainfall of between 45 and 65 inches. Its extremely fertile soils showed 'very little erosion' despite the cultivation of steep slopes. The consolidation of holdings proved impossible, as they were 'extremely fragmented, averaging three to four per cultivator and in some cases up to fifteen. Part of the holding is usually on the mountainside on steep land, and the balance on the floor of the valley.'[84] Peoples' houses, some of them brick, were scattered in the upper heights of the mountains near the high-altitude fields, rather than in the hot and humid valleys which were the only areas where 'lines' could be demarcated.[85] The density of settlement in Ngorima and the investment in coffee, tea, and fruit trees made it virtually impossible to reshuffle settlement patterns and fields.

In addition to these difficulties, Ngorima's interdependence with Mozambique and neighbouring commercial farms made nonsense of the NLHA's search for self-contained economic 'units'. Families lived, farmed and herded stock on both sides of the border, thus nullifying the procedures for assessing carrying capacity.[86] The forestry officer noted that timber was scarce in Ngorima, but there was 'unlimited timber available on European farms', and thus afforestation was unnecessary. In the end, no action was taken beyond recommending further research, promoting 'high value special crops', and developing roads and bridges.[87]

The NLHA's inflexibility also halted implementation on irrigation schemes. The NC had initially stressed that the three schemes were the areas in most urgent need of the Act's disciplining effects. They were the first to be assessed, in 1954. Villages were already centralised. The greatest problem was identified as overgrazing around the schemes and the sub-division of plots.[88] The NC wanted to fence off the schemes with their own grazing areas, cutting them off from the dryland economy. However, as in Ngorima, technical officials expressed reservations, and in 1956 the application of the Act to irrigation schemes was held up nationally pending an economic survey.[89] The survey, undertaken by S. M. Makings of the Department of Native Economics and Marketing, overturned many official assumptions about irrigation schemes. Makings held that of all the schemes in the country only two sections of the Nyanyadzi scheme were in 'a reasonably sound economic position'. Nyanyadzi was the centrepiece of irrigation policy and had received a disproportionate amount of investment. Five schemes failed to provide average plot-holders with an income that allowed them to pay maintenance charges. Only two produced surpluses. The original four-acre plots had been widely subdivided, with women generally farming the smaller plots. Makings considered them inefficient and recommended 're-examining their rights to land'.[90]

In addition, the irrigation schemes were inextricably linked to the dryland economy. Many irrigators relied on dryland farmers for wage labour, and 'grazing' areas served multiple purposes for both dryland farmers and irrigators: 'In practice, it is impossible to separate out the grazing areas for these schemes from the rest of the reserve. The land marked out for the irrigation scheme grazing areas is used by kraals in the dry land for grazing and for arable.' Though grazing land was fenced on the Nyanyadzi and Mutambara schemes, dryland farmers continued to cultivate and graze stock in the area. Finding discrete 'economic units' either on or off the schemes proved impossible.[91] As in Ngorima, the state's investment in producing knowledge so as to intervene instead cast sufficient doubt on the NLHA's applicability to halt its implementation. Major confrontations over destocking or land rights were thereby averted.

The Middle Veld and Lowveld: Compromise and Local Resistance

The only areas in Chimanimani where the NLHA was implemented were the low and middle veld regions of Muwushu and Mutambara reserves. The Act was first implemented in the middle veld zones. Much of this land was inaccessible, mountainous and lacked water supplies. Most people were settled along the Mutare–Melsetter road, which divided 'European' from African land, and along rivers. The middle veld economies were characterised by a mixed farming system of grain and stock, supplemented by migrant labour earnings.

Stockowners in the Muwushu middle veld had adopted official recommendations regarding the management of grazing land. In deference to their cooperation, no destocking was recommended, nor were arable acreages reduced in the majority of the zone; NLHA grazing rights were never issued and previous settlement patterns were allowed to stand.[92] In the Mutambara middle veld, no destocking was recommended, grazing rights were never issued and, though land allocations were demarcated, they were never legally 'confirmed' under the NLHA. Commenting on both the Mutambara and Muwushu middle veld, the NC wrote, 'In the early stages, as was to be expected, there were cases of beacon removal and ploughing outside the holding but it is hoped that prosecutions will have a salutary effect.'[93] Widespread prosecutions were used to enforce allocations, hitting women particularly hard as they were often the resident farmers. But they did not have the hoped for 'salutary effect'. Instead, where allocations interfered with previous farming patterns, they were widely flouted until the suspension of the Act two years later. In Mutambara, the nationalist activists based at the irrigation scheme, and the long history of non-compliance with demonstrators' edicts, contributed to the pervasiveness of resistance.

A similar fate awaited the NLHA in the lowveld zones. High rates of labour migration, illegal irrigation, stream-bank cultivation and a reliance on stock sales in drought years characterised the Save Valley strip of Muwushu and Mutambara Reserves. The 1958 Assessment Committee described the Muwushu zone as heavily over-grazed along the Save River but under-grazed elsewhere. The area had not been centralised nor were there any demonstrator cooperators. Farmers grew bull–rush millet and sorghum on the granite sand soils where erratic and low rainfall produced on average only one good season every five years. Of a population of 2,600, there were only 271 resident adult males; more than one in three landholders were women. The Mutambara lowveld shared similar characteristics, though it was also linked to the irrigation economies.[94] Information collected by the Assessment Committees was used to allocate fields, but stock rights were never issued and landholdings were never legally 'confirmed' due to widespread non-compliance and the subsequent suspension of the NLHA.[95]

The only area to experience severe disruption was densely settled Biriwiri. In Biriwiri's rocky hills people lived on steep slopes where they had constructed stone terracing on the insistence of the Land Development Officer. Despite their cooperation with conservation measures, it was these people who were to suffer the greatest dislocation. In an effort to avoid wholesale eviction, their fields were initially reduced, a measure which led some to complain 'bitterly about having their land taken away'.[96] It was then decided that 84 families would have to move to remote Chikwakwa in Muwushu Reserve. People complained that they had recently raised £90 for upgrading the Biriwiri Mission School which they would no longer be able to use. They protested at having to leave the stone terracing which they had constructed at officials' behest. As the NC pointed out, 'Many men have put in an enormous amount of work in the last two to three years and, in some cases, they employed others to help and, having incurred this expenditure in wages, are reluctant to abandon the result.'[97] As in Insiza, the adoption of technical advice, at no mean cost, was seen as the basis of a claim to land, as part of a negotiated agreement between the state's agents and local farmers. In contrast to other areas, however, the NLHA's rigid calculations rode roughshod over such notions in Biriwiri: in 1958, 82 families were removed to Chikwakwa.[98]

Overall, the NLHA had a limited impact on authority, tenure and production in Chimanimani. In dryland areas, previous centralisation patterns largely held, no destocking was undertaken, grazing rights were never issued and, where land allocations were made, they were rapidly flouted. The Act's own rigidity precluded its implementation on irrigation schemes and in the highveld Ngorima Reserve. The NLHA's most significant impact was to be its legacy of insecurity and distrust.

Conclusion

The NLHA succeeded in undermining the fragile relationships NCs had built with local leaders, and in provoking widespread resistance. It created disaffection and insecurity even where it was not in the end implemented. But the extent to which the Act achieved its goals was limited. Eleven years after the NLHA's introduction, a full 73 per cent of all African land had been proclaimed under the Act but stock rights were registered in only 36 per cent of all areas, residential sites in only 26 per cent and land allocations in only 39 per cent. Towards the end of the Act's implementation, land allocations were never, or only briefly, enforced. Destocking likewise had only a brief impact in many areas as people rapidly re-stocked with the relaxation of controls. The establishment of markets in land and grazing rights was also limited, most sales being concentrated in Victoria Province, possibly due to the migrations from this area to the northern frontiers.[99]

The effort to create full-time 'farmers' and 'workers' utterly failed. Nonetheless, the Act had a lasting impact on authority and the land. It added to the repertoire of means of claiming land; it created new ideas of community and settlement patterns that would shape debates in coming decades. It at the same time provided a tremendous boost to nationalism, and to the demands for a transformed state. The attacks on officials and the spread of nationalist parties into rural areas would constitute the most pressing force behind the NLHA's suspension. The Act underlined the potent ideological value of science to the settler state, but it just as clearly underlined the vast discrepancies between the technical imagination and state capacity.

Notes

1 Low and Lonsdale, 1976, 12-16.
2 See Cooper, 1996.
3 Yudelman, 1964, 117.
4 Drinkwater, 1989, 285.
5 Holleman, 1969, 54-5, 31-2. Also see Murray, 1970, 308.
6 Drinkwater, 1991, 77.
7 Holleman, 1969, 38-9, 33.
8 Quoted in Holleman, 1969, 39, fn 2.
9 Government of Southern Rhodesia, 1944, 46.
10 23.7.5R/93142, Internal Affairs Correspondence Files, Per 5/GEN, L. Powys-Jones, CNC, File No. 542, Circular No. 322, 1 July 1951; Weinrich, 1971.
11 See the views of NCs compiled in Howman, 1962, Part III. The CNC's views are quoted in Barber, 1967, 235.
12 Howman, 1963, paras 170, 173, cited in Holleman, 1969, 67-8.
13 Memorandum on African Local Government Bill, 2 June 1954, para 4(b), cited in Holleman, 1969, 68.
14 See Passmore, 1972, 58-63.
15 CNC's Annual Report for 1959, 158, quoted in Weinrich, 1971, 19.
16 See Phimister, 1988b, 238-9.
17 Quoted in Phimister, 1993, 231.
18 See Worby, 2000, 109.
19 S1217/9, Native Reserves Land Utilisation and Good Husbandry Bill, Introductory Note by A. Pendered (Marketing Officer), 10 April 1948, quoted in Phimister, 1993, 231. The sentiment that labour migration led to 'grossly inefficient' farmers and workers was reiterated repeatedly in the next decade. For example see 6.5.9R/84273, F. H. Dodd, Administrative Officer, NLHA, 'The Native Land Husbandry Act', October 1958.
20 6.5.9R/84273, F. H. Dodd, Administrative Officer, NLHA, 'The Native Land Husbandry Act', October 1958.
21 Quoted in the *Rhodesia Herald*, 19 May 1955.
22 Wilson, 1987b, 59.
23 Yudelman, 1964, 119.
24 See Chanock, 1991, 61-84.
25 Scott, 1998, 183-4.
26 Drinkwater, 1991, 66; Bulman, 1973, Appendices C and F.
27 The first use of aerial photography in classifying land was in the Nata Reserve in 1949-1950. Weinmann, 1975, 208.
28 23.7.5R/93142, Per 5/GEN, P. B. Fletcher, Ministry of Native Affairs, Memorandum by the Minister of Native Affairs, Proposed increases in Chiefs' and Headmen's subsidies and personal allowances, 21 October 1957.
29 23.7.5R/93142, Per 5/GEN, Memorandum by the Ministry of Native Affairs on increased subsidies for

Chiefs and Headmen, Salisbury, n.d. [1957].

30 Phimister, 1993, 227, 232, shows that the Cabinet's decision to speed the Act's implementation was motivated directly by concern over conservation.

31 See, *inter alia*, Floyd, 1959; Duggan, 1980; Bulman, 1973; Scoones, 1990.

32 Bulman, 1973, 33, 12.

33 Drinkwater, 1991, 67. Yields estimated by NCs and demonstrators were highly inaccurate. See Central Statistical Office, 1962.

34 Government of Southern Rhodesia, 1960, paras 130-7.

35 6.5.9F/84267, Native Land Husbandry Act, Standing Committee, Minutes of the Sixth Meeting, 7 January 1956. Also see Bulman, 1973, 13; Drinkwater, 1991, 68; 6.5.9R/84273, F. H. Dodd, Administrative Officer, NLHA, 'The Native Land Husbandry Act', October 1958.

36 That the Act undermined security of tenure is widely accepted. See Bulman, 1973, 22-3; Holleman, 1969, 62-3; Floyd, 1959, 119-120; Government of Southern Rhodesia, 1961b, paras 82-90 (the Mangwende Commission).

37 Floyd, 1959, Chapter 8, shows that there were far too few stock to maintain soil fertility under the assumptions of the Alvord production system in a wide variety of reserves and, pp. 303-4, estimates that over 60 per cent of right holders would have less than the recommended number of stock, many having none. Officials were aware of these problems. See 6.5.9R/84273, *Annual Report of the Director of Native Agriculture for the Year 1958*, R. M. Davies, Salisbury, March 1959, p. 5, for example.

38 On NCs' calls for more land, see, for example, 6.5.9F/84267, Meeting of the NCs, Manicaland, Umtali, 26 June 1959; Minutes of the Eighth Meeting of the Native Land Husbandry Act Standing Committee, 15 April 1957.

39 27.6.6F/100842, LAN/20/GEN, R. L. C. Cunliffe, 'Annual Report. Native Land Husbandry Act', Salisbury, May 1963.

40 See, *inter alia*, Bulman, 1973, 16, 21; Holleman, 1969, 63; Yudelman, 1964, 131.

41 Floyd, 1959, 8. Also see,for example, 6.5.6R/84266, PNC, Mashonaland East, to Under Secretary, Native Agriculture and Land, 28 January 1960.

42 6.5.9R/84273, *Annual Report of the Director of Native Agriculture for the Year 1958*, R. M. Davies, Salisbury, March 1959, pp. 4, 38-40.

43 See, for example, Bhebe, 1989a, 5-6; Weinrich, 1964, 17-18, and 1975; *The African Weekly*, 23 November 1960; *The Harvester*, 22 October 1958; Phimister, 1993.

44 27.6.6F/100842, Internal Affairs, LAN/20-LAN/22, NC N. A. Hunt, Gwelo, to PNC, Midlands, 4 November 1957; 6.5.6R/84266, Under Secretary, Native Agriculture and Land Husbandry, to Secretary for Native Affairs, 27 January 1959.

45 6.5.9F/84276, NC, The Range, to Assistant Commissioner, Land Husbandry, 29 April 1954.

46 6.5.9F/84267, Minutes of the Ninth Meeting of the Native Land Husbandry Act Standing Committee, 3 June 1957.

47 6.5.9F/84267, Native Land Husbandry Act Standing Committee, Minutes of Ad Hoc Meeting to discuss the common levy and destocking, 25 June 1957; R. L. C. Cunliffe, NLHA, Destocking, Memorandum prepared for the Native Land Husbandry Act Standing Committee, Ad Hoc Meeting to discuss the common levy and destocking, June 1957.

48 *Ibid.*, and see 6.5.9F/84267, R. M. Davies, Memorandum on Destocking in Native Areas presented to the Native Land Husbandry Standing Committee, 25 June 1957; 6.6.8R/84277, NLHA, Matabeleland, D. A. Robinson, Director of Native Agriculture, to Under Secretary, Native Agriculture and Lands, 2 June 1959; Drinkwater, 1991, 71.

49 Drinkwater, 1991, 72.

50 On irrigation schemes, see 6.1.9F/84256, S. M. Makings, Department of Native Economics and Marketing, 'Manicaland Irrigation Schemes: Economic Investigation', June 1958, and 6.5.6R/84266, Assistant Secretary to Administrative Officer, NLHA, 14 August 1956. On low rainfall areas, see 18.8.10R/88379, Arthur Hunt, Native Affairs Department Economist, 'Cattle in the Lower Rainfall Regions of Southern Rhodesia', 26 February 1959, and Bulman, 1973, 15. For higher rainfall areas, see comments of the Manicaland Provincial Agriculturalist and Arthur Pendered, Under Secretary, Native Economics and Marketing in 1957, cited in Bulman, 1973, 20, fn 1.

51 6.5.9R/84273, S. M. Makings, Department of Native Economics and Marketing, 'The Problem of the Communal Grazings', Salisbury, 13 October 1958, 11.

52 See discussion in Holleman, 1969, 325-8.

53 23.7.5R/93142, Per 5/GEN, Memorandum by the Minister of Native Affairs on increased subsidies for Chiefs and Headmen, Salisbury, Ministry of Native Affairs, n.d. [1957].

54 Phimister, 1993, 233-9.

55 See Werbner, 1991, 26-7 and, more generally, Beinart and Bundy, 1987, 29-30.

56 For example, see the Land Development Officer's report on opposition to proposed reductions in arable land from chiefs, headmen and village heads whom the Officer describes as 'land barons' in Chibi. 6.5.6R/84266, LDO, Chibi, to NC, Chibi, 11 April 1956. Similarly, in Wenlock, the NC charged that Chief Sigombe and other large cattle owners led resistance to destocking and tried to force small herd owners to destock to save their own herds. 27.6.6F/100842, Internal Affairs, LAN/20-LAN/22, NC W. D. R. Baker, Gwanda, to PNC, Matabeleland, 12 April 1957.

57 See letters to the editor in *The African Weekly*, 10 December 1958; objections raised at a meeting with the NC over destocking reported in *The Harvester*, 25 March 1959; Scoones, 1990; Scoones and Wilson, 1988.

58 *African Daily News*, 31 August 1960. Similar letters multiplied in the late 1950s.

59 See 27.6.6F/100842, Internal Affairs, LAN/20-LAN/22, NC R. S. Coleman, Tjolotjo, to PNC, Matabeleland, 2 September 1960. Also see Wilson, 1989; McGregor, 1991; Werbner, 1991.

60 27.6.6F/100842, Internal Affairs, LAN/20-LAN/22, PNC M. Campbell, Bulawayo, to the Secretary for Native Affairs, 7 September 1960.

61 *African Daily News*, 1 and 4 October 1960.

62 See Phimister, 1993, 228.

63 PER 5, Chief Maduna, Filabusi, A. M. Mansell for Secretary of Internal Affairs to Provincial Commissioner, Matabeleland South, 21 September 1965. Mansell was the NC for Filabusi between 1951 and 1955. Maduna's role was not unusual in Matabeleland. See Werbner, 1991, on Chief Bango, and Ranger, 1999, on Chief Sigombe.

64 See 35596, Assembly of Chiefs, Matabeleland, PNC to Secretary of Native Affairs, 9 December 1952.

65 6.5.9R/84273, Assessment Committee Report, Godhlwayo, Insiza District, 14 May 1956.

66 See S2827/2/2/3, NC's Annual Report for 1955, Filabusi.

67 Minutes of the Insiza Reserve, Godhlwayo and Glassblock Native Council (hereafter Godhlwayo Council), Avoca, 8 December 1953, 12 January 1954, Sibasa, 26 August 1954. Complaints about rates in part reflected debate over who should pay: some argued that only those with cattle should pay.

68 Minutes of the Godhlwayo Council, Avoca, 18 July 1955, 25 October 1955, 12 July 1956, 22 May 1956.

69 S2827/2/2/3, NC's Annual Report for 1955, Filabusi.

70 See Ministry of Internal Affairs, 1963, Delineation Reports, Sibasa Community: Chief Sibasa, Insiza Tribal Trust Land; Ndube Community: Chief Ndube, Glass Block Tribal Trust Land, Filabusi District, A. D. Elliot, Delineation Team.

71 6.5.9R/84237, Assessment Committee Report on Insiza and Glassblock, Filabusi, 14 May 1956. 'Re-centralisation' was required in areas throughout the country, proving a major obstacle to the speedy implementation of the Act and revealing how haphazard was much of the earlier centralization. See 6.5.9R/84273, *Annual Report of the Director of Native Agriculture for the year 1958*, R. M. Davies, March 1959, p. 41, and Bulman, 1973, 17.

72 Minutes of the Godhlwayo Council, Avoca, 10 January 1957, 15 August 1958; 5.2.8R/82725, Working Party D, Robinson Commission, District Survey, Insiza (Filabusi), 11 July 1962.

73 See 6.5.9R/84273, Assessment Committee Report on Godhlwayo S.N.A., Insiza District, Filabusi, 14 May 1956; Assessment Committee Report on Insiza Reserve, Insiza District, Filabusi, 14 May 1956; Assessment Committee Report on Glass Block and Panasequa (Insiza B) S.N.A, Insiza District, Filabusi, 14 May 1956. Only the tiny Ntabazinduna Reserve faced a higher rate of destocking than Godhlwayo.

74 A report submitted to the Insiza Assessment Committee estimated that 61 per cent of taxpayers were resident in Godhlwayo in contrast to 52 per cent in Insiza Reserve and 44 per cent in Glassblock; 58 per cent of taxpayers owned stock in Godhlwayo as compared to 46 per cent in Insiza and 50 per cent in Glassblock; the average number of Animal Units per owner in Godhlwayo was 17.2, as compared to 13.8 in Insiza and 12.3 in Glassblock. 6.5.9R/84273, Report: Insiza District Native Areas, 1956. Also see 18.8.10R/88379, Internal Affairs, Arthur Hunt, NAD Economist, 'Cattle in the Lower Rainfall Regions of Southern Rhodesia', 26 February 1959.

75 Minutes of the Godhlwayo Council, Avoca, 13 August 1957, 5 November 1957. In his study of lowveld production, Arthur Hunt found that 'although many appeared to own no cattle and held no dip cards' they often did own cattle but had loaned them to others while they sought work in urban areas or in order to take advantage of other grazing areas. Fathers often kept cattle intended for their sons. 18.8.10R/88379, Internal Affairs, Arthur Hunt, NAD Economist, 'Cattle in the Lower Rainfall Regions of Southern Rhodesia', 26 February 1959.

76 5.2.8R/82725, Working Party D, Robinson Commission, District Survey, Insiza (Filabusi), 11 July 1962; Minutes of the Godhlwayo Council, Sibasa Hall, 4 April 1961.

77 See 14.8.8F/69691, Working Party D, Arising from the Robinson Commission Report, 'The Tribal Authority and the Land', Paper No. 16, Salisbury, Annexure A, 2 September 1961.

78 See Minutes of the Godhlwayo Council, 18 June 1960; Bhebe, 1989b, 96; Ranger and Ncube, 1996, 38-9.
79 32.14.3R/35580, NC R. Cashel, 'Mutambara Native Council', 25 January 1955.
80 32.14.3R/35580, T. D. Baldwin, Auditor, 'Inspection Report Mutambara Native Council', 19 June 1956.
81 See correspondence in PER 5, Chief Mutambara, Melsetter.
82 Sithole, 1970, 22, 118-25; Bhebe, 1989b, 96.
83 In 1960, 46 people had 1,697 three-to-ten-year-old coffee trees. 6.5.6R/84266, Internal Affairs, Correspondence, Reports, etc., Land Development Officer's Report, Ngorima Reserve, Melsetter District, 18 February 1960.
84 5.2.8R/82725, Working Party D, District Survey, Melsetter, 2 November 1962; 6.5.6R/84266, Internal Affairs, Correspondence, Reports, etc., 1957-60, Land Development Officer's Report, Ngorima Reserve, Melsetter District, 18 February 1960.
85 6.5.6R/84266, Internal Affairs, Correspondence, Reports, etc., 1957-60, Land Development Officer's Report, Ngorima Reserve, Melsetter District, 18 February 1960.
86 5.2.8R/82725, Working Party D, District Survey, Melsetter, 2 November 1962.
87 See 6.6.5R/84266, Internal Affairs, Correspondence, Reports, etc., 1957-60, Pasture Officer's Report, Ngorima Reserve, 9 February 1960; Meeting of Assessment Committee, Ngorima Reserve, Melsetter District, 18 February 1960; Land Development Officer's Report, Ngorima Reserve, Melsetter District, 18 February 1960; 5.2.8R/82725, Working Party D, District Survey, Melsetter, 2 November 1962.
88 6.6.5R/84266, Internal Affairs, Correspondence, Reports, etc., 1957-60, Assessment Committee Report, Nyanyadzi, Zone B, 5 July 1954; Assessment Committee Report, Mutambara Irrigation Project, Zone E, July 1954.
89 6.5.6R/84266, Internal Affairs, Correspondence, Reports, etc., 1957-60, Assistant Secretary, Native Affairs to Administrative Officer, NLHA, 14 August 1956.
90 On Mutambara, 51 per cent of plots were two acres or less while the equivalent figure for Umvumvumvu was 37 per cent and on Nyanyadzi the figure ranged between 60 and 32 per cent. Women plot holders constituted from 17-36 per cent of all plot holders on Chimanimani's schemes. See 6.1.9F/84256, S. M. Makings, 'Manicaland Irrigation Schemes: Economic Investigation', Department of Native Economics and Marketing, June 1958. Also see 18.8.10R/88379, Arthur Hunt, 'Have Irrigation Schemes a Future?', *Makoholi Newsletter*, No. 13, January 1960.
91 See 5.2.8R/82725, Working Party D, District Survey, Melsetter, 2 November 1962; 6.1.9F/84256, S. M. Makings, 'Manicaland Irrigation Schemes. Economic Investigation', Department of Native Economics and Marketing, June 1958.
92 6.5.6R/84266, Internal Affairs, Correspondence, Reports, etc., 1957-60, Pasture Officer's Report, Mahkwe Zone, Muwushu, 16 August 1954; Assessment Committee Report, Muwushu Reserve, Zone 1, Melsetter District, 23 May 1956; 5.2.8R/82725, Working Party D, District Survey, Melsetter, 2 November 1962.
93 6.5.6R/84266, Internal Affairs, Correspondence, Reports, etc., 1957-60, Native Land Husbandry, Melsetter, Native Commissioner, 30 December 1957.
94 6.5.6R/842266, Internal Affairs, Correspondence, Reports, etc., 1957-60, Assessment Committee, Zone III, Muwushu, 20 November 1958; Assessment Committee, Zone A, Muwushu Low Veld, 1954; Assessment Committee, Mutambara Low Veld, Zone D, 1954.
95 5.2.8R/82725, Working Party D, District Survey, Melsetter, 2 November 1962; 14.8.8F/69691, Development and Land Returns, Annual Reports, 1962-64, Melsetter, 7 January 1964; Bulman, 1973, 15.
96 6.5.6R/84266, Internal Affairs, Correspondence, Reports, etc., 1957-60, Minutes of a Meeting at Biriwiri on 30th May 1957, to discuss problems arising from allocations.
97 6.5.6R/84266, Internal Affairs, Correspondence, Reports, etc., 1957-60, NC, Melsetter, to PNC, Umtali, 14 June 1957.
98 6.5.9R/84273, *Annual Report of the Director of Native Agriculture for the year 1958*, R.M. Davies, March 1959.
99 27.6.6F/100842, LAN/20/GEN, Annual Report, Native Land Husbandry Act, R. L. C. Cunliffe, Salisbury, May 1963. Over half of the 709 farming rights transferred in the country as a whole were in Victoria Province while a full 74 per cent of 19,617 grazing right transfers fell in the province.

3

Remaking Rural Administration
Knowing African Society

In the 1960s, the settler state rejected the high modernist goals of the NLHA in favour of settling the maximum number of Africans in the reserves under the 'customary' authority of chiefs and headmen. The central impetus behind this dramatic shift was the panic within government caused by its inability to enforce the NLHA, and the expansion of African nationalism. The turn to chiefs was intended to distance the state from its coercive role and to legitimise authority over people and land in customary guise. The transition required that African society be reconceptualised once again as communal, bound by irrational beliefs, and so incapable of modernisation. Blame for the failures of the NLHA was laid at the doorstep of Africans, not technical officials. Africans were reified as essentially different from Europeans, notably in regard to their relationship to the land. The response to crisis was, however, far from smooth: it was played out in intense ideological debates in which the human and natural sciences were deployed by different state bureaucracies. As in previous periods, contradictory policies co-existed uncomfortably, highlighting divisions within the state and the tenuousness of its knowledge of – and authority over – its charges and the land.

Administration and Order

In the late 1950s, the Rhodesian government increasingly turned to repressive measures to counter the spread of African nationalism. A State of Emergency was declared in early 1959. Immediately thereafter, parliament passed the Unlawful Organizations Act and the Preventive Detention Act. The ANC was banned under the former while the latter was used to detain over 300 nationalist leaders, mainly in rural areas. The 1959 Native Affairs Amendment Act made it a crime for any African to say or do anything 'likely to undermine the authority' of officials, chiefs or headmen, and prohibited meetings of twelve or more in the reserves save with the NC's approval. In 1960, the Law and Order (Maintenance) Act and the Emergency Powers Act greatly expanded the powers of the executive and security branches of government. The Law and Order (Maintenance) Act allowed for the banning of publications and meetings, arrest without a warrant, restriction without trial, and created new crimes, ranging from causing 'disaffection' in the police and publishing 'false news', to intimidation, sabotage and terrorism. Between 1958 and 1962, the personnel of the British South Africa Police (BSAP) and Ministries of Native Affairs and Justice nearly doubled, and the number of police stations rose from 102 to 134.[1]

In the reserves, the degree to which officials felt directly threatened by opposition to the NLHA was clearly expressed by the Native Affairs Advisory Board in early 1961. Members saw the last two years of resistance as 'nothing less than a challenge to the right of the Government to exercise any control'. CNC S. E. Morris ominously warned that 'there will be bloodshed' if destocking continued. The Board cited growing instances of resistance, 'such as opposition to veterinary measures, creating disturbances at cattle sales, breaking up Land Development Officers' extension meetings, assaults and threats of assaults to persons in authority, down to direct opposition to the application of the Native Land Husbandry Act and the deliberate flouting of its provisions after application'. The Board concluded on an apocalyptic note:

> *The Important point* in all this is the extent to which this criticism and opposition to what is Government policy is undermining and obstructing the administration of this policy and the whole maintenance of law and order. This can and will, unless it is strongly combated and counteracted, bring about the breakdown of administration and maintenance of law and order. This could all happen in a relatively short time. *This all important fact must be brought to the attention of the Government in the plainest terms.*
> The most urgent and dangerous aspect of this overall position is the determined and by no means unsuccessful campaign to penetrate the rural areas with planned political agitation in which every possible grievance, particularly in relation to land and stock, arc [sic] exploited to the full, emotions whipped to the point of violence and the fullest use made of intimidatory practices.[2]

In 1960 and 1961, strikes, demonstrations and riots in the urban centres mirrored the unrest of the rural areas.[3]

One of the Board's principal concerns was the position in which NCs had been placed. African 'agitation' engendered 'strong feelings of hostility towards the native commissioner, who is looked upon by the people as the person who decides whether or not a person may have land or stock rights. The most pressing and immediate problem is to direct these feelings of hostility away from the native commissioner.'[4] The attacks on NCs brought to a head the strains between technical and administrative officers. Arthur Pendered summarised the prevailing views.[5] Administrators felt that 'technical staff appear to want to proceed from an advisory to a directive capacity, but, on the other hand, do not want to accept responsibility for distasteful tasks, e.g. destocking, Native Land Husbandry Control, etc.' Technical officials drew attention to the NLHA's flaws, hurried implementation, and the complete absence of extension work. They stressed the difficult position of inexperienced staff, and argued that 'inspection, control and so-called quasi-police work in connection with [NLHA] control ... is incompatible with gaining and retaining the goodwill and cooperation of the African farmer'. Neither group wanted to shoulder the dangerous burden of enforcing the Act; both understood that the problem was inextricably linked to their own and the state's tenuous authority.

In early 1961, senior officials of the Ministry of Native Affairs perceived the NLHA as a threat to their officers, and to the government's very ability to rule. Their debates took place amidst a wider set of momentous changes. Southern Rhodesia stood at a crossroad. The northern partners of the Central African Federation were moving rapidly to majority rule, African nationalism boomed as never before, and the economic downturn threatened the push towards 'partnership' and away from segregation. As much of Africa achieved its independence, Southern Rhodesia clung fiercely to its own. But settler rule required new trappings, and a new claim to legitimacy if it was to present an acceptable face to this brave new world, and to rebuild the state. That it failed to find a *modus vivendi* with Britain and the international community led to the Unilateral Declaration of Independence in 1965, sanctions and isolation, but before this breach occurred there was an energetic search for new means of 'native rule', shaped by the international trends of the time.

The 'Human Factor', Chiefs and the Land

The air of panic that marked the early 1960s was met with a thoroughgoing overhaul of Southern Rhodesia's 'native policy' in the context of negotiating a new constitutional relationship with Britain. The government established a series of commissions to assess agricultural, administrative, economic and judicial policy.[6] They were strongly influenced by imported experts and assumed that Southern Rhodesia was moving towards both a gradual desegregation of land, as proposed in the 1960 Quinton Report and endorsed by Prime Minister Edgar Whitehead's government, and the adoption of a multiracial policy of community development.[7] While many of the experts who sat on the commissions came from Britain and the British colonial world, the initiative behind community development was American, itself a sign of shifts in world power.[8] By then engaged in community development across the globe, the United States Agency for International Development (USAID) approached the Rhodesian government in 1959. An American community development adviser arrived in 1960, and the policy was formally adopted in 1962. Key in the elaboration of community development were Dr James Green, an American 'consultant sociologist' engaged under the auspices of USAID, and Roger Howman, a senior member of the Ministry of Native Affairs and a well-travelled thinker on African administration and local government.[9]

In brief, the commissions' recommendations resulted in the creation of a new Ministry of Internal Affairs (MIA) to replace the Native Affairs Division in 1962. NCs became District Commissioners (DCs), and PNCs became Provincial Commissioners (PCs), thus expunging the now offensive term 'native' from government titles. Technical and judicial services were removed from the direct control of Native Affairs while the new MIA was left in the key role of coordinating services and running local government under the rubric of community development. The reorganisations were implemented and modified over the 1960s with varying effects, but with an overriding tendency toward returning the policy initiative to the administrative branch.

The return to prominence of administrative concerns was instrumental in redefining the causes of African opposition to the NLHA in terms of what were called 'human factors', rather than the Act's widely noted technical flaws. The 'human factor' gained currency in official discourse in the early 1960s, partly drawing on James Green's use of the term. Thus implementation of the NLHA had to be slowed down so as to 'deal with human factors'; resistance resulted from the neglect of 'human material'; technical development had produced 'a kind of human sand held together with little or nothing'.[10] In his influential review of technical development in 1961, a report strongly influenced by Roger Howman, CNC S. E. Morris condemned high modernist social engineering:

> What is the common factor that has produced results so different from the confident hopes of those who produced these schemes and threw finances, personnel and technical specialists into the battle to save the soil and increase production? As we now see it, the simple explanation of a vastly complex problem is that a barrier of human beings lay between technical knowledge and the soil. And that barrier comprises not a multitude of individuals living in isolation, not a crowd of units waiting to welcome benefits, but a cultural organisation with its own structure, organisation, patterns of thinking, feeling and acting.... The moral for planners seems plain ... that no long-term results are achieved by an individualistic approach which leaves the fabric, pattern and structure of social life out of account or undermined. The problem is not a technical one, nor is the crux of it the extent to which capital, management and labour are there to develop the land, as the economist would have it. It seems clear that the more a technical approach is adopted..., the greater becomes the cultural resistance. We must see it as a human problem.[11]

This soul-searching report laid the groundwork for the application of a new discourse of human science to the vague practices of customary rule. If resistance was 'cultural' and the problem 'a barrier of human beings', then the answer lay not with technical calculation or individual incentive, but in administrative solutions provided by community development and backed by a different band of experts – sociologists, anthropologists and administrators.

The community development policy, as formulated by Green, fitted well with this reconceptualisation of African society. He found that the ideal basis on which to 'delineate' communities to which responsibilities could be transferred was the 'judicial function', a function 'invariably' exercised by chiefs and headmen. By contrast, technical officers' attempts to create 'economic units, based on a balance of arable and grazing land' had been 'sociologically unwise' and hence 'doomed to failure'.[12] Green stressed community development's foundation in the sciences of sociology, psychology and anthropology. Under the community development philosophy, human growth was more important than 'purely economic development' brought about by the 'atomization of groups and compulsive measures'. People did not respond solely to the market place: they 'must want development'. The policy rendered local government responsible to an active community, engaged in democratic planning to meet its 'felt needs'. Experts would no longer set the agenda, but would act as 'servants of the people'.[13]

This was a policy with an illustrious international past and present. Green traced the origins of community development to a 1948 Cambridge conference for colonial administrators. It was used by social welfare organisations in the USA and Britain, and had been adopted by the UN, UNESCO, the UK Colonial and Commonwealth Relations Offices, and USAID. India had adopted community development in 1952, Pakistan in 1953, the Philippines in 1956, and it existed in various forms in Ghana, Uganda, Tanganyika, Nigeria, Northern Rhodesia, Nyasaland, Iran, South Korea, and Kenya.[14] Roger Howman constructed a more local genealogy, placing community development's origins in 1920s and 1930s Southern Rhodesia, in Harold Jowitt's work in the Native Education Department, in early NCs with a keen interest in 'social structure', and in his own thinking on administration in the 1950s.[15]

Green's findings and the beliefs of administrators were reinforced by the Whitehead government's need for an alternative voice to that of African nationalists. To this end, the government set about recruiting chiefs into national politics. Chiefs' first act was to deliver a badly needed measure of African approval for the 1961 constitution at a government 'indaba'. In return, parliament passed the Council of Chiefs and Provincial Assemblies Act, establishing a prestigious forum for consultation with selected chiefs; chiefs' salaries were raised, and additional concessions promised. At the same time, further repressive measures were enacted. The ANC's successor, the NDP, was banned in late 1961, and its successor, the Zimbabwe African People's Union (Zapu), was banned in September 1962. Hundreds were detained. Though the People's Caretaker Council, a front for Zapu, and the Zimbabwe African National Union (Zanu), which split from Zapu in 1963, continued to operate until they were banned in 1964, they were preoccupied with internecine strife. In effect, the 'open' nationalist period was brought to a close.

At all levels of government there was now a strong disposition to turn to chiefs, rather than to a more democratic system lacking the 'natural' cohesion Green sought for community development. Communal, not individual, rights in both economic and political spheres were the order of the day. The demands of nationalists were shunted aside in the process. So was the debate within the technical branches over the validity of their recommendations, a development which suited many technical officers, especially those who had expressed doubts over their expertise, suffered physical attacks, or desired a return to the less fraught business of agricultural extension.

Acceptance of an administrative solution to resistance nevertheless had to be given scientific validity. This was not to be the haphazard treatment of 'custom' of earlier decades: it would involve a huge programme of collecting information about 'traditional structures' and 'community'. In practice, the transition was far from smooth. Technical and community development co-existed during an awkward interim period, as the work of the Robinson Commission's Working Party D illustrated.[16] Dominated by administrative officers, including Howman and Green, and chaired by the chief architect of the NLHA, Arthur Pendered, it combined in a highly unsuccessful way the concerns of both policies. The Commission's brief was straightforward: 'to propose measures designed to fill a vacuum in the reserves and to retain the loyalty of the chiefs'.[17] The Working Party's recommendations led to a rejection of the tenurial and economic goals of the NLHA and the initial transfer of powers to chiefs. It was strongly influenced by its consultations with chiefs and DCs, and by an overriding sense of the urgency of the 'landless problem'. At the same time, it continued to draw on technical advice and methods.

Working Party D found that chiefs' loyalty was 'severely strained' by 'pressure being brought upon them by their followers as the result of political agitation or by what they consider to be legitimate grievances'. A bargain urgently needed to be struck: some concessions on land were deemed necessary and the status of chiefs needed to be bolstered with powers over land and in courts. A failure to 'return' powers to chiefs, in the Working Party's words, would lead them to 'swing to the extreme nationalist cause' along with their followers, causing 'a breakdown of good Government'. In the short term, the 'political menace' posed by those rendered 'legally landless' by the NLHA needed to be met by allowing chiefs to allocate land. Cabinet heeded the warning and hurriedly authorised allocation under amendment 22c to the NLHA. Hastily demarcated areas in grazing land were 'placed at the disposal of the tribal authorities', largely on the basis of multiplying the 'known number of landless' with the 'subsistence acreage per family for that region'. Considerations of economic productivity did not enter into this equation.[18]

Though regarded as politically necessary, 22c allocations were problematic. Chiefs on the newly constituted National Chiefs' Council initially strongly objected to them in the absence of land redistribution. Moreover, the 1961 constitution had entrenched NLHA rights in the Tribal Trust Lands (TTLs), as the reserves were tellingly renamed. Thus, where NLHA rights had been issued, the 'resuscitation' of what were called 'Tribal Land Authorities' could only come through the 'expressed desire of those concerned'.[19] The Tribal Land Authority had no codified function until 1967.[20] In the meantime, it was to operate according to what chiefs designated as 'tribal law and custom'. The Working Party adopted an extraordinarily *laissez faire* attitude: 'those who opt for the traditional tribal system in land allocation must be assumed to know what they are doing and to be prepared to accept the conse-quences'.[21] Chiefs were, however, often all too aware of the consequences, and they were to pose formidable obstacles to the Working Party's attempts to 'resuscitate' custom, as I explore in the next chapter.

The Working Party went on explicitly to reject individual tenure in the reserves, thus scuppering the basis on which the Quinton Report had envisaged the gradual desegregation of land, through the conversion of all categories to freehold status.[22] This meant rejecting the repeal of the Land Apportionment Act, a crucial measure promised by the Whitehead government, and backed by various members of the NAD as necessary to regaining a lost 'moral' platform. The Working Party countered that to enforce private tenure in the reserves would mean the 'sacrifice' of 'traditional tribal authorities' in the name of a discredited notion of economic progress.[23] The reserves were recast as a traditional bastion:

> We may even have to return for the time being to the old concept of the tribal lands as the 'secu-rity pool' of the tribe and 'reservoir of labour' until we can fill in some of these gaps (e.g. social security, adequate industrialisation, administrative-development approach, etc.), which exist in our society and economy as compared to that of a modern state.

But if Rhodesia was clearly not ready for modernisation, this did not explain the reasons for the failure of the NLHA. The Working Party interpreted resistance to the Act, and justified the 'return' to 'tribal tenure' in terms of Africans' 'spiritual' ties to land and cattle, arguing that these attachments were 'quite impervious to logical or other argument'.[24] This view was cited repeatedly by the commissions of the early 1960s; though the NLHA's wide-ranging economic and technical flaws were clearly identified, African objections were not linked to these deficiencies. There was a 'much deeper reason', i.e. 'the clash between the objectives of the Act and the traditional beliefs that the *Chiefs spiritually are the land*, that the *individual cannot have rights to ownership of the land*, and that *cattle, possessing a spiritual significance far transcending their intrinsic value, cannot be treated merely as animals providing services or for disposal for sale*'.[25] Such views were sanctioned by experts, and bolstered with reference to anthropological insight. They brushed aside NCs' more nuanced interpretations of earlier periods, and ignored the complex mix of individual and communal rights and claims, many of which were not based in the customary or spiritual, that characterised tenure in the TTLs.[26]

While the Working Party was firmly opposed to the conversion of Tribal Trust Land to private tenure, it was not opposed to land redistribution. It recommended using the Unreserved Area (i.e. unalienated former crown land) for 'tribal' settlement in order to 'quickly reassure the chiefs' and to deal with 'the problem of the landless on a communal basis'. This was a political, not an economic, strategy. The Unreserved Area was of little productive use and thus ideal for Africans who 'are not farmers in our economic sense, they simply want a stake in the land for a complexity of reasons which we may not fully appreciate but which means everything to them'.[27] But land redistribution was to fall victim to the pressures of the white electorate, with devastating repercussions for the political project of recruiting chiefs.

Working Party D followed its fateful short-term step of authorising chiefs' allocations with a more concerted effort to establish their powers as a long-term solution to the crisis of authority engendered by the NLHA. The Working Party set out:

> (1) to determine what was the traditional Native Authority in respect of the land according to tribal law and custom, and what were its methods and powers; (2) to list the ways in which Government policy and legal enactment has altered or eliminated these powers; (3) to consider whether and in what form this authority should be restored and what powers it should be given to make it effective in the changed circumstances of today.[28]

In its deliberations, administrators played an important role. They had earlier been extremely ambivalent about the authority of chiefs,[29] but now the 'overwhelming majority' were found to believe that 'traditional tribal authority is by no means dead, that its force and continuing viability reasserts itself strongly at every turn and that certainly for some time to come it has a very important part to play'.[30] Roger Howman put the vibrancy of chieftaincy down to the absence of indirect rule: chiefs had not been co-opted into inappropriate institutions and so had not been given a host of less than customary roles. Their 'genuine, inherent or traditional' power was thus maintained.[31] Working Party D argued that the 'tribal authority' would provide 'cohesion' in line with the community development goal to 'build upon and to develop from existing institutions'.[32] The language of Green's community development policy was used to cast the departure from technical development in the positive light of a more enlightened administrative philosophy, sanctioned by the human sciences, and given an earthy credibility by DCs' testimony to their hands-on experience with 'tribal custom'.

By the end of 1961, many of the policy decisions crucial to undermining the NLHA had been taken. The final blow came in 1962 when Working Party D commissioned a countrywide survey in a last and ultimately doomed attempt to dress up chiefs' land allocations in the trappings of technical development. In the style of the NLHA's implementation, Arthur Pendered stated that the survey 'obviously calls for the coordination of a vast amount of data'.[33] Technical officials hurriedly toured the country, assessing 'ecological risk' on the basis of the 'Annual Cropping Acreage' and the 'Recommended Livestock Equivalent' for each of 210 areas.[34] The former was calculated by reducing the 'Potential Arable' land (itself determined by excluding all land with over a twelve per cent slope or with less than ten inches of top soil) by factors which determined the amount of land on which productivity could be sustained under a given – but unclearly specified – farming system.[35] In order to create 'room to manoeuvre', the Working Party, in negotiation with technical officers, agreed to allow up to 30 per cent 'overstocking'. The Working Party assumed that a judicious measure of overstocking, and the use of what were felt to be more sophisticated technical methods, would allow increases in carrying capacities and arable land allocation, and thus allow for the political mollification of the 'human factor'. It was to be sorely disappointed.

Makoni District offers an extreme but not unrepresentative example of the problems that the surveys encountered in higher rainfall regions. The new stock-carrying capacity assessments were drastically lower than previous ones, leaving 'no room whatsoever to manoeuvre'. Though 'technically irrefutable', according to the Working Party, the assessments were strongly challenged by the NC and left the Provincial Agriculturalist, himself a pasture expert, 'somewhat taken aback'. The NC stated his case vehemently, and very much in keeping with the spirit of the day:

> As I have so often pointed out, the erosion of the soil is one thing, but with certain measures it can be healed, whereas the erosion of the goodwill of the Africans, which is likely to be caused by lack of arable land is an entirely different matter, and, so far as I know, once lost there is no remedy available to regain it. It would appear to me, therefore, that whatever the technical considerations are, the human ones completely outweigh them.[36]

In lower rainfall areas, where the stress lay on pastoral production, there were even more severe obstacles. No agreement could be reached between agricultural and administrative officers. The Working Party thus established an arbitrary measure of acceptable usage of arable land which it freely admitted did not have 'any technical merits'. The same problem arose with regard to stock: new technical assessments often lowered existing carrying capacities; administrators and technical officials proved unable to reach agreement. Thus the Working Party decided to disregard all previous stocking policy, resolving instead that 'recommended numbers must be regarded purely as a guide line because (a) the number of stock is constantly changing, (b) the carrying capacity differs from one year to another', views that had much more in common with those of African stockholders than with the sciences of technical development.[37]

In practice, throughout the country, technical officers' often contradictory recommendations were rejected at the behest of administrators and in the name of 'practical politics' and 'human factors'. In its attempt to rebuild rural administration, Working Party D set in motion processes that undermined many of the long sacrosanct tenets of technical planning, notably the enforcement of rigid carrying capacities, and the distinction between 'arable' and 'grazing' land. An important exception to this rule, however, was the commitment to mechanical conservation. This was from the outset rigorously defended as a 'prime duty of the Government'. Community development policy explicitly designated conservation as a 'national issue' not to be 'confused with voluntary felt needs of the community'.[38]

Within the space of a few turbulent years, a new orthodoxy had been entrenched within government. It rejected the possibility of 'modernising' the reserves on the grounds that Africans were too steeped in tradition to accept the rationality of western science, individual tenure, private property and the market. The turn to chiefs brought together the traditionalist beliefs of administrators and their desire to maintain order, the 'expert' advice of community development advisers seeking 'natural' communities, and white politicians' need for allies other than the nationalist leadership. It entrenched territorial segregation in the process, by underlining the essential difference between the relationship of Africans and Europeans to the land.

Community Development and the Rhodesian Front

The obstacles community development was to face lay in its alliance to segregation and its exclusion of nationalist demands. With the rise of the right-wing Rhodesian Front, these issues blossomed into political conflict, and fatally undermined attempts to remake the state. Though the 'liberal' Whitehead government had formally adopted community development, it was the Rhodesian Front that outspokenly endorsed it as a plank of its election platform. The policy was severely compromised in African eyes as a result, not least due to its association with South African apartheid.[39]

When the Rhodesian Front came to power in December 1962, it focused its energies on pleasing its white constituency of farmers, workers and petty bourgeoisie.[40] It dramatically rejected the rhetorical and real moves to desegregation of the Whitehead government, denouncing the multiracial aspect of community development in favour of a South African-style emphasis on 'cultural' (rather than biological) difference and separate development.[41] It also adamantly refused to consider land redistribution to Africans. The influential W. H. H. Nicolle, Deputy Director in the Ministry of Internal Affairs, heatedly defended the Land Apportionment Act as necessary to avoid 'racial difficulties arising out of differences in "psyche" between the races': 'There is no doubt whatsoever that if the Land Apportionment Act was repealed natives would move into the European areas, and in consequence large numbers of Europeans would leave the Country and in consequence property values would drop substantially and in consequence the economy of the Country would collapse.'[42]

There was a simple answer to African demands for land: the Primary Development programme. Launched in 1963, it acknowledged the political need to settle the unemployed landless, as Working Party D had, but applied the principle only to the TTLs.[43] Primary Development had two main planks: developing 'sparsely populated' TTLs and expanding irrigation schemes. The former required a huge programme of tsetse-fly clearance, road building and water development in thirteen districts, spanning the northern border of the country, though concentrating in Binga and Gokwe. Between 1963 and 1968, approximately 80,000 people moved to the northern frontier as a result of evictions and land pressure within TTLs.[44] These movements were termed 'voluntary', meaning the government offered no assistance in terms of transportation or resettlement. W. H. H. Nicolle, who ran the programme, gleefully told European landowners with unwanted tenants, DCs with overcrowded TTLs, and Africans facing eviction or demanding land that there was in fact no shortage of land: 'If ... people want more land we can easily accommodate them in the huge unoccupied tracts of Tribal land in the Binga and Gokwe districts.'[45]

The second plank of the policy involved an ambitious programme of irrigation development within TTLs. Irrigation schemes had come under severe criticism at the time of the NLHA's implementation due to their low incomes and the subdivision of four-acre plots. But in the 1960s and 1970s two-acre plots were standard issue, reflecting the change in focus from creating 'economic units' to absorbing the landless and unemployed. As A. K. H. Weinrich writes, these schemes were intended to 'tie men and women to the land throughout the year and so prevent them from seeking work in European areas'. An Internal Affairs official bluntly held 'our policy is to place as many people on as little land as possible.'[46] Between 1965 and 1969, the area under irrigation in TTLs increased from 5,700 to 14,000 acres.

THE THREE-LEGGED POT

Community development was in theory to conform to Roger Howman's metaphor of the 'three-legged pot'.[47] Councils and community boards formed the first leg and were to provide a secular and largely elected authority responsible for 'modern services' and intended to 'keep pace with the advanced fellow'.[48] Chiefs and headmen were to sit as ex-officio members of councils while also acting as the second and third legs of community development in the form of Tribal Courts and the Tribal Land Authority. They were to be responsible for an expanded judicial brief, land allocation and conservation, as well as serving as the leaders of a communal bulwark against the too rapid turn to individualism, a dangerous tendency that Howman pointedly noted had fueled the Mau Mau rebellion in Kenya.[49] Constituting any of these 'legs' proved difficult. In the first years of Rhodesian Front rule, the Green/Howman partnership struggled to defend community development against an onslaught from African nationalists, teachers, MPs, missions, and other government departments, notably Agriculture and Education, jealous of their terrain and suspicious of community development.

Internal Affairs officials were immediately faced with the challenge of finding an acceptable language with which to introduce community development, as well as a means of disguising civil servants' past (and present) coercive roles. Even the term 'community' provoked objections: as Roger Howman noted, it 'is so loaded with racial connotations that the less we see [it] in the headlines the better.'[50] The term 'council' was also compromised, through its association with the hated African Councils. Officials noted that 'it was better to avoid wherever possible the use of the term', but failed to come up with an alternative.[51] Changing the perceptions of the foot soldiers of community development, the Community Development (CD) agents, proved an additional challenge. CD agents were drawn from the ranks of agricultural demonstrators, men who had played much resented enforcement roles under the NLHA. Secretary for Internal Affairs Morris stressed that they 'must be immediately divorced from their past agricultural duties'. The name 'demonstrator' and its vernacular equivalents were to be replaced by new names. DCs would need to give their 'full weight and backing' to the CD agents, but 'It must be stressed that they are not "agents" of Government but agents of community action.'[52]

All this failed to convince even the trainee CD agents. In a question and answer session with James Green, they pointed out, 'In general, people do not like Government agents', and, in a wonderfully succinct turn of phrase, wondered, 'How will the people believe that the Community Development agent, who was a Demonstrator, is no longer a policeman?'[53] Moreover, CD agents faced hostility from other ministries, notably Agriculture, which resented their transfer to Internal Affairs.[54] The MIA could only advise the CD agents to overcome opposition '(a) By not over-estimating political influence. (b) By the use of extensive, carefully planned propaganda. (c) By encouraging the nationalists to participate.' Most importantly, the CD agents had to woo the chiefs: 'Within the TTLs, the traditional authorities are so strong today that without their support a community development agent will achieve little.'[55] But again the CD agents were unconvinced. They asked what they were to do in cases of conflict between government-appointed chiefs and headmen and 'the one recognised by the people'; 'What happens if a chief is hated by the community?'[56]

African Field Officers of the Information Service, charged with promoting community development through civics courses and cinema, raised a host of broader questions.[57] They stressed that the history of evictions meant people felt unable to invest in community projects: 'they know that what they've got, what they possess is not theirs'. They pointed out that people were afraid to form associations because 'once you have meetings', 'the police must be there'. They noted that community development did not really imply the ability to make choices or control finances: the DC was still in charge, and most rates and levies went to central government. People thought community development was 'a Group Areas Act in disguise'. It could not work 'where there is already a rigid policy like the Land Apportionment Act standing'. All officials were fatally tainted: 'when you take community development and try to associate it with … those officials in central government trying to give directives in a local community which you claim has got its own autonomy, I don't think it will work.'

Efforts to defend community development as based on culture not race and sanctified by the human sciences also faced heated objections. As a self-styled 'Moderate African' wrote to the *Rhodesia Herald*:

It is all very impressive to quote the opinions of eminent sociologists and anthropologists to justify the stand the Government is making, but these philosophical arguments will not make the plan feasible. The canons of the scheme are to maintain racial segregation and to intensify it…. It is unfortunate that this new move by the Government gives the lie to those Africans who thought co-operation, calculated to bridge the gaps between the two major races, would surely solve the problems of this country. One hopes that the Government will soon realise that whatever measures it chooses to impose from above in bureaucratic fashion are palliatives which will not cure our ills.[58]

Such views were backed by opposition MPs, including Africans elected under the 1961 constitution. They charged that the language of community development was little more than a smokescreen for 'apartheid, Bantustan, separate development', that Africans thought of it as a 'dreadful monster that had devoured their brothers in South Africa'. MP J. M. Gondo warned prophetically, 'that while discrimination and the Land Apportionment Act exist Community Development stinks in the face of the African…. The Minister will require an army to make it work.'[59]

Missionary and church leaders, responding to a seminar intended to gain their support, expressed deep concern over the implications for education, equity and racial separatism.[60] The key 'felt need' that the policy was supposed to address was primary education, run almost entirely by missions in African areas, with grants from government. Missions faced the spectre of community development authorities taking over education, but without adequate resources. Teachers were not any better disposed to the policy. At the Teachers' Association annual congress, President C. G. Msipa called community development 'Bantu Education' to cries of 'Apartheid', 'Bantustan', and 'divide and rule' from the audience.[61] Even officials of the Ministry of African Education were unconvinced of councils' ability to run schools, given their lack of funds and staff, and the fact that existing locally supported schools eschewed any links to councils. They were also uneasy about the politics of community development: 'the question is to what extent can the political system we are trying to set up compete with the African conception of one man, one vote and one party'.[62]

All these objections made the implementation of community development exceedingly difficult. Officials were unsure of even where to start. The mere act of sending delineation teams into the test district of Selukwe had built up a 'fairly solid block of opposition'.[63] They struggled to come up with new forms of propaganda, and new forms of statecraft, so as to 'market' the policy. The Information Department argued for a militarily organised advertising campaign: 'We are in the situation where we have manufactured a new kind of soap – it is in a variety of wrappers and no sales organisation has yet been created to market this product.' The 'order of battle' needed to be set out, 'soft' targets needed to be 'infiltrated', and 'saboteurs' taken care of. It was necessary to 'look at our ordnance store and see what armoury we have', and then to 'assault the press, radio and television, church councils, women's organisations and the African bodies of influence'. Roger Howman called for the Prime Minister to state clearly 'that this has nothing whatever to do with Bantustans or the Group Areas Act'.[64] But the PM was to stay silent until 1965. The delay in the Prime Minister's Directive on Community Development and opposition from other ministries led

Secretary of Internal Affairs Morris to complain bitterly that the policy had become 'some strange obsession' of his ministry.[65]

The situation on the ground was far from encouraging. From districts across the country, DCs reported opposition to community development, sometimes in the form of intimidation and attacks aimed at CD agents and chiefs and headmen who cooperated with them. As one DC explained, 'Over recent years political influences have been successful in inculcating an almost instinctive distrust of anything proposed or introduced by Gov't.' People told CD agents 'they know what they want and they have their own leaders'.[66] They preferred to dissolve existing agricultural and other projects than to put them under the community development rubric.[67] Little of value to 'communities' was at any rate placed within the purview of councils, and resources were in any case woefully inadequate.[68] The distinction made between 'land' and 'development' meant that councils, as opposed to Tribal Land Authorities, could not concern themselves with land allocation or use, or controls on stock, and neither councils nor chiefs could respond to the most consistently articulated 'felt need' – more land.

Minister of Internal Affairs J. H. Howman, younger brother to Roger Howman, tried to put a brave face on community development in late 1963. He scolded those ministries that were 'dragging their feet', and appealed to a sense of patriotic duty: community development was not 'party politics. This is national. This is Rhodesianism moving together.'[69] But 'Rhodesianism' was not moving together, even in the narrow world of the Rhodesian Front. Subsequent to the break-up of the Federal state, the question of independence deeply divided the party, leading to the resignation of Prime Minister Winston Field in April 1964. Importantly, J. H. Howman resigned with him, thus leaving Internal Affairs in the hands of a staunch member of the Rhodesian Front's right wing, William Harper. Harper favoured separate development and restricting African political representation to chiefs and headmen. He was vehemently backed by his influential deputy, W. H. H. Nicolle, who would take over from S. E. Morris as Secretary for Internal Affairs in 1965. Nicolle was an admirer of the South African homelands system and believed that 'the major part of the native populations is still in the kopjes and not ready to take its place in a modern democracy or civilisation'.[70] A demoralised James Green left in 1964 when the US government withdrew its support, to be replaced by a British adviser, T. R. Batten. While Nicolle welcomed Batten's approach as preferable to that of the 'Americans', Batten was not impressed: he found 'people's ideas about community development "woolly" and unclear'.[71]

THE TWO-LEGGED POT

Community development had come to mean something new. The long delayed Prime Minister's Directive on the policy, issued in July 1965, stressed the duty of DCs to 'inculcate a proper understanding of the disciplinary and penalizing influences of Government'.[72] The Rhodesian Front firmly rejected negotiation with the nationalist leadership in favour of chiefs: at the much vaunted 'indaba' of 1964, they unanimously backed the Rhodesian Front's call for a declaration of independence.

Their endorsement was accompanied by another round of severe repression of nationalists. The Front parlayed chiefs' backing into 'one of the largest and most prominently displayed banners proclaiming the African Majority's staunch support of the country's European leadership'. In return chiefs received salary increases and promises of more powers.[73] Chiefs now stood unambiguously at the centre of community development. As Secretary for Internal Affairs Nicolle proclaimed, 'Community Development as it is known and applied in other parts of the world is a premature concept for Africa.' In South African vein, he asserted that the answer lay in 'the Africans' own known, tried and understood system – the tribal structure of organization and leadership'.[74] The bald endorsement of 'tribal structure' marked a hardening of a trend present from the beginning, but now a massive investment was made in conceptualising African society as 'tribal' alone. Green's concern for 'human growth' through democratic 'social action' was no longer on the agenda, and nor was Howman's concern for balancing the needs of 'advanced' Africans with those of their 'tribal' brethren.

The concern for 'tribal structure' was given shape by the work of the Ministry of Internal Affairs' delineation teams. They set about identifying communities on the basis of the judicial authority of customary leaders. Chiefs and headmen were the principal and, in many cases, exclusive informants. Researchers travelled the length and breadth of Rhodesia in the mid-1960s, collecting chiefly histories, establishing the boundaries of 'traditional' communities, and noting down 'felt needs'. Administrators went to great lengths to identify 'legitimate' chiefs on the basis of traditional succession procedures. Clear distinctions were drawn between 'Shona' and 'Ndebele' institutions. The Ndebele were construed as 'a military organisation' made up of 'many tribes'. Headmen and village heads were simply chiefly appointees, while the chief's authority lay not in ritual or kinship or the ancestors but in his role as a commander. In contrast, Shona institutions were cast as a hierarchy of kinship groups in which the chief represented the ancestors, and in which authority travelled up through village heads and headmen in a tortuous process of ritually sanctioned consultation. In both cases, individual rights in the political sphere were rejected, just as they had been in the economic sphere: 'The notions, of European political habits, of decisions by vote, with its assumptions of the isolated individual making decisions of his own, of a majority of numbers overwhelming the minority, these are strange and objectionable foreign customs.' An 'aggregate of communities' not an 'aggregate of individuals' constituted 'the basis of the state'.[75]

The attempt to constitute chiefs as land authorities, never mind as 'the basis of the state' was to be no easy task. Bureaucratic conflict and delays in legislation posed one set of problems. Debate in the TTL Board centred on the conundrum of bolstering chiefs' authority over land while also enforcing conservation measures. The Natural Resources Board (NRB) complained of the vast acreages opened without conservation works.[76] It called for continued central government 'control of the block demarcation of arable land', but was firmly informed of the new dispensation by W. H. H. Nicolle: 'There is no such thing as arable land – even a kopje can be arable land if it is put under conservation.'[77] The NRB responded by focusing its attention on prosecutions and fines wherever land was opened without conservation works. DCs were less concerned with conservation than with the authority of chiefs and headmen. Part of their troubles lay in the delayed passage of the TTL Act which would give chiefs' legal authority over land allocation.[78] They urgently called for legislation providing punitive powers to back chiefs' 'tribal' authority.[79] The NRB's single-minded enforcement of conservation regulations compounded the problem: when it enforced conservation works on land farmed without the chief's authority, it was interpreted as 'a sign of condoning the illegal cultivation.'[80] Impassioned pleas from DCs led to an informal policy of prosecuting those cultivating without chiefs' authority, and preventing the NRB from ordering those facing prosecution to conserve the land.[81] Conservation work was also suspended where its enforcement was deemed a threat to public order.[82]

The TTL Board sought to find a compromise between conservationist concerns, the imperative of bolstering chiefs' authority, and the need to control the opening of land, by directly involving chiefs in conservation and attempting to disabuse them of the idea that land could be allocated to all. Chiefs were sent on tours abroad, the 'main objectives' of which, were 'to show that in no country in the world can everybody have all the land he required and everybody who wants land have land, and that provided extension services are available ... men can do with considerably less acreages of soil than he imagined he required.'[83] The NRB organised conservation courses for chiefs and tried to establish conservation committees under their control. It adopted Internal Affair's customary discourse by casting chiefs in an invented role as 'guardians of the soil'.[84] It also maintained its distinctly authoritarian tone, producing for example a pamphlet on contour ridging entitled 'Obey or Die' for chiefs' consumption.[85] Finally, the Ministries of Agriculture and Internal Affairs agreed to create the post of 'chief's pegger' to demarcate conservation works in new fields. It was hoped that, as chiefs' employees, the peggers would 'not be subject to the same antagonism, threats and intimidation as officers of the Ministry of Agriculture have been encountering.'[86] Chiefs were in effect expected to play the same policing roles they had under the NLHA, but now in the name of custom not science.

The confusion of the 1960s was partially resolved in favour of the MIA in 1969 when it resumed control over African agriculture. This was one of many moves intended to increase the control of DCs and chiefs. Amendments to the African Affairs Act in 1966, the long awaited TTL Act in 1967, the African Law and Tribal Courts Act in 1969, and the inclusion of chiefs in the house and senate under the 1969 constitution, all vastly increased the powers and duties of chiefs. As Roger Howman wrote: 'Through the Tribal Trust Lands Act government relinquishes its direct control over Tribal Trust land, restores traditional powers to traditional leaders and clothes them with legal authority.'[87] The Tribal Land Authority was nonetheless very vaguely described as 'the chief of the tribal area and such other tribesmen resident therein as the chief may nominate in accordance with tribal custom', the MIA retaining ultimate control should 'custom' prove obstructive.[88] Under the Tribal Courts Act, chiefs and headmen gained limited criminal jurisdiction, while the African Affairs Act gave chiefs new punitive powers and assigned them government-paid 'messengers' with powers of arrest.[89] The Land Tenure Act of 1969 subsequently reinforced land segregation and, according to Prime Minister Ian Smith, placed responsibility for the TTLs 'squarely where it belonged – on the people, represented by the tribal land authorities'.[90]

But neither these measures, nor the subsequent elevation of chiefs to Regional Authorities in 1973 and 'cabinet councils' in 1976, produced effective rural authorities. Chiefs proved highly unreliable as intermediaries, and councils barely functioned. The Rhodesian Front was forced to implement the threat, laid down in 1963, of withdrawing services in an effort to boost the formation of councils. The number of councils grew, but in practice most rapidly fell under the 'management' of DCs.[91] The community development policy failed to relieve the necessity and costs of management and coercion, as Secretary for Internal Affairs Nicolle admitted in 1968.[92] The retired Roger Howman looked on in horror as the last remnants of elected councils were dismantled: in 1971, chiefs were given the right of veto over council candidates; in 1972, councils became known as 'chiefs' councils'; in 1973 they were converted to wholly appointed bodies.[93] His warnings about the dangers of relying on the 'hypnotic attraction of "inherent" customary authority', on the 'cult of tribal custom' were ignored,[94] as was vividly illustrated by the administration's launch of one last, doomed effort to find the 'real' roots of 'tribal community' in 1973. The problem was that 'incorrect levels' of the 'tribal structure' had been used: 'sub-communities' had now urgently to be identified – at the level of the village – and only once this had been done could development and 'any effective planning' take place.[95]

The panoply of security legislation and punitive powers granted to DCs in this period belied any effort to infuse 'tribal structures' with authority. Rhodesia was entering the period of armed struggle, and administration became more militarised than ever before. After 1972, administrators assumed paramilitary powers under the much amended Law and Order (Maintenance) Act and Emergency Powers Act.[96] PCs could impose collective fines, and DCs could marshal forced labour for security reasons, control the movement of food and stock, administer corporal punishment, control entry to and exit from TTLs, and prohibit any meeting whatsoever. DCs' African District Assistants received military training; the paramilitary Guard Force was established in 1976 and the Security Force Auxiliaries in 1978. From 1973, people largely in the north and east but extending into western and central areas, were forced into militarily regulated 'protected villages'.[97]

Community development in its early days, just as in its ultra-traditionalist Rhodesian Front version, had failed: neither councils nor community boards nor chiefs nor village heads could deliver control over land and people. The effort to establish customary authority marked only a theoretical withdrawal of what remained an interventionist and centralised state, weakly rooted in African society.

Conclusion

This period in Native Affairs' thinking about authority and the land marked a key moment in the displacement of one discourse and practice with another. The most important impetus behind the shift was the political crisis provoked by the NLHA. In the search for a solution, vague views about custom and 'tribal' structure held by administrators were accorded a new validity by the work of commissions and international experts. The human sciences displaced those of economics and agriculture. The way in which this transition occurred had important consequences. Despite its widely noted flaws, technical development was not itself blamed for the demise of the NLHA. Rather, the newly scientific analysis of African society provided a neatly self-contained explanation for the NLHA's failure and a solution to the quandary. The NLHA's high modernism was not discredited – Africans, African society and African attachments to the land were simply too mired in irrationality and superstition for it to work. In the heyday of Rhodesian Front racism, the assumptions about the cultural 'otherness' of Africans established by community development advisers and expert commissions alike inspired an elaborate attempt to find the customary key to African authority on which the state might be built. The consequences for the land, and for rural authority, are explored in the following chapter.

Notes

1 See Kriger, 1992, 110-15; Weitzer, 1984; Martin and Johnson, 1981, 60-8.
2 See 6.1.9F/84256, C. J. Bisset, Acting Under Secretary, Native Agriculture and Lands, 'Working Party on the Immediate Future of the Land Husbandry Act', Annexure E to Special NAAB Meeting, Salisbury, 20-22 March 1961; Minutes of Special NAAB Meeting, Salisbury, 20-22 March 1961. Emphases in original.
3 Bhebe, 1989b, 70-84, 98-108.
4 6.1.9F/84256, Special NAAB Meeting, Salisbury, 20-22 March 1961, C. J. Bisset, Acting Under Secretary, Native Agriculture and Lands, 'Working Party on the Immediate Future of the Land Husbandry Act', Annexure E ; 'The Native Land Husbandry Act and Present Problems of Political Agitation', Annexure B.
5 See 6.1.9F/84256, Arthur Pendered, Deputy Secretary, Development, 'Departmental Organization for African Agricultural Development and Implementation of the Native Land Husbandry Policy', Salisbury, 25 January 1961, Annexure A to Special NAAB Meeting, Salisbury, 20-22 March 1961. For a clear statement of the administrative perspective, see 27.6.6F/100842, PNC Campbell, Bulawayo, to Secretary for Internal Affairs S. E. Morris, 7 September 1960.
6 The Mangwende Commission reported on the breakdown of local government in Mangwende Reserve. The Robinson Commission reported on the administrative and judicial functions of the Departments of Native Affairs and District Courts. The Paterson Commission reported on the public services and the Phillips Commission reported on economic development and African agriculture.
7 Government of Southern Rhodesia, 1960; Passmore, 1972, 71-4.
8 It should be noted, however, that American influences on Rhodesian policy were long standing. See Beinart, 1984.
9 Passmore, 1972, 74. See Holleman, 1969, 331, fn 1, on Green's extensive influence.
10 See 27.6.6F/100842, R. L. C. Cunliffe, Annual Report, Native Land Husbandry Act, May 1963; 6.1.9F/84256, Special NAAB Meeting, Salisbury, 20-22 March 1961; 6.7.5F/84279, Roger Howman, Deputy Secretary, Internal Affairs, 'The Application of the Philosophy of Community Development in Southern Rhodesia', 1963; and Passmore, 1972, 48-50.
11 Government of Southern Rhodesia, 1962c, 26-7.
12 See 6.1.9F/84256, C. J. K. Latham, District Officer/Delineation Officer, 'Community Development: Methods and Techniques', July 1963; 'Delimitations of Communities', Senga Community Development Centre, Gwelo, 1963; 28.10.8F/98431, J. W. Green, 'Community Development in Southern Rhodesia', Paper delivered to the Southern Rhodesia Information Service, March 1963; 6.1.9F/84256, James W. Green, 'Prerequisites to African Development – The Three R's', 1 June 1961.
13 S2820/X150, James W. Green, 'What is Community Development?', Opening Address at the Conference on Community Development, University College of Rhodesia and Nyasaland, Salisbury, 31 August 1962; Also see, James W. Green, 'Community Development in Southern Rhodesia', Gwelo, 1963.
14 *Ibid*. On the travails of Kenyan community development, see Berman, 1990, Chapter 7; Lewis, 2000, Chapter 6.
15 ORAL/HO 3, Henry Roger Howman, interviewed by M. C. Steele, 10, 26 August 1971; S2809/2450, R. Howman, 'Report on Visit to Kenya, Uganda, Tanganyika and Nyasaland', December 1951.
16 Four Working Parties were established under the Robinson Commission. Working Parties A, B, and C made recommendations regarding non-racial administration, a new department of African agriculture, and

'tribal' courts. All were influential in shaping policy change.

17 6.1.9F/84256, Minutes of the Meeting of the NAAB, Salisbury, 27-28 June 1961.

18 14.8.8F/69691, Working Party D, Arising from the Robinson Commission Report, 'The Tribal Authority and the Land', Paper No. 16, Salisbury, 2 September 1961.

19 14.8.8F/69691, Working Party D, 'Revision of the Native Land Husbandry Act', Paper No. 23, 24 December 1961.

20 The legislation proposed by the Working Party was accepted by Cabinet in mid-1962, but was found to be *ultra vires* the 1961 constitution. Five years and many drafts later, the legislation was finally passed.

21 14.8.8F/69691, Working Party D, 'Revision of the Native Land Husbandry Act', Paper No. 23, 24 December 1961.

22 See Government of Southern Rhodesia, 1960, paras 346-50, 232-54. Within reserves, the Quinton Report envisioned a gradual move to freehold tenure and desegregation through the consolidation of NLHA allocations. Outside the reserves, the Report recommended the desegregation of other categories of land by opening them up to purchase by all races on a freehold basis.

23 14.8.8F/69691, Working Party D, 'Revision of the Native Land Husbandry Act', Paper No. 23, 24 December 1961.

24 14.8.8F/69691, Working Party D, 'The Tribal Authority and the Land', Paper No. 16, Salisbury, 2 September 1961.

25 Government of Southern Rhodesia, 1962b, 148-52 (the Phillips Commission). Emphasis in original.

26 See Cheater, 1990, 188-206.

27 14.8.8F/69691, Working Party D, 'The Tribal Authority and the Land', Paper No. 16, Salisbury, 2 September 1961.

28 *Ibid.*

29 See Chapter 2. The NAAB had very recently expressed strong doubts about chiefs. See 44.11.8F/90496, Memorandum for Discussion on the Future of Chiefs: Native Affairs Advisory Board, 9 March 1961.

30 14.8.8F/69691, Working Party D, 'Revision of the Native Land Husbandry Act', Paper No. 23, 24 December 1961.

31 Howman, 1966, quoted in Ranger, 2001, 40.

32 14.8.8F/69691, Working Party D, 'Revision of the Native Land Husbandry Act', Paper No. 23, 24 December 1961.

33 *Ibid.*

34 The Working Party defined the Large Stock Equivalent as including all bovines, horses, donkeys and mules over 12 months of age. 5.2.8R/82725, Working Party D, Third Report, District Surveys of Land, Population and Stock, Introductory Chapter, 26 September 1962. According to Jordan, 1964, 69, fn 1, the Annual Cropping Acreage concept was first proposed by Conservation Planning Officer P. A. Colville in 1961.

35 Working Party D calculated on the basis of 'U' factors – land taken up by conservation works, roads and rocks – and 'F' factors – the minimal rotation necessary for the maintenance of soil fertility. The basis of the 'F' factor is unclear. No farming system is specified, nor is the use of fertilizers taken into account. Annual Cropping Acreages calculated by Jordan, 1964, 69-70, varied widely depending on the system used to maintain fertility.

36 5.2.8R/82725, Working Party D, District Survey, Makoni, October 1962.

37 5.2.8R/82725, Working Party D, Third Report, District Surveys of Land, Population and Stock, Introductory Chapter, September 1962, and, e.g., Working Party D, District Survey, Insiza (Filabusi), 11 July 1963.

38 14.8.8F/69691, Working Party D, 'Revision of the Native Land Husbandry Act', Paper No. 23, 24 December 1961; 25.10.6R/100839, Deputy Secretary, Development, W. H. H. Nicolle to Provincial Commissioner, Matabeleland North, 19 December 1961; 6.1.9F/84256, Draft Report of Working Party B, Establishment of Department of Agriculture, Working Paper on 'Land Husbandry Planning and Implementation', 14 September 1961.

39 Roger Howman admitted that he had underestimated the effects of an association with South African policy. See Passmore, n.d., xxi.

40 Munro, 1998, Chapter 4.

41 On South African 'community development', see Eiselen, 1959, cited in Passmore, n.d., xxi, and see p. xx. On the shift from an emphasis on racial to cultural difference in the apartheid era, see Dubow, 1989.

42 27.6.6F/100843, W. H. H. Nicolle, Deputy Director, Development, to Secretary for Internal Affairs, 17 February 1964.

43 The TTL Board was told in no uncertain terms that land transfers to TTLs were to be avoided at all cost. See 28.10.8F/98431, Tribal Trust Land Board, Third Meeting, Salisbury, 10 April 1963. The Unreserved

Area remained open to purchase by any race until 1969, but in practice little land was sold to Africans.

44 On the Gokwe frontier, see Nyambara, 2001b, 771-92; Worby, 1998, 561-78.

45 For example, see 25.10.6R/100839, File LAN/13, IA to MBO, W. H. H. Nicolle, Deputy Secretary, Development, to Mr Morris, 3 February 1964; W. H. H. Nicolle, Deputy Secretary, Development, to PC, Matabeleland South, 29 July 1963.

46 See Weinrich, 1975, 37-40, 229.

47 See Ministry of Internal Affairs, Circular No. 172, 'Tribal Land Authorities', Salisbury, 15 December 1966, signed by H. R. G. Howman in his capacity as Acting Secretary of Internal Affairs, quoted in Passmore, 1972, 160.

48 S2820/X150, Community Development Meeting at the Department of Internal Affairs, 9 September 1963.

49 6.7.5F/84279, Roger Howman, Deputy Secretary, Internal Affairs, 'The Application of the Philosophy of Community Development in Southern Rhodesia', n. d. [1963]. Howman cited the work of British psychiatrist J. C. Carothers on Mau Mau.

50 S2820/X150, Community Development Meeting at the Department of Internal Affairs, 9 September 1963.

51 S2820/X150, Minutes of a Meeting held in the Board Room, 31 August 1963.

52 S2820/X150, S. E. Morris, SIA to all PCs and DCs, 'Community Development Agents', Circular No. 101, 21 May 1963.

53 6.1.9F/84256, 'Community Development: Questions and Answers Arising from the C.D. Selection Courses at Senka Training Centre', Gwelo, 1963.

54 Holleman, 1969, 330-2.

55 6.7.5F/84279, Internal Affairs Seminar, 'Solutions to Problems of Implementation of Government Policy on Community Development and Local Government', n.d. [1963].

56 6.1.9F/84256, 'Community Development: Questions and Answers Arising from the C.D. Selection Courses at Senka Training Centre', Gwelo, 1963.

57 See 6.7.5F/84279, Group Reports and Questions on Speech by Dr Green: Community Development, March 1963.

58 *Rhodesia Herald*, 5 September 1963.

59 *African Daily News*, 24 August 1963, 28 August 1963; *Sunday Mail*, 1 September 1963; *Rhodesia Herald*, 22 August 1963.

60 See responses in 18.8.10R/88379, File C.D., Volume I, 1963. Ten missionary societies responded in writing to the seminar, all of them expressing their opposition to community development.

61 *African Daily News*, 30 August 1963. And see 18.8.10R/88379, Southern Rhodesia Teachers' Association to Secretary for African Education, 17 October 1963.

62 See S2820/X150, Minutes of a Meeting held in the Board Room, 31 August 1963, signed by A. M. Mansell, Assistant Secretary, Community Development; Community Development Meeting at the Department of Internal Affairs, 9 September 1963.

63 S2820/X150, Community Development Meeting at the Department of Internal Affairs, 9 September 1963. And see S2820/X150, Minutes of a Meeting held in the Board Room, signed by A. M. Mansell, Assistant Secretary, Community Development, 31 August 1963.

64 *Ibid.*

65 Quoted in Barber, 1967, 226.

66 6.7.5F/84279, District Reports on Community Development Implementation, 1963.

67 See Weinrich, 1975, 74.

68 See Bratton, 1978, 31.

69 S2820/X150, Foreword by Hon. J. H. Howman, MP, Minister of IA and LG, *C.D. and L.G. Bulletin*, No. 1, 25 November 1963.

70 6.1.9F/84256, W. H. Nicolle, Under Secretary, Native Economics and Marketing, to Secretary, Public Services Board (Working Party 'B', Robinson Commission), 6 September 1961.

71 28.10.8F/98431, W. H. Nicolle, 'Community Development: Report on Seminar with Dr T. R. Batten on Community Development and Local Government', 1965; Munro, 1998, 170.

72 Bratton, 1978, 29.

73 Holleman, 1969, 345-7.

74 Quoted in Munro, 1998, 167.

75 'Tribal Psychology and Tribal Structure', *NADA*, 1966, quoted in Ranger, 2001, 40-41. James Green had earlier reified administrators' views regarding the differences between 'Shona' and 'Ndebele' chieftaincy. See 28.10.8F/98431, J. W. Green, 'Community Development in Southern Rhodesia', 1963.

76 28.10.8F/98431, R. Cunliffe, Assistant Secretary, 'Provision of Peggers for Chiefs', Annexure to Paper 16/64, TTL Board, 18 December 1964.

77 28.10.8F/98431, Tribal Trust Land Board, Eighth Meeting, Salisbury, 13-14 January 1964.

78 For example, see 27.6.6F/100842, DC J. L. Fowle, Buhera, to PC, Manicaland, 11 February 1964.
79 27.6.6F/100842, PC R. P. Holl, Victoria, to Secretary for Internal Affairs, 19 September 1963; Notes on Minutes of DCs' Conference, Victoria Province, 19-20 August 1963.
80 27.6.6F/100842, Report of the DC Ndanga, Zaka, for the Quarter ended the 30th September 1963.
81 27.6.6F/100842, PC N. L. Dacomb, Matabeleland South to Under Secretary, Administration, 8 January 1964; SIA Circular Minute No. 146/63, 25 November 1963; R. L. C. Cunliffe to PC, Matabeleland North, 21 January 1965.
82 For example, see 27.6.6F/100842, Clive Hayes, Senior Inspector to Chief Inspector, Lands and Natural Resources, 7 August 1963.
83 28.10.8F/98431, Tribal Trust Land Board, Eighth Meeting, verbatim record, 17 August 1964.
84 See McGregor, 1991, 305; Weinrich, 1975, 35-6.
85 23.7.5R/93142, Provincial Assembly of Chiefs and Headmen at Seke: Mashonaland North and South, 23-4 August 1965.
86 28.10.8F/98431, R. Cunliffe, Assistant Secretary, 'Provision of Peggers for Chiefs', Annexure to Paper 16/64, TTL Board, 18 December 1964; Passmore, 1972, 160, 219-20. Chiefs' peggers were not effectively deployed until the late 1960s. 28.10.8F/98431, Tribal Trust Land Board, Estimate of Expenditure for 1965 and the Present Financial Position of the Board's Fund, Paper No. 16/1964, TTLB, Fourteenth Meeting, Agenda Item B, Arthur Pendered, Salisbury, 18 December 1965; Memorandum, Tribal Trust Land, Estimates of Revenue and Expenditure 1966: Reports and Accounts to 31st December 1965, Annexure A to paper 18 August 1966; Tribal Trust Land Board, Eighteenth Meeting, 18 January 1966.
87 Howman, 1967, 15, quoted in Weinrich, 1975, 35.
88 See Holleman, 1969, 334-5; Weinrich, 1975, 35-7.
89 Holleman, 1969, 357-66.
90 *Rhodesia Herald*, 8 July 1971, quoted in Weinrich, 1975, 43.
91 See Bratton, 1978, 22-33; Weinrich, 1971, chapters 9 and 10.
92 See Munro, 1998, 176.
93 Passmore, n.d., xxiv.
94 Howman, 1966, quoted in Ranger, 2001, 40; Munro, 1998, 189.
95 Alexander, McGregor and Ranger, 2000, 128.
96 Bratton, 1978, 37, notes that the Emergency Powers Act had been amended 32 times and the Law and Order (Maintenance) Act 12 times since 1965.
97 See Weinrich, 1977, 207-9; Bratton, 1978, 34-45.

4

Chiefs, Nationalism & the Land
Knowing the Colonial State

In the 1960s, chiefs stood at the centre of the Rhodesian state's struggle to remake its authority over land and people. The nature of the powers granted to chiefs would, however, do much to undermine the project of reconstituting rural rule. Chiefs were not willing converts to the merits of state-backed custom, and nor could the 'perpetual contest' over authority in the rural areas be contained within the discursive realm of custom. Chiefs and other rural leaders drew on alternative versions of history, on the now discarded technical discourses of officials, and on the flexible claims of nationalism to challenge and engage with the state, reshaping and undermining it in the process. The patterns of contestation that marked this period produced an unstable and contradictory set of claims to land and authority that would shape rural politics well after the end of settler rule.

Reassessing the 'Return' of Powers to Chiefs

In the era of Rhodesian Front rule, chiefs have been depicted as at best anachronistic, and at worst as willing tools of oppression. Contemporary anthropological literature cast chiefs as caught in an awkward half-way house between the demands of 'patriarchy' and 'bureaucracy', the traditional and the modern.[1] More recent literature has documented the diverse roles played by chiefs but is nonetheless almost unanimous in their dismissal. Michael Bratton confidently held that 'chiefs have lost claim to represent peasants because of their collective decision to join forces with the settlers against Zimbabwean nationalism'.[2] Ngwabi Bhebe argued that their co-optation in Matabeleland was 'the tragedy of Ndebele politics'.[3] Terence Ranger considered it 'pretty obvious' that chiefs were 'anachronistic and discredited'.[4] 'By accepting their lowly position in the government hierarchy', David Lan argued, 'chiefs had acquired the authority to receive a monthly salary, to collect taxes, to wear a flamboyant uniform and little else'.[5] In 'Shona' areas, Lan and Ranger argued, chiefs were rendered irrelevant by spirit mediums' transfer of the ancestors' legitimating power to guerrillas and nationalist committees.[6]

While some chiefs clearly did act as prominent proponents of minority rule, and many exploited their positions for personal gain,[7] the charge that they became discredited and irrelevant grants far too much success to Rhodesian officials' traditionalist project. The Rhodesian state did not 'win' the struggle for chiefs' allegiance, and it transformed chieftaincy into neither an effective instrument of control nor a legitimating stamp for settler rule. The individuals who occupied chiefly office brought with them diverse political views. Local histories of opposition and struggles for authority, land, and development resources shaped their attitudes to the state. Some chiefs were nationalists before occupying office; others turned against government, if not to nationalism, as a result of the disregard for their demands, notably for land; still others reluctantly obeyed nationalist dictums for fear of retribution. Nationalists preferred recruiting chiefs to attacking them: they were not opposed to chieftaincy *per se*, or to customary ideology, which formed an increasingly important component of cultural nationalism, but to its use in the service of government.[8] As DCs everywhere worried, chiefs' loyalty was 'tenuous and vacillating' in the face of the nationalist appeals of Zanu and Zapu.[9]

Not only were chiefs' political views diverse and subject to suasion, but chiefly office remained important to the expression of rural demands and the obstruction of state intervention. Chieftaincy held a strategic position precisely because Rhodesian policy left it as one of the few means of access to officials, and one of officials' key means of intervention. It was vigorously used to make demands, voice criticism and undermine state authority, at times on the basis of an interpretation of custom at variance with that of officials, at times on overtly nationalist grounds, and at times through invoking religious or scientific argument. This was the case until the guerrilla war intensified in the late 1970s, making any form of contact with the state dangerous and increasingly turning divisions within rural society into sites of violent conflict.[10] Chiefs were vulnerable due both to their contact with officials and to their privileged position within rural society. But the many attacks on chiefs during the war is evidence less of a rejection of chieftaincy than a repudiation of association with the state: even where individual chiefs were killed, powerful groups within rural society retained an interest in the institution itself.[11]

In order to set developments in Chimanimani and Insiza in the context of Rhodesia as a whole, the remainder of this section is devoted to an analysis of the 'return' of powers over land to chiefs in the 1960s. Though few authors consider this process in any detail, the politics of land within and outside the Tribal Trust Lands (TTLs) was central to the agendas of nationalists and chiefs, and powerfully shaped the constitution of rural authority.

LAND AND CHIEFS

As we have seen, in the early 1960s officials sought to re-establish order through the repression of nationalist activists, the elevation of chiefs as political representatives in their place, and the 'return' of powers over land to chiefs so that they might placate those rendered 'legally landless'. Far from simply 'reconstitut[ing] chiefs in their traditional roles',[12] these new powers often clashed with chiefs' interpretation of their office. They did not compliantly accept the new dispensation, or the customary ideology that went with it. Instead, they tried to exploit the government's need for allies by setting conditions for their exercise of powers, refusing some altogether, and seeking to manipulate the authority conferred on custom.

Chiefs at first sought a link to land redistribution. While they condemned the NLHA, saying it had 'shorn' them of 'their greatest claim to the loyalty of their followers', chiefs on the National Council 'all adamantly refused' to consider making allocations within the TTLs: 'They could not undertake to put this to their people or accept the responsibility to implement it.... They unanimously stated that additional land for the tribal areas was the only solution'.[13] Chiefs expected concessions, and throughout the country they used their many high-level meetings with officials to press their case.[14] They argued in terms of the historical claims of their chieftaincies and the requisites of customary land allocation, they attacked European land alienation as the source of their troubles and of support for nationalists, and they deplored the inadequacy of opening the Unreserved Area (unalienated crown land) for individual purchase, an option at any rate soon to be withdrawn. Chiefs' demands were firmly founded in the knowledge that TTLs were not blank slates on which one had simply to find 'room to manouevre', as in Working Party D's formulation, but personal and political landscapes scarred by bitter struggles to retain the integrity of family and community and access to adequate land in the face of decades of evictions and state intervention. The offer of land allocating authority in the absence of land redistribution gave chiefs neither credibility as 'Tribal Land Authorities' nor an opportunity to bolster their positions through patronage, except at the high price of offending existing landholders.

Chiefs feared returning from their consultations with officials empty handed. The openly nationalist president of the National Chiefs' Council, Chief Shumba, angrily warned, 'I have told my people we are going to hear the results of our meeting with the Prime Minister. We are anxious to hear that more land is being given to us.... People will kill us if we don't tell them anything on our return.'[15] Shumba listed the European farms from which his people had been evicted, calling for the restoration of his 'tribal land'. Largely in Matabeleland, chiefs tried to buy land, a reflection of wealth accumulated in cattle and of the need for more grazing land to support such accumulation. In Lupane, Chief Mabikwa, a member of the National Chiefs' Council, 'stated that he wanted and was able to purchase Pioneer Block' for a 'tribal grazing area'. Pioneer Block was 'the ancestral home of his family and of his people'.[16] Other requests to purchase land 'as a tribe' were made in Plumtree, Umzingwane, Insiza, and Zvishavane while in northern Matabeleland chiefs asked to lease land from 'European big ranch owners'.[17]

Despite Working Party D's fears of 'losing' chiefs in the absence of meeting at least some of their demands for land, their requests were almost wholly refused.[18] Most concessions were made between 1960 and 1962, usually simply involving redesignations of heavily settled areas as Tribal Trust Land; almost no concessions were made as rewards to 'loyal' chiefs.[19] At Chiefs' Assembly meetings in 1964, W. H. H. Nicolle merely 'explained the need for better farming practices' and 'left [chiefs] in no doubt the Government would not add any further land to the Tribal Areas'. In response, chiefs astutely charged 'that Government was throwing the land problem back to the Chiefs because they were finding it too difficult'.[20] Much to the frustration of officials, they 'repeatedly harped back to the "good old days" ... when there was plenty of land, when a person could have as much land as he wanted and everybody could have land and stock.... Their view was that if the Europeans gave them back their land there would be no problem.'[21]

Chiefs were well aware that allocation within the crowded TTLs would prejudice the interests of existing farmers, themselves included. In describing the allocation of land to 'outsiders' – whether 'landless unemployed' or evictees – they regularly used the nationalist term, 'sell out'.[22] Notably in Matabeleland, chiefs focused on protecting grazing areas. One chief who 'complained of having "landless" persons, subsequently opposed allocation when suitable land was demarcated, because it affected his private grazing area.'[23] The legacy of technical development further complicated matters. Many chiefs refused to make allocations because 'they believe, after years of agricultural advice on the subject, that it would lead inevitably to destocking'.[24] The NLHA had also politicised specific pieces of the landscape. In much troubled Nkayi, attempts to re-allocate land from which people had been evicted caused 'a period of unrest and no more applications [for land] came forward'.[25] Summing up a common range of reservations, chiefs in Lomagundi argued that 'where the Native Land Husbandry Act allocations had been made and where there was little room to manouevre and where people had been moved to places they didn't like it would be impossible for the Chiefs and the Government should retain control'.[26] Many chiefs simply stated that they did not want to 'deal with the complaints of the landless' – they 'would prefer if these complaints went to the Native Commissioner'.[27]

Chiefs faced other obstacles too, in the shape of claims to authority over the land made by figures subordinate to the chief. Only in Matabeleland did chiefs argue they could control allocation through the 'tribal structure' without official backing.[28] Elsewhere, chiefs argued that, 'if a kraalhead had vacant plots in his area he would not allocate them to people who did not belong to his kraal, because he was reserving them for his children and the children of the people of his kraal'.[29] In Charter, village heads refused to accept chiefs' allocations, instead listing 'their own people who might come forward for land – people away at work and children'.[30] Village heads invoked customary rights, maintaining 'that traditionally the Samusha [village head] had complete control over land in his Musha'.[31]

Given this range of difficulties, many chiefs were reluctant to step into the vacuum left by the retreat of the technocratic state. Changes in land use in the early 1960s were nonetheless dramatic, a sign of the pressure of pent-up demand. Under the rubric of chiefs' allocations, almost 20,000 people were given roughly 90,000 acres in the 1961/62 season, and a further 16,000 people were allocated 84,000 acres in the following season.[32] The PC, Victoria, estimated that 100,000 acres had been opened in that province by mid-1964.[33] Many of these allocations were made by village or household heads and went to existing landholders and landholders' children or relatives who had been away at work when the NLHA was implemented.[34] Other changes focused on settling scores where NLHA allocations had infringed on land claimed by others.[35] Everywhere, people expanded old fields and opened new ones near their homes. Stream-bank and wetland cultivation proliferated.[36]

These tendencies were fed by, and justified through, nationalist calls for 'freedom farming', that is rejecting state authority through abrogating restrictions on land use.

Rumours spread that the NLHA 'is finished and everyone can do as he likes'.[37] Nationalism became a powerful means of claiming authority over the land, sometimes against and sometimes alongside technocratic prescriptions and chiefs' customary claims. Chiefs in Midlands and Manicaland made an almost identical complaint in 1964: 'there was common talk in the Tribal Areas now on the lines of "nyika yaka zarurwa – nyika ngeyedu" – in other words, in regard to land there is freedom and the land is theirs. As a result there is a tendency to ignore the tribal authority and plough anywhere, anyhow.'[38] In areas where the NLHA had been implemented, most of the new cultivation was in addition to NLHA allocations which were in fact rarely abandoned. NLHA 'lines' – the linear 'villages' demarcated under the Act – shaped settlement patterns in many areas long after independence. Large-scale repudiations of Land Husbandry allocations were concentrated where they had separated communities, were particularly infertile or far from homes or water, or where nationalist activity was pronounced, factors that often went hand in hand.[39] Retaining NLHA rights provided security to labour migrants away at work and people engaged in 'illegal' cultivation.[40] That NLHA rights should be held as 'social security' by absent workers, as one DC put it, is one of the great ironies of the NLHA's legacy, given that its original intention was to 'pull workers' tentacles out of the soil'.[41]

The NLHA also played a role where land rights were threatened by allocation to outsiders, in some cases by chiefs who sought to exploit their new powers for personal or political gain. The DC, Zaka, reported that he was 'approached by three people from Nyakunowa's area complaining that their grazing had been allocated to complete strangers ... who were not in any way welcome but who had been given the land by the Chief'.[42] Chief Nyakunowa's profligate allocation led to violent conflict and an appeal to the state's technical planners: 'In some areas people allocated land by the Chiefs are being chased away and in many cases assaulted by the existing land/grazing right holders. Kraal-heads in Chief Nyakunowa's area have asked for the agricultural staff to be sent in to do Land Husbandry over again.'[43] The NLHA had, however, had its day: the investment in chiefs' authority, however capricious, now superceded such appeals.

In other cases, chiefs used their new powers in support of nationalist parties. Terence Ranger shows how Chief Makoni allied with nationalists and used his position to give land to those unhappy with their NLHA allocations, labour migrants, and young couples against the wishes of the DC and other chiefs and headmen.[44] Ranger attributes Makoni's actions to self-interest, and his allocations were certainly in part directed at undermining the authority of other chiefs, but they also answered to the nationalist call for 'freedom farming' in an area particularly resentful of previous state intervention. The fees Makoni and his son collected for allocating land were apparently deposited directly in the 'African Nationalists' coffers'.[45]

Conflict among people making different claims to the land was most virulent where evictions forced people into TTLs. Notably in Midlands and Victoria Provinces, customary leaders were inundated with requests for land from evictees.[46] In some cases, the threat of evictees caused pre-emptive allocation. Consequent on his telling chiefs in Victoria TTL that people were to be evicted into the area from Nuanetsi Ranch, home to one of the largest 'squatter' populations in the country, the

DC wrote, 'During the past few weeks I have had reports that Africans in Victoria Reserve have suddenly gone "wild" and are opening up new lands all over the place.... It appears that Chiefs and Headmen are allocating land wholesale in the grazing to the landless. Nuanetsi Ranch squatters have not yet come into the picture.'[47] In other areas, large-scale movements posed an insuperable problem of control. Zhombe crown land and Silobela Purchase Area in Midlands Province offer a vivid example. Since 1949, residents had been repeatedly warned of pending evictions.[48] No evictions had taken place by 1960, and rumours, which proved accurate, spread of the imminent conversion of both areas to Tribal Trust Land. To the horror of officials, massive influxes of evictees, farm workers, and people from other TTLs followed. Zhombe and Silobela were described as Zapu strongholds in 1962. Newcomers who opened land 'adopted the attitude that they had fought for and obtained the area and it was no concern of the Chief as to who settled in the area'.[49] Chiefs accused headmen, headmen accused village heads, and newcomers exploited the several rungs of authority. Competition for land fed into and was fed by nationalist claims, providing a divisive backdrop for intimidation and accusations of 'selling out'.[50]

The contention that chiefs compliantly aided the Rhodesian state in securing authority over the land, and that they were thus reduced to irrelevant and discredited leaders, is far off the mark. Chiefs were vigorous proponents of land redistribution and saw land allocation powers as a mixed blessing, given the interrelated factors of land scarcity, vested interests and animosities created by the NLHA, disruptions caused by evictions, nationalist mobilisation, and the authority claimed by village and household heads. The failure to address demands for redistribution strained chiefs' allegiance and prevented the pre-emption of nationalists' most powerful claim: that the land belonged to the people, and that they should farm it as they liked. Land claims drew on a bewildering range of grounds – nationalist, technical, historical, and customary – and they were made by an equally bewildering diversity of authorities, from the different rungs of the 'tribal' hierarchy, to nationalists, evictees, kin, and officials. By granting chiefs authority over land and calling it 'customary', officials could not hope to contain these forces.

Insiza and Chimanimani: Chiefs, Councils and Nationalists

In the following accounts of Insiza and Chimanimani districts, I broaden the focus from land allocation to the regulation of agricultural production, administration and political representation, all fields in which chiefs became increasingly important. Chiefs opposed community development from the beginning not, as many have argued, due to the threat posed to their customary authority by the inclusion of educated Africans on councils and community boards,[51] but rather due to its failure to address longstanding demands for land and authority. As the other 'legs' of community development fell away in the late 1960s, chiefs' elevation as virtually the sole representatives of African opinion left the state with a fatally flawed foundation.

THE END OF COOPERATION IN INSIZA

In Insiza as in other areas the failure to add land to TTLs meant chiefs' allocations impinged on existing landholders. The DC reported that chiefs and headmen were having 'a difficult time': they were 'continually under pressure from the landless and from political parties', in this case Zapu, as well as from NLHA right holders who 'want their existing interests protected'.[52] Chiefs responded in different ways. In 1961, Chief Maduna allocated over 924 three-acre fields; in 1962 he compiled a list of 1,497 people who needed land, a figure that included the children of those with rights and people away at work. In contrast, Chiefs Ndube and Sibasa responded conservatively.[53] In 1964, the DC reported that Maduna was 'giving out land to almost anyone who applies to him', sometimes in contravention of village heads' wishes, while Ndube and Sibasa held firm.[54]

Under the influence of Chief Maduna and his advisers, the Godhlwayo Council actively entered debates over land. Councillors proposed buying adjacent farms, repeatedly complained of inaccuracies in NLHA allocations, and requested authority for the widespread practice of opening and extending home gardens.[55] They complained bitterly that insufficient land had been made available for chiefs' allocations, and demanded land for widows and children.[56] The questions of grazing rights, cattle prices and dip fees also caused much anger. Councillors drastically reduced dip fees by taking over the service, a measure which forced them to return the by then bankrupt service to state control a year later.[57] They expressed great concern for people who had received land allocations but not grazing rights, and so 'had no oxen to plough'.[58] In 1963, the Secretary for Internal Affairs intervened: in line with the community development policy of separating 'development' and 'land' issues, he ordered that discussions of land allocations, grazing rights, the location of stands, home gardens – in short, the issues that dominated council debate – be restricted to Chiefs' Meetings. An unpopular council was thus rendered largely irrelevant.[59]

Alongside the running debates over land and stock, the council faced a crisis over rate collections.[60] In 1964, conflict over rates boiled over, fed by anger over the lack of drought relief. Chiefs withdrew their support for the council, while councillors reported that people 'hate the Council' and did not understand its purpose since 'in times of starvation no help was given'. The meeting became 'unruly' and had to be closed.[61] At this distinctly unpromising point, the community development policy was introduced in Insiza. It rapidly ran into trouble. The delineation officer blamed Chief Maduna's 'great sway' for the 'repulsive attitude of the people toward council'. Headman Velapi and his village heads argued that community development was another form of council, an institution 'which has eaten our money and given us no return'. In Chief Sibasa's area, 'word has circulated that community development is government's method of harnessing them into another council. This comes at a time when the inhabitants are trying to shed the burden of council.' Throughout the district, people refused to have anything to do with community development.[62]

Hostility to the council presented a formidable challenge. A second obstacle emerged when the delineation team sought to ascertain people's 'felt needs'. Headman Velapi 'invok[ed] the idiom "Never chase two impala at the same time". Presumably the first impala is land and increased stock holdings!' In Chief Sibasa's area, elders held that, 'primarily people do not feel needs other than for more land and stock rights, this, they feel, is the ultimate in life.' Another strongly articulated 'felt need' outside community development's remit was for secondary schools.[63] The delineation team concluded on a dour note: 'The impression has been gained throughout the Filabusi district that the desire for land has so clouded their outlook that they see no other need for themselves. Due to the land factor and the breakdown of the council little progress in community development is envisaged in the near future.' The only hope lay in reducing government expenditure on services and thus inducing 'a change of heart'.[64]

The failure to constitute community development institutions forced a greater reliance on 'Tribal Authorities'. In Matabeleland, the elaborate debates about custom that characterised other regions were rare. Officials here saw a properly customary leader as little more than one who was able and willing to enforce policy.[65] Finding such leaders was nonetheless far from easy. Chiefs had scant incentive to aid officials, not least due to the failure to meet their demands for land. In Insiza, the official answer to land pressure was the Silalabuhwa Irrigation Scheme, established under the Primary Development policy in 1965. Schemes introduced in the 1960s were administered directly by the MIA: plot-holders were in effect employees of the officials who ran the schemes.[66] Far from placating chiefs or their followers, Silalabuhwa was resented for removing land from local control and for cutting into grazing areas. The DC had to resort to forcing office workers onto the scheme, while much of the physical work was carried out under drought relief projects. Drought was the main motive for taking up plots. With the arrival of guerrillas in Insiza, the scheme became a favoured target for attack.[67]

While irrigation fell outside the jurisdiction of chiefs and headmen, controls on stock and land use came increasingly under their authority. As in the case of the irrigation scheme, the droughts of the 1960s and 1970s played a key role. During the droughts, 'European farmers were heavily subsidized by government, African peasants were encouraged to sell their stock'.[68] 'Encouraging' sales was considered particularly urgent in Godhlwayo where herds had grown rapidly.[69] Chiefs and headmen, however, rejected sales in favour of lobbying for access to additional grazing land. Their preferred response to drought was, as in the past, to move stock to nearby ranches, Purchase Areas and better favoured TTLs.[70] The DC sought to use the threat of a ban on such movements to force chiefs to adopt that other staple of state intervention – the grazing scheme. A number of schemes were established under the stewardship of chiefs or headmen in the early 1970s, but they regularly came under siege from those whose cattle were excluded.[71] Finally, the deteriorating security situation led to a retreat: NLHA grazing rights were formally abolished in 1975 and chiefs were allowed to allocate dip cards, i.e. the right to depasture cattle, at their discretion. They did so with great vigour, much to the DC's consternation.[72]

The attempt to cast chiefs in a punitive and restrictive role with regard to conservation and controls on land allocation also came to little.[73] Chief Maduna and

Headman Ngomondo argued that conservation controls were not part of their 'tribal custom'. Insiza was unusual in that government employees had constructed contours under a 'special project' as a means of gaining compliance with the NLHA. Chiefs argued not only that conservation should remain the state's responsibility but that officials should construct contours for people in new fields.[74] The DC also struggled with the establishment of Tribal Land Authorities (TLAs). In practice, the active arm of the TLA consisted of 'chiefs' peggers', operating under the supervision of agricultural officers not chiefs. Peggers rarely lasted long. Conflict among chiefs, headmen, village heads, peggers and agricultural officers over boundaries, authorisation for allocations, and enforcement of conservation measures abounded. Lands Inspectors merely added to the confusion: people took their orders to construct contours as authority to cultivate land.[75] By 1972, village heads were routinely refusing to attend TLA meetings, while chiefs and headmen varied between avoiding responsibility and interceding where prosecutions threatened.[76] As with stock, after 1975 concern for security meant the administration retreated from its regulatory functions.

As the guerrilla war intensified, gaining chiefs' participation in the rituals and institutions of state took on a new importance. As the Maduna chieftaincy illustrates, this was a strategy that frequently left the state exposed. Before the expansion of the war, Chief Jim Mafu Maduna had set a poor precedent from the official point of view. Though he was eventually deposed, he retained his post for most of the 1960s due to officials' belief in his great sway, and their lack of alternatives. The delineation team wrote that Maduna exercised a powerful influence: he directly administered matters normally channeled through headmen; his 'community' was 'not based entirely on ties of traditional allegiance around the leader, who, by force of his personality and influence has had the community gather around him'. In 1965, when the DC requested the withdrawal of Maduna's allowance, officials advised caution. Certainly, Maduna was 'drunk and dirty' but, they warned, 'we may be risking a loss of Maduna's good will and we may tempt him into showing us just how much control and influence he has on his own.'[77]

In 1966 and 1967, guerrilla incursions, a flurry of Zapu meetings, and the repeated sabotage of dips and fences, increased the premium put on chiefs' cooperation. They were informed of 'terrorist' activities regularly and warned of their obligation to report 'illegal political meetings'.[78] Maduna, however, remained uncooperative: at ceremonies marking the opening of the Silalabuhwa Dam, he appeared too drunk to stand, and then deliberately snubbed the Minister for Internal Affairs.[79] His refusal to attend district meetings earned him a formal warning. When he did attend, he arrived drunk and shouted repeatedly for his assistants.[80] Maduna caused further outrage by supporting a religious revival. He gave notes to prophets and healers, authorising their activities throughout the district. The BSAP complained: 'Through allowing these various unreliable types to stay at his kraal, and thus giving permission to practice all sorts of odd religions in the area, our crime rate, in regard to witchcraft, is on the increase.'[81]

Maduna's refusal to cooperate in the establishment of community boards and councils, a policy now firmly backed by the threat of withdrawing services, finally led to his fall.[82] There followed a series of criminal cases against him, relating to the use of his car and the possession of *tototo* (illegal grain alcohol), and against his wife, who was charged for asking a CD agent if he was 'ruling with the Europeans'. Maduna declared himself 'too tired, old and sick to be a chief' and said that his son, Vezi, would be 'prepared to take over the reins'.[83] He died shortly thereafter. Vezi Maduna was representative of another generation and illustrated the diverse networks in which chiefs were engaged. An active nationalist, Vezi was literate and a Zionist, though he also supported the propitiation of the Mwali cult. Born in 1938, he studied at Moeng College in Botswana, completing Form III in 1958. Subsequently, he worked as a clerical assistant and received medical training. His active support for the NDP led to his arrest in 1960. After the NDP was banned, he joined Zapu. Though the DC expressed trepidation over his appointment, he was confirmed as acting chief in 1969, in part simply because he was the only claimant to the title.[84]

Vezi Maduna's relations with the administration were tense from the beginning. Shortly after his appointment, he claimed he was too ill to attend a Chiefs' Assembly meeting and refused to have a medical examination, despite his own medical training, on the grounds that he was a Zionist and therefore could not accept treatment. In 1970, the DC ordered chiefs to attend a meeting at which they were to elect national representatives. Vezi replied: 'I should like to extend to you the fact that I have decided to keep out of politics because politics is a dirty game. Voting is part of politics, so I am not going to [the meeting] for voting in the forthcoming general elections'. As the DC commented, 'This man seems to be running with the hare and hunting with the hounds.' Subsequently, Maduna was demoted for sending people to cultivate in Chief Sibasa's area against the DC's orders.[85]

In 1972, the PC delivered a reprimand to Insiza's chiefs and headmen. While maintaining that chiefs were the 'leaders of their people', he threatened to remove those who did not 'perform as they should'. Unimpressed, Maduna refused to support the formation of a council later in the year.[86] Maduna's behaviour delayed his appointment as substantive chief. In 1974, however, the administration changed tack, calling for his rapid appointment so he might be 'welcomed into the club' by the Council of Chiefs, and then be persuaded to aid in the formation of a council.[87] Maduna received high praise at his installation: 'Few Chiefs, if any in Rhodesia, command from their people such respect as he does.'[88] A period of relative calm followed, but no council was formed and Maduna continued to fall ill whenever a Chiefs' Assembly meeting was scheduled. More seriously, guerrilla incursions and illegal meetings multiplied, but went unreported by chiefs.[89]

The year 1976 marked a turning-point for chiefs in Insiza. In that year, the escalation of the war effectively brought to a close the period in which chiefs could mediate with the state. Vezi Maduna became increasingly active in Zapu. The DC reported that 'an unlawful meeting attended by Maduna was held in a public place outside his dwelling and that his role at this is under investigation. His property was recently subjected to an unsuccessful police search for illegal documents.'[90] Maduna was subsequently detained for failing to report 'a known terrorist presence', and was then sent into restriction and deposed.[91] In Maduna's place, the DC urgently requested the promotion of Headman Ngomondo, a highly successful farmer, professional painter and Jehovah's Witness: 'every day's delay strengthens the belief that Maduna is inviolate'.[92] Ngomondo was never effective as chief; soon after his appointment his 'village was burnt down.... He has been unable to carry out any of his functions as Chief and none of his followers have ever sought his audience.' Even his once popular court was undermined by the non–cooperation of his advisers.[93] The DC could do little more than warn chiefs and headmen 'that the terrorists in Rhodesia were communist backed'.[94]

As guerrilla activity increased, customary leaders were placed in an impossible position. In August 1977, Headman Nhlogotshane was killed. In September, Headman Labe was arrested on suspicion of not reporting guerrillas. Chief Ndube was arrested a month later. The DC regularly complained of the lack of security intelligence coming from chiefs and headmen, and informed them that, though it was the guerrillas' goal to cause a breakdown in services, 'the terrorists would not do these things, because the District Commissioner would instead'. Cattle sales, stores, dips, tax collection, bus services and schools operated erratically or not at all. Chiefs and headmen were unable to hold meetings; TLAs did not function; stock theft from European ranches boomed. Despite his dependence on state protection, Ngomondo criticised government soldiers, saying that people ran from them 'because they are beaten up by them at their kraals'. Headman Mapenka added that 'property was also taken by the security forces and the people were very confused'.[95]

Though the escalation of the guerrilla war was ultimately responsible for the breakdown of rural authority in Insiza, chiefs and headmen had confounded the state's customary vision much earlier. Chiefs' attitudes to land use and land redistribution had far more in common with nationalist views than with those of the Rhodesian Front. They used their positions not to enforce policies but to mitigate their effects or obstruct them. The Maduna chiefs refused to serve as political representatives within the Rhodesian regime; Vezi Maduna played an active role in nationalist mobilisation. The fact that many of Insiza's chiefs and headmen were ousted from office, placed in detention or killed in the 1970s indicates not that chieftaincy had been discredited, but a rejection of its role in the government's attempts to root the state in customary authority. The Maduna chiefs in fact carried on a tradition unappreciated in the official canon – that of allying with political movements, as they had from the days of the ICU and Voice.

LAND, CUSTOM AND CHIEFS IN CHIMANIMANI

Chimanimani's chiefs served the state's purposes no better than those of Insiza, but for different reasons. Negotiation between chiefs and the administration was conducted in an elaborate customary idiom, not in the relatively straightforward language of Insiza. Custom became a central tool in competition among elders, as well as in efforts to mediate state intervention. The battles over land use also took a different shape, with irrigation schemes once again playing a key role. Finally, Chimanimani's cross-border links undermined community development's search for bounded 'communities', much as it had made the NLHA's 'economic units' so hard to find, and put Chimanimani at the forefront of Zanu's guerrilla war.

Chimanimani's chiefs shared with their peers the problems associated with the 'return' of land allocation powers. In 1962, they were described as 'very much in favour' of allocations on grounds of equity – they wanted to vary allocations according to family size. Most chiefs made limited allocations in 1961 and 1962.[96] As elsewhere, however, they did not see their allocations as a solution to land shortage. They blamed European land alienation for their problems, maintaining that 'if there had been no buying of land, there would be plenty of land for everybody.' Their main concern was to acquire more land. Chief Chikukwa, who lived on state forestry land, made a 'strong plea' for a TTL. Chief Mutambara demanded additional grazing land, and Chief Muwushu asked to allocate land in the Nyamasundu Purchase Area. Chief Ngorima stated he was 'very glad' that part of the Vimba Purchase Area was redesignated as a TTL, 'as he could comfort people who wanted land'. All of these requests were refused. Working Party D held that expanding irrigation schemes was the only way to absorb the landless. Where chiefs failed, objections to evictions and land pressure, notably as a result of the expansion of the district's forestry industry, came in the form of a spate of arson attacks.[97]

In the TTLs, the most significant changes in land use came under the authority of village and household heads, largely in the form of extensions of arable land and home gardens, stream-bank cultivation, and a refusal to maintain conservation works. Throughout the district, hundreds of gardens were opened, 'often only at the kraalhead level'. These did not necessarily go to people without land. According to the DC, and in keeping with reports from other Manicaland districts, 'many of these new gardens are by persons who already have a registered holding but who are now practising shifting cultivation', reflecting a desire to fallow and expand fields as well as move them closer to homes.[98]

By the time delineation teams toured the district, it had been the site of one of the first guerrilla infiltrations. Chimanimani suddenly seemed politically dangerous. Four men recruited in Zambia by Zanu arrived in Chimanimani in 1964 intending to launch a series of attacks in protest against Ian Smith's impending declaration of independence. They launched a petrol bomb attack on the by then notorious police camp at Nyanyadzi and assassinated a Rhodesian Front branch chairman before most of them were caught and sentenced to death. Their activities led to widespread arrests, close surveillance, and a massively expanded military presence in the district. The brutal suppression of nationalist activists in the aftermath of the attacks drove the party organisation underground.[99]

The tensions created by political violence in combination with the district's unusual geography, economy and settlement patterns led to a substantially different focus for community development in Chimanimani as compared to Insiza. The delineation team was particularly concerned by obstacles to establishing the bounded, 'natural' communities on which it believed a state able to withstand nationalist pressure could be built. A formidable obstacle to 'delineating' such communities was the distribution of people among different categories of land. Chiefs had many followers living precariously as 'squatters' on white farms: 'They have no clearly established tenurial rights and their position within their tribes is made difficult as they live in two worlds and belong to neither.'[100] This situation caused friction and was open to abuse: that the district 'has been the scene of unpleasant hostilities is glaring proof of this.' The delineation team recommended making 'squatters' subject to the authority of chiefs, even suggesting that white farmers ask them to allocate land. This would encourage a 're–identification' with chiefs and thus, in the logic of the official mind, 'hostilities created by misunderstandings would be minimised and the Afro-Nat influence consequently reduced (for do they not always concentrate their efforts in areas where there is confusion and a lost sense of direction?)'. Most of Chimanimani's chieftaincies also had large followings in Mozambique and other districts, much complicating the search for 'functional communities' with clear boundaries.

The delineation team could, however, do little more than recommend marginal concessions and highlight dangers. In the case of Dzawanda Dzingire, an unrecognised headman and former agricultural demonstrator, the 'community' had been separated from the rest of the chieftaincy by a swathe of European farms on which many of Dzingire's followers lived. As we have seen, Dzingire had long been involved in the struggle for land: unsurprisingly, his single 'felt need' was more land. The delineation team recommended his recognition as a headman: 'Dzingiri is a known (and quite open) Afro-Nat. Making him a headman ... may prove a good way of satisfying his ambitions and guiding his undoubted energy and intelligence into more beneficial channels.' The unsettled state of the Chikukwa chieftaincy also caused concern: 'Unless their tenurial rights are worked out or they are resettled they must present a security risk. They are not happy with their present circumstances and resent their deprivation of rights to their ancestral area.' In an eleventh-hour bid for allegiance, Chikukwa was granted a tiny TTL in 1975, a measure that entailed little cost as commercial forestry operations had been shut down by the war.

The young Chief Garai Ngorima worried the delineation team for other reasons. Garai was a prominent member of the Chiefs' Council and had gone on high-profile chiefs' tours abroad. At home, however, he was not popular: 'The impression gained is that he has more prestige outside his district than in it. He is, apparently, resented by some of his people because he surrounds himself with strongmen (he himself is never without his loaded pistol) and appears to distrust his followers.' The delineation team was right to worry. In practice, Garai's half-brother, Mubhango Mwandihamba, acted as chief: 'whilst Garai ran away' during the war, elders commented after independence, 'all customary issues were solved by him'. Mubhango was praised as a 'loyal supporter of freedom fighters'.[101]

As the 1960s wore on, the contrast to the strategy employed in Insiza grew increasingly stark. Where officials treated chiefs like Maduna largely as secular political leaders, administrators in Chimanimani delved deep into the process of discovering chiefs' 'real' customs, succession procedures and spiritual functions. They 'developed an almost mystical belief that where there was nationalist agitation in any area this was because the tribal system was not operating in a "traditional" manner'.[102] The very complexity of succession procedures, as they were manipulated by elders and codified by administrators, made them fertile ground for dispute. The seemingly arcane debates over custom were not, however, simply the mumblings of elders left behind by history: custom provided an arena in which a host of other questions, from conservation policy to nationalist allegiance, were contested.

The search for 'genuine' chiefs took a particularly convoluted shape in the case of the Mutambara chieftaincy. Theoretically, the chiefly title remained within one house, passing from elder to younger brother and then to the eldest son of the youngest brother.[103] The chief's installation, as painstakingly recorded by the newly custom-aware DC, involved a large number of actors: the Chiesa house had to 'crown' the chief; the head of the Nezandonyi house acted as the 'doorway' or *samusuwo* to the chieftaincy, along with two other senior headmen; elders of the ruling house and headmen and senior village heads had to approve the candidate. Finally, the chieftaincy's spirit medium had to ritually sanction the elders' choice. Most of these actors lived far from the chief himself and exercised autonomous influence in the territory in which they resided. In the late 1960s, a crisis over Chief Dindikwa Mutambara's legitimacy involved almost all these actors as well as the DC, agricultural officers, nationalists and the American Methodist Mission near to the Mutambara Irrigation Scheme. While arguments centred on the question of whether Dindikwa had been properly installed, the substance of debate concerned the balance of power among factions of the chieftaincy, state intervention, and nationalist mobilisation. This was not a conflict which fell into the 'commoners' versus 'royals' divide outlined by Kriger: members of leading houses opposed one another, in alliance with other groups.[104] Nor did it follow the model propounded by Lan and Ranger in which spirit mediums separated themselves from discredited chiefs. Instead, mediums remained allied to factions within the chieftaincy, and chiefs were perfectly capable of allying with nationalists.[105]

Dindikwa had been appointed acting chief in 1947. Elders responsible for sanctioning his appointment prevaricated for years, until the NC forced them to approve someone against pleas for more time to 'allow the spirits to speak'.[106] Dindikwa's rushed installation proved open to challenge. He had two younger brothers: James Ngani and Samuel Mutambara. Dindikwa and James Ngani saw their youngest brother, Samuel, as the most dangerous competitor. He had been sent to Mozambique in the early 1960s, ostensibly to 'look after' factions of the Mutambara chieftaincy located there. In his absence, Dindikwa brought in his trusted spirit medium, Namire, to confirm his position as chief. However, seven of the concerned elders refused to recognise Namire's ceremony: opposition to Dindikwa, notably from James Ngani and members of the Chiesa house, themselves known nationalists, continued in Samuel's absence. James Ngani 'used every opportunity to throw [Dindikwa] into disrepute' with officials, followers, and the American Methodist Mission. When Samuel returned in 1966 he proceeded to cause such 'discord' on the irrigation scheme, in large part in response to the enforcement of new regulations, that he was banned from the TTL. Subsequently, Dindikwa himself took up a stance of non-cooperation.

As in Insiza, the additional powers given to chiefs put pressure on DCs to ensure their cooperation in administrative and agricultural policy. Dindikwa presented a great problem in this respect. The DC decided to make an alliance with Dindikwa's competitors, notably James Ngani and Chiesa, in a bid to depose him, citing his 'improper' installation and exclusion of elders from his *dare* or council, as evidence that he was not ruling in a customary manner. Open conflict erupted in 1970 and Dindikwa subsequently refused to attend meetings or to establish a Tribal Land Authority.[107] In 1972, Dindikwa stopped trying to convince other elders to recognise his installation. Instead, with nationalist backing, he organised opposition to increases in dip fees and attempts to issue new Permits of Occupation on the irrigation scheme, and then openly sided with nationalists in opposing independence under the Rhodesian Front's new constitution. As the DC commented: 'The events of the last 12 months provided the present chief with an opportunity to ... capitalise on weaknesses in our present administrative system, making particular use of the ... rise in popularity of the A.N.C. in his own area.'[108] Dindikwa was evicted from the irrigation scheme and had his subsidy withdrawn.[109] But, as the frustrated DC wrote, all this

> had little effect and he has continued to use every opportunity to frustrate our efforts to bring about a change of attitude in the area. Previous attempts to form a Tribal Land Authority have always been unsuccessful as a result of the chief's refusal to have anything to do with any group or body which he deems to be connected with Government in any way. Recently the chief refused to attend a conservation course for tribal leaders.[110]

James Ngani and Samuel Mutambara betrayed no such qualms about attending conservation courses, and they used their cooperative stance to further undermine Dindikwa's precarious hold on office.

In response, Dindikwa launched attacks on other customary leaders. He informed the DC that he intended to revoke James Ngani's authority over the area surrounding the irrigation scheme.[111] He also refused to grant recognition to the leader of the Nezandonyi house. Nezandonyi, a plot holder on the Nyanyadzi irrigation scheme, had started a campaign for a headmanship in 1972. Failing recognition, he threatened to withdraw from his now highly valued role in the succession of the Mutambara chiefs.[112] The pattern of obstruction on Dindikwa's part and cooperation on the part of his brothers came to a head in 1973. When the DC called a meeting of all 'tribal leaders', Dindikwa told him that he would 'rather have his case referred to the Police and be prosecuted than attend the meeting'. He distinguished between his role as a civil servant, which he no longer felt obliged to perform due to the withdrawal of his subsidy, and his position as chief.[113] Thinking public opinion was with him, the DC lodged charges against Dindikwa. At a meeting with the 'tribal network' he stressed that Dindikwa's non-cooperation had left the TLA leaderless, making it impossible to peg lands for conservation. James Ngani warned them, however, that 'they should all know that whoever is going to lead the people will be hated by the chief.' They decided that the government would have to resolve the situation as it had incorrectly installed Dindikwa in the first place.[114]

Charges were subsequently brought against Dindikwa for refusing to obey the DC's orders. DC Peters' statement indicated the extent to which Dindikwa had managed to disrupt administration: 'The disunity which exists amongst tribal leaders and the inability of the chief to provide positive leadership and direction has been directly or indirectly responsible for administrative problems in the past an[d] in particular has frustrated all efforts to properly conserve the land.'[115] Though Dindikwa was duly convicted, his suspended sentence allowed him to claim victory. He left the courtroom with his family 'while singing a song of victory', bought a supply of beer to celebrate and proclaimed that the DC had been found guilty.[116] A frustrated Peters wrote:

> Following advice given by two prominent ngangas (witchdoctors) the Chief considered it was unnecessary to obtain the services of a lawyer to defend him and his general attitude both

before, during and after the trial has been one of complete vindication of his actions and belief in his ability to counteract any attempts to discredit him. On the announcement of the judgment there were cries of jubilation from members of the Chief's family outside the courtroom and the Chief spoke to me as he left saying in effect 'I told you I would win'.

The government now looked 'weak, ineffective, unable to implement our policies in the face of opposition and worst of all in the present case, obviously having less influence and power than the Chief'. Dindikwa continued with a campaign he had started in the previous year to prevent people on the Mutambara scheme from planting the Devuli wheat recommended by officials, threatening 'that anyone planting and reaping such wheat would have his or her grain bins burnt down.' Peters concluded: 'The difficult times which lie ahead will require us to modify our policies and approach to enable us to strengthen the administration, regain the confidence of the people and most of all provide us the teeth to bring pressure to bear when this is needed.'[117]

Dindikwa's victory proved ephemeral. He had become too isolated from the majority of elders, relying almost exclusively on his sons and the spirit medium Namire.[118] He was deposed in June 1973 for 'not following proper customs', and James Ngani was appointed acting chief.[119] James would remain acting chief, the DC declared, until the 'real' medium of the 'real' spirit could be found, as Namire was 'nothing more than the ex Chief's personal swikiro [spirit medium]'.[120] A period of calm followed during which the DC wrote optimistically of the prospects for finally establishing a TLA. But once he had succeeded in wresting the title from Dindikwa, with the collusion of other elders and the DC, James Ngani himself turned to opposition. He refused to pay increased charges on the irrigation scheme in 1974, organised protests, and took up a stance of non-cooperation similar to that of Dindikwa. He was deposed in 1977 on charges of supporting guerrillas, and died the following year.[121] Samuel Mutambara's record was even worse. Though he had co-operated in the deposition of Dindikwa, attended TLA training courses, and accepted the position of secretary to James Ngani, he simultaneously organised Zanu committees and guerrilla recruitment through his extensive contacts with schools, churches and Mutare-based nationalists. His experiences in Mozambique, in traveling as an evangelist and then teaching in mission out-schools in the eastern districts, put him in an ideal position to recruit school children and to organise their passage across the border. In one such incident, over 500 students crossed the border. Samuel was detained in various police camps and prisons between 1974 and 1979, ending up in the nationalist-filled WhaWha detention centre in the Midlands.[122]

The administration's growing ideological and administrative reliance on chiefs raised the stakes in local disputes and gave officials a pressing interest in determining their outcome. In such circumstances, the language of custom took on weighty political implications. But Rhodesian Front policy manifestly failed to remake chiefs as 'the basis of the state' and as authorities over the land. Cooperation with officials was but one strategy among many: while it might be deployed at one stage, it was often later abandoned or accompanied by contradictory alliances. In Mutambara, chiefly office was certainly valued, but so was the prevention of state intervention on the irrigation scheme and support for nationalism and the guerrilla war. The elaborate debates about custom provided a malleable space for pursuing divergent ends.

Conclusion

In the 1960s and 1970s, chiefs played a central role in the politics of land and state-making. The stark dichotomy drawn between compromised and anachronistic chiefs and radical nationalists ignores the varied roles that individuals who held chiefly titles commonly played, and the complex politics of rebuilding the state in the wake of the NLHA. Chieftaincy served as an important platform from which demands for land could be made and policy obstructed. Chiefs drew on flexible versions of custom that more often undermined than bolstered the state, and they commonly participated in a host of other social and political organisations. The debates over chiefs' land allocations, and the attempts to constitute them as land authorities, illustrated the varied appeals to custom, nationalism, and technical development in local struggles over land, and vividly demonstrated the potent legacy of decades of state intervention for rural authority. This period produced and transformed a diversity of ideologies and institutions in African rural areas, none of which held a monopoly on legitimacy or power. Instead, a range of competing claims to authority over the land survived into the post-independence period, marking land as a pre-eminent resource through which state-making would continue to be contested.

Notes

1 See Weinrich, 1971, for the strongest statement of this case. For a more nuanced view, see Holleman, 1969.
2 Bratton, 1978, 50.
3 Bhebe, 1989b, 92, and 1989a, 126.
4 Ranger, 1982b, 24, passim. Ranger has revised his views. See Ranger, 1999, and compare to Maxwell, 1999.
5 Lan, 1985, 146.
6 Lan, 1985; Ranger, 1982b and 1985b.
7 Reports of chiefs using their offices to extract fees were common. Chiefs' messengers reported cases of chiefs charging fees for leases on business sites, hearing civil cases, applications for land, and applications to move from one place to another. See 23.7.5R/93142, Acting DC M. J. Spies, Gwelo, to DC, Gwelo, 'Chiefs' Messengers Training, Senka', 22 January 1965; DC M. R. Parker, Gwelo, to PC, Midlands, 29 January 1965.
8 See Ranger, 1985b, chapters 4 and 5, and 1999; Ranger and Ncube, 1996; Bhebe, 1989b, 100-101; Kriger, 1992, 95-101; Wienrich, 1975.
9 23.7.5R/93142, DC A. Wright, Nuanetsi, to PC, Fort Victoria, 14 July 1965.
10 See Kriger, 1992, Chapter 6; Ranger, 1985b; Alexander, McGregor and Ranger, 2000, Chapter 7, on wartime struggles.
11 See Alexander, 1996.
12 Weinrich, 1971, 22.
13 14.8.8F/69691, Working Party D, Arising from the Robinson Commission Report, 'The Tribal Authority and the Land', Paper No. 16, Salisbury, 2 September 1961; Working Party D, Robinson Commission, Second Report (First Draft), 'Revision of the Native Land Husbandry Act', A. Pendered, Deputy Secretary, Development, Paper No. 23, 24 December 1961. The quotation is drawn from the Working Party's consultations with chiefs in Masvingo and Matabeleland Provinces. The view was deemed 'typical' of the country as a whole and was much repeated.
14 Chiefs met with the Quinton Committee in 1960; cabinet ministers consulted chiefs in Gwelo in May 1961 and met the Chiefs' Council in Salisbury later in the year. These meetings and those held by Working Party D led chiefs to complain they were tired 'of talking about the land problem and its solution'. See 14.8.8F/69691, Working Party D, 'The Tribal Authority and the Land', 2 September 1961. Also see

5.2.8R/82725, Working Party D, District Surveys for Buhera, 18 July 1962; Mrewa, 13 April 1962; Mtoko, 11 April 1962, for explicit statements regarding chiefs' expectations of a response to their demands for land.

15 5.2.8R/82725, Working Party D, District Survey, Victoria, Annexure B, Record of a Meeting of Working Party 'D' Committee with the Chiefs of Victoria District, 15 January 1962. Chief Shumba was eventually ousted from the Chiefs' Council for the stridency of his views. See Weinrich, 1971, 21.

16 5.2.8R/82725, Working Party D, District Survey, Lupane, 11 October 1962.

17 See 5.2.8R/82725, Working Party D, District Surveys for Plumtree, 23 August 1962; Umzingwane, 3 July 1962; Shabani, 15 July 1962; Nkai, 20 September 1962. For Insiza, see below.

18 See 14.8.8F/69691, Working Party D, 'The Tribal Authority and the Land', 2 September 1961.

19 Despite worries over creating a precedent of buying land for 'squatters', heavily populated land was purchased in Chilimanzi, Charter and Gweru, among other areas. Many more people were simply evicted. The only case I could find of a land transfer justified as a reward to a chief was that of Chief Kayisa in the tiny Ntabazinduna TTL. The land in question had at any rate long been used as a grazing area, and thus fitted the pattern of buying occupied land. See 5.2.8R/82725, Working Party D, District Surveys, Nuanetsi, 21 August 1962; Chilimanzi, 6 November 1962; Charter, 28 July 1962; Gwelo, 2 May 1962; Inyati, 19 September 1962; 14.8.8F/69691, The Land Situation, Development and Settlement Reports, Vol. 2, 1963, Bubi.

20 28.10.8F/98431, Summary Report on Chiefs' Provincial Assembly Meetings, W. H. H. Nicolle, Deputy Secretary, Development, 20 April 1964.

21 5.2.8R/82725, Working Party D, District Survey, Wedza, 16 August 1962.

22 See, for example, 5.2.8R/82725, Working Party D, District Survey, Marandellas, 11 August 1962; Lupane, 11 October 1962.

23 5.2.8R/82725, Working Party D, District Survey, Plumtree, 23 August 1962. Also see Weinrich, 1975, 68-72.

24 *Ibid.* and see 5.2.8R/82725, Working Party D, District Surveys, Selukwe, 2 May 1962; Sipolilo, 14 April 1962; Mazoe, 14 August 1962; Victoria, 8 June 1962; Mzingwane, 2 July 1962; Inyati, 19 September 1962; Working Party D, 'The Tribal Authority and the Land', 2 September 1961.

25 5.2.8R/82725, Working Party D, District Survey, Nkai, 20 September 1962; also see Mrewa, 13 April 1962.

26 5.2.8R/82725, Working Party D, District Survey, Lomagundi, 1 April 1962.

27 5.2.8R/82725, Working Party D, District Surveys, Chilimanzi, 6 November 1962; Gwaai, 4 October 1962; Bindura, 19 September 1962.

28 See 18.8.10R/88379, First Meeting of the First Council of Chiefs, Salisbury, 21 November 1962; 28.10.8F/98431, Summary Report on Chiefs' Provincial Assembly Meetings, W. H. H. Nicolle, Deputy Secretary, Development, 20 April 1964.

29 5.2.8R/82725, Working Party D, District Survey, Marandellas, 11 August 1962.

30 5.2.8R/82725, Working Party D, District Survey, Charter, 28 July 1962. Also see Surveys for Buhera, 18 July 1962, and Wedza, 16 August 1962.

31 Such claims were made in, for example, Zaka, Bikita, and Gutu, and very widely in Manicaland. See 27.6.6F/100842, Minutes of District Commissioners' Conference: Victoria Province, held in Fort Victoria on the 19th and 20th August, 1963; N. J. Brendon, Acting PC Manicaland, to Secretary for Internal Affairs, 2 June 1964.

32 Weinrich, 1975, 35.

33 27.6.6F/100842, Acting PC M. E. Hayes, Victoria, to Deputy Secretary, Administration, 24 June 1964.

34 See 27.6.6F/100842, Minutes of District Commissioners' Conference: Victoria Province, Fort Victoria, 19-20 August 1963; N. J. Brendon, Acting PC Manicaland, to Secretary for Internal Affairs, 2 June 1964. And see Andersson, 1999.

35 In Zaka District, village heads 'chased away' right holders. See 14.8.8F/69691, Development and Land Returns, Annual reports, 1962-1964, Zaka, 2 January 1964. Also see Holleman, 1969, 336; Weinrich, 1975, 37.

36 See the Working Party D District Surveys for 1962 and evidence of vast increases in this phenomenon in 1963/4 in 14.8.8F/69691, Development and Land Returns, Annual Reports, 1962-1964.

37 5.2.8R/82725, Working Party D, Third Report, Chapter 11, Sinoia, 30 July 1962. Also see discussion in Nyambara, 2001b, 782.

38 28.10.8F/98431, Summary Report on Chiefs' Provincial Assembly Meetings, W. H. H. Nicolle, Deputy Secretary, Development, 20 April 1964.

39 DCs recorded large-scale movements in Makoni, Gutu and Semokwe TTLs and smaller movements in much of Manicaland and Victoria Provinces, Kana and QueQue TTLs. 27.6.6F/100842, Acting PC N. J. Brendon, Manicaland, to Secretary for Internal Affairs, 2 June 1964; DC, Matobo, to PC, Matabeleland South, 4 May 1964; DC, Gutu, to PC, Victoria, 17 June 1964; DC, Bikita, to PC, Victoria, 12 May 1964;

DC, Zaka, to PC, Victoria, 15 June 1964; DC, Gwelo, to PC, Midlands, 8 June 1964; PC E. D. F. Dawson, Midlands, to Under Secretary, Administration (B), 23 June 1964.

40 See 27.6.6F/100842, DC, Marandellas, to PC, Mashonaland South, 15 June 1964; DC, Wedza, to PC, Mashonaland South, 8 May 1964; DC, Mrewa, to PC, Mashonaland South, 28 May 1964; DC, Umvuma, to PC, Midlands, 26 May 1964; DC, QueQue, to PC, Midlands, 26 May 1964.

41 27.6.6F/100842, PC J. R. Inskipp, Mashonaland North, to Undersecretary Administration (B), 'Report on alleged misuse of land in the TTLs – Mashonaland North province', 11 May 1964.

42 27.6.6F/100842, Report of the DC Ndanga, Zaka, for the Quarter ended the 30th September 1963.

43 27.6.6F/100842, DC, Zaka, to PC, Victoria, 15 June 1964.

44 Ranger, 1982b, 24-30.

45 14.8.8F/69691, Acting DC J. H. Fynes-Clinton to Secretary for Internal Affairs R. L. D. Herbert, 27 March 1963; Acting DC to PC, Manicaland, 30 March 1963. CID reports recorded similar practices in Inyanga.

46 The biggest 'squatter' populations in the 1960s were on lowveld ranches. For complaints from chiefs regarding evictees' requests for land see 5.2.8R/82725, Working Party D, District Surveys, Chilimanzi, 6 November 1962, Gatooma, 25 August 1962, Nuanetsi, 21 August 1962; 28.10.8F/98431, Summary Report on Chiefs' Provincial Assembly Meetings, W. H. H. Nicolle, Deputy Secretary, Development, 20 April 1964.

47 27.6.6F/100842, DC M. E. Hayes, Fort Victoria, to PC, Southern Mashonaland, 28 June 1963. In the preceding years, Nuanetsi Ranch had sold over a million acres to largely Afrikaans-speaking South Africans who were, 'to say the least very unpopular with the tenants and squatters'. Roughly 1,100 families, with their 7,000 cattle, faced eviction. See 5.2.8R/82725, Working Party D, District Survey, Nuanetsi, 21 August 1962.

48 25.10.6R/100839, NC, QueQue to PNC, Midlands, 26 March 1959.

49 28.10.8F/98431, Summary Report on Chiefs' Provincial Assembly Meetings, W. H. H. Nicolle, Deputy Secretary, Development, 20 April 1964. For background, see 25.10.6R/100839, NC, QueQue, to PNC, Midlands, 27 April 1960; R. F. Robins, Member in Charge, BSAP, Silobela, to S. D. O., BSAP, QueQue, 1 June 1962.

50 23.7.5R/93142, Minutes of Chiefs' Meeting, DC's Office, QueQue, 15 January 1965.

51 This argument has been made by, *inter alia*, Weinrich, 1975 and 1971; Bratton, 1978, and contemporary Internal Affairs officials.

52 14.8.8F/69691, Report of the DC, Filabusi, for the year ended 31st December 1963. For chiefs' complaints over the conflict caused by allocations see 5.2.8R/82725, Working Party D, District Survey, Insiza (Filabusi), 11 July 1962.

53 5.2.8R/82725, Working Party D, District Survey, Insiza (Filabusi), 11 July 1962.

54 27.6.6F/100842, DC B. N. Gaunt to PC, Matabeleland South, 22 April 1964. Also see PER 5, Chief Maduna, Filabusi, Reign Mpuli, Extension Assistant to Extension Officer, Filabusi, 6 October 1967.

55 Minutes of the Godhlwayo Council, Sibasa Hall, 4 April 1961; Avoca, 29 August 1961, 17 May 1962. Several different names were used for the council: I use Godhlwayo Council throughout.

56 See Minutes of the Godhlwayo Council, Avoca, 20 September 1962, 22 November 1962; 27.6.6F/100842, R. L. C. Cunliffe for Secretary for Internal Affairs to PC, Matabeleland South, 6 December 1962; DC W. D. R. Baker, Filabusi, to PC N. L. Dacomb, Matabeleland South, 10 January 1963.

57 Issues concerning cattle were raised repeatedly in council meetings. See Minutes of the Godhlwayo Council, April 1961 to March 1963, and 14.8.8F/69691, Report of the DC Filabusi for the year ended 31st December 1963. The council's tactics regarding dip fees were common. See Government of Rhodesia, 1974.

58 Minutes of the Godhlwayo Council, Filabusi, 17 May 1962; Avoca, 20 September 1962; Sibasa, 21 March 1963.

59 Minutes of the Godhlwayo Council, Glassblock, 23 May 1963.

60 A simultaneous debate raged over the collection of government taxes due to violent confrontations between officials and sabhukus reluctant to collect taxes in the hostile political atmosphere. Minutes of the Godhlwayo Council, Avoca, 17 January 1963; Glassblock, 23 May 1963 and September 1963.

61 Minutes of the Godhlwayo Council, Avoca, 6 and 20 February 1964.

62 Unless otherwise noted, references in the remainder of this section are drawn from the delineation reports for Insiza District, Ministry of Internal Affairs, 1963a-d, 1964a-f.

63 See 14.8.8F/69691, Report of the DC, Filabusi, for the year ended 31st December 1963, 5 January 1964.

64 The response to community development differed in the prosperous purchase areas which had openly nationalist Farmers' Associations. They saw community development as a way of gaining control of African Development Fund Grants and schools. See Weinrich, 1975, 141-226, on other purchase areas.

65 E.g., see DCs' characterisations in 14.8.8F/69691, The Land Situation, Development and Settlement Reports, Vol. 2, 1963, Nyamandhlovu, Matobo.
66 See Weinrich, 1975, 37-40, and Chapter 3.
67 Chiefs' and Headmen's Meetings, Filabusi, 1 March 1966 to 20 January 1978; Interview, D. Bing, Filabusi, April 1989; 27.6.6F/100843, Quarterly Progress Report: Primary Development: Item 'P', Insiza, 30 September 1968; Secretary for Internal Affairs Circular No. 2, Addendum 'I', Insiza District, Quarterly Progress Report: Primary Development item 'P', December 1968; Insiza District Conference: Filabusi Minutes, 6 November 1968.
68 Weinrich, 1975, 97.
69 The DC recorded 18,135 Large Stock Equivalents in Godhlwayo in 1963, as opposed to 12,690 in 1961. The increase may have been aided by purchases from evictees and tenants in the north of the district who were forced to sell their cattle. 14.8.8F/69691, Report of the DC Filabusi for the year ended 31st December 1963, 5 January 1964. African-owned cattle herds as a whole grew dramatically between 1961 and 1965.
70 See Chiefs' and Headmen's Meetings, Filabusi, 5 May 1968, 26 March 1971.
71 Chiefs' and Headmen's Meetings, Filabusi, 26 January 1973, 23 March 1973, 20 March 1974, 24 July 1974, 24 October 1974. Earlier attempts to establish grazing schemes had failed, despite the allocation of £2,000 to construct paddocks. 27.6.6F/100843, Quarterly Progress Report: Primary Development: Item 'P' for Quarter ended 31st January 1970, District Insiza, SIA Circular No. 2, Addendum 'I', 9 January 1970; Chiefs' and Headmen's Meeting, Filabusi, 28 May 1971. Also see Weinrich, 1975, 107-8; Cousins, 1987.
72 Chiefs' and Headmen's Meetings, Filabusi, 25 July 1975, 24 September 1975, 23 January 1976, 23 April 1976, 21 October 1976.
73 Chiefs' and Headmen's Meetings, Filabusi, 2 November 1965, 30 November 1965, 1 March 1966, December 1968.
74 5.2.8R/82725, Working Party D, District Survey, Insiza, 11 July 1962.
75 Chiefs' and Headmen's Meeting, Filabusi, 1 December 1967; PER 5, Chief Maduna, Filabusi, Reign Mpuli, Extension Assistant, to Extension Officer, Filabusi, 6 October 1967.
76 See Chiefs' and Headmen's Meetings, Filabusi, from January 1970 to August 1973.
77 PER 5, Chief Maduna, Filabusi, DC B. N. Gaunt to PC, Matabeleland South, 4 August 1965; PC W. D. R. Baker, Matabeleland South, to Under Secretary, Administration, 23 September 1965; A. M. Mansell for Secretary for Internal Affairs to PC, Matabeleland South, 21 September 1965; Acting PC B. B. FitzPatrick to DC, Filabusi, 25 October 1965; Secretary for Internal Affairs to DC, Filabusi, 22 November 1965.
78 Chiefs' and Headmen's Meetings, Filabusi, 8 September 1966, 3 November 1966, 1 December 1966, 3 February 1967; Insiza District Conference: Filabusi Minutes, 23 February 1966.
79 PER 5, Chief Maduna, Filabusi, District Officer R. Goosen to DC, Filabusi, 18 October 1966; PC FitzPatrick, Matabeleland South, to Secretary for Internal Affairs, 2 November 1966; Acting Secretary for Internal Affairs H. R. G. Howman to PC, Matabeleland South, 23 November 1966.
80 PER 5, Chief Maduna, Filabusi, Order from Secretary for Internal Affairs; B. Martindale to DC, Filabusi, 4 September 1967.
81 PER 5, Chief Maduna, Filabusi, BSA Policeman Hunter Hardy to Member in Charge, BSAP, Filabusi, 1967.
82 Chiefs' and Headmen's Meeting, Filabusi, 29 December 1967. The government would maintain main roads, and run dips and cattle sales: 'all other projects, people must do, by formation of Boards or Council'.
83 PER 5, Chief Maduna, Filabusi, DC W.B. Rooken-Smith to PC, Matabeleland South, 10 July 1968; DC, Filabusi, to PC, Matabeleland South, 14 November 1968; Chiefs' and Headmen's Meeting, Filabusi, 31 January 1969.
84 Interview, Vezi Maduna, Avoca, 14 April 1989; PER 5, Chief Maduna, Filabusi, DC, Filabusi, to PC, Matabeleland South, 14 November 1968; DC, Filabusi, to Secretary for Internal Affairs, 19 December 1974.
85 PER 5, Chief Maduna, Filabusi, Vezi Maduna to DC, Filabusi, 12 February 1970, 9 April 1970; DC, Filabusi, to PC, Matabeleland South, 17 April 1970; Chiefs' and Headmen's Meetings, Filabusi, 25 September 1970, 9 October 1970.
86 Chiefs' and Headmen's Meetings, Filabusi, 28 April 1972, 25 August 1972, 29 September 1972. Councils were formed in Glassblock TTL in 1969 and Insiza TTL in 1971.
87 PER 5, Chief Maduna, Filabusi, PC, Matabeleland South, to Secretary of Internal Affairs, 27 March 1974; Secretary for Internal Affairs to PC, Matabeleland South, 2 April 1974; DC James Coetzer, Filabusi, to PC, 17 April 1974.
88 PER 5, Chief Maduna, Filabusi, DC, Filabusi, to Secretary for Internal Affairs, 10 October 1974, and see 19 December 1974.

89 Chiefs' and Headmen's Meeting, Filabusi, 20 December 1974; 23 April 1976; PER 5, Chief Maduna, Filabusi, Secretary for Internal Affairs to PC, Matabeleland South, 2 April 1974; DC James Coetzer, Filabusi, to Vezi Maduna, 24 September 1975.

90 PER 5, Chief Maduna, Filabusi, DC, Filabusi, to PC, Matabeleland South, 1 June 1976.

91 PER 5, Headman Ngomondo Hwadalala, Filabusi, DC, Filabusi, to PC, Matabeleland South, 6 July 1976, 9 August 1976; Insiza District Conference: Filabusi Minutes, 6 August 1976.

92 PER 5, Headman Ngomondo Hwadalala, Filabusi, DC, Filabusi, to PC, Matabeleland South, 9 August 1976. Also see Report by DA Philip Bhebe, 30 March 1983.

93 PER 5, Chief Maduna, Filabusi, DC A. Q. Cosens, Filabusi, to PC, Matabeleland South, 10 April 1980; Chiefs' and Headmen's Meeting, Filabusi, 27 May 1977; PER 5, Headman Ngomondo Hwadalala, Filabusi, Report by DA Philip Bhebe, 30 March 1983.

94 Chiefs' and Headmen's Meeting, Filabusi, 25 June 1976.

95 Chiefs' and Headmen's Meetings, Filabusi, July 1976 to December 1977.

96 5.2.8R/82725, Working Party D, District Survey, Melsetter, 2 November 1962.

97 See Sinclair, 1971, 172-4.

98 27.6.6F/100842, Acting PC N. J. Brendon, Manicaland, to SIA, 2 June 1964; 14.8.8F/69691, The Land Situation, Development and Settlement Reports, Melsetter, Vol. 2, 1963 and Development and Land Returns, 1962-1964, Melsetter, 7 January 1964. Compare to Andersson, 1999.

99 Sithole, 1970, 146-76; Martin and Johnson, 1981, 23-4.

100 Unless otherwise noted, references in the rest of this sub-section are drawn from the delineation reports for Melsetter district, Ministry of Internal Affairs, 1965a-h.

101 PER 4, Ngorima Chieftaincy, Ngorima Chieftainship Meeting, 4 June 1991; Chief Ngorima, New Incumbent, n.d.; Meeting of the Ngorima Chieftainship held on 18 May 1991; Minutes of the Ngorima Chieftainship held on 4 July 1991, DA's Conference Room.

102 Ranger, 1982b, 22.

103 Most of the Chimanimani chieftaincies did not follow the ideal model for 'Shona' collateral succession, the title more often having been dominated by brothers and then sons of one house, as in Mutambara, or following rules of primogeniture as in Ngorima and Chikukwa, owing to the influence of the Gaza Kingdom.

104 Kriger, 1992, 196-206.

105 PER 5, Chief Mutambara, PC Noel Hunt to DC, Melsetter, 18 January 1972. Also see Maxwell, 1999.

106 Paragraph based on PER 5, Chief Mutambara, G. R. Broderick to Mr. Thorpe, 29 June 1972.

107 PER 5, Chief Mutambara, DC J. R. Peters, Melsetter, to PC, Manicaland, 13 January 1972; MIA Memorandum, Per.5/Mutambara/7, 'Removal From Office of Dindikwa Dandiwa, Mr., 431, as Chief Mutambara, Melsetter District'.

108 PER 5, Chief Mutambara, DC J. R. Peters to PC, Manicaland, 13 April 1973.

109 PER 5, Chief Mutambara, MIA Memorandum, Per.5/Mutambara/7, 'Removal From Office of Dindikwa Dandiwa, Mr 431, As Chief Mutambara, Melsetter District'.

110 PER 5, Chief Mutambara, DC J. R. Peters to PC, Manicaland, 13 April 1973.

111 PER 5, Chief Mutambara, DC J. R. Peters to PC, Manicaland, 13 April 1973.

112 PER 5, Chief Mutambara, Nezandonyi the 6th (Chomwandoita), Nyanyadzi irrigation project, to DC, Melsetter, 5 June 1972. Other chiefs and headmen also tried to take advantage of the official emphasis on custom to claim recognition. For example, Mutare-based members of the Saurombe chieftaincy, which had been abolished in 1945, hired lawyers and negotiated with the DC and Chief Muwushu for reappointment. See PER 4, Saurombe File, DC J. R. Peters to Messrs. Ternouth, Lawton and Murnane, advocates, 4 January 1973; DC J. R. Peters to PC Manicaland, 4 July 1973, 17 August 1973, 10 October 1973.

113 PER 5, Chief Mutambara, DC J. R. Peters, 'Statement concerning the prosecution of Chief Mutambara (Dindikwa 5588 Melsetter)', 19 April 1973. Also see F. F. Tsorai, 'Meeting of Muchinda and Makota of Mutambara TTL', 16 April 1973.

114 PER 5, Chief Mutambara, F. F. Tsorai to DC, Melsetter, 'Meeting of District Commissioner and Dare Renyika of Mutambara TTL: Held on the 12th April 1973', 16 April 1973.

115 PER 5, Chief Mutambara, DC J. R. Peters, 'Statement concerning the prosecution of Chief Muttambara (Dindiikwa 5588 Melsetter)', 19 April 1973.

116 PER 5, Chief Mutambara, Ministry of Internal Affairs, Pass Office, to DC, Melsetter, 28 May 1973.

117 PER 5, Chief Mutambara, DC J. R. Peters to PC, Manicaland, 28 May 1973.

118 See PER 5, Chief Mutambara, Ministry of Internal Affairs, Pass Office, to DC, Melsetter, 28 May 1973.

119 PER 5, Chief Mutambara, MIA, Pass Office to DC, Melsetter, 23 June 1973.

120 PER 5, Chief Mutambara, DC J. R. Peters to PC, 11 September 1973.

121 PER 5, Chief Mutambara, DC J. R. Peters, to PC, Manicaland, 21 June 1973; Chief Mutambara, Acting

Chief Mutambara for Mutambara Plotholders to DC, 19 September 1974; Minutes of the Mutambara Chieftainship held at Independence Church, Mutambara Communal Land, 19 July 1988.

122 Interview, Chief Mutambara, Guhune, 6 November 1988, 10 November 1988; PER 5, Chief Mutambara, Chief Mutambara's Installation Speech by T. A. Kazembe, n.d. [1990]; DA T. A. Kazembe to PA, 9 November 1988.

5

Governing the Land in Independent Zimbabwe

The end of settler rule in 1980 heralded a transformation in the politics of land and state-making.[1] The newly elected Zanu(PF) government promised a democratisation of power and a large-scale redistribution of land. It sought to establish a new basis for order and legitimacy. To do so, it had to grapple with the legacy of the settler state. Nationalist hostility to Rhodesian institutions, officials and symbols had reached an extreme by the end of the war, removing space for the tactics of negotiation and cooperation. These were the strategies of 'sell-outs', and they risked the lives of those who employed them. The rejection of Rhodesian rule had not, however, wiped the slate clean in the eyes of rural people or in those of Zimbabwe's new leaders. Instead, nationalism sat uncomfortably alongside other claims to land and authority, rooted in the technocratic and customary, and in local histories of eviction and migration. The meanings of nationalism itself were the subject of heated struggle. As in the past, the politics of land would stand as a central challenge to the process of building and legitimising the state.

Negotiating Independence

In 1979, the leaders of Zanu and Zapu – temporarily united under the banner of the Patriotic Front – entered British-brokered negotiations with the Rhodesian authorities to end the guerrilla war. Land was the central sticking-point: under pressure from the countries that hosted the guerrilla armies, and placated by promises of British aid in the acquisition of land, the Patriotic Front accepted significant constraints on redistribution.[2] The Lancaster House constitution protected property rights for 10 years, and dictated that 'European' land be acquired under a 'willing buyer, willing seller' agreement. Moreover, the constitution guaranteed a white monopoly of 20 seats in the 100-seat parliament for seven years.

A disbanded Patriotic Front contested the elections in April 1980. Voting patterns largely followed the operational areas of the two guerrilla armies. Robert Mugabe's Zanu(PF) won a decisive 57 seats and was thus in a position to form the new government, while Joshua Nkomo's Zapu won 20 seats, largely in the western Matabeleland Provinces. The Zanu(PF) leadership espoused a recently acquired Marxism-

105

Leninism, but its ideological commitment had not been translated into programmes and policies, remaining instead at the level of slogans and broad goals.[3] The Zanu leadership had been pushed to adopt a more radical ideology as a consequence of wartime challenges from the left, challenges that were brutally suppressed and which had left an authoritarian political culture in their wake.[4] Marxism–Leninism came to serve as a 'symbolic system' that legitimised Zanu(PF)'s role as a crusader for social justice in the interest of a homogenous constituency – the *povo*, people or masses.[5] In practice, the ruling party's nationalism took the populist and pragmatic form of the 'moderation and reconciliation' policy.

In political terms, 'moderation and reconciliation' applied to whites who were willing to work with the new government and, initially, to Zapu. In economic terms, it translated into the 'Growth with Equity' policy.[6] Growth with Equity stressed the constraints that the Lancaster House constitution placed on redistributive policies, and emphasised the central role whites would continue to play in the economy. With an eye to the case of Mozambique, the new government sought to avoid the high costs of a white exodus, as well as the potential for intervention from South Africa or the former Rhodesian army that such an exodus might provoke. Particular emphasis was given to the 'indispensability' of white farmers: in 1980, they produced 90 per cent of marketed food requirements as well as a significant part of exports and supplies to the manufacturing sector. As Robin Palmer writes, white farmers 'had suddenly become something of a protected species'.[7] If 'growth' was largely to be the province of the white and foreign-owned sectors of the economy, alleviating the inherited inequalities of the Rhodesian era fell to the state. Thus 'equity' would be achieved through the centrally planned redirection of public and donor resources to the black majority.[8]

Moderation and reconciliation had other significant implications. First, it left much of the Rhodesian state's bureaucracy, as well as former officials, in place. In 1980, 29,000 of 40,000 civil servants were black, but whites dominated the senior echelons. Africanisation was concentrated at senior levels of the state and in fields such as education; many whites who chose to stay kept their influential positions, at least during the first crucial years of independence. They were able to draw on their experience and training to great effect, especially given Zanu(PF)'s lack of clear policies.[9] Moreover, Africanisation did not necessarily mean the introduction of new attitudes and practices, as many blacks promoted in the post-independence civil service received their training within the Rhodesian state. Newly trained civil servants were imbued with a powerful strain of bureaucratic professionalism, founded in high levels of education, and technical and legal expertise.[10] Second, 'reconciliation' was a fragile concept which was all too easily abrogated in the name of maintaining 'regime security'. Despite promises to dismantle repressive legislation, the new government maintained, and then expanded, the extensive powers it inherited under the Emergency Powers Act, the Law and Order (Maintenance) Act, and other legislation, as well as the formidable police and intelligence apparatus built by Rhodesian governments.[11] The State of Emergency introduced by the Rhodesian Front in 1965 was 'faithfully and ritualistically' renewed each year throughout the 1980s.[12]

The Zanu(PF) government justified the maintenance of the state's repressive capabilities in terms of the real threat posed by South Africa and disgruntled whites. But it was not whites who bore the brunt of state repression. Even if they were condemned for their failure to change their political allegiances,[13] their dominant economic position and constitutionally guaranteed seats in Parliament left them – for the moment – beyond the reach of Zanu(PF). Such was not the case for other groups, most notably Zapu. Between 1982 and 1987, the Zanu(PF) government subjugated and eventually absorbed Zapu through a brutal campaign of repression that far exceeded any response that could be justified in terms of threats to state security. The campaign targeted those who lived in areas that voted for Zapu; it recast loyalty to Zapu as part of an illegitimate ethnic identification with the 'Ndebele', and portrayed the 'dissident' violence of members of Zapu's armed wing as part of an even more illegitimate South African project of destabilisation. The attack on Zapu formed part of Zanu(PF)'s attempts to consolidate control over the nation, and to create political 'unity', goals that squared with its often-voiced desire for a one-party state.[14]

Zapu was the primary target of violent repression, but Zanu(PF) also tried to extend centralised control over a variety of other organisations and social groups, ranging from trade unions to ex-combatants to 'traditional healers', and from spirit mediums to Zanu(PF) village committees to churches to the production of history itself.[15] The practices of the new government combined an authoritarian populism with the political habits of the war years, when dissent was equated with 'selling out'. They also drew on Rhodesian institutions. In an ironic twist, Zanu(PF)'s preoccupation with 'regime security' transformed its erstwhile enemy – the Rhodesian state – into its most effective ally. The interaction between Zanu(PF)'s political agenda and the institutions of the Rhodesian state were also to have significant implications for reforms in local government, development planning and agrarian policy.

Remaking the State

At independence, the Rhodesian government's policy of community development lay largely moribund. Councils barely functioned, and in areas where the war was closely contested chiefs had been forced to withdraw from their often ambivalent cooperation with officials or face violent attack. The destruction of the state had stood high on the nationalist agenda. The new government thus faced a major challenge of state-building, encompassing the need to legitimise the state, to give it institutional form, and to meet the urgent demands of economic recovery.

The government's first step was symbolic of later reforms, in terms of its pre-independence genesis and its top-down implementation. District councils, established in lieu of the chieftaincy-based African councils, were designed by the transitional government and adopted just before independence.[16] To implement the measure, the thin veneer of senior Zanu(PF) officials relied on an uneasy combination of the former officials of the Ministry of Internal Affairs and rural party committees. Party committees at first played a key role in distributing aid, reconstruction, and communication with officials. But though they were instrumental in the creation of councils, they found themselves rapidly displaced by them, and by the re-establishment of state bureaucracies in rural areas. Senior Zanu(PF) officials were suspicious of rural party committees for a number of reasons: they did not represent all members of rural society, as councils theoretically did; they acted with an autonomy from the Zanu(PF) leadership that reflected both the lack of middle-level party representatives and the disparity between local demands and official policy; and, notably in Matabeleland, they were not loyal to Zanu(PF). In 1980 and 1981, the demands of rural party committees were routinely brushed aside, with the effect of 'demobilizing' them.[17]

Subsequent to the establishment of district councils, a number of other reforms were instituted with the goal of replacing customary authority with democratic institutions. In 1981, the Customary Law and Primary Courts Act replaced chiefs' and headmen's courts with elected presiding officers; in 1982, the Communal Lands Act gave district councils authority over land allocation, thus displacing the Tribal Land Authorities. Proposals for decentralisation below the level of district councils were mooted in 1982, but it was not until 1984 that a Prime Minister's Directive created village and ward development committees, known as vidcos and wadcos. These new 'democratic institutions of popular participation' were, in the populist language of the time, to promote 'the advancement of development objectives set by Government, the Community and the People. They would ensure that opportunities are created for greater participation by the mass of the people in decision-making processes which lead to the setting of development objectives.'[18] The directive also created district and provincial development committees, comprised of civil servants and chaired by administrators, and the office of Provincial Governor, a particularly powerful political appointee.[19] A final initiative sought to redress the division between white and black rural government. The Rural District Councils Act of 1988 provided for the amalgamation of the new district councils with rural councils, the local authorities representing formerly European farming areas.

This was to be a modern, unified state, linked from village to national level, in which citizens participated in democratic, non-racist channels of planning and policy-making. Communities were redefined and identified with the nation and state, not the customary groupings of Rhodesian rule. Vidcos bore the strongest stamp of bureaucratic origin: they were based on the arbitrary unit of 100 households, a unit that did not necessarily share resources, interests, or a common identity. They were intended to create an entirely new basis for rural authority. This reification of citizenship contained anomalies, however, in terms of both race and custom. Even with the long delayed implementation of the Rural District Councils Act, farm workers on formerly 'white' farms remained disenfranchised, beyond the borders of the nation.[20] The extent to which the Act would redistribute resources from 'white' to 'black' local government, and thus mark a real alteration of racial inequalities, was also questionable.[21] Moreover, within African rural areas, the displacement of customary authority was decidedly ambiguous. Pronouncements at district level were contradictory, and the central government instituted or perpetuated a number of measures that retained chiefs' status, if not, initially, their late-colonial powers.

The continued status granted chieftaincy was significant, though it has been underplayed due to the tendency to dismiss chiefs as discredited collaborators and to focus on the 'modernising' aspects of state-building.[22] In the first chaotic year of independence, before new legislation had been enacted, a key source of support for chiefs and headmen lay in the former officials of the Ministry of Internal Affairs. They responded to the idea of excluding chiefs from their previous roles with horror, envisioning 'anarchy' or worse.[23] In the end, the new Ministry of Local Government, inheritor of the Internal Affairs' mantle, required that chiefs sit as ex-officio members of the new councils, even where their presence was opposed by rural party leaders.[24] Chiefs' and headmen's salaries were maintained, thus leaving them better off than either elected councillors, who received a fraction of the chiefs' salary, or party and vidco leaders who received no remuneration. A 1982 handbook designed to explain the District Councils Act to civil servants employed a familiar dichotomy between 'traditional' and 'modern' institutions, much as Roger Howman had done: the Act was to 'marry traditional methods of administration [i.e. chieftaincy] ... to a modern system of local government'.[25]

Prominent nationalists and senior officials defended the recognition given to chiefs under the mutable rubric of reconciliation and through an appeal for the preservation of culture and custom. Minister of Local Government Eddison Zvogbo argued: 'We felt, in the end, that we could not do away with our traditions. If we had done so we would have looked like people who do not know where they come from. We would have lost our tradition and dignity if we threw that away. We therefore agreed that chieftainship was part and parcel of our culture.'[26] This rationale had roots in cultural nationalism, but the ways in which the new government sought to 'preserve and conserve' culture drew heavily on Rhodesian precedent. Echoing the practices of Rhodesian Front politicians, Prime Minister Mugabe held a series of 'indabas' with chiefs in 1980. At another 'indaba' just before the 1985 elections, Mugabe promised chiefs the return of control over courts, thus undermining one of the democratic reforms of the independence era.[27] The Ministry of Local Government acted to protect 'tradition and dignity' by perpetuating the use of static rules of customary succession in making appointments. The 'interference' of local party committees, which sought to introduce nationalist criteria to the appointment process, was explicitly rejected: custom was the province of an impartial and expert state.[28] New legislation was ambiguous, even in the realm of land tenure. Thus, 'where appropriate', district councils were instructed to 'have regard to customary law relating to the allocation, occupation and the use of land'.[29]

Other aspects of Rhodesian community development also persisted. As in the 1960s, district councils' 'driving force' was to be the 'felt needs of the people', but this did not mean that 'the people' knew what was best for them:

> Much of the initiative and drive will be found in the executive [the district admini-strator and other civil servants] who themselves are often stimulated by the ideas promoted by Central Government Officials. For a long time to come District Administrators will have to lend their authority and prestige to bolster the efforts of councils and to give them confidence in their powers. However, it is important that communities should feel that the results achieved are due to their own efforts and have not merely been imposed from above.

Civil servants were warned that, while councils were allowed to reach decisions contrary to their advice, 'this approach must not be taken too far.'[30] Zanu(PF)

Ministers regularly employed the 'felt needs' vocabulary and stressed the role of councils as implementers of centrally formulated policies, at times seeking to use control over service delivery as a threat to induce cooperation.[31] The District Councils Act also retained some of the conveniences of the Rhodesian era, such as the right of the Minister to assign any or all powers of the council to a civil servant. In practice, District Administrators (DAs), who sat as chief executive officers on councils, exercised great sway and remained answerable to the Ministry of Local Government, not elected authorities.[32]

The conditions that had made the rhetoric of 'democracy' and 'felt needs' so empty under Rhodesian community development were also perpetuated in other respects. Councils and vidcos were heavily dependent on centrally generated and controlled resources, a weakness that reflected the failure to expand councils' impoverished resource base or to allow local control over central government resources. The small gains in locally generated revenues in the 1980s were largely a result of the government's attempts to pass down costs, rather than of increased independence.[33] The lack of control over resources was reproduced in the lack of control over planning. Theoretically, vidcos submitted plans to wadcos which were then passed on not to the elected district council, but to the civil servant-run district development committee. Ministry representatives on the development committees were supposed to incorporate ward plans into a district plan which would then be 'approved' by the council. In practice, vidcos rarely came up with more than lists of 'needs', wadcos hardly functioned, and councils were not in a position to challenge plans produced by officials. In the controversial field of land use, 'both the supervising agency and the epistemes of authority lay outside the community', as William Munro writes.[34] Vidcos were charged with implementing land-use plans produced by experts. The same applied to by-laws regulating the use of natural resources.[35] As in earlier decades, local authorities were free to articulate 'felt needs', but they could not redress them. Ministries regarded local authorities primarily as implementing agencies, while planning and policy formulation remained the realm of 'experts' who all too often reproduced interventions that had long been at the heart of rural resistance.

The failure to decentralise power to elected local authorities was paralleled by failures to achieve the lesser goals of devolution within ministries and the coordination of ministry activities through development planning. Despite the creation of the Ministry of Economic Planning and Development, and the rhetorical emphasis on national planning to direct the transition to socialism, planning capabilities remained weak. In practice, the pre-independence Ministry of Finance continued to dominate the allocation of resources, and hence the paths which policy followed. As Colin Stoneman writes, 'plans amounted to not much more than elaborations of how the paths to the desired ends would look if they occurred, but offered little help in *making* them occur'.[36] In recognition of the Ministry of Finance's key role, it absorbed the Ministry of Economic Planning and Development in 1985.

Below the national level, the Ministry of Local Government dominated development planning, devoting considerable resources to producing provincial and district plans. These were, however, almost totally ignored and had no legal authority.[37] The obstacles to decentralised planning were deeply resented. One Provincial Administrator explained, 'If you are going to plan and plans are going to be workable you also need to control the budget. Power still remains in Harare and they still think that money cannot be decentralized.' Another underlined the point: 'The system of vidco to [Provincial Administrator] ... was brought from another country but they forgot to bring the authority. They just brought the structures in a bag. There is no use talking of decentralized structures when decision-making staff is at head office.... We are just carrying out directives.' Such views were strongly backed by DAs. [38] To add insult to injury, the Ministry of Finance did not allocate funds for the physical production of plans: administrators had to divert funds allocated to other tasks.

In practice, the competition and conflict among centralised and autonomous ministries and departments that had characterised the Rhodesian era continued in 1980s Zimbabwe. Policies of decentralisation simply disguised other goals, notably easing the implementation of centrally formulated policies and control. But this was a problematic way to remake the state, as was abundantly clear in the field of agrarian reform where the politics of land were central.

Governing the Land

In the early 1980s, the government sought to redress the discriminatory legacy of Rhodesian agrarian policy. It vastly expanded services in the former TTLs, repealed discriminatory legislation, and initiated an ambitious programme of land redistribution. These measures certainly responded to popular demands, but they allowed for little in the way of popular participation, particularly when it came to land. Only the state was deemed capable of ensuring that redistribution occurred in a rational and productive manner. As in the 1950s, it staked a moral claim to ensuring that the nation's resources were used 'properly', and thus assumed the authority to act as the arbiter of land rights, which fitted neatly with the nationalist construction of land as inalienable, held in trust by the state.[39]

Immediately after independence, economists, technical officials, and politicians, as well as donors such as the British government, agreed on the need for a quick redistribution of resources, financed through public and donor funds. At the Zimbabwe Conference on Reconstruction and Development, a forum at which the government sought to secure donor support, the political importance of land redistribution was stressed above all else. Minister of Lands Sydney Sekeramayi argued that 'a failure on the part of Government to meet these expectations [for land] could well degenerate into a cancer relentlessly eating away the promising foundation upon which all of us ... are trying to build a genuinely democratic, non-racial and egalitarian society in Zimbabwe'. The resettlement programme was necessary to 'neutralize a looming crisis of expectation on the part of a land-hungry population.'[40] Land redistribution was cast as a political imperative, central to creating the stability required for economic growth: in the Minister's metaphor, the demand for land was a disease that needed to be 'neutralized'.

Recognising the political need for land redistribution did not, however, necessitate challenging the settler state's representation of black farmers as subsistence-oriented and inefficient, in contrast to their white counterparts. The distinction between the two sectors took on symbolic form in the renaming of TTLs as 'communal areas' and of European land as 'commercial areas'. Here, as Michael Drinkwater argues, the legacy of technical development weighed heavily.[41] The unquestioned efficacy of 'expert' knowledge and technical solutions constituted a running theme in post-independence agrarian policy. Resistance to technical prescription in the past was explained in terms of its coercive implementation, rather than its inherent flaws, an analysis which put a nationalist spin on the Rhodesian state's own interpretation of resistance as 'cultural'. Thus the answer to 'bad land distribution, poor soils, poor farming methods and overpopulation' was to be found in a combination of resettlement and the inculcation of 'good farming methods'.[42] 'Good farming methods' would be identified through 'considerable investigation, research and planning, through the employment of special expertise and skills'.[43] The concession to participation consisted in a recognition that plans would need to be 'adequately sold to the people'.[44] Popular participation was reduced to an exercise in convincing people that the experts knew best; a means of gaining compliance.

The Riddell and Chavanduka Commissions set the tone for the agrarian reform debate in the early 1980s.[45] They recognised a pervasive demand for land, and endorsed land redistribution, but also went on to make proposals that echoed the Native Land Husbandry Act (NLHA), slating in particular the dangers of 'communal' tenure and labour migration. The Riddell Commission recommended consolidating arable land into blocks, fencing grazing areas, registering land with a title, and abolishing labour migration, thus creating permanent farmer and worker populations.[46] The Chavanduka Commission put the blame for low productivity on the shoulders of 'traditional' tenure, poor farming practices and labour migration.[47] In 1985 the Ministry of Lands revealed its *Communal Lands Development Plan*, a document which drew heavily on the Chavanduka Report. The plan relied on 1970s research, ignoring the increased communal area contribution to marketed crops in the post-independence years. It condemned communal tenure once again, seeing a solution in the creation of surveyed and planned 'economic units', consolidated villages, and state control over tenure through a leasehold system that would exclude those who were not full-time farmers.[48]

In these documents, customary leaders were cast as the conservative guard of an unproductive system, and came in for especially vehement attack. The Ministry of Lands saw the new legislation on land and courts as key in undermining them: 'If successful, the measures will leave the traditional, conservative leaders with little more than spiritual functions ... and will allow substantive innovation'.[49] This, of course, contradicted the continued status accorded chiefs by the Ministry of Local Government and politicians. The image of communal tenure as static and opposed to the market was also a highly misleading reading of history. The label 'communal' disguised a wide range of practices and claims to land in which individual rights sat alongside social obligations, and in which the regulation of access to land was far from the sole prerogative of 'traditional' leaders operating according to customary rules. As Pius Nyambara writes, communal tenure was characterised by 'multiple, overlapping and sometimes internally inconsistent sets of rights and means of access and control', all of which were subject to contestation.[50] Nonetheless, as the officials behind the NLHA had been forced to admit, such tenure was a great deal more secure than tenure dependent on the state. What 'communal' implied in the rhetoric of the Ministry of Lands was a space beyond state control. Characterising this space as customary and backward, and so inimical to productive and rational land use, obliged the state to intervene.

Official criticism of labour migration also echoed the blind spots of the NLHA era. It ignored the role that wages played in successful agricultural production and that land played in providing a safety net for urban workers.[51] And, as with the NLHA, officials were overly optimistic regarding the capacity of the formal sector to employ those excluded from land. The 'numbers game' failed to add up.[52] The Riddell Commission, for example, calculated that the communal areas could sustain 325,000 of their 780,000 families. Of the 'excess' of 455,000 families, 235,000 were believed to be headed by migrant workers. These, it was assumed, would voluntarily move to the cities with the (again assumed) introduction of higher wages, social security and better housing. Resettlement would absorb an additional 35,000 families. Much as in the fateful calculations of the NLHA, the remaining 185,000 'excess' families had only the slim hope (bolstered by the fast-growing economy of the early 1980s, much as a similar hope had been supported after World War II) of a sustained boom in the industrial sector. No such boom occurred, or was even envisioned in national development plans.

The official characterisation of rural land use and rural authority thus justified extensive state control in the mould of high modernism, a project nowhere more apparent than in the newly created arena of resettlement.

Resettling the Land

The resettlement policy vividly illustrated the contradictory forces with which the Zimbabwean state and polity grappled. Nationalism had promised a return of the land, and it had promised it on people's own terms. The resettlement policy offered redistribution, but cast the land not as the historical right of a dispossessed people, but as productive space in need of close state regulation. Within resettlement schemes, planners' imaginations had freer rein than anywhere else, and they sought to constitute a fundamentally new society: rational, disciplined and productive.

In the early 1980s, resettlement targets and criteria fluctuated widely. In 1980, the target was set at 18,000 families. In 1981, the number was tripled to 54,000, and in 1982 was tripled again, to 162,000 families. In 1985, the *Five Year Plan* set a target of 15,000 families per year over the 1986–1990 plan period. Initially, resettlement criteria focused on need, giving priority to the landless, unemployed and refugees. In 1982, Master Farmers, usually better-off communal area farmers with good farming certificates issued by the agricultural extension service, were included, a focus on wealthier farmers that was repeatedly reiterated in later years.[53] An aspect of resettlement that fluctuated very little was the imperative of productivity, and the commitment to state regulation as the means of achieving it. From the outset, the ministries concerned with resettlement stressed that the measure of the programme's success lay in its ability to produce marketed surpluses, an ability that they firmly believed did not exist within the 'subsistence-oriented' communal areas. Land had to be redistributed on a 'planned and organized basis': 'the objective of land redistribution is not merely to give land to the landless masses, but to create an agricultural community on land which will no longer be just subsistence but commercial in orientation.'[54]

Resettlement schemes were envisaged as self-contained islands of modernisation. In effect, settlers were expected to sever all social and cultural ties with their past lives in order to achieve new levels of productivity under the tutelage of the state. As a 1983 Department of Rural Development (DERUDE) report put it:

> The resettlement process discourages spontaneity in settlements and fights against attempts at reversion back to traditional methods of agriculture.... [Thus] resettlement can never be about extending the boundaries of existing communal areas ... creating new power bases for the restoration of traditional authorities, such as chiefs, headmen etc.[55]

A corollary to this was that historical claims to restitution could not be recognised. As Manicaland's Provincial Administrator explained: 'People wanted specific pieces of land because their forefathers lived there. But everyone used to live somewhere.... We are bitter but we can't reverse.... You must follow the procedures of the resettlement programme. You must believe that the government knows how to give land. Otherwise there would be chaos.'[56] A failure to acknowledge the state's expertise and authority could only bring disorder.

The battery of rules and conditions formulated to regulate production in resettlement schemes relied heavily on pre-independence plans, in part because of the inexperience of the newly created Ministry of Lands. Jeff Herbst quotes an official who graphically recalled conditions just after independence: 'When the Ministry was first established we had no files, no phones. Everything was new.... Everyone asked, "What are we supposed to do?" It took us six months just to learn the issues.'[57] Even after the Ministry had acquired files and phones, it remained reliant on the pre-independence Ministry of Agriculture for much of its technical expertise.[58] Despite the stated commitment to cooperatives, by far the most dominant resettlement model, Model A, closely followed the pattern of the NLHA and the resettlement plans produced by the Rhodesian Ministry of Agriculture.[59] Settlers were allocated individual five hectare fields, with provision for common grazing. Draconian conditions of tenure were to be enforced by DERUDE's resettlement officers. As Bill Kinsey writes,

> Settlers occupy land, plant crops and graze livestock on the basis of a series of permits. The permits are neither leases nor title deeds, convey no security, and appear open to political pressure. If the permit to reside is revoked, which it may be at the sole discretion of the minister, the holder is entitled to no compensation for any improvements made – far harsher treatment than that received by white farmers whose land is acquired for resettlement.[60]

Resettlement areas did not fall under the jurisdiction of district councils: like commercial farm workers, settlers had no local representation. Their economic dependence was in theory equally extreme. To be eligible for resettlement, settlers had to foreswear employment and any claim to communal area land; within schemes they relied on state marketing and service provision.

The extensive state controls on resettlement schemes proved a disincentive to potential settlers, many of whom chose to migrate to the frontier regions of the north or to cities, and encouraged the widespread abrogation of conditions.[61] A great deal of negotiation surrounded the enforcement of regulations: as in earlier periods, compliance with technical regulations often had less to do with their merit than with the power of the state. People also played on contradictions in policies, such as those between the status accorded chiefs and the rejection of chieftaincy-based claims to land, between the populist pronouncements of politicians regarding the 'lost lands' and attempts to exert control on the part of technical bureaucracies. As I explore below and in subsequent chapters, the state's high modernist pretensions constituted but one aspect of the process of state-making, and always relied on contradictory alliances in practice.

The resettlement programme quickly fell short of its plan targets. As Herbst argues, targets such as the famous figure of 162,000 families, were 'ideological state-ments' devoid of detailed plans and budgets.[62] Resettlement proceeded most rapidly in the first three years of independence. The 1981/82 and 1982/83 financial years accounted for over 70 per cent of all land purchases up to 1989. By 1985, 35,000 families had been settled on eleven per cent of formerly 'European' land, mostly in drier regions. By 1990, 52,000 families had been resettled on three million hectares or sixteen per cent of formerly white land.[63] The official explanation for failing to meet plan targets focused on the economic constraints of world recession and drought. As the 1980s progressed, Zimbabwe suffered from a growing balance of payments and debt crisis, inflation, and declining growth. Officials also cited the increasing scarcity and expense of land,[64] as well as the shortages of trained staff and difficulties in coordinating the many ministries, departments and NGOs involved in the programme.[65] All these factors were important, but they did not fully explain the slowdown in resettlement: the recession-inspired cuts in resettlement were far deeper than those in other redistributive programmes; while land did become scarce, the government failed to purchase much of the land that was on offer, even when it met its criteria; and finally, staff shortages and coordination problems were in part self-imposed constraints reflecting the commitment to extensive state control.[66]

The resettlement slowdown had more complex roots. As Sam Moyo and Tor Skalnes note, the debate over land redistribution rapidly shifted from a focus on the 'normative and political' to 'arguments in terms of a broader economic signifi-cance'.[67] Reports by the World Bank, Whitsun Foundation and others fed a growing consensus among policy-makers that land redistribution could not solve rural Zimbabwe's problems. Officials pointed out that resettlement would not keep up with communal area population growth even if it met plan targets. For resettlement to have any significant impact, it would need to use the majority of previously European land, an idea considered impractical given the economic role of commer-cial farm production. Thus, the argument went, agrarian policies should focus on improvements within the communal areas, not land redistribution.[68]

The debates over the efficiency of commercial and communal land use which surrounded these arguments relied on sketchy data and controversial assumptions. In the late 1980s, the commercial sector accounted for roughly 80 per cent of marketed agricultural production and the bulk of agricultural exports which were responsible for 35–40 per cent of foreign exchange earnings. It was a key supplier to and buyer from the manufacturing sector.[69] In large measure, the 'indispensability' of the commercial farm sector was taken for granted, while debate focused narrowly on gauging the extent to which commercial land was underused. Numerous calculations were made, from those of the 1982 *Transitional Plan* (4.2 million hectares unused, three million hectares underused), to a 1991 World Bank report which concluded that at least three million hectares in the high potential regions alone were underused. As the report commented, 'This 3.0 million hectares is equal to the total amount of land resettled during the 1980s.'[70] All of these estimates relied, in part, on the problematic assumption that using better rainfall regions for cattle grazing constituted underuse. This 'underused' land usually formed only part of a farm that would otherwise be considered productive, making acquisition difficult, and cattle production in higher rainfall areas was encouraged by the prolonged droughts of the 1980s as well as Zimbabwe's entrance into the European Community beef market.[71] Beef production in higher rainfall regions could be defended as a foreign exchange earner, much as the increasingly extensive use of lowveld land for wildlife farming was. Whether or not land was 'underused' depended on the government's wider economic strategy, notably the extent to which export promotion-led growth could justify the land extensive and capital intensive variants of commercial farm production.

The debate over communal area productivity focused on two contradictory features, both of which were used to argue against further resettlement – the unreliability of production in drought years, and post-independence increases in marketed production. The fear that further resettlement would lead to a loss in agricultural production received a powerful boost from the dramatic drop in communal area production during the early 1980s drought. The drought cost the government dearly in food relief and public works. In response, policy focused on boosting communal area productivity through a 'green revolution' package of inputs and credit.[72] The strategy seemed to be vindicated by the bumper crop of the post-drought 1984/85 year: the communal area share of marketed maize jumped from eight to 38 per cent and of cotton from seven to 42 per cent between 1980/81 and 1984/85. Cliffe, writing in 1986, commented: 'There is a current of thought that feels resettlement is not worth pursuing, and that [Communal Land] farmers will go on responding, as in 1984/85, to new economic opportunities now that they have inputs, credit and access to markets.'[73] The increases in production were cast as an unqualified success, but in fact they were severely limited, both geographically and socially. Production in drier areas remained precarious; state relief was necessary even in average years and took on an institutionalised form.[74] Most estimates put the percentage of farmers to benefit from increased marketing at 15–20 per cent, largely in the better-watered regions, and even these faced serious problems of debt owing to their use of credit and input packages. It was not at all clear that communal area 'successes' were sustainable.[75]

The unresolved nature of these debates was partly owed to wider political processes. The government did not wish to risk the ire of international financial institutions and donors by acquiring land outside the 'spirit' of Lancaster House. It was also, many argued, influenced by the Commercial Farmers' Union (CFU), which represents the commercial sector, and by the accumulation of land on the part of the ruling elite. The CFU constantly stressed that land acquisition outside the 'willing buyer, willing seller' format would undermine its 'confidence'. The government refrained from foreclosing on commercial farmers who became heavily indebted to the parastatal Agricultural Finance Corporation as a result of the mid-1980s drought, while the 1985 Land Acquisition Act, which was intended to aid in the acquisition of land for resettlement, was scarcely used.[76] Robin Palmer argues that the Act in fact aided in the accumulation of land by the black elite: farms offered to the government were refused and went onto the private market, eventually ending up in the hands of 'senior members of the government and the new black ruling elite.'[77] Moyo estimated in 1986 that 300 black farmers had joined the commercial sector.[78]

The declining pace of resettlement and the failure to meet official targets rightly sparked debate, but they also made it all too easy to lose sight of the fact that Zimbabwe's resettlement programme was vast, the biggest of its kind in sub-Saharan Africa. The significant scale of resettlement needs also to be understood. Explanations have focused on the combination of land abandoned during the war, and the movement onto such land by 'squatters'. Land acquisition in the early 1980s was dominated by purchases of abandoned and heavily occupied land. Dan Weiner estimated that 'squatters' comprised half of all those resettled by 1989.[79] Most commentators have argued that a crucial factor in the slowing of resettlement was the state's increased control over, and a reduction in, squatting, alongside falling demand for land. Michael Bratton suggested that people in communal areas saw the lack of access to agricultural services as a constraint on a par with land scarcity, and that they placed a great premium on access to education. Thus the government could shift its focus from resettlement to services without risking political support.[80] Herbst stressed the lack of an organised lobby for resettlement, noting that the National Farmers' Association, which in theory represented communal area farmers, focused its demands on service provision, not resettlement.[81]

These analyses are problematic for a number of reasons. Bratton makes his distinction between pressure for land redistribution and for services on the basis of a static snapshot of communal area demands. He does not explore people's percep-tion of future needs – for their children, for example – or how priorities changed from year to year in response to drought or unemployment. Herbst limits his consid-eration of pressure for land redistribution to squatters and the National Farmers' Association. He leaves out actors such as chiefs, councils and local party leaders, all of whom were significant both in negotiations for land and in constituting the state and its authority over the land. Moreover, the implication that illegal land occupa-tions had ceased to be significant is misleading: in the late 1980s, Mashonaland West and Manicaland Provinces both recorded squatter populations of over 35,000 people. Squatters continued to dominate available resettlement land, while encroachment remained an important tactic in the battle for control over resources. The ongoing struggles over land constituted a real threat to both the state's authority and the ruling party's legitimacy, thus ensuring that the question of land distribution did not leave the political agenda, as I explore in subsequent chapters.

Land and State-making in the Communal Areas

In the second half of the 1980s, extensive state intervention in the communal areas, a measure effectively de-linked from land redistribution, sat firmly on ministerial agendas. Debates focused on how to build authority over the land so as to enforce the package of spatial reorganisation and land use that was to deliver 'development'. The content of the policy went largely unquestioned, despite the lack of any convincing evidence that it was capable of addressing the economic and social difficulties of the communal areas.[82]

The mid-1980s marked a watershed for the idea of agrarian reform. The Chavanduka Report was released to the public in late 1984, and in 1985 the Ministry of Lands revealed its *Communal Lands Development Plan*. The ideas expressed in these documents were incorporated into the *First Five-Year Plan* in which agrarian reform came to mean two things: 'translocation resettlement', meaning what had previously been called simply resettlement, and 'internal resettlement', meaning reorganisation within the communal areas. In communal areas, 20,000 families were to be moved into 'consolidated villages' annually, arable land was to be planned in blocks and rotational grazing schemes and irrigation were to be introduced. The plan stated that 'the reorganization of settlement patterns in the Communal Areas will become part and parcel of the resettlement programme' but, in practice, 'internal' and 'external' resettlement were de-linked.[83] The disengagement of the questions of land access and land use was, as in the Rhodesian era, a pre-eminently political step that was cloaked in technical garb.

The separation of internal and external resettlement was reinforced by a reshuffle of the ministries concerned with agrarian reform, also in 1985. The Ministry of Lands, Resettlement and Rural Development, a new ministry created to facilitate resettlement, was divided between the long established Ministries of Local Government and Agriculture. DERUDE, which administered resettlement areas, was transferred to the Ministry of Local Government while other branches went to the Ministry of Agriculture, now renamed the Ministry of Lands, Agriculture and Rural Resettlement. Responsibility for agrarian policy was thus split between two powerful pre-independence ministries. The (post-1985) Ministry of Lands was responsible for land acquisition and the majority of technical agricultural planning and extension while the Ministry of Local Government was responsible for physical planning, aspects of infrastructural development, and administration.

In this somewhat chaotic context, one aspect of 'internal' resettlement gained prominence. The *First Five-Year Plan* allocated funding for the Ministry of Public Construction to launch a rural housing programme.[84] The 'consolidated village', in which the improved houses were to be built, was the lowest rung in a seven-tier settlement hierarchy which drew on earlier traditions of physical planning. As Gasper writes,

The emphasis given to the programme reflects the relative ease with which it can present *visible*

118

results of 'development' to rural areas.... Physical planning was one tool of settler social engineering. Its typical concern with a clear cut settlement hierarchy may also match the social
vision of some of the new leaders, of a single and well-defined social tree – orderly, controlled,
simple (and, if necessary, simplified).[85]

The Minister of Lands maintained that economic development and state-building
would follow automatically from spatial reorganisation: villagisation would serve as
the basis for 'development committees' which would in turn ensure 'the promotion
of both land and labour productivity in the peasant sector'.[86]

Villagisation went ahead following a 1986 directive requiring a pilot village in each
district. The Deputy Minister of Public Construction declared: 'My Ministry is
resolved to phase out haphazard and scatter-based settlement pattern[s] prevailing
throughout the country and establish properly planned villages.'[87] Promises of, or
more accurately, threats to withhold, water, electricity and housing loans were used
to 'encourage' people to move into the planned villages.[88] The Department of
Physical Planning was asked to provide village layouts. Councils and DAs were told
to identify village sites, and did so with a minimum of consultation.[89] The
Department of Physical Planning prepared the only kind of layout it was trained to
do, as the Deputy Director explained: 'Our tradition was town plans because we said
we are not worried about the rural housing development.... We tried here and there
to accommodate a kraal but basically the concept was a town plan.'[90] The sites chosen
were generally far from established villages. People were expected to move without
compensation and then take out a loan, which would leave them in debt for years, to
cover the costs of housing construction.

Not surprisingly, the pilot villages were greeted with hostility. Objections made at
the District Council Association Congress indicated the extent of misgivings. To
applause from the house, one council chairman raised the question of compensation:
'He asked the Minister to look closely into the issues as he was finding it difficult to
understand for example how someone with a house worth around ten thousand
dollars, (a life investment) would agree to leave such [a] house and ressettle [sic] at
the proposed village site.' Nor were councillors willing to accept the *de facto* separation of land redistribution and villagisation: the Congress resolved, 'that in order for
effective villagisation/land reform to take place, the resettlement programme has to
be speeded up. This was because in some areas there was still not enough land to
move people to'.[91]

In practice, villagisation proceeded slowly. The Deputy Minister of Public
Construction complained that councils had failed to 'mobilize and educate the
people on the rural housing programme, as well as make them understand and accept
the concept of planned villages'.[92] In some areas, coercion accompanied the
programme.[93] Non-cooperation from other ministries was also blamed. The technical planning departments were slow to produce plans, and the Ministry of Local
Government refused to guarantee housing loans on the grounds that a high default
rate would leave councils deeply in debt. Nor did the promised infrastructure mate-
rialise: the Ministry of Water objected to reticulated water because its policy was to
develop boreholes; the Zimbabwe Electricity Supply Authority, a parastatal, was
only prepared to put in electricity on a cost-recovery basis, the funds for which were

unavailable. The model villages remained almost wholly unoccupied in late 1988, and the Department of Physical Planning subsequently refused to plan new villages.[94] Underlying the non-cooperation of some departments were different views regarding rural development. Most significantly, both DERUDE and the Department of Agricultural and Technical Extension Services (Agritex) saw focusing on housing in advance of formulating a broader agrarian reform programme as a case of putting the cart before the horse.[95]

In the end, villagisation survived as a component of the agrarian reform policies of the Ministries of Local Government and Lands. These policies stressed changes in production and tenure, seeing villagisation as a secondary goal. In the late 1980s, DERUDE tried to take the lead in agrarian reform, in part so as to guarantee the Department a continuing role in the context of declining resettlement.[96] DERUDE took up Lionel Cliffe's 1986 report on agrarian reform, organising two inter-departmental conferences: the Nyanga Symposium in 1987, and the Harare Agrarian Reform Seminar in 1988.[97] The Nyanga Symposium's main conclusions were loosely based on Cliffe's recommendations but with a bias toward regulation. Basically, DERUDE sought to extend resettlement scheme controls into communal areas: land reorganisation was 'aimed at emulating the planned land-use patterns within the resettlement areas in the communal areas [which are] to be replanned and assisted by Government to develop for purposes of optimising production from the land.'[98] Under this system, 'land tenure shall be guaranteed within communal and resettlement areas on an individual permit basis. These permits shall guarantee succession, prevention of sub-division, abidance by environmental regulations and acceptable land husbandry practices.' Those who did not farm their land holdings would have their rights withdrawn, while those in employment would be given last priority in land access.[99]

These steps implied extensive state intervention in the name of productivity. Echoing the Godlonton Commission of 1944, DERUDE called for legislation that would 'emphasise that it is the duty of every cultivator, owner or occupier of any land to cultivate such crops or rear such breeds of livestock as are best suited for the land ... according to certain specified standards with the objective of improving the productivity and monitoring efficient standards of production as to both the quality and quantity of the produce'.[100] The technical side of the programme fell to Agritex, which was responsible for producing land use plans. These relied on a familiar combination of spatial reorganisation and rigid carrying capacities:

> blocks for residence, arable, grazing and other are identified and isolated in land use plans. Land availability in the cropping area will determine the number of users and should also determine the siting and size of residential area.... [Land use plans] will determine the location and extent of grazing which will determine carrying capacities and stocking rates per village.

In short, the land use plan 'must be the starting point in the reorganisation process, with residential and grazing needs merely falling in place subsequently.'[101]

Few officials questioned the merits of reorganisation, but many worried over the state's capacity to implement such measures. DERUDE's approach was by far the most extreme, reflecting its experience of administering resettlement areas. The director expounded on the benefits of the resettlement permit system, contrasting it to the problems the department had encountered elsewhere:

> we have been having problems because in communal lands people have got rights which don't derive from government legislation. They have always occupied that land, it is theirs, it is not state land. They say they have got traditional rights to it and some stubborn communities will say, 'No we don't want anyone to come and dictate to us how we will live. We will live how we have always lived and that is it.'

From the director's point of view, rights to land that were not derived from the state were simply obstructive. Only the state had the right to take decisions about land access and use: 'Government has the resources and the people take a back seat. We tell people what we are doing and they tell us their fears.'[102]

DERUDE's authoritarian views were not uniformly popular among those departments that (unlike DERUDE) had extensive experience of the communal areas. One DA told me that administrators' endorsement of DERUDE's plans had been 'rammed down our throats'. Nor was Agritex convinced. Agritex was crucial in all this due to its extensive field staff and technical expertise. The department was aware that implementing the proposed measures would be no easy task: the state had first to create the capacity to intervene. The Nyanga Symposium had recommended that land allocation and other powers should be devolved from councils to vidcos, and that vidcos should be strengthened with legal powers enabling them to enforce penalties for failures to farm productively or follow conservation rules. They also needed to be redefined. Agritex argued that the effort to create new communities, and authority over them, through the arbitrarily defined vidcos was beyond the capacity of the state. Thus, in a reversal of the earlier hostility to customary authority in the planning departments, and sounding remarkably like the community development ideologues of the early 1960s, the symposium recommended that 'VIDCOs should be re-constituted to include whole village head units (sabhuku areas) so as to avoid fragmenting communities and thus make these units identifiable communities occupying a given geographic space, with defined boundaries.' In addition, 'to resolve the potential conflict between the traditional local leadership and … VIDCOs and WADCOs, the sabhuku and headman should be incorporated into these institutions as ex-officio members as is the case with chiefs at the District Council level'.[103]

Agritex officials had a host of additional worries. They had misgivings about enforcing technical calculations of carrying capacity, pointing out that there was simply not enough land in the communal areas: 'In reality, in terms of land area, we can't depopulate by that kind of margin.'[104] They raised further questions related to struggles over resources, turf and credibility, complaining about the lack of support from other departments, as well as their own shortages of both staff and resources. The immense task of producing land use plans had forced field staff to abandon, or at least marginalise, their duties in extension, much as had been the case during the NLHA's implementation. Moreover, because Agritex was most closely associated with the land use plan, it felt it suffered a disproportionate loss of credibility when plans did not receive the promised support.[105] Its critical views notwithstanding, Agritex at the national level retreated into the safety of calling itself simply a 'technical adviser'. The department's chief planning officer commented, 'we are the extension service so we feature at implementation but we are not the makers of policy'. He realised the importance of Agritex's contribution – 'the base situation which the land use plan shows is the basis for the whole debate on agrarian reform' – but maintained, 'we act only as consultants in the debate.'[106]

By the end of the 1980s, the agrarian reform debate within the central state focused on the methods of implementing a policy that closely paralleled the high modernism of the NLHA. Though land redistribution was ritually endorsed in all policy documents, it was not coordinated with interventions within communal areas. The ironies of such a policy were great: resistance to the NLHA and the kind of state it implied, alongside demands for land, had constituted a key force behind rural nationalism. There were, however, political and administrative imperatives which fed other tendencies, and which also drew on Rhodesian legacies. From the outset, official attitudes to chiefs, particularly within the Ministry of Local Government, had reflected continuities with past practices. Agritex's attempts to incorporate 'traditional' leaders into the 'modern' institutions that were to constitute authority over the land paralleled the roles that chiefs, headmen and village heads had performed under the NLHA, and which they had been called on to carry out much more explicitly under community development. The contradictory forces that shaped policy regarding customary authority and agrarian reform were symbolised in a concession intended to bolster the political allegiance of chiefs in 1990: just prior to national elections, Mugabe promised chiefs involvement in the selection of people for resettlement, a concession that placed 'customary' prerogatives in the midst of a programme administered by the most uncompromisingly technocratic of departments, DERUDE.[107]

Conclusion

The challenges of state-making in independent Zimbabwe centred on the question of exerting authority over the land, of who should use it and how. Some writers have echoed James Scott in depicting the state as a modernising intruder. Thus Drinkwater identified continuities in the 'purposive rationality' of bureaucracies that remained unable to 'understand' African farmers and intent on defining land use and access in technical terms. He noted in particular the threat that technical experts saw in the 'traditional land tenure system' and in customary leaders.[108] Munro likewise stressed the state's attempts to 'reorient the political identities of rural communities away from local and traditional forms of authority that challenge the state'.[109] These analyses highlighted the practices of some ministries and the ways in which customary and modern were used to constitute one another, but they underplayed the uses of custom itself in state-making and neglected the vital role of nationalism in its varied forms as a means of claiming land and power. Constituting authority over people and the land also needed to contend with the diverse and historically rooted ambitions and demands of rural people. In the following chapters I turn to the contrasting fortunes of Insiza and Chimanimani districts.

Notes

1 A different version of this chapter is published as Alexander, 1994.
2 Palmer, 1990, 164-7.
3 See Mandaza, 1986a; Stoneman, 1988b; Stoneman and Cliffe, 1989.
4 See Moore, 1991 and 1995; Chingono, 1992, 454.
5 Drinkwater, 1991, 93-8. And see Sylvester, 1986, 229; J. Moyo, 1991, 88.
6 Government of Zimbabwe [GoZ], 1981a.
7 Palmer, 1990, 167.
8 GoZ, 1982c, i.
9 See Bratton, 1981, 452; Murapa, 1984, 72; Herbst, 1990, 30-33.
10 See Roe, 1995.
11 Weitzer, 1984.
12 Ncube, 1991, 159-60.
13 Kriger, 2005, 11-12.
14 See Werbner, 1991, 158-62; Alexander, McGregor and Ranger, 2000.
15 On trade unions, see Wood, 1988, 289-90; Sachikonye, 1986. On Zanu(PF) village committees see below and subsequent chapters. On the government's response to 'traditional healers' and spirit mediums, see Ranger, 1991, 158-62. Kriger, 1995, describes the Zanu(PF) elite's attempts to exert control over the history and memory of war.
16 See Gasper, 1991, 23.
17 See subsequent chapters and Kriger, 1992, Chapter 6; Ranger, 1985b, 319; Lan, 1985, 220-1.
18 Ministry of Local Government and Town Planning, 1985, 1.
19 Ministry of Information, Posts and Telecommunications, n.d., 1. The pre-independence Provincial Authorities, constituted by chiefs and council chairmen, were replaced by Provincial Councils in 1985 under separate legislation.
20 See Rutherford, 2001b.
21 See Helmsing *et al.*, 1991; Roe, 1995.
22 Drinkwater, 1991, and Munro, 1995, stress the state's rejection of customary authority.
23 Chimanimani District Ministry of Local Government (MLG) Records, DC, Melsetter, to PC, Manicaland, 27 June 1980; PC, Manicaland, to Secretary for District Administration, Harare, 8 July 1980. Kriger, 1992, 228 and 228, fn 44, writes that by 1981, 25 of 58 white DCs remained in office. They were eventually absorbed by the District Development Fund.
24 See discussion in 'Memorandum. Implementation of the District Councils Act', Division of District Administration, Salisbury, 9 May 1980, and PER 4, Headman Saurombe, Chimanimani, J. D. White for Secretary of Local Government and Housing to Under Secretary, Development, Manicaland, 4 September 1981.
25 GoZ, 1982a.
26 *Herald*, 18 January 1982, quoted in Kriger, 1992, 234.
27 *Sunday Mail*, 27 July 1980; *Herald*, 3 October 1980; *Herald*, 17 March 1985.
28 Kriger, 1992, 233, notes a Local Government circular that warned political parties 'that Government will not, under any circumstances, permit elements of political parties to remove Chiefs from office, or to inter-fere in the normal selection procedures, for purely political reasons'. Circular Minute No. 1/1981, 'Statement by the Minister on Chieftainships', Division of District Administration, 9 January 1981.
29 Communal Land Act of 1982, quoted in Cheater, 1990, 201.
30 GoZ, 1982a.
31 See, for example, Association of District Councils, 1986, Annexes 4 and 11, which reproduce the speeches of the Minister of Local Government and the Minister of Community Development and Women's Affairs; Thomas, 1991, 23.
32 See Gasper, 1991, 18-23; Murapa, 1986, 53-8.
33 District councils were, nonetheless, significantly better funded than their African council predecessors. See Wekwete and Helmsing, 1986, and De Valk and Wekwete, n.d. [c.1985], 11.
34 Munro, 1995, 119.
35 Thomas, 1991, 15 and passim. Councils were to approve by-laws in consultation with a range of depart-ments. After their approval, vidcos were given 30 days to report any objections. Objectors had to be named.
36 Stoneman, 1988a, 53, emphasis in original. Also see Kadhani, 1986, 111, and GoZ, 1982c, 46.
37 See De Valk, 1986, 12.
38 Interviews, Provincial Administrator, Matabeleland South, Gwanda, 23 August 1988; Provincial

Administrator, Manicaland, Mutare, 24 November 1988; District Administrators, Chimanimani District, Chimanimani, 21 November 1988, and Insiza District, Filabusi, 26 September 1988.

39 See Nyambara, 2001b, 788-9; Cheater, 1990, 189.

40 Ministry of Economic Planning and Development [MEPD], 1981, 124. And see Minister of Economic Planning and Development Bernard Chidzero's comments, 49.

41 Drinkwater, 1991, Chapter 3.

42 Bernard Chidzero in MEPD, 1981, 52-3, and see GoZ, 1982c, 54, 64-71.

43 Sydney Sekeramayi in MEPD, 1981, 123.

44 Director of Devag, the pre-independence extension agency concerned with the TTLs, in MEPD, 1981, 138-9.

45 GoZ, 1981b and 1982b. For a prescient early critique of the Riddell Commission, see Williams, 1982, 114-20. Also see Drinkwater, 1991, 100-101, and Ranger, 1988, 15-16.

46 GoZ, 1981b, 147-9.

47 GoZ, 1982b, 9-13, 62-3 and see 29, 35.

48 Ministry of Lands, Resettlement and Rural Development [MLRRD], 1985, 121-4.

49 *Ibid.*, 20, and see 16-20.

50 Nyambara, 2001b, 772. Also see Cheater, 1990; O'Flaherty, 1998; Andersson, 1999; Scoones and Wilson, 1988, 41-4.

51 See, for example, Drinkwater, 1991, Chapter 5; Cousins, 1990, 6; Potts and Mutambirwa, 1990; Cousins, Weiner and Amin, 1992, 5-24.

52 See Bush and Cliffe, 1984, 84-5.

53 See Alexander, 1991, 605-6.

54 MEPD, 1981, 124, 132. And see GoZ, 1982c, 66.

55 Department of Rural Development, 1983, 1-2, quoted in Drinkwater, 1991, 100.

56 Interview, Provincial Administrator, Manicaland, Mutare, 24 November 1988.

57 Herbst, 1990, 71. Also see Weiner, 1988, 81-2; Riddell, 1979, 26-7.

58 See Gasper, 1990, 7.

59 There were three other models: Model B collective cooperatives; Model C collective 'core estates' with additional individual smallholdings; and Model D which involved adding paddocked ranchland to replanned communal areas.

60 Kinsey, 1983, 190.

61 Kinsey, 1983, 190; Drinkwater, 1991, 100; Gaidzwana, 1981; Gasper, 1990, 12.

62 Herbst, 1990, 45.

63 See Moyo and Skalnes, 1990, 3.

64 For figures, see Cliffe, 1986, 47.

65 Drinkwater, 1991, 85; GoZ, 1982c, 66.

66 See Bratton, 1987, 190; Palmer, 1990, 171.

67 Moyo and Skalnes, 1990, 4.

68 For commentary, see Cliffe, 1986, 56; Drinkwater, 1991, 86-8; Moyo, 1986, 171-81.

69 See Moyo and Skalnes, 1990, 5; Riddell, 1988, 76-9.

70 GoZ, 1982c, 65; World Bank, 1991, 45, and see 37-46. For other estimates, see Cliffe, 1986, 45-6, 125-7; Weiner, 1988, 74-9; Weiner *et al.*, 1985, 251-85; Moyo *et al.*, 1989; Moyo, 1986, 175.

71 Weiner, 1988, 76-7.

72 See Drinkwater, 1991, 88-9.

73 Cliffe, 1986, 67-8; Moyo, 1986, 181.

74 According to Gasper, 1990, 15, in an average year one million people participated in public works programmes. The Minister of Local Government commented in 1987 that 'Government has already adopted the Food-For-Work Programme as a permanent feature of rural development.' Department of Rural Development *et al.*, 1987, 81.

75 See Moyo, 1986, 166; Moyo and Skalnes, 1990, 8; Cliffe, 1986, 14-39; Weiner, 1988, 63-89; Cousins, 1990, 3-10; Jackson and Collier, 1988; Drinkwater, 1991, 89.

76 On these issues, see Stoneman, 1988a, 45-50; Palmer, 1990; Moyo and Skalnes, 1990, 10-11. The Land Acquisition Act gave the government the 'right of first refusal' on all land offered for sale as well as the power to nationalise unused land. Part of the Act's ineffectiveness was due to the fact that the decision to purchase a farm offered for sale had to be made within 30 days, too short a period for government to act.

77 Palmer, 1990, 170. Moyo and Skalnes, 1990, 12-13, imply corruption in the acquisition of land.

78 Moyo, 1986, 188; Palmer, 1990, 174-5.

79 See Weiner, 1989, 401-28.

80 Bratton, 1987.

81 Herbst, 1990, 57-9, 75-7.
82 Drinkwater, 1991, Chapter 7, makes this point forcefully.
83 GoZ, 1986, 28, and see 11-12, 27.
84 See GoZ, 1986, 33, and GoZ, 1988, 44.
85 Gasper, 1988, 435, emphasis in original.
86 Association of District Councils, 1986, Annexe 6, 3.
87 Quoted in Gasper, 1990, 16.
88 See, for example, Association of District Councils, 1986, Annexe 4, 4.
89 Interview, Provincial Planner, Department of Physical Planning, Matabeleland South, Bulawayo, 20 July 1988.
90 Interview, Harare, 6 September 1988.
91 Association of District Councils, 1986, 1, 4-5, 8.
92 *Ibid.*, Annexe 8, 2-3.
93 See Drinkwater, 1991, 140-50, and Gasper, 1990, 17.
94 Interview, Deputy Director in Charge of Regional Planning, Department of Physical Planning, Harare, 6 September 1988.
95 Interviews, Director, DERUDE, Harare, 5 September 1988; Assistant Director (Technical), Agritex, Harare, 21 September 1988.
96 Between 1986/7 and 1990/91, allocations under the heading 'Communal Area Reorganisation' became an increasingly important part of DERUDE's budget while allocations for resettlement stagnated. See GoZ, 1988, 15.
97 See Department of Rural Development *et al.*, 1987, and Department of Rural Development *et al.*, 1988. DERUDE also set up eight pilot reorganisation projects with UNDP funding. Interview, UNDP Technical Adviser, DERUDE, Harare, 22 March 1989
98 Department of Rural Development *et al.*, 1987, 84, and Interview, Director, DERUDE, Harare, 5 September 1988.
99 Department of Rural Development *et al.*, 1987, 28-9, 49-52.
100 *Ibid.*, 95.
101 Gonese, 1988, 3-4. Gonese was then the Assistant Director, DERUDE.
102 Interview, Harare, 5 September 1988. Also see Department of Rural Development *et al.*, 1988, 15.
103 Department of Rural Development *et al.*, 1987, 51-2, 28. And see Agritex, 1988.
104 Interview, Assistant Director (Technical), Agritex, Harare, 21 September 1988.
105 Agritex, 1988, 6-8.
106 Interview, Chief Planning Officer, Agritex, Harare, 6 April 1989. Also see the nuanced discussion of Agritex in Drinkwater, 1991, Chapter 7.
107 *Herald*, 27 March 1990.
108 Drinkwater, 1991, 98-105.
109 Munro, 1995, 108.

6

Political Conflict, Authority
& the Land in Insiza

The party committees that emerged from the liberation war constituted a vital source of authority in independent Zimbabwe, expanding the range of rural institutions and ideologies and the means of making claims on the state. In Insiza, however, nationalists were loyal to Zapu, not the ruling Zanu(PF), and this was to act as a formidable obstacle to remaking the state. The Zanu(PF) government's efforts to coerce allegiance undercut new development institutions and derailed debate over agrarian change. Technical officials explained resistance to their modernising plans as rooted not only in an unproductive set of customary social relations, but also in party allegiance. The failure to meet demands for land and the persecution of Zapu drove Insiza's communal area farmers to seek out illegal and informal means of gaining access to land, a process that produced deep division and at times violent conflict. The state was itself deeply divided by economic interests, party politics, and strategies of directing agrarian change. I begin with a consideration of land redistribution before turning to the communal areas.

Resettling the Land

Settler land alienation had been particularly severe in Insiza, placing land at the heart of the district's politics. Unsurprisingly, a return of the 'lost lands' was a central expectation at independence. But land acquisition in this region proceeded slowly: in early 1981, the Matabeleland provinces accounted for only ten per cent of land purchased for resettlement.[1] The slow start was in part due to the small number of abandoned farms: Insiza's white ranchers had weathered the war largely intact because Zapu's military strategy had not targeted them.[2] There was also little pressure to increase the speed and scope of resettlement from the large-scale 'squatter' occupations of commercial land that would play such an influential role in districts like Chimanimani. The role of cattle in agricultural production meant that it was additional grazing, not arable, land that communal area farmers perceived as their most pressing need. 'Squatters' were largely drawn from the ranks of farm and mine workers, and they monopolised the resettlement land that was available.[3]

The resettlement of unemployed workers was in line with official goals, but it clashed with the expectations of Zapu activists in the communal areas. They rejected official criteria in favour of claims to land based on histories of eviction, the claims of chieftaincies, and their need for grazing land. They were slow to respond to calls for participation in official schemes: in late 1981, only 2.7 per cent of 88,000 resettlement applications circulated in Matabeleland South had been returned. A Ministry of Lands official blamed councillors for hoarding the forms, chiefs who wanted to move with their followers, and the fact that, 'people did not agree that the resettlement scheme worked out by the Government would redress their problems, mainly in grazing'.[4] Zapu-dominated councils communicated this view repeatedly to officials.[5] In Insiza and elsewhere in the region there were numerous attempts to purchase neighbouring ranch land, indicating a desire to expand the resource base of communal areas outside state control.[6] Such initiatives mirrored attempts to purchase land in the 1960s, and received a similarly hostile response from officials, despite the removal of legal obstacles to black land purchase.

Initially, officials recognised the inappropriateness of resettlement models in this region, and sought to come up with alternatives.[7] But the space for negotiation rapidly disappeared as the fragile coalition between Zapu and Zanu(PF) broke down in 1981. Armed 'dissident' groups multiplied following clashes between the two guerrilla forces in Assembly Points and thereafter in response to the persecution of Zipra (Zimbabwe People's Revolutionary Army) guerrillas in the army and in their homes, as well as due to South African intervention. The 'discovery' of arms caches on Zapu-owned properties and elsewhere in February 1982 led to the dismissal of Zapu leader Joshua Nkomo and other Zapu ministers and the detention of Zipra leaders. As armed attacks increased, Zanu(PF) came to view any opposition in Matabeleland as tantamount to treason, and it responded with military force.[8] The escalating conflict was accompanied by severe drought. In mid-1982, officials reported that the lives of 120,000 people were threatened by drought and that they might need to feed as many as two million.[9] Cattle began to die in their thousands in 1982; by 1985, over a third of Insiza's cattle had died.[10]

Under these pressures, demands for land, driven by the desperate need for relief grazing, turned to threats; officials responded with accusations of subversion. On a tour of Matabeleland in 1982, Deputy Minister of Lands Mark Dube met stiff opposition to official resettlement plans. In Gwanda, 'one district councillor after the other rose to demand that resettlement priorities be reversed to give priority to grazing land'. An 'angry peasant' responded uncompromisingly to Dube's plea for help in protecting resettlement officers: 'The intimidation of the resettlement officers is not our responsibility until we get grazing for our cattle. Don't talk to us about policing this area. We will do so as soon as we have been given more land for grazing.' Dube blamed opposition on Zapu members who wanted to 'achieve their own political goals'.[11] Objections were interpreted not as genuine expressions of people's views and needs but as politically motivated sabotage.

By the end of 1982, many of the factors that would shape land redistribution and the government's relations to people in the communal areas were in place: official accusations of support for 'dissidents' were common, people had become dependent on state-supplied drought relief, and dissidents had launched attacks on government personnel and property, resettlement schemes and commercial ranchers. The most

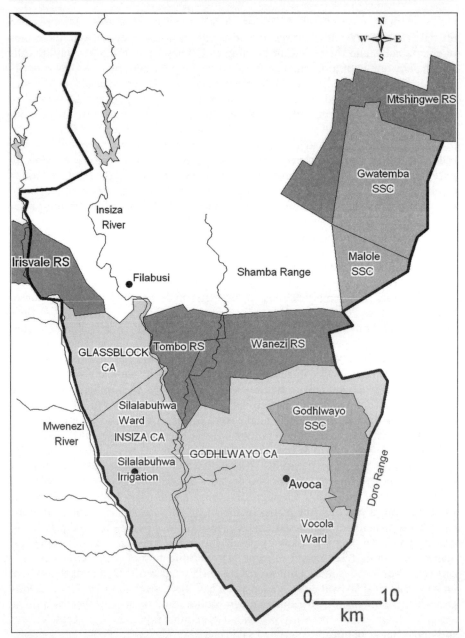

Map 6.1 Southern Insiza District, 1990.
CA – Communal Area, RS – Resettlement Scheme, SSC – Small Scale Commercial Area.

severe repression fell between early 1983, when the notorious Fifth Brigade was sent into Matabeleland, and 1985 when national elections were held. Made up of mostly Shona-speaking ex-Zanla guerrillas, the Fifth Brigade reported directly to Mugabe.

It was responsible for the murder of thousands of civilians. The extent of repression far exceeded the threat posed by the relatively small number of armed 'dissidents' operating in the western regions, and extended well beyond the government's own assessment of the end to South African intervention. Military repression greatly increased the vulnerability of a rural economy already reeling from drought as a consequence of dawn-to-dusk curfews, implemented in 1984, and the withholding of food from areas accused of supporting dissidents. Rural production was further disrupted by flight: thousands of people, particularly young men, fled to Bulawayo, Botswana and South Africa.[12]

In Insiza, the stage for heavy-handed repression was set in 1982 when guerrillas stationed at Silalabuhwa irrigation scheme clashed, and an 'arms hideout as big as a football pitch' was reportedly discovered at the scheme.[13] Captured dissidents allegedly told rallies that they had hidden arms in Insiza to be distributed to army deserters.[14] The context of suspicion and conflict placed a distorting lens over district councillors' demands for land. A Ministry of Lands official informed the council that: 'Records indicated that people did not want to be settled yet this was not the case. It was because individuals who wanted to be settled were regarded as sell outs.... It appears people have preferred to cut fences and steal things from farms bought by the government.'[15]

Claims to land, and authority over it, that could not be made through councils were made, in some cases, by dissidents and the threat of dissident violence. A series of attacks on Matabeleland's Model A schemes were reported in the press. They reflected the volatile combination of the anti-government agenda of the dissidents and the distribution of benefits from the schemes. In Plumtree, dissidents attacked a resettlement village in Dombodema, beating the settlers and burning their homes. The settlers said they were accused of being 'sell-outs', and alleged that the dissidents had been incited to attack them by their communal area neighbours whose cattle they had tried to drive off the scheme.[16] On the Hollins Block scheme in Gwanda, communal area cattle owners had been allowed access to the land by the commercial rancher. When settlers were brought in and tried to exclude the cattle, the scheme's fences were cut and its villages burned.[17] At the Mbembesi scheme in Lupane, dissidents burned settlers' huts to the ground because, settlers recounted, they opposed the village system of settlement.[18] In Insiza, the ex-miners and farm labourers on the Tombo scheme were harassed and cattle were driven onto the scheme. According to the resettlement officer: 'The problem is when communal lands border resettlement and people take the fencing. It was because of politics and people were afraid of the dissidents. You can't enforce rules in that situation.'[19]

Dissident attacks also had a significant impact on commercial farm ownership. In 1982, the Commercial Farmers' Union reported that 30 of its members or their relatives had died as a result of armed attack since 1980; ranchers who rounded up communal area cattle on their land received death threats. Attacks led to the movement of white ranchers to Bulawayo, the resumption of the 1970s 'agric-alert' security system and the introduction of militias seconded from the army.[20] During the conflict as a whole, 80 white ranchers and missionaries were killed, many more than in the 1970s.[21] Ranchers were also hard hit by drought. Large numbers of Matabeleland South's commercially owned cattle were moved to grazing in

Mashonaland or sold under the Cold Storage Commission's (CSC's) Operation Cattle Rescue. Many ranchers sold up, greatly increasing the quantity of land in state hands.[22]

Where the liberation war had failed to drive out white ranchers, the violence and drought of the 1980s succeeded. The political potential of land redistribution as a means of building legitimacy for the new state nonetheless went unrealised. Instead, a considerable proportion of land intended for resettlement was put to other uses. By 1989, only 1,878 families had been settled on less than half of the 500,000 hectares purchased for resettlement in the province.[23] Some of the land was leased, often to officials and politicians, a practice that only came under public scrutiny after the end of the conflict. The Minister of Lands retrospectively defended the practice as a means of protecting the land from destructive squatters, and serving the patriotic purpose of 'saving the national herd' by providing drought-relief grazing to ranchers – at the price, of course, of denying it to communal area cattle owners. In late 1988, at least 64,000 cattle were on leased land, judging from the fees collected,[24] though local officials considered the number to be far higher.

The leasing policy acted as a block to land redistribution and an aid to elite accumulation. The thirteen leased farms in Insiza were divided among 33 individuals and syndicates, among whom, in 1987, were senior administrators, local businessmen and teachers, several local ranchers and a large number of Bulawayo residents.[25] Many lessees had acquired herds through the CSC in order to take advantage of the available land, thus creating powerful interests in forestalling resettlement. When a provincial official tried to begin planning Insiza's unsettled land in 1986 he found information and funds were not forthcoming. Many of the officials involved had a stake in the *status quo*, including the DA, Provincial Administrator, and members of the Provincial Development Committee tasked with looking into the issue.[26] When the leases were cancelled at the end of 1988, district officials remained sceptical of the prospects for resettlement. Insiza's newly appointed DA commented: 'I'm not sure [the land] will be released as some big guns moved in to use it. People became cattle ranchers as a result of those farms being available.'[27] With a hint of irony, the district resettlement officer added: 'It is just like squatters. Where will they go when they are asked to leave?' Moreover, the funds necessary to settle most of the leased ranches remained unavailable.[28]

The delays in resettlement thus allowed the well-connected to accumulate wealth through the use of resettlement land at a time when the drought was taking a heavy toll on communal area cattle. It divided the state between those who wanted to settle the land and those who benefited from its unsettled status. The delays also allowed a new generation of black commercial farmers to purchase land. In the north of Insiza District, 57 of 114 ranches were black-owned by 1988.[29] Elsewhere in the province, potential resettlement land went to the parastatal Agricultural Development Authority (ADA). In Kezi and Marula, ADA retained almost 70 per cent, roughly 135,000 hectares, of the land acquired at the height of the conflict.[30]

On land which was not leased, redistribution was slowed by continued controversy over resettlement models. As an alternative to the Model A schemes, the cattle-oriented Model D was proposed. A pilot project was to be implemented from 1984 to 1986 in Gwanda district. Three ranches would be used for rotational grazing while the beneficiary communal areas were villagised and paddocked.[31] The goal of

Model D was to boost marketed beef production. Close state regulation was justified by once more casting communal area farmers as the victims of a 'cattle complex' that left them with an irrational desire to accumulate cattle for prestige purposes.[32] As in the past, communal area farmers had a fundamentally different view of both the purpose of cattle ownership and the means of management. Cattle formed the basis for a range of social relationships, and served multiple purposes within the agricultural economy – from transport to draught power to milk and manure production – alongside their role as beef producers. They were essential to overcoming both fertility constraints and labour shortages. Range management was shaped by the role cattle played in arable farming, and the need to move cattle so as to exploit uneven grazing resources and thus maximise the number of cattle. These strategies were 'efficient' and 'rational', but not in the ways officials desired.[33]

On the Model D pilot in Gwanda, the initial land-use plan envisioned moving 90 per cent of households and was rejected out of hand. A new plan was formulated but did not get underway until late 1987 due to security threats. On the ranches, dissidents repeatedly attacked labourers, cut fences and destroyed property. They were also blamed for preventing local participation: as an ADA report put it, participation in the scheme 'tended to endanger the lives of those identifying with the project'. The implementation of the most controversial aspect of the model – destocking – was delayed. Even with the addition of ranch land to the communal area, ADA planners estimated that stocking rates would be double the desired level. They feared that access to the ranches would lead to the accumulation of additional cattle, not to their sale: 'logically, therefore, ranch development would have had to be complemented by stock limitations'.[34] From participants' point of view, the point of Model D was to increase cattle holdings, and they were unlikely to accept such restrictions.

Despite many remaining questions concerning the Gwanda project, Model D schemes were proposed for a range of other districts. They fared little better. The Bulilimamangwe scheme was held up due to foot-and-mouth disease restrictions.[35] In Matobo, land designated for Model D went unused because the council refused villagisation.[36] A similar problem was encountered in Beitbridge where the Model D scheme's 'constraints' included the 'reluctance' of participants to comply with land use plans in the communal areas, poach-grazing, and a lack of funding.[37] In Insiza, the Wanezi Model D scheme was proposed for eight farms bordering the northern edge of Godhlwayo communal area. Planning for the scheme was slow to get underway. In the meantime, the farms were stripped of their infrastructure and overrun with cattle.[38] A massive capital investment was necessary even if plans for reorganising the communal areas succeeded; that was far from assured, as I explore below.

Despite experiments with the Model D scheme, many of the ranches bought for resettlement remained designated for Model A settlement, causing ongoing tensions. In a familiar refrain, Insiza's councillors objected vehemently to the use of any land for Model A in 1987. They had rejected the model and had told their constituents as much: 'Therefore how could they, the councillors, go back to the people and tell them that they had agreed on [the model], this would cause some quarrels between the councillors and the people.'[39] Plans nonetheless went unchanged, in part because of the utility of Model A in settling 'squatters'. There were over 1,300 squatters on mines, ranches and state lands, but only room for 200 on resettlement schemes.[40] The pressure on officials to resettle squatters was strong, and communal area people who were not squatting found it difficult to compete. A similar polarisation between communal area residents and squatters developed in other areas as land abandoned during the 1970s ran short, but the difference in Matabeleland was that squatters from communal areas had never dominated resettlement.

In the 1980s, land redistribution in Matabeleland failed to meet the demands of local leaders. They faced a government that distrusted them politically, and officials who disparaged their demands for grazing land as an attempt to extend an inefficient system of production. Their inability to influence the state, and the state's inability to build authority, moved the battle over land outside formal channels.

Encroachment and Land Access

People in Matabeleland turned to the 'weapons of the weak' in their quest for additional grazing land. They justified encroachment tactics with reference to nationalism, the moral imperatives of survival, and the desire to defend communities constituted through kin and patronage relationships. Dissident attacks or the threat of them was one such strategy, as we have seen. Others were less dramatic but no less important.

The 1989/90 provincial plan's review of resettlement schemes listed fence-cutting, tree-cutting and poach-grazing as serious problems almost everywhere: 'It has so far proved difficult to construct boundary fencing at many of the Resettlement Schemes because of the stiff and hostile opposition from communal farmers who want to continue to use the schemes as extended grazing for their cattle.'[41] The exclusiveness of schemes was one source of conflict. Related to this was technical planners' desire to transform the role of cattle on Model A schemes from suppliers of arable inputs like manure and draught power to producers of beef. The CSC's 'Livestock Improvement Scheme' was intended to allow settlers to start their own commercially managed herds with loans from the Commission, thereby undermining arrangements whereby neighbouring farmers loaned cattle to the often cattle-poor settlers.

Insiza's Mtshingwe resettlement scheme provides an example of the conflicts that ensued. Implemented in 1987, the scheme was planned on a modified Model A basis, i.e. with 2.5 hectares of arable land rather than five and increased provision for grazing land so as to allow for beef production. In the interests of beef production, the resettlement officer had tried to ban loaned cattle from the scheme. From his point of view, such cattle were unproductive because they could not be sold. He depicted loaning as part of an inegalitarian social system, and argued that state regulation could convert 'unproductive' customary networks into a modern, market-oriented system.[42] The neighbouring farmers in the staunchly nationalist Gwatemba Small Scale Commercial Area (formerly African Purchase Area) saw matters differently. Some of them had been evicted from Mtshingwe in the 1950s. They saw the settlers as occupying land that was rightfully theirs, and which they had been able to use as grazing land before the scheme's settlement. By loaning cattle to the settlers they could at least use the scheme for relief grazing. Attempts to keep loaned cattle out led to a poach-grazing and fence-cutting battle. The resettlement officer responded with a vigorous fencing programme, but his fences signally failed to make good neighbours. On the Tombo Model A scheme, which bordered all three communal areas, he was pushed to even more drastic action. Settlers on the scheme instituted by-laws allowing them to impound outsiders' cattle and hold them to ransom for one dollar a head, money that was used to repair damaged fences. The scheme nonetheless remained besieged.[43]

The movement of cattle outside the communal areas was commonplace and, despite its illegality, openly defended. As a vidco chairman explained, 'to deal with the shortage of grazing land we take our cattle across the river to government farms [the Tombo scheme] for a few months.... It was never organized by anybody and I think it was illegal. But we lost a lot of cattle during the drought so we took them there.'[44] Councillors argued that the movement of cattle outside the communal areas was morally justified due to the pressures of drought and the government's refusal to respond to their demands for land on acceptable terms: 'We have never had land given to us. Many animals died.... We had to steal. It was self-resettlement. We were not helped – it was each man for himself.' Insiza's neglect was due to 'political confusion': 'They would say, "you can't accept our party so you will be given no land". People couldn't get land without party allegiance.'[45]

Another tactic employed by both resettlement and communal area farmers was that of poaching animals from commercial ranches. Ranches bordering communal areas and resettlement schemes were most vulnerable. An Insiza rancher who lived adjacent to a resettlement farm commented, 'I lost seven sheep in the last eight or nine months. [My neighbours] have had huge problems with cattle theft. In the last two years they have lost thirty head.... I don't think you can control it.'[46] Stolen animals were usually sold to local butchers, a market that flourished due to CSC inefficiencies in allocating beef to rural outlets.[47]

The 'weapons of the weak' undermined unpopular resettlement schemes, helped to save cattle during droughts, and provided a means for supplementing incomes, but they entailed high risks in terms of fines, imprisonment, reprisals from settlers and officials, and loss of cattle.[48] This was especially true in the mid-1980s when attacks on resettlement schemes and ranches incurred military retaliation. Moreover, it was the people in resettlement schemes who suffered the brunt of these tactics as 'willing' sellers of ranch land often lived adjacent to communal areas where attacks and encroachment were concentrated.

Resettlement in Insiza underlined the political failings of 1980s' land redistribution. It was seen as the province of outsiders, in whose interests it was controlled using arguments that cast communal area farmers as not only illegitimately opposed to resettlement due to their political affiliation, but engaged in a farming system that threatened the state's imperative of production for the market, here narrowly defined in terms of beef.

The achievement of political Unity in December 1987, through which Zapu was absorbed into Zanu(PF), and the quick return to peace in 1988, brought these issues into the open, and sparked a new debate on the use of resettlement land. The outspoken formerly Zapu MP Sydney Malunga raised the issue of leased land in parliament almost immediately.[49] In subsequent speeches, he charged that Ministry officials had 'abused their authority by entering into grazing schemes with the Cold

Storage Commission'.[50] Resettlement models also came under renewed scrutiny. The 1989/90 Matabeleland South Provincial Plan noted, 'a serious drawback emanating from the reinterpretation of the Model D concept by some city dwellers, off farm workers' who now claimed that Model D 'was limited to relie[f] grazing and as such should not be allowed to interfere with the way people are presently settled. At this point even the former proponents of the model were beginning to join the bandwagon and started questioning the way things were being done.'[51] Local opponents of Model D were backed by former Zapu MPs who called for the straightforward extension of communal area grazing land under local control and without paddocking, on the grounds that this was what nationalists had fought for. Their calls were derided by the Minister of Local Government who accused them of 'cheap politicking', and ridiculed their defence of what he called 'nomadism': 'Surely we must argue that nobody during this modern age can call for nomadism in today's Zimbabwe just because it was practiced traditionally.' Officials did not yield to local demands. Instead they introduced a new Model that offered access to land only to those with over ten head of cattle and technical qualifications, so as 'to discourage communal farmers from keeping cattle for traditional purposes and prestige reasons'. The result was an ongoing battle of encroachment, which eventually resulted in the demise of the flagship Gwanda scheme.[52]

The surrender to encroachment in the Gwanda case indicated not only a weakened state but also the declining acceptability of coercion. In the aftermath of Unity, squatters suddenly received better treatment. For example, squatters on a Lonhro-owned farm in the north of Insiza came under public scrutiny in early 1989 when the Senator for the area claimed they were to be evicted without provision for resettlement.[53] In an attempt to gain local support, he arranged for a visit by the Provincial Governor and lobbied on their behalf. The Provincial Administrator's response highlighted the touchy nature of the issue in post-Unity Matabeleland: in sharp contrast to the 'seek and evict' army operations employed in the same area in 1983, he stressed 'we never evict people without providing alternative areas'.[54]

Despite this newfound sensitivity, the return to peace did not produce an expansion of resettlement on locally acceptable terms. The resources necessary to speed implementation were not made available, as I explore further in Chapter 8. Nor did technocratic views change: the commitment to beef production was in fact bolstered, even if planners' schemes remained unimplemented. Post-Unity changes in Matabeleland consisted largely in an expansion of encroachment on commercial and state land, tactics that evoked strong protests from ranchers but that were treated more indulgently by officials and politicians than those of the mid-1980s.[55] The lean fruits of encroachment notwithstanding, the failures of land redistribution over the first decade of independence were to weigh heavily on the process of remaking the state within the communal areas.

Governing Insiza's Communal Areas

In 1980, nationalism was central to constituting rural authority. Zapu dominated every level of elected local government. Nationalist credentials were essential to legitimating new leaders, whatever their standing in terms of customary or other claims to authority, and leaders commonly bridged new and old institutions. When political conflict resulted in a concerted attack on Zapu, it undermined the whole range of rural institutions.

Prior to the outbreak of conflict, the fate of Insiza's customary leaders was tied to their relationship to Zapu. Headman Ngomondo, who had assumed the deposed Chief Vezi Maduna's office in the late 1970s and now lived in Bulawayo, 'flatly refused to go back to the people because he fears they might kill him'.[56] Chief Maduna, by contrast, had spent the late 1970s in detention and held a senior position in Zapu. His reception could not have been more different. In June 1980, the DC reported that it was the desire of the people that he be re-appointed as chief. A committee consisting of Zapu 'senior party representatives and others' acted as 'liaison between people and the chief'. At several massive rallies, the call for Maduna's return was reiterated and a 'large welcome' planned. He was duly re-installed, despite the fact that in most of the country officials stubbornly refused to make any concessions to party lobbying.[57] Chiefs Maduna and Sibasa were elected to serve on the first Insiza council (rather than being appointed as ex-officio members) in 1980. Councillors chose Maduna as their chairman, and he was crucial to legitimising an institution that looked all too much like the hated councils of previous decades.[58] In the early 1980s, he was, once again, a key negotiator with officials and a link to Zapu politicians.[59]

Customary leaders were also commonly elected as the presiding officers of village courts. The elections were seen as an unwanted imposition. A councillor explained: 'The directive ... came from government but people were very happy with chiefs settling disputes and were very disturbed by having to choose others.' He, like many other elder men, objected to the government's legal 'interference' in, most notably, the status of women.[60] On the whole it was customary leaders who dealt with disputes, mostly involving fighting, cattle encroachment on fields, and adultery. Other leaders did not perceive this as problematic but, instead, saw it as important to maintaining social order.

Though chiefs and headmen received official sanction as customary leaders, the role of the village head (the sabhuku or 'kraal head') was more controversial. Local Government officials in Matabeleland, though not elsewhere, derided their claims to customary authority. They held that sabhukus 'started with the Land Husbandry Act.... Sabhukus were not traditional. Headmen and chiefs were.' They were a 'historical problem'; their post had been created 'because the chiefs and headmen sided with the people'.[61] Local leaders agreed that sabhukus had no customary standing. Their office was depicted as one of stewardship over a 'line', the linear 'villages' established under the Land Husbandry Act, and liaison with chiefs and headmen.[62] They nonetheless did not reject them outright, but rather judged them on the basis of their behaviour. In some areas, sabhukus were depicted as having been irredeemably corrupt and authoritarian in the past, and as no more than troublesome 'members of the public' in the 1980s; in others, they were described as weighty leaders and nationalists, deserving of respect. Though village heads received neither official recognition nor salaries, their authority was not wholly eclipsed officially: some ministries, such as Home Affairs, continued to work through them.[63]

In the first years of independence, the vague delineation of authority among different institutions, and the fact that leaders commonly held several posts at once, created combinations of new and old roles, and space for continued debate under the rubric of Zapu's nationalism. This situation was to be rapidly transformed by the onset of political conflict. In concert with extreme military repression, Zanu(PF) launched a direct attack on Zapu members and councils. A recruitment drive was initiated in 1983: in just three months, Zanu(PF) claimed that the party's Matabeleland South membership jumped from 20,000 to 120,000. A district Zanu(PF) committee was formed in Insiza in June 1983.[64] Just before the council elections of the same year, Mugabe accused Zapu councillors of obstructing development and aiding dissidents.[65] Insiza's council chairman, Chief Maduna, was detained on charges of caching arms, thus ending his tenure just three years after his triumphal return to the district. Remaining councillors were ordered to leave office and the DA was appointed as 'manager'.[66] DA Martin Simela, himself a recent Zanu(PF) convert, held that all but two councillors elected in 1983 were loyal to Zanu(PF).[67] Mugabe touted the elections, which gave his party majorities in four of six councils in Matabeleland South, as a triumph over tribalism and as a vindication of the government's development policies, a view that found little local resonance.[68]

In the mid-1980s, Vezi Maduna stood at the centre of inter-party conflict. As repression escalated, he drew strategically on his several offices and diverse alliances. In March 1983, DA Philip Bhebhe wrote a revealing evaluation of Maduna, then 'in Police hands'.[69] He warned that 'people's respect of him might be too much': 'Chief Maduna has had full control over the entire population of Godhlwayo. People say that a word from him is sufficient to keep everyone on the move.... People say that he is ready to listen to their problems at any time of night or day and under any circumstances.' A 'prominent farmer', Maduna supported 'all forms of development'. He also retained his eclectic influence in other realms: while maintaining his Zionist affiliation, he contributed in cash and kind to rain-making ceremonies at the homes of local adepts of the Mwali cult: 'The Chief sends his personal representative to such ceremonies as a sign of appreciation of his peoples' mores.'

After his release from police custody, Maduna sought refuge in Bulawayo, fearing for his life, until just before the 1985 parliamentary elections. Insiza's Zanu(PF) candidate was Enos Nkala. Born in Insiza, he was the most prominent of the Ndebele-speaking Zanu(PF) Ministers and had launched some of the most vitriolic of attacks on Zapu. Zanu(PF) placed great weight on his campaign. But Vezi Maduna soon intervened. 'To the dismay of government officials', the DA reported, 'it surfaced during Minister E. W. Nkala's campaign that people could not vote for ZANU(PF) because the chief was PF ZAPU'. Nkala was resoundingly defeated. In July, police called Maduna to a meeting near his home. DA Simela told those present that Maduna 'was being given a last chance to reform'. An unrepentant Maduna 'said he wanted to be free like anybody else and cannot commit himself that he will leave PF ZAPU politics as he knows the government still allowed a multi-party state'.[70] However, the continued attacks on Zapu did force a transformation in Maduna's role. Unable to carry on as a Zapu politician and perform his duties as chief, he publicly renounced his party position. In September 1985, Simela reported the proceedings of a meeting with Maduna and 'kraal heads': 'Kraal head after kraal head pleaded that the chief resigns from politics in favour of his traditional role as Chief. The kraal heads concurred that they had put the chief in politics and therefore they were taking him out of politics.' According to Simela, Maduna agreed to abstain from party politics, stating: 'No politics anymore. I will work with government and my people.'[71] The retreat to his customary office allowed Maduna a continued, if much narrowed, public role.

Maduna's concession indicated the extent to which Zapu had been driven underground and the state politicised. Even Insiza's nominally Zanu(PF) councillors were not free from accusations of being 'camouflaged ZAPU' or 'ZAPU in heart'. Nor were they free from attacks from Zapu members and 'dissidents'. Much as in the 1970s, holding public office in a time of armed conflict carried heavy risks. The turnover in council membership was extremely high, and councillors regularly complained of intimidation by officials, as well as the danger in which their posts placed them at home.[72] Local Government Promotion Officer (LGPO) John Mbedzi led the attack. He regularly came into conflict with councillors, threatening one with a gun, beating up another, firing council employees he accused of supporting Zapu, and aiding in the detention of councillors and others.[73] Formerly Zapu himself, Mbedzi was a fanatical Zanu(PF) convert. In Zanu(PF)'s quest for loyalty, appointees like Mbedzi were catapulted into prominent positions. He became the party's provincial vice-chairman, and stood as the parliamentary candidate for Beitbridge in 1985. A firm believer in the one-party state, he held that 'the police and the civil servants had to join the party and attend meetings since there was no neutrality'.[74] Matabeleland South's newly appointed Provincial Governor, Zanu(PF) stalwart Mark Dube, felt much the same way: he introduced a motion in Parliament to ban Zapu.[75] The state was, however, far from united in its commitment to partisan politics. Many civil servants, including policemen, sought to defend their professional status. Mbedzi regularly clashed with his peers. Insiza's other LGPOs did not endorse his practices, and even the Zanu(PF) DA Martin Simela angrily remonstrated with Mbedzi, telling him that 'he is not allowed to make decisions for the council, even issuing directives to the councillors'.[76]

Vidcos were established in this context in 1984 and quickly became a focus of partisan conflict. Provincial Governor Dube placed vidcos at the heart of a strategy of surveillance. He told councillors: 'The menace of dissidents is going to be destroyed. With the establishment of the new vidco system we will know each other at village level. This will help us to identify strangers.... This will help to root out robbers who steal from us and kill us.'[77] Vidcos' party affiliation was extremely touchy. In an emergency council meeting in 1984, one councillor 'wanted to know if the youth and women [vidco] representatives are political appointees or is it somebody liked by the people?' A provincial official replied that they could be 'either Zanu or Zapu' but soon found himself under attack from Mbedzi.[78] Not surprisingly, people were reluctant to serve on or support vidcos: much like the council, they suffered a high turn-over in membership. People adopted strategies intended to control their influence, such as nominating 'camouflaged' Zapu candidates or people of low status.[79]

In 1987, Zapu meetings were banned on the heels of an upsurge in violence,[80] and Insiza's council was put under the 'management' of officials for a second time.

For most of the 1980s, the pressures of inter-party conflict thus prevented Insiza's local institutions from representing people's views, much less exercising effective authority. The partisan uses of the council and vidcos had the additional effect of giving new life to the offices of customary leaders: in periods when the council was disbanded or disrupted people sent representatives to the district offices unilaterally or used the customary hierarchy to express their views. Some Zapu politicians, such as Vezi Maduna, retreated to the relative safety of a customary office while sabhukus had ample grounds for criticising vidcos as an illegitimate imposition.

Development and Political Conflict

Party conflict profoundly shaped local understandings of development. In the first years of independence, the provision of infrastructure and services expanded rapidly in Matabeleland as elsewhere. But unlike in Zanu(PF) areas, local institutions were not credited with their delivery. As the drought took hold and national growth declined after 1983, service expansion was curtailed in most areas. But perceptions differed again: in Zapu areas declining investment coincided with political persecution and was perceived as deliberate neglect, not austerity. In the mid-1980s, political violence greatly limited the disbursement of what development resources there were. Schools had trouble functioning, cattle feed lots, inspections and sales were disrupted, borehole drillers refused to operate, and of course resettlement was greatly compromised.[81]

An important form of state patronage in Insiza during the mid-1980s was drought relief and food-for-work programmes. Between 1982 and 1984, the government annually distributed food to the vast majority of communal area households.[82] Though the Department of Social Welfare and Agritex assessed the need for drought relief, councillors and vidcos (often working with village heads) identified recipients, potentially giving them control over an important resource. But instead of bringing them support, distributing drought relief led to conflict with constituents and officials, again along party lines, as it was used as yet another tool of political control.[83] Most of the accomplishments claimed by vidco chairmen in the late 1980s were projects completed under the food-for-work programme. These were few and far between. Many vidco chairmen held that they had accomplished nothing at all; some said people were not even aware of the vidcos. They complained bitterly of the lack of support for development initiatives and of the often futile work they carried out. One vidco chairman commented: 'We haven't had any development in our area except for the roads,' and these he suspected served a military purpose. Another held that 'the vidco has only increased the way of implementing government policy.'[84] Sabhukus used the lack of development to discredit vidcos, drawing unfavourable comparisons with the expansion of dams and boreholes under the primary development policy of the 1960s.[85]

The council, as well as vidcos, had difficulty not only in securing and claiming credit for development, but also in exercising authority over issues of central concern to the agrarian economy. An issue that preoccupied the council for much of the 1980s was cattle theft. Drought meant cattle were moved long distances in search of better grazing and water, usually onto occupied, leased or vacant resettlement land. Large numbers were reported to be wandering unattended. Political conflict meant services related to cattle management were disrupted. Both drought and conflict contributed to lawlessness. Theft was sometimes directed at Zapu sympathisers.[86] In the mid-1980s, the council sought to enforce order by introducing a series of measures to regulate cattle movements and sales. Implementing the measures proved impossible, however, due to the 'security situation', and resistance to controls from people who 'fear government will take the cattle'. Councillors accused police of freeirg thieves for bribes which, they complained, 'favours rich thieves who can buy off the poor'.[87] The inability to control stock theft led to the emergence of local 'kangaroo courts'.[88] These courts, as well as the problem of stock theft, survived the advent of political Unity, in part due to the black market in beef created by a national beef shortage.[89] A vidco chairman explained: 'People take cattle to butcheries and the police don't stop them. Local people steal so locals should deal with the cases.' Stock theft was commonly explained in terms of a decline in 'respect' for elder men, and of the failure of the vidcos, council and police to enforce rules, both developments that were contrasted unfavourably with the past.[90]

The return to peace in 1988 brought an ambiguous mix of political change. Security imperatives were overtaken by the need to build support, and to absorb long-excluded Zapu leaders. An immediate effect was the fall of the senior Ndebele-speaking Zanu(PF) faction in Matabeleland.[91] At district levels, (now former) Zapu members once again dominated councils and all other levels of local government. In Insiza, only two members of the pre-Unity council continued in office. Some newly elected councillors greeted Unity with high hopes for peace and development, but others remained fearful and pessimistic. Many Zapu leaders were no longer present or withdrew from politics. Chief Maduna devoted his time to the Chiefs' Council, to which he was elected in 1986, and his village court, though he was to rejoin party politics in later years.[92] A suspicious apathy greeted efforts to establish 'united' Zanu(PF) committees.[93] Unity was often cast as a deal cut between national leaders with little to offer ordinary people,[94] a view that seemed to be vindicated as expectations of a boom in development were disappointed. Peace did not rejuvenate local authorities, and nor did it give the state the capacity to intervene in the most vexed of arenas: communal area land tenure.

Authority and the Land in the Communal Areas

In the 1980s, the government's repressive capacities were not matched by an ability to build authority over land and people. Officials found mobilising people and enforcing policy difficult due to the disruptions of, and distrust for, development institutions, and the severe constraints of the 'security situation'. Little happened until the latter half of the 1980s, and even then communal area land use remained largely beyond the control of the state.

Councils were supposed to have assumed land allocating powers in 1982, but the issue was not directly addressed in Insiza until 1986 when the Ministry of Local Government issued a circular on the topic. The circular stressed that 'Chiefs,

Headmen, Politicians or Chairmen of Village and Ward Development Committees' were not permitted to allocate land. Only the council as a whole could: 'If any person other than the District Council allocates land to anyone, that person who does the allocation will be prosecuted and severely punished. The illegal occupant will be regarded as a squatter and will be removed'.[95] As surprised councillors attested, the council in fact played no role whatsoever in land allocation.[96] Rights to land were shaped by the legacies of decades of state intervention and political struggle, and mediated by the competing claims of families, customary leaders, nationalists, vidcos, councillors and officials.

The circular coincided with the focus on 'internal' resettlement in the communal areas, a policy that by necessity brought the question of the state's authority over the land to the fore. As explored in Chapter 5, the policy was the subject of intense debate at the national level, not over its merits as such, but over the means by which it might be implemented.[97] At district level, Local Government and Agritex were the most influential actors, but their views did not necessarily reflect either national or provincial attitudes. In Insiza, LGPOs had drawn vidco boundaries at the height of political conflict, mapping them in the office due to security threats, with no reference to actual patterns of resource use or social ties. LGPOs were aware that vidcos were unpopular, and as political conflict subsided, they tried to strengthen them by encouraging the co-optation of sabhukus onto committees.[98] LGPOs' pragmatism did not, however, influence Insiza's Agritex officials who insisted on undertaking the technical work of land-use planning on the basis of the original vidco boundaries, on the grounds that they were 'political' and hence beyond their remit.[99]

Attempts to implement land-use planning were disastrous. The first step here as elsewhere involved the establishment of model villages. In early 1986, the council was asked to identify sites for three such villages, but instead chose sites for three houses. When officials realised the mistake, an alternative site was chosen by driving around in Glassblock communal area and consulting Chief Ndube. People refused to move to the stands, and so the council nominated a Small Scale Commercial Area as an alternative site, though the policy only applied to communal areas. The council was subsequently disbanded and the civil servant-run District Development Committee chose a site at Avoca in Godhlwayo, where people were to be displaced by the construction of Siwaze dam. Few people agreed to move to the village; long after it was supposed to be settled, no services had been provided.[100] A councillor explained: 'The way [villagisation] was brought was more or less as an order so people couldn't accept it. People must accept it first or they will try to sabotage it.'[101]

Political conflict no doubt undermined progress, but the return of peace did not dissipate the suspicion that greeted the policy, now cast as a much more wide-ranging measure involving paddocking grazing areas and consolidating arable land. Even politicians with the prestige of former Zapu leader Joshua Nkomo had difficulty drumming up support. At a rally at Avoca in 1988, Nkomo was greeted with stony silence when he endorsed villagisation. 'People had expected him to be in opposition,' explained an LGPO.[102] When the fourth Insiza council was elected shortly thereafter, councillors simply claimed ignorance of the policy.[103]

A final factor behind the slow progress of the policy was the delay in resettlement. The offer of access to grazing land under the Wanezi Model D scheme, which would theoretically benefit Insiza's communal area wards on a rotational basis, might have been used as a carrot to gain compliance, much in the same way as compliance with the Native Land Husbandry Act had been achieved. But the conflicts surrounding resettlement prevented such an exchange: instead, people sought relief grazing independently. As the following case studies illustrate, control over land-use practices remained largely outside the ambit of state and council. Land use was shaped far more powerfully by the legacies of earlier state interventions and local responses to drought. Re-establishing and policing Land Husbandry Act 'lines' often formed the locally negotiated basis for cooperation between sabhukus and vidcos. The lines had largely survived in Insiza until the 1970s when people moved into grazing land and expanded fields under the rubric of 'freedom farming'. In the late 1980s, they served a number of purposes: they were invoked to illustrate shortages of arable land, they were used as a means of preventing encroachment on grazing land, and they were deployed as a rhetorical tool useful in warding off new state interventions.

VOCOLA WARD

Vocola Ward is located in the remote southeast corner of Godhlwayo communal area. All local leaders were male, in their 40s to 60s, and said they owned cattle, though in small numbers ranging from two to eleven.[104] Almost every vidco chairman had drawn sabhukus onto their committee while in three areas sabhukus had been elected as vidco chairmen. The number of sabhukus per vidco was about average, that is, between three and five, each heading a 'line' of from 20 to 40 homesteads. In the late 1980s, Vocola had had little attention in terms of development resources or extension work, and local leaders complained bitterly of their inability to procure particularly dams and boreholes.

Authority over land allocation in Vocola was rarely a source of conflict, in part because pressure to allocate land had not been great for most of the 1980s. Young men had been particularly vulnerable to political persecution: many had fled the district; others had left to seek work due to the pressures of drought. This had begun to change in the late 1980s, however, as peace returned, unemployment grew, and the cost of living in cities rose rapidly, forcing people onto the land.[105] Local leaders used the original Land Husbandry Act allocation of eight acres per household as a measure of arable land shortage and as the ideal for new allocations. One vidco chairman commented: 'Government has promised each person eight acres but some have only four.... Eight acres were promised under the Land Husbandry Act in 1954. People are many now and that is why there is not enough land.'[106] In most vidco areas land was not being allocated because the Land Husbandry lines were 'full' and, as a vidco chairman explained, 'no one dies without heirs'.[107]

Inheritance and the subdivision of fields was the most common way for young people to gain access to land, causing concern both over the reduction in the size of fields and the pressure to move into grazing areas. Allocations outside families or of new land were a rarity: in only one vidco had land been allocated to 'outsiders', in this case to four families displaced by the construction of Siwaze dam at Avoca. The families had refused to go to the 'government's place', meaning the model village.

A sabhuku had authorised the allocations after consultations with Chief Maduna, from near whose home the people came, and after informing the vidco chairman who in turn informed the councillor and Agritex. All local leaders agreed that while 'informing' other authorities was necessary in order to prevent 'misunderstandings', ultimate authority for the allocations lay with the sabhuku.

The pressure on arable land evoked concerns for the future. Though local leaders were not themselves interested in Model A-style resettlement, meaning the movement of households to new areas, they, like leaders in many other wards, argued that shortages in arable land threatened the next generation's livelihood and could only be solved through the resettlement of the young, or increased employment and better rains. Resettlement was nonetheless seen as problematic: many leaders worried about breaking up families, stressing that they would 'lose' their children.[108] In a strongly worded criticism, one councillor argued: 'People couldn't accept [Model A] because it meant isolation.... People objected because it is far away, with other people. It is more like restriction', a reference to the Rhodesian government's detention of political leaders in remote camps.

Indicating the lasting, and mutable, influence of the Land Husbandry Act, the Vocola leadership agreed that policing the 'lines' was a primary concern. Vidco chairmen and sabhukus cooperated in trying to stop the extension of fields and in reversing the breakdown in the lines that had resulted from people building homes and cultivating in grazing areas in the 1970s and early 1980s. Their desire to preserve 'lines' was linked to their interests as cattle owners and leaders: they sought to prevent further encroachment on grazing land and to ensure that the young only obtained land with their approval. Where land access was mainly a consequence of inheritance, as it was here and in most of the district, elder males were able to control arable land within groups of households.[109] The defence of 'lines' was, however, at least in part rhetorical: lines could be redefined; establishing who was outside a line, and hence subject to pressure to move, was a political process that centred on competing interpretations of history.[110]

The principal land shortage perceived by Vocola's local leaders concerned not arable but grazing land, a shortage worsened by drought and obstacles to transhumance. The lack of rain was described as an intractable problem, related not least to the government's uses of violence and lack of legitimacy.[111] Adequate rain would rejuvenate grazing areas, alleviate the need to move cattle to other areas, and allow re-stocking. Drought and transhumant strategies had created such a severe shortage of cattle within Vocola, and many other wards, that the ability of cattle owners to provide for the cattleless, or even themselves, was threatened. 'Loaning is a tradition but there aren't enough cattle left to practice it', explained a vidco chairman.[112] Some said that, under the pressures of economic hardship, cattle owners felt that others could not be trusted with cattle as they might sell them, pretend they were stolen, or even eat them. Instead of benefiting from loaning arrangements, people without cattle hired them in exchange for cash or labour, or hoed their fields by hand. Leaders concurred that there were not enough cattle left for everyone to gain access to them in time and many had to plough late with devastating consequences; some people also suffered due to a lack of ploughing implements.[113]

Cattle deaths, and their impact on both social relations and production, underlined local leaders' perception of the most appropriate form of land redistribution: adding grazing land to the communal areas. People here were heavily involved in the encroachment tactics described earlier. In late 1988, cattle from Vocola and several of the other Godhlwayo wards were on state land north of Godhlwayo, or in the Gwatemba Small Scale Commercial Area. In effect, cattle owners had instituted their own version of land redistribution outside official control. This practice was, however, less than ideal. In 1988, people were trying to bring their cattle back in time for the coming rainy season but were unable to do so due to an outbreak of foot-and-mouth disease which had trapped them on the wrong side of veterinary department fences.

Local leaders did not see land-use planning as a solution to any of their problems. They invoked the Land Husbandry Act 'lines' as evidence of a previously established contract with the state, and used them as an argument against further intervention. Most leaders worried that villagisation would lead to social conflict and require the costly relocation of homes. They expressed concern that paddocking would be used to restrict cattle movements and numbers. The idea of destocking was greeted with horror. Though some benefits to fencing were perceived in terms of keeping cattle out of fields and reducing herding labour, problems which had led vidcos to institute strict regulations on seasonal cattle herding, paddocking was considered too expensive and evoked fears of exclusive grazing areas.[114] A vidco chairman explained: '[Paddocks are] not a good idea because it means cattle from one vidco can't go to another. Grazing land overlaps. We share the grazing land.'[115] Local leaders defended at great length the necessity of using the varied resources of grazing areas 'opportunistically', a view endorsed by grassland researchers, but not by Agritex.[116]

Establishing exclusive grazing areas posed a formidable obstacle to Agritex's plans for paddocking, as it had for pre-independence grazing schemes.[117] Vidcos were meant to be self-sufficient units but in practice some had no grazing at all within their official boundaries. According to Insiza's Agritex officer, 'from the planning we are doing now we see that some vidcos won't have any grazing at all. So if they do some fencing in the future we don't know how they are going to sort that problem out.'[118] Agritex simply denied any responsibility for the consequences: 'We are not redrawing the boundaries. They are political boundaries made by Local Government.'[119] Agritex's strict restriction of its role to the technical was utterly self-defeating: it was left with plans that could not be implemented.[120]

Local leaders in Vocola largely cooperated in authorising land allocation and, for a complex variety of reasons, in defending the land-use patterns based, at least rhetorically, on the Land Husbandry Act 'lines' of the 1950s. Their responses to drought endorsed the right of stockowners to make use of state land denied them under the resettlement programme. Official interventions fed insecurity and perpetuated the deep distrust for the state, but they failed to muster the authority necessary to reshape land-use practices.

SILALABUHWA WARD

Silalabuhwa Ward, located in the northern half of Insiza communal area, differed from Vocola on a number of counts. It was the site of the district's only irrigation

143

scheme and, as a result, had a far larger official presence. Initiated in the 1960s, the scheme had been deeply unpopular. People had come to value access to irrigated land in the droughts of the 1980s, but the scheme still faced many problems: it did not function until 1985 due to drought and its role in the arms caches saga, and until then it was overrun by cattle, enclosures were built on it and trees torn up. Subsequently, friction over Agritex's recommended crop rotations was common.[121]

The vidco chairmen located near to the scheme differed from those in Vocola in that several claimed to have had vigorous disputes with sabhukus, especially in the volatile first years after the establishment of vidcos when 'people were not sure who was in charge.'[122] Some vidcos had made alliances with extension workers in order to assert their authority in the late 1980s. None, however, acted without the sabhukus' involvement, instead seeking to minimise conflict by sharing power and granting sabhukus 'respect'. Vidco chairmen were unanimous in seeing advantages to the new system: 'The improvement now is that the vidco is not an individual', and thus less open to corruption and authoritarianism. Another commented, 'with the chiefs' rule as it was we were not electing a person with knowledge. It was just blood. Now we elect a person who can do things.'[123] But the extent to which the council and vidco had failed to 'do things' was their Achilles' heel. Vidco chairmen and councillors were vociferously critical of the government's neglect, while sabhukus and chiefs were given grounds for criticising the new institutions.

Land was allocated largely to young people in the ward and, in the north, to people from the defunct Pangani Mine. In the latter area, far from the irrigation scheme, sabhukus authorised the allocation of land to newcomers, though vidco chairmen and Agritex were often consulted, sometimes after the fact. As in Vocola, there was concern to defend Land Husbandry lines: 'During the war we rejected all the rules of the government but now we don't accept building houses anywhere anymore.'[124] Close to the irrigation scheme, vidco chairmen said they had excluded sabhukus from decisions about land allocation. Their 'allocation' consisted largely in monitoring young people's inheritance. They also at times drew on Agritex's authority to stop extensions of fields into grazing land, a tactic common among vidco chairmen where movements into grazing areas were widespread.[125]

Save in the vidco which had lost land to the Silalabuhwa school and business centre, arable land was not considered in short supply. Most leaders saw access to irrigated land, which fell under Agritex control, as more important. 'When there is enough rain we depend on the irrigation scheme. When there is a drought we depend on drought relief,' as one vidco chairman succinctly put it.[126] Leaders worried there would not be enough irrigated land in future. Grazing land, however, was perceived to be desperately inadequate, in part because of the irrigation scheme's encroachment on former grazing areas.

Local leaders' reactions to land-use planning in Silalabuhwa highlighted the kinds of controversies likely to surround its implementation. The policy was well known here because of the greater contact with extension officers. Villagisation met with a unanimous and vigorous refusal.[127] Local leaders considered paddocking acceptable only if more land was added to the grazing area. Citing the high stock mortalities and the need to use resettlement land as relief grazing, they argued that communal area grazing was inadequate for a rotational system, especially under drought conditions. They saw fencing as a way of keeping cattle out of fields, not as a way of managing grazing land. Concern about paddocking was also linked to a fear of destocking. People were at pains to show that there were not enough cattle at present. As in most areas, vidco chairmen greeted the idea of destocking with angry responses: 'We are not working. We are starving. You can't accept a reduction when you depend on cattle'; 'It would be better to reduce the number of children than the number of cattle'; 'We need more land. Reducing the number of cattle would mean a war.'[128]

The district Agritex officer's views on stock management stood in sharp contrast. He had tried to stop local fencing initiatives, fearing they would undermine his plans; he depicted cattle mortalities not as a devastating tragedy reflecting the dearth of land but as a lesson to cattle owners that their herds were too large: 'People will see the benefits of decreasing livestock numbers in improved conditions, improved off-take.... So we think the drought is a blessing in disguise for our purposes.'[129] Only one vidco chairman, himself cattleless, had any sympathy for Agritex's point of view. He agreed that people would never voluntarily destock, but felt that large cattle owners could reduce their herds in order to improve the grazing.[130] His views reflected two changes. First, as in Vocola, local leaders said that cattle loaning was rare, that it was more common for cattle to be hired for ploughing. Weakened patronage ties had undercut the identification of the cattleless with cattle owners.[131] Second, the vidco chairman hoped to acquire his own cattle under a state scheme and only wished to reduce the numbers grazed by others given this eventuality. It was, however, unlikely that the state would assume the role of a cattle-loaning patron on a wide scale, or that it would favour those without cattle. The Cattle Finance Scheme was geared to individuals who would be good credit risks and willing to devote herds to beef production. It required substantial investment in dips, water and paddocking, and sometimes required moving cattle to distant state land.[132]

The most dramatic development in Silalabuhwa had nothing to do with state policy. It sprang from local initiative and sparked new conflicts among communal area farmers, police, the district administration, conservation bodies, Ministry of Mines and council.[133] The source of division was alluvial gold-panning along the Insiza river which feeds Silalabuhwa dam and, in turn, the irrigation scheme. Gold-panning started in early 1989; by 1990 it had grown into a booming business involving over 1,500 panners, many of them women seeking an independent source of income. The dramatic rise of gold-panning reflected the lack of economic returns to agriculture during the prolonged droughts of the 1980s and early 1990s. It illustrated the rapid spread of new technologies and production practices, and the striking ways in which such opportunities transformed local economies.[134]

Panners first dug up the bed and banks of Insiza river, and then moved down the river to the irrigation scheme. In 1990, officials alleged that people were blocking and panning in the canal between the dam and irrigation scheme and that 'hundreds' of people were digging up the scheme itself where an old mine shaft was located. An Mberengwa woman known as Magumbo allegedly acted as buyer. She was accused of illegally exporting some 400 ounces of gold from the district. Police held that many of those arrested in raids referred to her as their 'employer'. Officials faced difficulties in stopping her due to her adept manipulation of the cumbersome bureaucracies that regulated mining. Police action against panners was also ineffective. Over 150 people were arrested in August, but they simply paid their fines and returned to the river. Like poach-grazing, panning was vehemently defended as a moral right under drought conditions: panners took a defiant stand, posting lookouts along the river banks, and refusing to speak to officials.[135] Panners came to Insiza from Mazoe, Mberengwa, Bulawayo and Zvishavane; panning spread through large areas of the south west and further afield. A *Herald* article explained: 'People have left commercial farms where they were employed on a contract basis and opted for gold panning. Some have left drought stricken areas, unproductive communal lands and taken to the gold trail. Some are in it simply because of unemployment, which affects most people.'[136]

Panners sought to protect their position by playing various authorities off against each other. Depending on who asked, they claimed authority for their activities from the Ministry of Mines, Agritex, Local Government or Chief Sibasa. The council chairman alleged that Sibasa had given his approval to panning, and received a cut of the profits in return. Where conflict such as this emerged, it brought the various communal area leaderships into competition, and may also have had the effect of bringing panning, initially an activity dominated by women, under the control of male office-holders as panners sought protection.

In Vocola and Silalabuhwa, locally initiated and historically shaped responses to drought, land shortage and wider economic pressures had a greater impact on production practices and social institutions than did state policy. The period of political conflict made official mobilisation difficult and compromised new institutions, while the lack of development and delays in resettlement meant there were few resources that could be exchanged for support and compliance. Opposition to land-use interventions also stemmed from the fact that local leaders saw production constraints in terms of a combination of land shortage, especially grazing land, the dearth of rain and water supplies, and the contraction of other opportunities like employment, not, as had officials both before and after independence, in terms of 'customary' land-use practices. In an ironic twist, the previously much maligned Land Husbandry Act served as a means of warding off new state interventions, and of highlighting the state's obligation to redistribute land.

Conclusion

Nationalism had promised the land. It had also promised a better state. The Zanu(PF) government's difficulties in rebuilding authority over the land in Insiza was owed to failures on both counts. The range of institutions that claimed and exercised authority over land and people were shaped by the struggles of previous decades, the ecology and economy of this region, and the political conflict that erupted after independence. A Zapu pedigree was a crucial means for all post-independence institutions to attain legitimacy. With the persecution of Zapu, and Zanu(PF)'s attempts to command the political allegiance of council and vidcos, the new hierarchy of democratic governance was severely compromised. Customary office achieved greater importance over the course of the 1980s, acting as a place of retreat from political persecution, and as a position from which new institutions could be criticised.

The council and vidcos were the means by which a modern state was to be instituted from village on up, and land use practices transformed. Their effectiveness was undercut not only by political conflict, but also by continuities in technocratic ideology and practice. Technical prescriptions failed to offer solutions to communal area problems, instead reproducing a critique of African farmers that cast them as unproductive and backward. This was not, however, a monolithic state intent on enforcing a singular vision of 'development'. Civil servants were divided here more than anywhere else by the politicisation of the state and its use in elite strategies of accumulation. State bureaucracies were also divided over the means of implementing technocratic prescription. Thus LGPOs promoted institutions that would combine what they saw as the customary and modern, while Agritex retreated into a narrowly technical role from which it rejected any involvement in what it saw as the political.

Neither compromise nor repression gave the state the ability to intervene effectively. Instead, agrarian and social change was dominated by locally initiated strategies. Courts were run by customary leaders. Land allocation was dominated by local debates over history and justice. People took their own initiatives in defending their livelihoods. They panned for gold and migrated throughout the region in search of work. They threatened ranchers and resettlement schemes, literally, and through a campaign of encroachment justified through need and the denial of nationalist demands. The political conflict and drought of the 1980s drove white ranchers off the land far more effectively than the liberation war, but the region's Zanu(PF) elite used much of the land to accumulate cattle, not meet the demands of popular nationalism. State institutions struggled to build legitimacy, while the strategies of communal area farmers left them subject to insecurity, losses of livestock and violent reprisals. As Insiza entered the 1990s, the land remained not a basis for state-making and source of political capital, but a site of conflict.

Notes

1 Minister of Lands Moven Mahachi, *Hansard*, 2 January 1981.
2 Nkala, 1989, 43. Insiza fell in Zipra's 'Southern Front'. It formed part of a transit route through which casualties, supplies and recruits were moved to and from Botswana. To avoid drawing a heavy Rhodesian presence into the area, Zipra did not target white ranchers. Interview, former Zipra Security Officer, Bulawayo, 20 July 1991.
3 Ex-miners from the many defunct mines surrounding Filabusi and farm workers facing eviction dominated Insiza's first resettlement scheme. Interview, Resettlement Officer, Insiza District, Filabusi, 7 October 1988; *Herald*, 26 July 1982, 5 January 1983; *Sunday Mail*, 5 December 1982.
4 *Herald*, 22 October 1981. Also see *Herald*, 26 October 1981.
5 Interview, Chief Vezi Maduna, Avoca, 14 April 1989. Maduna was the first chairman of the Insiza Council.
6 For examples, see 'Background to Model D Resettlement Schemes in Gwanda District', 1990, 2; Cliffe, 1986, 66; Drinkwater, 1991, 142; Cousins, 1987, 82; Wilson, 1987a, 17. Jeanette Clarke, Forestry Commission Research Officer, pers. comm., 7 August 1990, reported such an initiative in Ntabazinduna.
7 See Herbst, 1990, 71, and comments of the Deputy Secretary for Rural and Cooperative Development, *Herald*, 16 August 1982.
8 These developments are explored in detail in Alexander, McGregor and Ranger, 2000, Chapter 8, and in Alexander, 1998.
9 *Zimbabwe Project News Bulletin (ZPNB)*, No. 18, Month In Zimbabwe, 17 July 1982.

10 *ZPNB*, No. 16/17, Month in Zimbabwe, 4 June 1982; Agricultural and Rural Development Authority, 1985, 14, 18-24.
11 See reports in the *Herald*, 4, 5, 29 June 1982; 3, 27 July 1982.
12 See Alexander, McGregor and Ranger, 2000, Chapter 8; Alexander, 1998, 166-7. For the most thorough account of human rights abuses in this period see Catholic Commission for Justice and Peace/Legal Resources Foundation [CCJP/LRF], 1997.
13 *Herald*, 8 February 1982. Also see Mnangagwa, 1989, 237.
14 *ZPNB*, No. 26, Month in Zimbabwe, 3 April 1983; No. 24, Month in Zimbabwe, 18 February 1983.
15 Minutes of the Insiza District Council, Filabusi, 1 February 1985.
16 *Herald*, 17 June 1983; *Sunday Mail*, 21 August 1983.
17 Interview, Provincial Planning Officer, Department of Physical Planning, Bulawayo, 8 August 1990. Also see Sibanda *et al.*, 1986.
18 *ZPNB*, No. 28, Month in Zimbabwe, 6 July 1983; *Herald*, 7 July 1983.
19 Interview, Filabusi, 7 October 1988.
20 *ZPNB*, No. 15, Month in Zimbabwe, 30 August 1982; No. 21, Month in Zimbabwe, 14 October 1982; No. 28, Month in Zimbabwe, 8 July 1983; *Herald*, 12 October 1982; Interviews, local ranchers, Filabusi, August 1988.
21 Nkala, 1989, 43. Mnangagwa, 1989, 241, cites the figure of 61 commercial ranchers killed in the 1980s.
22 See *ZPNB*, No. 30, Month in Zimbabwe, 16 September 1983; Ranger, 1989; *Herald*, 4 February 1984. The Lawyers' Committee for Human Rights, 1986, 26, estimated that, by early 1984, 500,000 acres of commercial land had been abandoned in Matabeleland.
23 Figures calculated from Matabeleland South Provincial Development Committee [PDC], 1989, and Matabeleland South PDC, 1988. Also see Matabeleland South PDC, 1985, 8, 36-7.
24 See the *Herald*, 10 December 1988.
25 Mberengwa Rural Council, List of Lessees as of 10 September 1987. Other prominent officials leased land elsewhere. For example, the *Herald* of 18 November 1988 reported that Provincial Governor Mark Dube grazed cattle he had acquired under the CSC's Cattle Finance Scheme on a partially settled scheme in Beitbridge District.
26 Interview, Provincial Planning Officer, Department of Physical Planning, Bulawayo, 8 August 1990; Minutes of the Insiza District Development Committee and Sub-Committees, Filabusi, various dates from 1986 to 1988. The DA had formed the MSM Syndicate with local commercial farmer Jack Mclaren and leased a ranch under this title. Additional light was shed on his connections with Mclaren during the Sandura Commission's investigations into the resale of vehicles allocated to MPs and Ministers. The then former DA (he had become a Zanu(PF) MP) was found to have abused his privilege by buying a vehicle for Mclaren. See the *Herald*, 13 April 1989.
27 Interview, Acting District Administrator, Insiza, 26 September 1988.
28 Interview, Resettlement Officer, Filabusi, 7 October 1988, and see Matabeleland South PDC, 1989, 39.
29 Interview, Nsiza Rural Council Chairman, Bulawayo, 11 October 1988.
30 Matabeleland South PDC, 1989, 14-15; *Herald*, 9 and 13 June 1989.
31 *Herald*, 28 March 1983; Matabeleland South PDC, 1985, 48.
32 See Robins, 1998, and 1994.
33 A large literature has highlighted the advantages to household production of communal area cattle management over the strategies of technical planners. See, for example, Drinkwater, 1991, Chapter 4; Cousins, 1987; Scoones, 1990; Sandford, 1982.
34 See Mbelesi and Ngobese, 1990.
35 Interview, Provincial Planning Officer, Agritex, Bulawayo, 10 October 1988; Matabeleland South PDC, 1989, 15.
36 Ranger, 1989.
37 Matabeleland South PDC, 1989, 14.
38 Interview, Acting District Administrator, Filabusi, 26 September 1988.
39 Minutes of the Insiza District Council, Filabusi, 8 May 1987.
40 Insiza District Squatter Control Committee, 'Squatters Return', July 1988; Interview, Acting District Administrator, Filabusi, 26 September 1988; Minutes of the Insiza District Development Committee, Filabusi, 17 July 1987.
41 Matabeleland South PDC, 1989, 39, 10-17.
42 Interview, Resettlement Officer, Filabusi, 7 October 1988. Also see Minutes of the Insiza District Council, Filabusi, 10 April 1987.
43 Interview, Resettlement Officer, Filabusi, 7 October 1988; and see Matabeleland South PDC, 1989, 11-12; Minutes of the Insiza District Development Committee, Filabusi, 20 July 1988.

44 Interview, V16, Silalabuhwa. In references to interviews with local leaders (members of vidcos, councillors, chiefs and their subordinates, party leaders), I use a coding system, followed by the ward.

45 Interview, C4/6, Ntunte.

46 Interview, Rancher, Mberengwa Rural Council, 25 August 1988.

47 The CSC's 'beef crisis' started in 1986. See S. Moyo, 1991, 29–30; *Herald*, 5 December 1986, 13 January 1987, 21 June 1989, 16 June 1990.

48 For example, *Herald* articles of 13 and 20 December 1983 reported that 20 people from Godhlwayo communal area had accused Resettlement Officer Charles Gumbo of assaulting people for driving cattle onto state farms. One complainant alleged that Gumbo had beaten him up, driven off his cattle, and fined him $42.

49 See *Parliamentary Debates*, Vol. 14, No. 51, cols. 2807-10, 2 March 1988.

50 *Chronicle*, 10 August 1990. Also see Malunga's criticisms in the *Herald*, 2 August 1991.

51 Matabeleland South PDC, 1989, 16. For other new demands see, 'Background to Model D Resettlement Scheme in Gwanda District', 1990, 2, fn 4.

52 See Robins, 1998, on these debates.

53 *Chronicle*, 28 April 1989.

54 *Herald*, 29 April 1989, and see the *Herald*, 2 February 1983, on earlier evictions.

55 See discussion in Alexander, 1991, 608-9.

56 See PER 5, Headman Ngomondo, Filabusi, DA to Under Secretary, Matabeleland South, 14 June 1983. In the same file, also see report by DA Philip Bhebhe, 30 March 1983. Ngomondo was subsequently deposed.

57 PER 5, Chief Maduna, Filabusi, DC, Filabusi, to PC, Bulawayo, 20 June 1980; DC, Filabusi, to PC, Bulawayo, 14 July 1980.

58 See Alexander, McGregor and Ranger, 2000, chapter 8, on Zapu's role in overcoming suspicion of new institutions.

59 Interview, Chief Vezi Maduna, Avoca, 14 April 1989.

60 Interview, C4/4, Silalabuhwa, and, for example, C4/4, Ntunte. It does not necessarily follow that the content of judicial decisions would have changed had elected courts exercised more influence, nor that the courts as they operated in Insiza had not changed their practices from previous periods. The anger with which new legislation giving women additional rights came under attack indicates that change was both underway and the subject of struggle.

61 Interviews, Provincial Promotion and Training Officer, Matabeleland South, Gwanda, 23 August 1988, and Acting District Administrator, Filabusi, 14 April 1989, respectively.

62 For example, interviews, V19/3, Mbondweni; V33/3, Mashoko; TV22/3, Sidzibe.

63 Interview, Provincial Promotion and Training Officer, Matabeleland South, Gwanda, 23 August 1988.

64 *ZPNB*, No. 26, Month in Zimbabwe, 24 April 1983, pp. 8-9; *ZPNB*, No. 28, Month in Zimbabwe, 15 June 1983, p. 5, 29 June 1983, p. 10.

65 *ZPNB*, No. 25, Month in Zimbabwe, 18 March 1983; *Herald*, 17 May 1983.

66 *ZPNB*, No. 28, Month in Zimbabwe, 3 June 1983, p. 2.

67 *ZPNB*, No. 29, Month in Zimbabwe, 17 August 1983; no. 30, Month in Zimbabwe, 21/9/83. By 1984, only one Zapu councillor still held office. See Minutes of the Governor's Meeting with the Insiza District Council and Representatives of Government Departments, Filabusi, 29 March 1984 and Minutes of the Insiza District Council, Filabusi, 6 November 1984.

68 *ZPNB*, No. 32, Month in Zimbabwe, 21 November 1983, p. 7.

69 Paragraph based on PER 5, Chief Maduna, Filabusi, DA P. Bhebhe, Filabusi, 30 March 1983.

70 See PER 5, Chief Maduna, Filabusi, DA Simela, Filabusi, to PA, Bulawayo, 31 July 1985.

71 PER 5, Chief Maduna, Filabusi, DA, Filabusi, to PA, Bulawayo, 19 September 1985.

72 The Minutes of the Insiza District Council from 1984 to 1986 contain numerous such complaints.

73 Minutes of the Insiza District Council, Filabusi, 14 November 1984, 1 February 1985; local interviews, 1988.

74 *Herald*, 17 November 1984.

75 *Herald*, 22 November 1984.

76 Minutes of the Insiza District Council, Filabusi, 4 November 1985, 13 December 1985. See discussion in Alexander, McGregor and Ranger, 2000, Chapter 9.

77 Minutes of the Governor's Meeting with the Insiza District Council and Representatives of Government Departments, Filabusi, 29 March 1984.

78 Minutes of the Insiza District Council, Filabusi, 3 October 1984. And see minutes for 6 November 1984.

79 Interview, Local Government Promotion Officer, Filabusi, 4 October 1988, and interviews with vidco chairmen and councillors in 1988 and 1989.

80 Ranger, *Review of the Press*, No. 33, 17 July 1987, pp. 6-9; Mnangagwa, 1989, 240.

81 Running complaints of these types are recorded in the Minutes of the Insiza District Council, various dates, 1984 to 1986.

82 Interview, Department of Social Services Officials, 28 September 1988; Minutes of the Insiza District Council, Filabusi, 31 August 1984.

83 See Minutes of Insiza District Council, Filabusi, 27 January 1984, 1 February 1985. The use of drought relief for political purposes is documented in CCJP/LRF, 1997, Lawyers' Committee for Human Rights, 1986, and Sibanda *et al.*, 1986.

84 Interview, V18/3, Mbondweni, and V25, Vocola, respectively.

85 For example, interviews, TV22, Sidzibe.

86 The council minutes record that two councillors who were accused of Zapu sympathies had their cattle stolen, one while in detention. See Minutes of the Insiza District Council, Filabusi, 27 January 1984 to 28 February 1986.

87 See Minutes of the Insiza District Council, Filabusi, 27 January 1984 to 25 April 1986.

88 Minutes of the Insiza District Council, Filabusi, 28 February 1986.

89 Interview, Officer in Charge, Zimbabwe Republic Police, Filabusi, 14 April 1989, and see *Herald*, 8 December 1986. A comparison of police records of cattle and donkey theft for January to September 1988 showed that donkey theft was much easier to detect, largely because donkeys were not slaughtered.

90 Interview, V31, Mashoko, and, for example, interview, TV37/4, Bekezela.

91 Many lost their posts as a result of the Sandura Commission's investigation into corruption in the distribution of vehicles allocated to MPs and Ministers. See GoZ, 1989. The investigations led to the resignation of Minister of Industry Callistus Ndlhovu, former Minister of Defence Enos Nkala, Provincial Governor of Matabeleland North Jacob Mudenda, and Insiza's former DA, MP Martin Simela.

92 Interview, Chief Vezi Maduna, Avoca, 14 April 1989. See Chapter 8.

93 See Ncube, 1989, 312-15; *Herald*, 24 February 1989; 13 October 1989.

94 See Alexander, McGregor and Ranger, 2000, 229-31, on interpretations of Unity.

95 Ministry of Local Government, Rural and Urban Development, 'Policy: Allocation of Land Within Communal Lands', Circular Minute 1/1986, Annexure E to Minutes of the Insiza District Council, 20 February 1986.

96 Minutes of the Insiza District Council, Filabusi, 25 April 1986.

97 Debates at provincial levels were also acute. A provincial Local Government officer told me that policy was to conform to village head boundaries and to co-opt village heads onto vidcos. When I interviewed provincial Agritex officials, they expressed disbelief, holding that this official in particular, and his Ministry more widely, was blocking their attempts to implement just such a policy. Interviews, Provincial Promotion and Training Officer, Gwanda, 23 August 1988; Provincial Agritex Officers, Bulawayo, 10 October 1988.

98 Interview, Senior Local Government Promotion Officer, Filabusi, 18 August 1988. The LGPOs cited here worked in the district for most of the 1980s. However, they had not participated in political repression as their colleague John Mbedzi had, in fact acting to limit the damage he inflicted. These officials, along with the newly appointed DA, were among the most sympathetic to the views of local leaders.

99 Interview, Regional Agritex Extension Officer, Filabusi, 18 August 1988.

100 Account based on interviews with Provincial Planning Officer, Department of Physical Planning, Bulawayo, 29 September 1988; Local Government Promotion Officer, Filabusi, 30 August 1988; settlers at the model village, Avoca, 3 October 1988; Minutes of the Insiza District Council, Filabusi, 31 January 1986, 26 June 1987; Minutes of the Insiza District Development Committee, Filabusi, 11 November 1987.

101 Interview, C4/4, Ntunte.

102 Interview, Local Government Promotion Officer, Filabusi, 30 August 1988.

103 Minutes of the Insiza District Council, Filabusi, 9 September 1988. Council officers complained that the new councillors were ignorant of policy in general. Interview, Executive Officer for Administration, Insiza District Council, Filabusi, 15 August 1988, 27 September 1988.

104 Establishing the number of cattle people 'own' is difficult in part because of loaning practices but also because of fears that such information will be used to control stock numbers. See Scoones and Wilson, 1988, 23, passim.

105 The perceived pressure on arable land was variable with some seeing it as a serious problem and others, e.g. V11/2, Gangabezi, arguing it was not a problem, 'because so many left during the drought'. Also see Werbner, 1991, 162 and passim, and Wilson, 1992.

106 Interview, V25/2, Vocola. Similar arguments were made elsewhere; for example, C1, Sanali.

107 Interview, V27/2, Vocola.

108 Also see Wilson, 1987a. The strongest demand for Model A resettlement lay in Insiza's Small Scale Commercial Areas where the expansion of families was seen as a major threat to the viability of farms.

109 This process was more complicated than a focus simply on vidcos and sabhukus indicates: as Wilson, n.d., and 1987a, argues, inheritance involved a wide range of members of an extended family, and included the rights of women to inherit and pass on land to their sons.

150

110 See Drinkwater, 1991, Chapter 5; Wilson, 1987a; Andersson, 1999, on pressures to move back into lines, and disputes over lines, in other lowveld areas.

111 Explanations for the dearth of rain varied widely and were hotly contested. See Alexander, McGregor and Ranger, 2000, 264-76; Werbner, 1991, 162 and passim.

112 Interview, V30, Vocola.

113 Interviews, V25, V26, V27, V28, V29, Vocola. See Scoones and Wilson, 1988, and Drinkwater, 1991, chapters 4 and 5, on the importance of timely ploughing and access to stock for arable production in low veld areas.

114 Most vidcos set dates after which cattle had to be herded away from fields. One chairman said his vidco imposed a fine of one goat on those who failed to keep cattle out of fields, and that the vidco had helped people to fence fields. Interviews, V30/3, V28/3, V29/3, Vocola.

115 Interview, V29, Vocola.

116 See Drinkwater, 1991, Chapter 4.

117 Encroachment was a significant problem in grazing schemes established, or revived, after independence. See Cousins, 1987, 48, 54-6.

118 Interview, Regional Agritex Extension Officer, Filabusi, 18 August 1988, and see Agritex, n.d. [1988].

119 Interview, Regional Agritex Extension Officer, Filabusi, 18 August 1988.

120 Compare to Drinkwater, 1991, 116-20.

121 Minutes of the Insiza District Council, Filabusi, 27 November 1984, 3 May 1984, 29 September 1988.

122 Interview, C2, Silalabuhwa.

123 Interview, V16, V6, Silalabuhwa.

124 Interview, V6, Silalabuhwa.

125 For example, in Bekezela Ward. The reasons for moving into grazing land were diverse: in most wards the process was explained as a hangover of freedom farming, or as the result of in-migration and land shortage. In Bekezela, however, leaders said that the movement into grazing land was due to land infertility, not shortage, reflecting the different soil type found in the area. Bekezela leaders also held a more positive opinion of Model A resettlement, seeing it as a way to gain access to fertile land.

126 Interview, V15, Silalabuhwa.

127 Interviews, V6, V15, V16, Silalabuhwa, for example. In most wards such views were echoed, though criticisms were sometimes tempered by fear of coercion and by the hope of trading compliance for the development resources promised in conjunction with villagisation.

128 Interviews, V6, V14, V15, V16, Silalabuhwa.

129 Interview, Regional Agritex Extension Officer, Filabusi, 18 August 1988.

130 Interview, V15, Silalabuhwa.

131 However, even where loaning was curtailed, cattle ownership could still serve as a source of patronage: people could be given preferential access to cattle or hire cattle at concessionary rates. Most leaders stressed the obligation of the better off to aid poorer neighbours and relatives. Also see Scoones and Wilson, 1988, and Wilson, 1992.

132 See the *Chronicle*, 31 August 1988; *Sunday Mail*, 29 January 1989, on the scheme. Some local leaders, e.g., TV22, Sidzibe; C4/2, Ntunte, strongly criticised the CSC scheme (as well as Agritex initiatives) as elitist. Also see S. Moyo, 1991, 38, on resistance to cattle finance schemes.

133 This account is based on my attendance at a meeting of representatives of the Mberengwa Intensive Conservation Area, Rural Council, Natural Resources Board, Agritex, Ministry of Mines, Zimbabwe Republic Police, Insiza District Council and Ministry of Local Government on 10 August 1990 in Filabusi and discussions with representatives of the Rural Council and Provincial Council; the Officer in Charge, Zimbabwe Republic Police, Filabusi; the Insiza District Council Chairman; and the DA, Filabusi, in August 1990. Also see the *Herald*, 31 January 1990, 15 August 1990, 6, 7 September 1990; *Chronicle*, 23 August 1990.

134 Compare to Wilson, 1992, 4-5; Yeros, 2002a, 218-26.

135 Such tactics were described by the acting DA who tried to negotiate with panners. Also see the *Herald*, 7 September 1990, and comments of the President of the Chamber of Mines in the *Herald*, 6 September 1990.

136 *Herald*, 6 September 1990.

7

Nationalism, 'Squatters' & Chiefs in Chimanimani

Remaking authority over the land in Chimanimani was not dominated by the partisan violence that so powerfully shaped Insiza's politics. Instead, a subtler process of redefining the meaning of nationalism was unevenly launched. Nationalism was not to be about the popular expectations of the war years, but about the establishment of a bureaucratic state able to discipline its citizens, both through technocratic prescription and state-backed custom. This shift was not easily achieved. Local interpretations of nationalism were difficult to dismiss in the face of avowals of political allegiance, the workings of patronage, and the massive occupations of land that characterised this region. The customary also emerged as a difficult to control and influential realm of knowledge and authority that acted not as a space of retreat from repression as in Insiza, but as a sphere for making and contesting claims on the state and the land. Chimanimani's politics was shaped by a multiplicity of interlinked claims to authority, each seeking its 'room to rule'.[1] I begin with a consideration of land redistribution before turning to communal area institutions.

The 'Lost Lands'

Chimanimani seemed well placed to realise nationalist promises of returning the 'lost lands'. In the 1970s, white farmers had been trapped between the Tribal Trust Lands and the Mozambican bases of Zanu's guerrilla army. As in much of Manicaland, and in contrast to Insiza, the war drove the vast majority of white farmers from the land.[2] People in Chimanimani's communal areas perceived well watered arable land, not grazing land, as their greatest need, and they were quick to occupy vacant land. Occupations created facts on the ground in a way that Insiza's poach-grazing could not, and they were not incompatible with official resettlement models. Moreover, Chimanimani's loyalty to Zanu(PF) meant local leaders were able to appeal to the ruling party. Manicaland's Provincial Governor played an influential role as a defender of land claims, in striking contrast to his equivalent in Matabeleland South.

The experience of Insiza and Chimanimani was not, however, solely one of contrasts. Popular nationalism was not just about reclaiming the lost lands but also about remaking the state. In both districts, people rejected the state's claims to technocratic authority over the land in favour of local versions of nationalism, histories of eviction, chiefly claims and need. When their objections were ignored, they resorted to extra-institutional tactics that vividly expressed their unwillingness to accept the new state's authority.

Official resettlement policy was only slowly explained in Chimanimani, and even more slowly enforced. At first, the district's party leaders expected the state to act as their benefactor. The newly constituted Zanu(PF) Steering Committee pressed for faster land redistribution through official channels, repeatedly requesting information about resettlement and reporting demands for land in expectation of support.[3] But it was not until early 1981 that Deputy Minister of Lands Moven Mahachi arrived in the district to explain policy. He informed the newly established council that the government intended to buy 49 farms in the district, but in an early expression of distrust, refused to disclose their location. Much to the surprise of councillors, he stressed that unproductive farmers would be evicted from resettlement land, and emphasised that the state was in charge of settling people: claims to land based on past evictions or chieftaincies were 'not practical'.[4] The Minister's views also diverged from those of some politicians, chiefs and officials. In 1981, for example, MP Bishop Joshua Dhube pressed for official recognition of 'Chief' Saurombe, whose title had been abolished in 1950, and for recognition of his people's claims to land from which they had been evicted. Members of the chieftaincy began returning from Mutare and elsewhere to stake their claims. A district official wrote: 'The general belief is that if government buys the farms, the Saurombes will be given priority in settling as this land was originally theirs.' Sceptically, he added, 'they will not settle until they are told to do so, they say.' In fact, 'Chief' Saurombe did not wait.[5]

Cases such as that of Saurombe were common because resettlement criteria had not been fully explained at the outset, and because they were considered unacceptable when they were explained. It was not until mid-1981 that councillors were told that those wishing to be resettled had to fill out forms. They 'were not pleased because when Mahachi had spoken there were no such conditions'. They 'said that the situation was tense with the inhabitants and that the councillors were unpopular because the people's wishes were not being fulfilled'. When the forms finally arrived, they were treated with distrust: only 1,400 of 8,000 were returned.[6] As a district official explained: 'People refused to fill forms or move on the initial mobilization due to their fear of the permits being revoked and their loss of control on the schemes. Rumours were rampant on the government's plans to take the crops grown on resettlement. They didn't trust the government and were suspicious of its motivations.'[7] Chimanimani's experience was mirrored in Manicaland as a whole: of 93,000 forms, only 10,909 were returned.[8] Though this response was significantly better than that in Matabeleland South, it nonetheless indicated a profound distrust of official intentions. Half of those who did fill out forms in Chimanimani were anyway judged ineligible for resettlement. Officials explained that people who were employed, owned ten or more cattle, had more than six acres of land or were unmarried did not qualify. Astounded councillors objected that, 'some people had eight acres but it was on a stoney, hilly, slopey or unproductive piece of land. Others were employed as casual labourers in Coffee Estates and Forestry and could be sacked at any time.'[9]

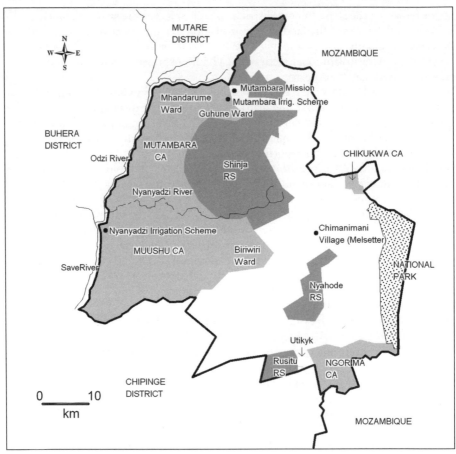

Map 7.1 Chimanimani District, 1990.
CA – Communal Area, RS – Resettlement Scheme. Rusitu resettlement scheme is not fully shown.

As the 1981 rainy season approached, objections to resettlement criteria and the speed of resettlement led to a large-scale movement onto the vast areas of vacant farm land in the district, a movement paralleled in much of the province.[10] Councillors continued to appeal for official approval for the occupations. They wrote to the Ministry of Lands requesting at least temporary access to 'old fields in abandoned farms' in order to 'alleviate the landless plight caused by the delay in the resettlement programme'. Along with party leaders they constantly requested services for 'squatters' and pressed for speedier resettlement. Delays were making them unpopular, and people were 'confused'.[11] In the meantime, people occupied land, often under the aegis of local party leaders and chiefs, and often with the encouragement of politicians and officials.[12] Movements were especially common during the three years of drought that followed the 1980/81 season when the imperative to move out of the arid western parts of the district was strongly felt.[13] Such occupations were largely successful. When Resettlement Officer Butsu arrived to run the Shinja Scheme in 1983, 'squatters' were automatically included, leading councillors to

154

query whether filling out forms really was the way to gain access to land.[14]

While official concern over squatting grew, policies remained largely sympathetic: squatters had regular access to ministers and politicians, police were instructed not to arrest them, and land redistribution was speeded through the 'accelerated' resettlement programme, the distinguishing feature of which was its lack of planning and infrastructure. As Bill Kinsey put it, 'sceptics among the technical planners refer to the programme as a "squatters' license"'.[15] At a Chimanimani council meeting, a Ministry of Lands official explained that squatters 'would be resettled and they would be given certificates of registration to fill in so that they might not be moved until the Ministry resettled them on accelerated resettlement schemes.'[16] Squatters made particularly effective use of their party allegiance, as Mutare's frustrated DA attested: '"If you want to see them you have to go through party structures before you can speak to them," he said.... "Some even leave me with their donations for the new ZANU(PF) headquarters"'.[17]

Though squatters who had occupied resettlement land in the early 1980s were largely left in place, the attitude to new occupations, and particularly people on commercial land, hardened. In late 1982, Deputy Minister of Lands Mark Dube declared 'total war' on Manicaland's squatters, while the Secretary of Lands announced the formation of a 'joint force' 'to show these people it is the whole of the government against squatting.'[18] The effectiveness of squatting as a means of claiming resettlement land declined as vacant land grew scarce, resettlement schemes fuller, and state bureaucracies stronger. The early 1980s marked a transitional period at the end of which the demands of outspoken local party leaders, chiefs and others were increasingly rejected in favour of central state control. This shift required the marginalisation of the political institutions that had emerged from the war, and a redefinition of nationalism from the top down. Nationalism was not to be about the popularly controlled restitution of the lost lands but about productivity, delivered through a technocratic bureaucracy for the benefit of a disciplined citizenry. Enforcing this transition was, however, far from easy.

SQUATTER CONTROL COMMITTEES

Following the early 1980s boom in resettlement, squatters were recast as a threat to central planning, to the environment, and to commercial farm production. The shift was justified in terms of protecting the foreign-currency earning potential of commercial farms. Minister of Lands Mahachi described squatters as 'undisciplined and criminal elements' who intended to 'frustrate the agricultural industry and resettlement process'. He stressed the importance of evicting squatters in terms of their 'detrimental effect' on 'foreign exchange earners'.[19]

A report from Mashonaland West typified these tendencies.[20] It blamed the 'squatter menace' for the 'destruction of natural resources', damage to the 'production potential of land', 'undue pressure' on social services, rising crime, and the 'disruption of proper resettlement demarcations'. Contradictions in the report highlighted the extent to which this characterisation constituted an ideological attack intended to justify the imposition of control. The depiction of squatters as a disorderly 'infestation' sat uneasily alongside passages in which the reasons for the same squatters' success was outlined: 'They display a high degree of self-reliance in the provision of services such as schools.... Some are very productive farmers and a lot of their produce has gone to the GMB [Grain Marketing Board].' The Provincial Administrator defended squatters as heroes of the liberation war and land-starved peasants, but his moral rectitude faltered under the pressure of coping with the estimated 36,000 squatters in his province: 'morality breeds a soft approach to dealing with squatters and this invites more and more squatters who probably will run away from those areas where seemingly tougher action is taken.' Moral argument gave way to administrative imperatives.

The hardened official critique of squatting was accompanied by the introduction of new control measures. Following the reorganisation of the ministries concerned with rural development in 1985, the Ministry of Local Government took the central role, and rapidly instituted a number of changes. Squatters were denied the automatic access to ministers and politicians they had previously enjoyed (in Zanu(PF) areas), and powerful Squatter Control Committees were established, the 'sole function' of which was 'to remove squatters'.[21] These committees were designed to coordinate the actions of all ministries involved in evictions and resettlement, alongside the party leadership. The Minister of Local Government stressed that 'land grabbers' would be 'ruthlessly removed'.[22] Developments in the mid-1980s were singularly inauspicious for popular land demands: resettlement no longer held pride of place in agrarian policy, a formidable ministerial machinery was devoted to squatter control, and a hostile – if ambivalent – critique of squatters pervaded the state.

Squatter Control Committees faced their greatest challenge in Manicaland, long host to the country's largest squatter population. The 1985 *Manicaland Provincial Development Plan* estimated that there were 50,000 squatters in the province, a figure that rivalled the officially resettled population of 60,000, and this in the region with the largest resettlement programme in the country.[23] Most squatters were on private farms, with the rest on resettlement and state land. The plan blamed a 'lack of political will' for the magnitude of the problem, but also admitted that resettlement could not 'absorb a large number of persons who cannot currently or are unlikely in the Plan Period to be supported on Communal Farmland or in Rural Employment'. In Chimanimani, the number of squatters roughly equalled the 400-odd officially resettled families.[24] The prospects for acquiring more land were poor: much of the remaining commercial land belonged to parastatals or subsidiaries of multinational companies. These estates produced timber, coffee, tea, wattle and fruit. They were unlikely to come up for sale and, if they did, were unlikely to be divided into smallholdings.

In the context of land shortage, growing unemployment, and huge 'squatter' populations, the responsibility for controlling squatters was passed down to district levels. DAs found themselves, as chairmen of the Squatter Control Committees, with the unenviable task of enforcing evictions, but with little resettlement land at their disposal. Few issues proved as contentious. DAs complained of their lack of control over land acquisition, and of the criteria applied by technical planners. They worried over the consequences of evictions, complaining that 'the causes of squatting were not considered when directives were issued to DAs to evict, e.g. closures of mines, retrenchment, abandonment by former farm owners and so on'.[25] Refusing to resettle such people only created further problems as they occupied land elsewhere. Land that DAs felt was needed for resettlement was often judged better suited to other purposes. In Chimanimani, an official angrily explained: 'Land hunger is very high.... [But] most of the land bought here has gone to the Forestry Commission. If that land had been given to people we wouldn't have a problem. [But] squatters aren't productive and timber is foreign currency'.[26] DAs' problems were compounded by the transformation of Manicaland's border into a war zone. As Renamo's insurgency in Mozambique expanded, it provoked an exodus from border regions, creating new demands for land.[27]

DAs' views brought them into conflict with technical officials who derided their desire to use 'every piece of land', with no concern for the requirements of land-use planning.[28] They insisted that 'the problem of squatting is a question of a lack of discipline not a function of overcrowding'.[29] All officials also faced pressure from politicians. Chimanimani's Agritex officer commented on the Shinja scheme:

> Kraal head Saurombe has 18 settlers in village 12. Another kraal head also disputes the boundary so 11 to 12 settlers move in. They build nice houses. [Officials] will say these people are squatters but these people will say, 'no, this is our motherland'. The [Resettlement Officer] has a lot of power but he knows if he moves these people the politicians will criticize him.... The politicians don't move squatters because it's political dynamite. Local politicians hide behind local traditions, they use the kraal head's argument that this land was ours long back. The squatters keep quiet and don't talk to anyone. They get vicious if you call them squatters.[30]

DAs complained that 'politicians viewed evictions of squatters as inhuman and will always view the DA as a heartless person who originates his own eviction ideas whenever he feels like it'.[31]

In practice, district Squatter Control Committees compiled lists of people occupying land and lists of farms that might be available for resettlement, and then sought to match the two in such a way as to clear commercial land, forestall further squatting, and avoid offending politicians. Committee debates largely excluded consideration of those who had filled out resettlement forms while councillors were kept in the dark regarding land purchases on the grounds that they 'would immediately tell people to rush into farms and put in their stakes'.[32] People who remained in communal areas had little chance of gaining access to resettlement land. As the district Agritex officer explained: 'Squatters are getting priority for resettlement, not people who filled resettlement forms. The battle between the commercial farmers and the government is about squatters. Squatters take advantage of the DA who wants to resolve the conflicts so he settles the squatters and the communal area people don't have a chance.'[33]

Councillors deeply resented their exclusion from decisions regarding land redistribution. They felt resettlement land, which was less heavily populated and stocked than communal areas, was 'used for nothing', and they still keenly felt the unequal distribution of land, as a councillor explained: 'There is a white farmer who owns 11 farms.... It is not fair for him to keep 11 farms for himself and then we have people living on mountain tops with no land.'[34] One consequence of the council's margin-alisation was that customary leaders played an increasingly important role in making demands for land. They came into the open as critics of resettlement criteria and Squatter Control Committee practices. At a Manicaland Chiefs' Council meeting, they 'complained that all farms bought are geared towards the resettlement programme at the expense of the people in the communal areas'. Drawing on the promises of the guerrilla war, they argued, 'they need the land that their children liberated from the hands of the white commercial settlers'.[35]

In the late 1980s, Chimanimani's Squatter Control Committee closely supervised processes of squatting, eviction and resettlement in an attempt to solve short-term crises. The results were highly variable. In the case of the residents of Saurombe West, a small farm located in the district's central highlands, no one save the farm owner favoured eviction. The roots of the eviction lay in the confusion surrounding resettlement at independence. In 1981, former farm workers and 'squatters' had formed a cooperative which was duly registered by the Department of Cooperative Development. Agritex did not, however, deem the farm suitable for resettlement, and it was subsequently sold to John Heyns.[36] A prominent farmer, Heyns was popu-larly known as 'Masoori' due to his reputed propensity for making people sorry. In this case, he did not disappoint. Heyns obtained an eviction order. The Squatter Control Committee then added the farm's residents to its list of people needing resettlement, but it was soon sidelined by Provincial Governor Dhube whom coop-erative members had approached. The Committee's plans were thrown into limbo: 'One morning they are going to move, the next they are going to stay. It is highly politicised and we don't touch it.'[37]

In this instance, officials welcomed the intervention of politicians. They objected to being 'used by one rich man to oppress others'.[38] But the protests of politicians served only to delay the eviction until late 1988, at which time the evictees' homes were burned and they were moved to Chimanimani village. The evictees gathered outside the DA's office to sing liberation war songs; women threatened to take their clothes off, a deeply shaming form of protest. The evictees received sympathetic press coverage, while the MP and Governor Dhube loudly pronounced the eviction 'intolerable'.[39] The resettlement bureaucracy quickly offered five farms close to the Mozambican border for resettlement, but the evictees responded by arguing that 'there are too many bandits there. We think "Masoori" Heyns should go to the land we have been offered.'[40] A reporter visited the few families who had agreed to be resettled in 1989. He found them living in Red Cross tents. A 62-year-old woman invoked the promises of the war: 'We thought the liberation war was fought to give us back our land. My grandfather was born on that land, my husband died there and now they throw us off.'[41] Such a resolution was obviously an unhappy one for the evictees. It was also far from satisfactory for the MP and Governor, who found them-selves unable to secure patronage for their constituencies, as well as for the DA who feared the evictees would simply occupy land elsewhere. Even 'Masoori' Heyns complained of the court costs he had incurred.

The Saurombe case demonstrated the precedence of private landowners' claims and technical land use considerations over nationalist appeals and political patronage. A very different outcome emerged from a dispute between residents of the Dzingire section of Ngorima communal area and the Roscommon Development Company, owner of neighbouring Uitkyk farm. As we have seen, the border conflict between Dzingire and Uitkyk dated back to the 1940s when the boundary had been redrawn over the protests of Headman Dzingire and his mission–educated sons. In this case the salience of historical land grievances, the relationship between different evictions in the context of land scarcity, and the intractable problems that farms bordering on communal areas faced with encroachment were all highlighted. It also underlined the changed status of the Mozambican border, which no longer acted as an escape route. Instead, and as in the Saurombe case, it was avoided as dangerously subject to armed attack.

The boundary between Roscommon's Uitkyk farm and Dzingire surfaced constantly in council meetings. The ward was represented by a voluble councillor who campaigned for land and denounced Roscommon for impounding squatters' cattle and burning their huts.[42] The dispute simmered until it was dramatically heightened by an influx of people evicted from the nearby Rusitu resettlement scheme in 1985.[43] They angrily 'pushed their way' into Dzingire's grazing area and onto Uitkyk; Roscommon responded by destroying crops and shooting dogs.[44] The Squatter Control Committee decided to solve the problem by moving the Uitkyk 'squatters' to the unplanned Nyahode resettlement scheme to the north. The movement of over 70 families did not, however, resolve the dispute. Shortly thereafter, Roscommon complained that the land was being cultivated by people from Dzingire. The Committee charged the councillor with encouraging 'civil disobedience'. He countered that the Dzingire residents were in desperate need of land, and that they had filled out resettlement forms to no avail.[45]

In this instance, the concerned parties forged a compromise, laying to rest, at least in the short term, a dispute that had simmered for the better part of half a century. Roscommon agreed to donate the disputed area for resettlement if settlers agreed to become out-growers on its tea estate, which they duly did.[46] The Dzingire case illustrated the interconnected nature of evictions, resettlement, communal area land pressure, and people's historical claims to land, as well as the singular determination behind the use of encroachment tactics.

The case of the Nyahode valley illustrated the contrasting role that unplanned resettlement land played. The Nyahode farms were located in the high rainfall mountains. Like Saurombe West, they were occupied by a mixture of former farm workers, people from communal lands and, subsequently, evictees from Uitkyk and workers from nearby forestry estates.[47] The first wave of settlers had formed nine cooperatives, usually under Zanu(PF) leadership. The state subsequently purchased the farms, intending to plan them as cooperatives. But planning did not get underway until 1987, and in the interim the land was an easy mark for both the Squatter Control Committee and the 'self-resettled'. Officials recognised that shuffling people from one area to another was bound to create new problems but perceived it as unavoidable: 'You have commercial farms and you have state land and you have squatters all around in Chimanimani. The law says if a private landowner complains the government must remove the occupants but the state land is open so you put the squatters there.... There isn't a choice. Planning is going on and another problem will be created when we try to implement.'[48]

In Nyahode, it was likely that there would be serious problems when it came to implementation. The people moved into the area from Uitkyk did not accept resettlement criteria, especially as they pertained to employment. And, like others who had moved in of their own accord, they were not interested in cooperatives. Moreover, the estimated 780 families who lived in the valley – that is, more than on all other district resettlement schemes combined – far exceeded the number for which Agritex was planning. While Agritex recognised that evictions would be 'administrative dynamite', its officials were content to simply 'do the plan and then hand it to the Ministry of Local Government'.[49] In the meantime, relations with people in the valley deteriorated. Officials requested police escorts to go with them to the valley because 'people are resistant'.[50] Agritex complained that it could not enforce conservation measures because people were 'hostile', and 'they can find sympathy higher up'.[51] Officials avoided intervening in conflicts over access to land in the valley, even when they were a direct result of state evictions into the area: 'People will think they will be permanent if we interfere in their conflicts and we don't know who will be permanent.'[52]

From the point of view of the people in the valley, conflicts with officials were overshadowed by conflicts among themselves. Kwirire Cooperative, one of the older and more productive cooperatives, illustrated these disputes. Despite what the cooperative thought was a clear claim to the land, it had come under siege from self-appointed village heads. The cooperative chairman, who was also a Zanu(PF) branch chairman, said he intended to resign because of the enmity and witchcraft accusations that trying to enforce rules had brought him. Those he refused land simply approached a village head, paid a fee and, as he put it, 'I look like a fool.'[53] Those who were not Kwirire members argued that the cooperative had unfairly monopolised the best land. To them, village head allocations were just and egalitarian.[54] Other farms faced similar conflicts, between cooperative members and non-members, farm workers and Zanu(PF) youth leaguers and village heads. In the midst of a resettlement scheme, an area the state intended as the pre-eminent space for modernist engineering, a vast range of conflicting claims to land were deployed, largely beyond the state's control.

Though the nature and outcomes of conflict in these three cases differed, all illustrated the tremendous diversity in claims to authority over the land, and means of making claims, as well as the extent to which, from the state's point of view, resettlement had become a means of resolving conflicts over commercial land. Those who dutifully filled out resettlement forms were ignored in the rush to solve crises caused by evictions or encroachment disputes. In practice, the question of land pressure within communal areas went unaddressed. The state's management of land redistribution bred deep resentment, and placed local institutions at odds with the state and their own constituencies, acting as an obstacle to legitimising authority over the land. The consequences for the communal areas fed into other struggles over state-making.

'Who is Today's Government?'

In Chimanimani, party loyalty was not at stake as it had been in Insiza. Rather, the new government's first challenge lay in defusing and channelling the popular demands made through Zanu(PF). State-building at first focused on bringing the multitude of autonomous and outspoken local Zanu(PF) committees under a semblance of control. In Chimanimani, they were rapidly reorganised into a hierarchy of village, branch, and 'district' (the equivalent of a council ward) committees. The Zanu(PF) Steering Committee, made up of the eighteen district chairmen, sat at the top. All levels of party leadership were dominated by older men, not by the youth and women who had gained authority in the war, marking what Terence Ranger has called a 'conservative revolution'.[55] At first, party leaders played a key role in mediating with central authorities and expressing local demands, in distributing development resources and relief, and in settling disputes and allocating land.[56] The authority that they wielded did not, however, imply uncontested local support. Nor did Zanu(PF)'s electoral victory guarantee official favour.

The second step in bringing order was the creation of a district council. Chimanimani's Zanu(PF) Steering Committee was centrally involved in the difficult task of building support. The Committee complained of the 'hard job they met'. Popular 'reservations' were rooted in suspicions of continuities with the Rhodesian regime, and in expectations of immediate redress for nationalist demands.[57] The Committee was energetically questioned on a tour of the district. People asked, 'Who is today's government?' They wanted to know 'whether the District Commissioner was still there and what his role is now that the [Zanu(PF)] chairman for the district has been elected?'; 'When the money promised the people by Government to rebuild their homes, buy food and clothing shall be coming'; 'When shall land be given to the people?'; 'Why the present government is still in use of [the] old Council Act, Warrant and Advisers'; 'Why has it been found necessary by the present government to keep in employment the same Policemen and Civil Servants...?' An official worriedly commented, 'People have wild expectations which will breed frustration and resentment if their state of mind is not collected now.'[58]

The first hurriedly organised council elections proved controversial. Council wards were delineated by Zanu(PF) political commissars on the basis of party districts; Zanu(PF) nominees ran unopposed in all wards. Complaints of inadequate consultation and charges that candidates had been imposed followed: people 'didn't feel represented'.[59] Nonetheless, the establishment of a council, however tenuously, provided officials with a means for restricting the role of the party. The council rapidly became the principal development authority and channel for communication. Local Government Promotion Officers (LGPOs), many of whom were drawn from the ranks of guerrillas and political commissars, were particularly influential in diverting Zanu(PF) committees from work delegated to the council.[60] Party committees were also undermined by their failure to meet popular demands, such as for war reparations and speedy resettlement. Party chairmen were demoralised by their lack of remuneration, in contrast to the salaries given higher level party officials, councillors and chiefs.[61] The initiative from within Zanu(PF) increasingly came not from grassroots committees but from the District Party Coordinator, a salaried appointee, and from provincial and national officials.[62] The establishment of a council and the centralisation of the party were key steps in re-asserting government control over its rural constituency – in creating the means for 'collecting' people's 'state of mind'.

Interventions with regard to chieftaincy constituted another aspect of this process.

The role of chieftaincy in the early 1980s highlighted the diverse legacies of earlier policies and politics. Contrasts between official views in Insiza and Chimanimani paralleled pre-independence patterns: where Insiza's officials remained largely unconcerned with customary criteria for succession and considered village heads an illegitimate creation, Chimanimani's officials accepted village heads as legitimate and plunged into the process of investigating succession procedures on the basis of Rhodesian records. They stressed that neither councillors nor Zanu(PF) leaders influenced succession, instead depicting the process as apolitical by right of its reliance on customary criteria.[63] As in the past, the intense politicking that surrounded chieftaincy belied such a claim. Debate over customary appointments was much complicated by the long history of demotions and depositions, evictions and migrations, and, latterly, the Rhodesian Front's search for pliable and 'genuine' chiefs, and war. Claimants to chiefly titles lobbied politicians, officials and councillors, solicited the help of lawyers, and received the backing of urban constituents: titles were highly valued and hotly disputed.[64] Claims to lower level offices were particularly difficult to regulate. A Local Government official lamented: 'Now no one knows who is the kraal head. There are so many disputes. Some kraal heads died before the struggle and some died during the struggle and other people registered as kraal heads.'[65] Though district officials were sympathetic to demands for redress against past depositions, no provision was made for the creation of new titles, thus maintaining a late Rhodesian *status quo*.[66]

Policy on chieftaincy ran counter not only to the expectations of deposed chiefs and the constituencies they mustered, but also to the views of local Zanu(PF) leaders who sought to distinguish between good and bad chiefs, and to redefine chiefs' prerogatives. In 1980, the Zanu(PF) Steering Committee demanded that Tribal Land Authorities be removed from the council warrant because they 'are no more functioning in the rural areas because the committees set up by the masses are the ones operating in the people's day to day lives'.[67] Party leaders objected to the policy requiring that chiefs sit as ex-officio members of the council, 'on the grounds that they are not democratically elected and so do not represent the masses'.[68] They did not, however, wholly reject chieftaincy. A Steering Committee member commented that, 'as chiefs, the people recognised them as their traditional leaders', but to ask them to undertake council work would be 'unrespectful' and would take them away from the 'great demand of work awaiting them at home'.[69]

Committee members' views reflected the complexities of nationalist mobilisation: they were well aware that some customary leaders had formidable nationalist credentials, that the reason Tribal Land Authorities were defunct was in part due to chiefs' opposition to them, and that there had been cooperation between Zanu(PF) committees and village heads in allocating land and settling disputes during the war.[70] They sought not to reject customary authority but to make a clear distinction between their own democratically legitimated authority and that of hereditary leaders. Thus they argued that chiefs' role should be limited to the 'spiritual' sphere where their expertise was pertinent. The council in fact relied heavily on customary leaders' expertise in its development work. They were consulted over the requirements of 'local spirits' at the Hotsprings resort, over taboos in sacred forests, over the 'traditional implications' of cracks in roads, over the handling of grave sites near building projects. When the fish in a fish pond project were believed to have been 'hidden traditionally', funds were allocated in order to obtain customary advice on the pond's 'cultural requirements'.[71]

In fact, the only chief named as a wholly unacceptable member of the council was Garai Ngorima, who had worked so closely with the Rhodesian Front. His nomination angered party leaders: 'There was a great deal of opposition from ZANU (PF), who say Chief Ngorima is unpopular, should not sit on the Council, and that his presence would wreck its future prospects.'[72] Their objections were ignored. In the end, it was an appeal to custom, not nationalism, that proved effective. Drawing on events dating from the 1950s, elders in Ngorima argued that Garai was the son of an illegitimate marriage, and that he been improperly installed. They held that Garai's half-brother, who had remained in the district during the war as a Zanu activist, was the 'real' heir. Local Government officials accepted their argument on its customary merits, though they were well aware that such arguments disguised other agendas: the tactics that elders had honed under Rhodesian rule proved far from outdated.[73]

Central government interventions thus rode roughshod over local efforts to create a changed political order: popular suspicions of the council were ignored, attempts to discriminate among chiefs were brushed aside in favour of the maintenance of state-backed custom, and the party's demands went unheard. The primary local authority, the district council, uneasily yoked together a faction of the party and of customary leadership, neither of which commanded uncontested support and both of which claimed authority on distinct bases but in overlapping spheres. From its shaky start, Chimanimani's council found its authority limited by its financial dependence, popular distrust, and challenges from 'traditional' and party leaders. The council's efforts to collect rates illustrate the obstacles it faced.

People had angrily rejected rates in 1980,[74] and officials did not press for rate collection again until 1982 when they were faced with cuts in council grants. Councillors initially rejected the proposal as 'tantamount to political suicide',[75] but relented a year later, cautiously calling for a tour of the district to introduce the measure. Though the tour met heated opposition, the council proposed that Zanu(PF) committees collect annual rates of two dollars per adult for a ten per cent commission. When rate collections got underway in 1984 the results were dismal: party leaders proved reluctant to embrace such an unpopular task, people were 'uncooperative', and only a paltry sum was collected.[76] It was deemed wise to 'shelve' collections in the run-up to the 1985 national elections. The council then tried to solve the problem by transferring rate collection duties to the newly established vidcos.[77] However, and in striking contrast to Insiza, vidcos were drawn almost entirely from party ranks – sometimes Zanu(PF) committees were simply rechristened as vidcos – and faced similar popular pressures to the party.

The failures of the party and vidco in rate collection were not just a result of their concern for popularity. They were also undermined by sabhukus who argued that rate collection was properly their duty, as it had been before independence.[78] In 1986, the council, in common with councils throughout the province, bowed to their pressure.[79] But this simply provoked a new dispute with party leaders who argued they had not been properly consulted. Under pressure from the District Party Coordinator and the Zanu(PF) provincial leadership, vidcos were reinstated.[80] These tensions did nothing to improve rate collections. Councillors were forced to intro-duce other unpopular ways of raising revenue. With considerable desperation, they declared that it was 'worthless to keep discussing' among themselves: the problem was political.[81] A joint council and party meeting was called at which the low rate collections were blamed on drought, unemployment, and the failure to address the 'landless problem'. There was a 'lack of good communication between vidcos, wadcos, party and traditional tribal leadership' as well as pervasive opposition to women paying rates and to paying rates at all. In the end, councillors appointed 'tribal leaders' as rate collectors for a second time, stressing that the party and vidcos should 'reinforce the collection of subscriptions, in order to avoid defaulters hiding behind any one leadership'. Chiefs 'welcomed the resolution stating that it had been the responsibilities of the traditional tribal leaders' in the past.[82] Village heads in fact only marginally improved rate collections, but nonetheless touted their appointment as an important recognition of their customary authority.

The troubled conclusion to the rate collection debate was symptomatic of wider changes in the relationships among local leaders. By the late 1980s, economic decline and corruption scandals fed disenchantment with Zanu(PF). Chimanimani's District Party Coordinator was removed from office on corruption charges in 1988. Far from the assertive and autonomous party of the early 1980s, chairmen faced an apathetic constituency. Tasks such as collecting membership fees and 'mobilising' people for rallies grew onerous. In border areas, party leaders described their main role as ensuring security: army units used the youth wing to 'identify suspicious characters'.[83] The party was not, however, wholly sidelined. Invoking the name of the party and holding Zanu(PF) office was important in local power struggles and in claiming patronage. Party membership remained a key prerequisite to positions in other institutions and some individuals retained influence as a result of personal links to MPs and ministers. In addition, struggle over the meaning of nationalism continued: local leaders commonly reiterated the phrase 'we are all Zanu(PF)' when expressing anger over policies or to legitimise evasion, a tactic unavailable in Zapu areas such as Insiza.

The council and vidcos occupied a difficult position. They were the officially recognised lowest rungs of popular representation and drew their membership from Zanu(PF) ranks. They assumed the development role briefly played by the party at independence, and were able to claim some credit for the expansion of agricultural and social services in the early 1980s, the distribution of drought relief, and projects carried out under the food-for-work programme. Councillors and vidco chairmen (and this included many party and customary leaders) were also often in a position to benefit from the expansion of services and infrastructure in rural areas, creating a basis for an alliance between local leaders and the state. However, the vidcos and council depended on central government resources, and were excluded from policy-making. Council meetings were peppered with accounts of failures to collect school fees, the collapse of income-generating projects, and complaints about the exclusion of the council from control over services, and about the lack of consultation by offi-cials. Their role as policy implementers left them vulnerable where policies were unpopular. Moreover, the divisions among leaderships, each with different historical and epistemic claims to authority despite the many overlaps in membership, offered opportunities to undermine one another. Notably, the weaknesses of vidcos and the apathy within the party created space for the emergence of customary leaders as, at one and the same time, populist critics of state policy and a pivotal means for officials to implement policies and for politicians to build support. Their ability to mobilise the ideological field of custom proved a powerful tool.

Courts and the Politics of Custom

Immediately after independence, both party and customary leaders exercised judicial authority. Government attention focused on stamping out Zanu(PF) courts (Zapu presented far fewer problems in this regard). At a meeting with party leaders, Chimanimani's MP railed against 'kangaroo courts' and threatened to prosecute anyone who participated in them.[84] The district Magistrate explained: 'The party courts were abolished at independence because they were kangaroo courts and only believed in beating. It was trial by ordeal.' The establishment of the new village courts further undercut the party's role. Officials 'did a lot of work' intended to 'channel' the party away from its judicial role, much as it had been diverted from development work with the creation of the council.[85]

Official explanations of the new courts were contradictory and, from the local point of view, unsatisfactory. In part due to the continued recognition given chiefs, officials found it difficult to define their role in relation to the new courts. The Deputy Minister of Lands told party leaders that there 'will be a village court, community court then Magistrate court.... People will see by themselves that the chief automatically will have no power and duty to perform.'[86] But shortly thereafter the Deputy Minister of Justice stressed that the new courts did 'not imply that there is an end to Chieftainship'. He advised councillors and the party to consult 'tribal elders' when choosing presiding officers, advice that caused little protest: chiefs and headmen were almost all elected to run village courts, as were many village heads.[87] The only chief who was left out was the unpopular Garai Ngorima: his half-brother, and eventual successor, was elected in his place. Customary leaders nonetheless bitterly objected to the elections as an affront to their hereditary authority. The Deputy Minister of Justice's edicts regarding the kinds of cases the courts could hear also provoked controversy. Councillors and chiefs held that the greatest number of cases would likely concern witchcraft, while the Minister stressed that, under the Rhodesian Witchcraft Suppression Act, 'nobody is allowed by law to accuse another of being a witch and if you do you are liable to go to jail'. He tried to dodge the issue by suggesting that such cases be referred to the Ministry of Health, now responsible for 'traditional' healers, a view that evoked both protest and laughter from his audience.[88] Witchcraft cases, and the related 'healing' of individuals and communities subject to wartime violence, had the effect of bolstering customary leaders, including spirit mediums, as they were deemed uniquely qualified to handle such cases.[89] Cases involving accusations of witchcraft and of 'bad spirits' haunting families remained prevalent in subsequent years.[90]

As the 1980s progressed, chiefs and headmen in Chimanimani pressed for official recognition of their judicial authority. They argued that the three-year drought following independence was a consequence of the ancestors' displeasure with their loss of recognition, a view that was widely shared.[91] They sought to exploit the vacuum created by the party's growing malaise and government concern to bolster support as the 1985 elections approached. Chimanimani's DA held a pre-election meeting with customary leaders at which he appealed for their political allegiance. He thanked them for the good rains of 1984/85 and stressed that the government was not 'throwing chiefs overboard': chiefs were still paid salaries and provided with uniforms; they were necessary to development and to 'ceremonies required by custom'. He called on chiefs to exercise their 'spiritual powers' on behalf of Zanu(PF) and not to allow opposition parties to entice them 'to perform spiritual rituals designed to influence spirits of the land to support those bad elements'.[92]

Chiefs' lobbying paid off: just prior to the elections, Prime Minister Mugabe promised to give official sanction to chiefs' and headmen's courts, not on the basis of elections but on the basis of their customary authority. Legislation was not passed until 1990, but the increased attention paid chiefs allowed them to join more effectively an existing chorus of criticism directed against legal changes granting women new rights, particularly the Legal Age of Majority Act. The Act's passage had provoked vitriolic denunciations in the national press: it was depicted as 'corrupting and unafrican'.[93] Chimanimani's councillors argued that it was 'a departure from our culture and would increase the stubbornness amongst girls and women'.[94] Chiefs complained that the Act undermined 'traditional values': it led to baby dumping, divorce and disputes.[95] MPs endorsed chiefs' views, arguing that the 'return' of powers to chiefs was necessary to protect African culture; many called for a repeal of the Legal Age of Majority Act on the same grounds.[96] The government sought to tread a middle path. Thus while chiefs were given control over courts, their jurisdiction did not extend to the controversial sphere of family law. Nonetheless, laws which were already difficult to enforce looked set to face new obstacles. During the legal training sessions for chiefs and headmen, Chimanimani's Magistrate commented: 'It is central government policy to keep them involved but the chiefs don't accept the new laws.'[97]

The 1990 Act had other, unanticipated effects on relations among local leaders. Long before its passage, it heightened competition among customary leaders. In anticipation of the Act, the government pressed for all vacant Rhodesian-era posts to be filled while reiterating its refusal to create new titles.[98] Offices in Chimanimani were largely filled by the late 1980s, highlighting unmet claims. According to the district's Magistrate, the 'social conflict' surrounding outstanding claims prevented nearly half of the district's village courts from functioning.[99] The promised recognition of courts raised the stakes in competition for titles, provoking bitter conflicts which impinged on efforts to implement development projects and agrarian policies, and which drew party and vidco leaders into heated disputes. The conflicts and compromises which characterised struggles over judicial authority also featured in the struggle to constitute authority over land.

Authority and the Land

State interventions with regard to land allocation and use within the communal areas were probably less effective than in any other sphere. After independence, the council, like chiefs before it, was unable even to monitor land allocation in the vast area under its jurisdiction. Instead, and with the DA's backing, the council called for Zanu(PF) chairmen to allocate land – but they faced a stiff challenge from customary leaders.[100] DAs throughout Manicaland were confused: in 1983, they requested head office clarification on 'the working relationship of District Councillors and traditional leaders in so far as allocation and use of land was concerned'.[101] Conservation also proved a difficult nettle to grasp. The council proved reluctant to take punitive action, arguing that conservation was a 'touchy issue' that should be solved through land redistribution.[102] State efforts to intervene in land use and allocation only slowly gained momentum.

As elsewhere, the first intervention involved villagisation. Chimanimani's 'Village Settlement Housing Scheme' was the first in the country, and intended solely as a means of improving housing.[103] The council nominated the tiny Chikukwa communal area as the project site. Chikukwa was unusual in that it had been created in the midst of the liberation war and so had relatively little investment in homes. Nonetheless, local enthusiasm fell well short of expectations: only 33 of 500 stands were taken up, owing to people's reluctance to take loans, and objections to the proximity of houses and their placement in areas considered sacred.[104]

The broader land use planning exercise that followed was initially a source of confusion. As the district Agritex officer explained: 'Local Government came in and said everyone should be in straight lines. Community Development says they want closer settlement for piped water. We come in and say it is a total land use plan with the use of all areas.... [The policy] had so many different interpretations.'[105] A consensus that intensified intervention was necessary was, however, entrenched by 1986: the Chimanimani Five Year Plan stressed that policy was aimed not only at promoting 'modern housing' but also 'at persuading people to abandon scattered settlements and demarcating areas for grazing, cultivation and settlement'.[106] This call coincided with other changes in official and local attitudes to land. Competition for land in communal areas had sharpened owing to curtailed opportunities for 'squatting' and resettlement, localised pressure from evictees and Mozambican refugees, and declining formal employment. These pressures interacted with the rising influence of customary leaders. Village heads were set to win the struggle over rate collection and increasingly sought to make exclusive claims to authority over land allocation, often cultivating a constituency among the land hungry. Chiefs had been promised courts and they used forums like the Manicaland Council of Chiefs to argue that judicial authority could not be divorced from land authority, a view that found sympathy among officials and MPs.[107] At the same time, pressure to enforce land use regulations increased. After years of prevarication, the council passed land use by-laws in 1986. Echoing the shift in official attitudes in the 1940s, the Natural Resources Board argued that it was time education was backed by force. Lands

167

Inspectors warned councillors that 'they should expect tough measures by the Department against conservation law breakers'. A spate of prosecutions, fines and crop destruction followed.[108]

Revived concern over the issue of land allocation illustrated the effects of these changes. Debate focused on village heads. In 1986, conservation committee members complained of a district-wide problem of village heads allocating land on slopes and stream banks.[109] The District Party Coordinator and councillors attacked them as corrupt and irresponsible, charging that they took money for allocating land. Chiefs called for 'stern measures'.[110] Officials also believed village heads acted with undue autonomy: 'The kraal head used to report to the chiefs in the old days but the new kraal head doesn't have to and the chief doesn't control him. The kraal heads solicit money from settlers and give lands on slopes and in forests'.[111] The council resolved that land allocation be channelled through vidcos, councillors and chiefs, thus excluding village heads. Interestingly, Zanu(PF) chairmen went unmentioned, in contrast to 1983 when they were appointed as the key local land authority.[112] The resolution was not, however, put to the test as the council was informed that it fell foul of the law: only the council as a whole could allocate land. Councillors dutifully repealed their resolution, though neither they nor officials had any illusions that the letter of the law could be enforced.[113]

In this context, land use planning was formally introduced. Agritex officials drew explicit parallels with some of the most hated of Rhodesian policies. They told councillors that the land use plan was based on the Native Land Husbandry Act which had been 'overturned because of politics', and on the wartime Protected Village which 'was good, for all people were together and security was seen at one place'.[114] Land use planning followed directly in this lineage: 'It was all the old idea but the difference is that in the past people were forced but now its all put to the community to decide for themselves.' The extent of local decision-making was, however, limited to consideration of a completed plan: formulating land use plans was a technical exercise for which only experts were qualified.[115]

Despite officials' endorsement of land use plans, most were well aware of, and often sympathetic to, popular objections to the policy. They held that the major cause of opposition was the lack of compensation for those who would be displaced: people who had invested in houses and orchards were loath to move or take on loans.[116] Officials worried that movements would hit recent migrants and the poor hardest, because they were more likely to be in grazing areas and less likely to have invested in housing, and they did not want to be 'accused of favouring the rich over the poor'.[117] The land use plans had also provoked fears of destocking and limits on field sizes, and concern that the young would be excluded from land.[118]

As elsewhere, officials' awareness of objections to land use planning led them not to reconsider its merits but to seek strategies for easing its implementation. One tactic was to offer services in exchange for cooperation. In Chimanimani, these were available as a result of a NGO-funded 'water and sanitation' project which provided boreholes and Blair toilets. However, in practice, Agritex's production of land use plans lagged far behind the provision of services, and they were thus effectively pre-empted.[119] A second strategy consisted in a policy of co-optation intended to unite all leaders. As with land allocation, rates and courts, officials were well aware of local leaders' capacity for disruption, and their own need for allies. Extension workers tried to gain the support of 'influential leaders' before introducing policies more widely, so that 'no one will confuse people'.[120] Officials agreed that customary leaders were the most effective spoilers. Some saw them as 'resistant to all development' – 'There are names and ancestral beliefs to be followed and by this people resist' – while others depicted them as 'in favour of development', so long as their authority was respected.[121]

The district Agritex officer was the most outspoken proponent of granting customary leaders authority in support of implementing land use plans. He went significantly further than Local Government officials, who stressed the need to bolster vidcos. His views on elected development institutions were derisory: 'The vidcos are a political imposition on traditionalists.... The vidco helps the kraal head and not the other way around.' The council was 'only an arm of the chief': 'We are going back to the old times, we are giving the chiefs the power. Wherever we have success in the land use plan, there is hidden evidence that a chief is behind it. If the chief opposes it, it won't happen.'[122] With regard to land use planning, he held that co-opting village heads was necessary to identify boundaries and manage resources. In fact, and in contrast to Insiza, Agritex and Local Government officials had cooperated in demarcating vidco boundaries such that they reflected those claimed by village heads. Neither Agritex nor Local Government were, however, complacent about the problems of implementation. As in Insiza, Agritex retreated from taking responsibility for the implications of its plans, notably with regard to setting limits on stock and arable land: 'That is planning dynamite. We restrict ourselves to the technical field and leave that to Local Government after our plans are done'.[123] Local Government officials were, as usual, left in an invidious position. Their views were pessimistic: 'we explain, people accept in principle, but implementation will be a problem.'[124]

District officials effectively acknowledged the authority of customary leaders to a far greater extent than was enshrined in the law. In part, their attitudes reflected continuities with past practices; in part, they were a response to, and also reinforced, the limited authority of vidcos and the council. Relations among local leaders and officials were in practice diverse and mutable, as the following case studies illustrate. Nonetheless, several generalisations can be made. First, agrarian interventions were interpreted as highly political, despite their pretence of technical neutrality. Second, they shaped the language and tactics that local leaders adopted in struggles for authority and resources, reinforcing distinctions between different forms of knowledge of, and so authority over, the land. Finally, the cases illustrate the limited authority that the state was able to exercise over the land: 'communal' tenure was determined through a process of political negotiation and conflict, not by the state's rule-making.

MHANDARUME WARD

Mhandarume ward is located in the north-west corner of the district. It has neither the irrigation schemes nor the high rainfall of other wards. All local leaders were men over the age of 40 who had been born in the area. They had relatively large herds of stock and fields in comparison to both newcomers and young people. Membership in local institutions frequently overlapped: almost all vidco chairmen and customary leaders were also Zanu(PF) chairmen. Though some customary leaders held vidco posts, in this area vidcos tended to be dominated by people who were neither members nor allies of the 'royal' Chiesa lineage.[125] In late 1988, land use planning was central to competition among local leaders and their relationships to officials.

Customary leaders in Mhandarume were extremely disgruntled by post-independence policies and had fought to assert their authority. 'Chief' Chiesa was officially recognised as a village head but had lobbied for a chiefly title since the 1970s.[126] Chiesa had not been elected to the village court in 1981, but had adjudicated cases nonetheless and eventually succeeded in wresting the court from the elected presiding officer.[127] Other customary leaders, most of whom were closely related to the Chiesa house, waged a vitriolic campaign against vidco chairmen over land allocation, while vidco chairmen used the introduction of land use planning to attack 'customary' authority over the land.

Conflicts varied. Several vidco chairmen reported cooperation with sabhukus in enforcing a ban on new allocations, thus restricting land access to inheritance.[128] In other areas, village heads had asserted their authority by authorising the settlement of Mozambican refugees and evictees from commercial farms.[129] Concern over village heads' practices had led vidco chairmen to endorse land use planning, and so the authority of expert knowledge over the customary. They argued that land use planning would help to solve a severe shortage of grazing and arable land, which they attributed to sabhukus' allocations. One chairman, a member of the council's conservation committee and a former Zanu(PF) political commissar, explained:

> The sabhukus give land. I cannot lie and say the vidco is doing it. We were told to be together but the sabhukus refuse to be with us. They allocate on their own to people from Chipinge and Mozambique. People pay money for land to the sabhuku and chief. We don't have enough grazing land or land for cultivation but the sabhuku continues to give land…. If we need to brew beer that is for the traditional leaders but the control of land should be with the vidco and we should decide which area is for grazing.[130]

The councillor expressed similar concerns: 'Now the very big conflict is between the sabhukus and vidco chairs on land allocation. Government's policy really conflicts with the sabhukus' decisions. The vidco will demarcate land into cultivation, grazing and housing but the sabhuku puts people into grazing areas so there is no grazing left…. They want to keep allocating because they get money from it.' He felt customary leaders needed to be 'educated' into compliance because 'even though government is backing the vidcos, people respect kraal heads and chiefs. They will be very angry without their powers.'[131]

Customary leaders' views were very different. Those interviewed were all, with two exceptions, related to 'Chief' Chiesa and very much arguing his case. They justified their authority over land in terms of history and customary expertise. 'Chief' Chiesa's representative explained: 'The chief is giving land to people who are being chased off of some farms. We don't want a newcomer giving land. He won't know what land is sacred. Now, the chief doesn't give land by himself.... We are not happy about this.... We want what had been happening a long way back.'[132] The view that the vidco and councillor were not competent to allocate land was widely voiced by customary leaders. They also explained land shortage in different terms: it was not the result of their own profligate allocation but of the alienation of the northern part of the chieftaincy by whites in the 1930s. The remedy lay not in a land use plan but in the return of 'their' land. In fact, this land, which was part of a resettlement scheme under the jurisdiction of Mutare district, had been used for grazing during the post-independence droughts.[133]

A historical view also shaped customary leaders' position on the land use plan. Chiesa's son recalled a history of resistance: 'I remember in the '50s when the government tried to move us into lines. We refused that and we are still not happy about lines.' He nonetheless invoked the legitimating strength of lines: 'Land is being given in lines but not the way government wants to put people in lines.'[134] Laughing, one village head commented, 'I don't think *you* would see the lines.'[135] Customary leaders tried to out-manoeuvre officials by adopting and adapting their terminology. Official land use plans in fact evoked considerable fear of restrictions on field sizes, of social conflict attendant on living closer together, and of the costs of moving homes. Vidco chairmen shared these fears, but downplayed them in order to use an alliance with officials and their technical knowledge to bolster their claim to authority.

Land shortage and productivity constraints were seen very differently by the Agritex officer responsible for planning the area. He held that concerns over land shortage were wholly unfounded: 'The resources are adequate to support the population. They are more than enough. That is a fact.... More could be produced with better management and use of resources. That is what the land-use plan will achieve. That is another fact.' He denied that his technical interventions had political implications, either by undermining claims to land redistribution or in terms of the planned movement of an estimated 30 per cent of households. Instead, he held that 'the kraal heads are very cooperative: they have nothing to fear', a perception that said more about village heads' political tactics than it did about their attitudes to the plan.[136]

In Mhandarume, land use planning acted as a lightning-rod for conflicting claims to authority over the land, based on different kinds of knowledge and interpretations of history. Customary leaders' claims to authority were contested by vidco chairmen, in part because the vidcos were dominated by outsiders to the Chiesa family, and in part because 'Chief' Chiesa invoked his 'customary' authority to settle newcomers in grazing areas. For customary leaders, allocating land was a source of prestige and wealth as well as a challenge to the authority of vidco chairmen and an act of opposition to an official policy that rejected land redistribution in favour of technocratic planning. The councillor and vidcos meanwhile turned to the alternative authority of officials and their technical plans in the hope of preventing further settlement. Both claims to authority remained heatedly contested, feeding conflict over the land.

GUHUNE WARD

Located in the north-east of the district, the densely settled Guhune Ward is better watered than Mhandarume and is home to the Mutambara irrigation scheme, Mutambara mission and a business centre. Leadership in the ward was dominated by three exceptionally charismatic men: the chief, the councillor and the Zanu(PF) branch chairman. Chief Mutambara had powerful economic and political resources under his control. He drew legitimacy from his history of nationalist activism, both locally and in the eyes of officials. The DA described him in glowing terms: 'He was an active and loyal supporter of the freedom fighters during the war of liberation which led to his detention.... He supports the present government to the hilt. He commands great political respect of the people and chiefs in this district. The people love him.'[137] He was elected as the village court's presiding officer in 1981, and chaired the committee of irrigators responsible for running the Mutambara scheme. He personally held 60 acres of irrigated land as 'chief's land', and was a frequent patron of development projects.[138]

For all his power, Chief Mutambara nonetheless claimed he was 'under' the party leadership. The councillor and Zanu(PF) branch chairman modestly said they were 'under' the chief. In fact, all three cooperated: the councillor acted as an assessor in the chief's village court, and all three leaders pressured vidcos, Zanu(PF) chairmen and village heads to cooperate in allocating land. No leaders made the vitriolic attacks on one another common in Mhandarume. Chief Mutambara held that 'when people are quarrelling they won't have progress. You can't ignore anyone's office or power.'[139] Cooperation among local leaders with regard to land consisted in a decision to end arable allocation, though stands for houses were authorised. Local leaders considered land shortage to be extreme. One vidco and Zanu(PF) chairman complained that people had stopped coming to his vidco meetings 'because they say since independence we haven't been given enough land to plough so we won't go to the meeting.... We are just waiting for the government to give us land. When it does we will be free.'[140] Land shortage was seen as particularly hard on the young: 'Young couples are suffering. They are ploughing where their parents are.'[141]

Though the councillor saw a solution to land shortage in the resettlement of young couples, almost all other leaders put their trust in the chief's ability to persuade the government to return what they considered to be the chieftaincy's former lands. Chief Mutambara was an outspoken critic of resettlement:

> We tell the DA that he needs to buy a farm for the landless. He says they will only settle people who sign forms. Some people don't want to fill the forms and leave here.... People shouldn't be forced to join [resettlement]. We should have freedom of talking and freedom of tillage. Government emphasis shouldn't ignore the communal land people. We are all Zanu(PF).

The chief along with many other local leaders considered resettlement unacceptable because it undercut chiefly authority as well as kin and community ties. They preferred to make the historically based claims to land that were endorsed by custom and nationalism, but which the resettlement policy rejected.[142]

Chief Mutambara had argued the case for customary power in land and courts with vigour since independence: 'Right after independence the powers were taken from the tribal courts. From that year the people leading looked to the Prime Minister to see if he would accept giving the trial of cases back to the chiefs.' The promised return of courts was a welcome victory, but 'the chiefs say courts are not enough. We want the allocation of land – where to live and till and build. The power of land is our tradition, in our ancestral spirits. It is all one thing – land and cases.'[143] Vidco and Zanu(PF) chairmen supported the chief in his quest for customary power. This was not without good reason: the chief and his allies in the party leadership had obtained temporary access to grazing land in precisely the resettlement areas they claimed by making an appeal to the Provincial Governor.

With regard to land use planning, there was no open rejection of reorganisation as in Insiza or other wards in Chimanimani. Almost all leaders endorsed the plan in theory, but argued that it could not be implemented without the addition of land to the ward. Vidco chairmen argued that the grazing area was too small to be paddocked and pointed out that people cultivated outside their vidcos because of land pressure. Moreover, under the water and sanitation programme, boreholes and improved toilets had been provided at existing homes, thus acting as a powerful disincentive to move. Under such circumstances, the land use plan could not work. Local leaders thus sought to link compliance with the policy and demands for land, a link which existed only theoretically in official policy.[144]

In Chimanimani, local leaders sought to establish claims over the land both in cooperation with and in opposition to officials. Their attitudes were shaped by local conflicts, not the technical merits of policies. Officials' ability to enforce policies was limited, even where they gained the nominal cooperation of factions of the local leadership. Local leaders set conditions for the acceptance of state interventions, and proposed their own versions of land use planning. In practice, land allocation fell outside the control of state and council. Nonetheless, official interventions reshaped local discourse and claims to authority, hardening divisions among local leaders in some cases, and underscoring the state's failure to build legitimacy through land redistribution in others.

Conclusion

In Chimanimani, the relative power of local leaders and their means of claiming authority shifted dramatically in the years after independence. Zanu(PF) committees were marginalised not through repression as with Zapu in Insiza, but as a result of their inability to deliver on wartime promises, exclusion from decision-making and lack of financial support. Zanu(PF) dominated the council and vidcos, but this proved an ambiguous victory. These institutions were unable to collect rates effectively, control land use or influence policy. In the late 1980s, customary leaders emerged as important lobbyists for land redistribution, populist critics of technocratic interventions, and proponents of mutable versions of 'customary' land use and law. They officially regained control over courts in 1990, though many had exercised judicial powers since independence. As in previous decades, they represented most clearly the uneasy relationship between the government's 'modernising' goals and its appeals to custom in search of political support and state capacity.

Land played a complex role in this period. The 'squatter' occupations of the early 1980s relied on a unique set of circumstances, and were a powerful expression of popular nationalism defined in terms of the reclamation of the lost lands. They just as importantly expressed a desire for a new relationship between state and people. Local party leaders at first assumed that their demands would be met. But while some politicians remained sympathetic, the development bureaucracies rejected their authority over the land. This choice was central to the process of state-making, and to the redefinition of nationalism from the top down as a modernising and increasingly neo-liberal project. The rapidly instilled lack of state accountability in this realm undid popular attempts to build a new relationship between government and people. Instead, suspicion, distrust and a host of informal means of claiming land flourished. The efficacy of squatting declined after the first years of independence, as private landowners and a technocratic bureaucracy gained the upper hand. Land redistribution was reduced to a closely managed process of moving squatters from private to state and communal land. It ignored both communal area land pressure and the institutions that represented the rural areas.

If Chimanimani's nationalists, customary leaders and councillors failed to remake the state, that did not mean that the state succeeded in establishing its authority. The state's technocratic policies could not offer solutions to locally conceived needs, and nor could they displace nationalist and customary claims to land. A multiplicity of overlapping institutions claimed authority over the land, shaped tenure and reshaped the state. Land claims, inside and outside the communal areas, remained the subject of intense political conflict. It was in this unstable ground that the politics of 1990s Zimbabwe and the crisis of 2000 took root.

Notes

1 The phrase is from O'Flaherty, 1998.
2 Between 1976 and 1978, the number of functioning commercial farms dropped from 105 to eight. See Caute, 1983, 271-83; Martin and Johnson, 1981, 223-4.
3 Minutes of the Second Meeting for the Formation of a District Council in Melsetter, District Commissioner's Conference Room, 25-26 June 1980. Also see Minutes of the Third Meeting for the Formation of the Melsetter District Council, District Commissioner's Conference Room, 15 September 1980.
4 Minutes of a Meeting at the District Commissioner's Conference Hall, Melsetter, 27 February 1981. See Minutes of the Mabvazuwa District Council, Chimanimani, 20 May 1982, for examples of demands for land made on the basis of past evictions.
5 PER 5, Saurombe, Chimanimani District, J. M. Gabaza, Assistant Secretary (Development) to Under Secretary (Development), Mutare, 4 December 1981. Also see interviews, Senior Administrative Officer, Chimanimani, 24 October 1988; 'Chief' Saurombe, Biriwiri, 13 November 1988.
6 Minutes of the Mabvazuwa District Council, Melsetter, 27 May 1981, 30 July 1981.
7 Interview, Local Government Promotion Officer [LGPO], Chimanimani, 31 October 1988.
8 Minutes of the (Provincial) Meeting with the Deputy Minister of Lands, Resettlement and Rural Development at the Office of the Under Secretary (Development), Mutare, 1 October 1981.
9 Minutes of the Mabvazuwa District Council, Chimanimani, 27 August 1981.

10 The number of 'squatters' in the early 1980s is difficult to pin down. Estimates for Manicaland include MP Des Butler's figure of 70,000 people in September 1981, quoted in Ranger, 1985b, 305; a *Moto*, July 1982, estimate of 75,000 people; and the Mutare DA's estimate of 90,000 people reported in the *Herald*, 20 September 1982.

11 Minutes of the Conservation Committee, Mabvazuwa District Council, Chimanimani, 13 October 1981; Minutes of the Mabvazuwa District Council, Chimanimani, 29 October 1981, 31 January 1983.

12 See Ranger, 1985b, 305-8 for sympathetic statements on squatting from Deputy Minister of Lands Moven Mahachi, Prime Minister Mugabe, and Minister of Local Government Eddison Zvobgo in 1981 and 1982. Also see Herbst, 1990, 71-5.

13 See, for example, Minutes of the Mabvazuwa District Council, Conservation Committee, 16 November 1983, 15 February 1984; PER 5 chiefs' and headmen's files, Chimanimani District.

14 Interview, Assistant Resettlement Officer, Shinja, 26 October 1988; Minutes of the Mabvazuwa District Council, Chimanimani, 13 April 1983.

15 Kinsey, 1983, 176-7. Also see Minister of Lands Mahachi's comments in the *Herald*, 23 November 1982.

16 Minutes of Mabvazuwa District Council, Chimanimani, 29 October 1981.

17 *Herald*, 20 September 1982. Such appeals were common and effective in Zanu(PF) areas. See Mashonaland West Provincial Development Committee [PDC] *et al.*, n.d. [1987]; Herbst, 1990, 73-5.

18 *Herald*, 17 December 1982, 22 December 1982. Compromises nonetheless remained common: the intransigence of squatters, and the sympathy for them among politicians and officials, proved an ongoing obstacle.

19 *Herald*, 23 December 1983. Also see Ranger, 1985b, 309.

20 See Mashonaland West PDC *et al.*, n.d. [1987]. Also see Yeros, 2002a, 151-2.

21 Ministry of Local Government, 1985, Circular No. 10, Addendum A (circulated to district councils).

22 Ministry of Local Government Policy Statement, 7 May 1986, quoted in DERUDE, 1987. Also see the *Sunday Mail*, 21 September 1986.

23 See Manicaland PDC, 1985, 48-9, 213-14.

24 See Chimanimani District Development Committee [DDC], n.d. [1986]; interview, Senior Administrative Officer, Chimanimani, 24 October 1988; Minutes of District Resettlement Meeting, 11 November 1987.

25 Minutes of the Provincial District Administrators' Meeting, Chimanimani, 30 October 1987.

26 Interview, Senior Administrative Officer, Chimanimani, 24 October 1988.

27 In Chimanimani, this was the case particularly at the northern and southern ends of the National Park. An escalation in armed attacks in late 1987 and 1988 caused large movements from borderland resettlement schemes, communal areas and forestry estates. See Minutes of the Provincial District Administrator's Meeting, Chimanimani, 30 October 1987; Resettlement Meeting, DA's Office, Chimanimani, 15 April 1988; Minutes of the Squatter Control Committee, Chimanimani, 2 August 1988.

28 Interview, Provincial Planning Officer, Mutare, 24 November 1988.

29 Interview, District Agritex Extension Officer, Chimanimani, 4 November 1988.

30 *Ibid.*

31 Minutes of the Provincial District Administrators' Meeting, Chimanimani, 30 October 1987; Minutes of a Provincial Meeting of District Administrators of Manicaland, Mutare, 7 August 1987.

32 Minutes of the Provincial District Administrators' Meeting, Chimanimani, 30 October 1987.

33 Interview, District Agritex Extension Officer, Chimanimani, 4 November 1988.

34 Interviews, C7, Guhune; C4, Biriwiri, respectively. In reference to interviews with the local leaders, I use a coding system, folowed by the ward.

35 Minutes of the Manicaland Provincial Council of Chiefs, Mutare, 5 January 1989.

36 *Herald*, 3 December 1988; Interviews, Senior Administrative Officer, Chimanimani, 24 October 1988, 14 March 1989; LGPO, Chimanimani, 15 March 1989.

37 Interview, Senior Administrative Officer, Chimanimani, 24 October 1988; Minutes of the Squatter Control Committee, Chimanimani, 2 August 1988. And see Thornycroft, 1989b, 7-8.

38 Interviews, Provincial Administrator [PA] and Provincial Planning Officer, Mutare, 24 November 1988.

39 *Herald*, 30 November 1988, 2 December 1988.

40 Thornycroft, 1989b, 7; *Herald*, 9 April 1989.

41 Maier, 1989.

42 Among others, see the Minutes of the Mabvazuwa District Council, Chimanimani, 29 October 1981; Minutes of the Conservation Committee, Mabvazuwa District Council, Chimanimani, 15 February 1984.

43 Interview, PA, Mutare, 24 November 1988, and see the *Financial Gazette*, 6 July 1990.

44 Interview, LGPO, Chimanimani, 24 October 1988; Minutes of the Conservation Committee, Mabvazuwa District Council, Chimanimani, 15 January 1986, 17 September 1986, 18 November 1987.

45 Minutes of the Squatter Control Committee, Chimanimani, 30 September 1988; Minutes of the Mabvazuwa District Council, Chimanimani, 31 October 1988.

46 *Herald*, 2 August 1990. Also see the *Manica Post*, 3 February 1989; *Chronicle*, 5 March 1989.
47 Interview, District Agritex Extension Officer, Chimanimani, 4 November 1988. An Agritex survey of 59 families in Nyahode revealed that many residents were employed, and that it was common for an employed man to send his family into Nyahode to claim land in his absence. Many families 'had well-planned houses, very expensive. They have money, they can buy cement, tile, asbestos. That squatter is just probably a clever man making use of the confusion.'
48 Interview, Provincial Planning Officer, Mutare, 24 November 1988.
49 Interview, District Agritex Extension Officer, Chimanimani, 4 November 1988.
50 Minutes of the Squatter Control Committee, Chimanimani, 2 August 1988.
51 Interview, District Agritex Extension Officer, Chimanimani, 4 November 1988. Also see Minutes of the Mabvazuwa District Council, Conservation Committee, 17 June 1987.
52 Interview, LGPO, Chimanimani, 21 November 1988.
53 Interview, Kwirire Cooperative Chairman, Nyahode, 18 November 1988.
54 Interviews with a village head who was allocating land in Kwirire and with 'squatters' in Kwirire, 18 November 1988. The village head did not answer save nominally to a hierarchy of chiefs and headmen.
55 Based on a review of the membership records of Chimanimani's Zanu(PF) committees, and local interviews. Ranger, 1985b, 291-2. Also see Cliffe *et al.*, 1980, 52-4.
56 Also see Kriger, 1992, 214-5, 221; Brand, 1991, 90.
57 Minutes of the Second Meeting for the Formation of a District Council, Melsetter, 25-26 June 1980; interview, District Council Chairman, Mhandarume, 7 November 1988.
58 Minutes of Trips Made Through Out the District to Brief People on the Formation of the Melsetter District Council, 16-22 June 1980. Suspicion over the presence of Rhodesian officials and the introduction of councils was common. See Kriger, 1992, 217, 228-30; Ranger, 1985b, 296-7.
59 See Minutes of the Special Meeting of the Council, Chimanimani, 2 August 1982; DC A. Macfarlane, Melsetter, to PC, Manicaland, 27 June 1980, 22 December 1980; Third Meeting for the Formation of the Melsetter District Council, Chimanimani, 15 September 1980.
60 See discussions in Brand, 1991, 91-2; Lan, 1985, 221; Ladley, 1985, 290-3, 415-23
61 See Report for a Meeting held at Ngangu Stadium, Chimanimani, 9 August 1980, at which local party leaders vigorously questioned MP Bishop Joshua Dhube and a provincial party representative on the question of salaries. Zanu(PF) committees were also demoralised by a series of tedious reorganisations at the behest of national leaders. See Kriger, 1992, 221-8.
62 The increasingly active role played by provincial and national Zanu(PF) officials and the District Party Coordinator is apparent from a study of council and other meetings. The provincial party presence was much strengthened following the creation of Provincial Governors.
63 Interview, Senior Administrative Officer, Chimanimani, 24 October 1988.
64 For example, see PER 5 and PER 4 files, Chimanimani, for Headman Saurombe and Chief Mutambara.
65 Interview, Senior Administrative Officer, Chimanimani, 24 October 1988.
66 In mid-1982, all new appointments were frozen for two years. In late 1984, there was still 'no definite policy regarding the appointment of new Headmen, upgrading Chiefs etc.'. See PER 4, Headman Saurombe, Chimanimani, J. D. White for Secretary for Local Government and Housing to Under Secretary, Development, Manicaland, 4 September 1981; J. M. Gabaza for DA to Under Secretary, Development, 27 October 1983; J. D. White for Secretary for Local Government and Town Planning to PA, Manicaland, 20 December 1984.
67 DC, Melsetter, to PC, Manicaland, 23 December 1980; Minutes of the First Meeting held for the Formation of a District Council in Melsetter, 11 June 1980.
68 See DC A. Macfarlane, Chimanimani, to PC, Manicaland, 27 June 1980.
69 First Meeting Held for the Formation of a District Council in Melsetter, Melsetter, 11 June 1980, and see DC, Melsetter, to PC, Mutare, 27 June 1980.
70 This was widely held to be the case in Chimanimani. For example, interview, District Council Chairman, Chimanimani, October 1988.
71 See Minutes of the Mabvazuwa District Council, 27 May 1981, 30 July 1981, 20 May 1982, 30 January 1985; Finance Committee, 7 September 1983, 26 September 1984, 17 October 1985, 16 January 1986.
72 DC A. Macfarlane, Chimanimani, to PC, Manicaland, 23 December 1980.
73 See J. M. Gabaza for the DA, Chimanimani, to PA, Mutare, 23 November 1987. Compare to Maxwell's discussion (1999, Chapter 6) of succession disputes in Nyanga.
74 DC A. Macfarlane, Melsetter, to PC, Manicaland, 27 June 1980.
75 Minutes of the Mabvazuwa District Council, Finance Committee, 28 June 1982.
76 See Minutes of the Mabvazuwa District Council, Finance Committee, Chimanimani, 7 September 1983, 11 January 1984, 27 November 1984 to 29 May 1985; Mabvazuwa District Council, Chimanimani, 15

September 1983; Special Meetings, Mabavazuwa District Council, Chimanimani, 24 September 1983, 9 and 25 January 1984.

77 See Minutes of the Mabvazuwa District Council, Chimanimani, 30 April 1985, 24 July 1985, and Finance Committee, 29 May 1985.

78 Interviews, LGPO for western Muusha and Mutambara; Senior Administrative Officer, Chimanimani, 24 October 1988.

79 Minutes of the Mabvazuwa District Council, Chimanimani, 29 January 1986, and Finance Committee, 16 January 1986; Minutes of a Meeting of Executive Officers, Finance, and Senior Executive Officers, Mutare, 15 January 1987.

80 See Minutes of a Special Full Council Meeting, Chimanimani, 9 April 1986; Special Meeting, Mabvazuwa District Council, Chimanimani, 22 April 1986; Special Full Council Meeting, Chimanimani, 18 May 1986.

81 Special Full Council Meeting, Chimanimani, 29 October 1986. At a provincial meeting of council executive officers Chimanimani's representatives, 'pointed out politicians should be involved in collections as they had been denounced under the previous regime and people didn't understand why they should pay'. Minutes of a Meeting of Executive Officers, Finance, and Senior Executive Officers, Mutare, 15 January 1987.

82 Special Full Council Meeting, Chimanimani, 30 March 1987, 14 April 1987.

83 Interview, Commanding Officer, 12th Infantry Batallion, Mutambara, 26 October 1988. In 1988, army units were stationed in northeast Mutambara and in Ngorima.

84 Report of Meeting held at Ngangu Stadium, Melsetter, 9 August 1980. Also see attacks on party courts in Parliament, *Parliamentary Debates*, 3 February 1981.

85 Interview, Magistrate, Chimanimani, 3 November 1988. Also see Kriger, 1992, Chapter 6.

86 Minutes of a Meeting at the District Commissioner's Conference Hall, Melsetter, 27 February 1981.

87 Minutes of the Mabvazuwa District Council, Melsetter, 27 May 1981; Minutes of a Meeting with the Deputy Minister of Justice and Constitutional Affairs, Melsetter, 21 July 1981, appended list, 'Elected Members, Mabvazuwa District Council, Melsetter District, Village Courts'; interview, Magistrate, Chimanimani, 3 November 1988.

88 Minutes of a Meeting with the Deputy Minister of Justice and Constitutional Affairs, Melsetter, 21 July 1981.

89 This view was widely expressed by local leaders in Chimanimani. On cases of chiefs and spirit mediums, sometimes with the backing of the party, handling cases of witchcraft and 'healing' see Kriger, 1992, 232; Lan, 1985, 210; Reynolds, 1990; Maxwell, 1999, Chapter 7.

90 See Chimanimani DDC, n.d. [1986], 72.

91 For example, Interviews, Chief Samuel Mutambara, Guhune, 6 November 1988; District Council Chairman, Mhandarume, 7 November 1988. Also see Ranger, 1988, 12.

92 Minutes of the First Meeting held with Chiefs, Headmen and Kraalheads, Chimanimani, 31 January 1985. Also see Maxwell, 1999, 176–80.

93 The promise of judicial authority to chiefs in 1985 coincided with a much publicised test case (Katekwe v. Muchabaiwa) in which it was ruled that a father could not sue for seduction damages on behalf of a woman over 18. As Batezat *et al.*, 1988, 159, write, a 'hysterical debate' followed: 'It was suggested that the law had gone too far too soon, or more catastrophically, that family life would break down and that women would now enter lives of unbridled and irresponsible promiscuity!'

94 Minutes of the Mabvazuwa District Council, Chimanimani, 17 December 1981.

95 Minutes of the Manicaland Provincial Council of Chiefs Meeting, Chiefs' Hall, Mutare, 5 January 1989.

96 *Parliamentary Debates*, Vol. 16, No. 54, 18 January 1990.

97 Interview, Chimanimani, 3 November 1988. Also see Chimanimani DDC, n.d. [1986], 73.

98 See J. D. White for Secretary for Local Government and Town Planning to all DAs and PAs, 11 January 1985, and M. S. Mukuchura for the PA, Manicaland, to all DAs, 7 February 1989.

99 Interview, Magistrate, Chimanimani, 3 November 1988.

100 Minutes of the Mabvazuwa District Council, Conservation Committee, 15 June 1983.

101 Minutes of the Second District Administrators' Provincial Meeting, Nyanga, 2 September 1983.

102 See Minutes of the Mabvazuwa District Council, Chimanimani, 30 June 1982, 30 January 1985, 30 October 1985; Conservation Committee, various dates.

103 See Minutes of the Mabvazuwa District Council, Chimanimani, 10 November 1982.

104 Interviews, Senior Administrative Officer, Chimanimani, 24 October 1988; Agritex Extension Officer, Chikukwa, 5 November 1988. And see Minutes of the Mabvazuwa District Council, Chimanimani, 15 September 1983, 30 November 1983, 21 May 1984, 27 June 1984.

105 Interview, District Agritex Extension Officer, Chimanimani, 28 November 1988.

106 Chimanimani District Development Committee, n.d. [1986], 44.

107 Minutes of the Manicaland Provincial Council of Chiefs Meeting, Chiefs' Hall, Mutare, 5 January 1989. On MPs' views, see *Parliamentary Debates*, Vol. 16, No. 54, 18 January 1990.

108 Minutes of the Mabvazuwa District Council, Chimanimani, 29 January 1986; Minutes of the Mabvazuwa District Council, Conservation Committee, Chimanimani, 18 February 1987. For instances of enforcement, see cases reported in Minutes of the Mabvazuwa District Council, Conservation Committee, Chimanimani, 15 April 1987, 17 June 1987. The council remained wary of punitive action, insisting on reduced penalties for offences.
109 Minutes of the Mabvazuwa District Council, Conservation Committee, Chimanimani, 19 March 1986, 18 June 1986, 17 September 1986.
110 Minutes of a Special Conservation Committee and Heads of Committees Meeting, 7 October 1986.
111 Interview, Senior Administrative Officer, Chimanimani, 20 October 1988. Also, for example, Interview, Agritex Extension Officer for Ngorima, Chimanimani, 28 October 1988.
112 Minutes of Special Conservation Committee and Heads of Committees Meeting, 7 October 1986.
113 Interviews, Senior Administrative Officer, Chimanimani, 20 October 1988; LGPOs, Chimanimani, 24 October 1988; Senior Agritex Extension Officer, Chimanimani, 24 October 1988; PA, Mutare, 24 November 1988; Minutes of the Mabvazuwa District Council, Chimanimani, 7 October 1987.
114 Minutes of the Mabvazuwa District Council, Chimanimani, 3 June 1987; Conservation Commitee, 15 April 1987. The analogy to protected villages was all too close in Chipinge where Renamo attacks had been intense. The provincial administrator commented on their beneficial side effects: 'The areas affected by Renamo bandits are the ones offering easier solutions in terms of the pattern of settlement.... The schemes in Chipinge were facilitated by Renamo.' Interview, PA, Mutare, 24 November 1988.
115 Interview, DA and Senior Administrative Officer, Chimanimani, 21 November 1988.
116 For example, Interviews, LGPO, Chimanimani, 24, 25 October 1988; District Agritex Extension Officer, Chimanimani, 28 November 1988.
117 Interview, Senior Administrative Officer, 20 October 1988. Also Interview, PA, Mutare, 24 November 1988; Gasper, 1991, 21.
118 Minutes of the Water and Sanitation Workshop, Chimanimani, 13-15 July 1988; Interviews, District Community Development Officer, Chimanimani, 26 October 1988; District Agritex Extension Officer, Chimanimani, 28 November 1988; Senior Agritex Extension Officer, Chimanimani, 24 October 1988.
119 See discussions in Minutes of the Water and Sanitation Meetings held at the DA's Office, Chimanimani, 8 September 1988, 10 November 1988; Minutes of the Water and Sanitation Subcommittee Meeting held at Mashonjowa School, Mhandarume, 9 March 1989; J. M. Gabaza, 'Villagisation reconnoitre exercise for preparation of layouts', 30 September 1988.
120 Interview, LGPO for Ngorima and Chikukwa, Chimanimani, 21 November 1988; LGPO for western Muusha and Mutambara, Chimanimani, 24 October 1988; Senior Agritex Extension Officer for Ngorima, Chimanimani, 28 October 1988.
121 Minutes of the Water and Sanitation Workshop, Chimanimani, 13-15 July 1988; Interviews, District Agritex Extension Officer, Chimanimani, 28 November 1988; District Community Development Officer, Chimanimani, 26 October 1988.
122 Interview, District Agritex Extension Officer, Chimanimani, 28 November 1988.
123 *Ibid.*
124 Interview, Senior Administrative Officer, Chimanimani, 20 October 1988.
125 Compare to O'Flaherty, 1998; Andersson, 1999.
126 See PER 5 file for Chief Mutambara, Chimanimani.
127 Interviews, C2, T9/2, Mhandarume.
128 Interviews, V46, V47, Mhandarume.
129 See debates in Minutes of the Mabvazuwa District Council, Conservation Committee, Chimanimani, 18 February 1987, 19 August 1987, 18 November 1987, and Hughes, 1999.
130 Interview, PV52/2, Mhandarume.
131 Interview, C2, Mhandarume.
132 Interview, T9/2, Mhandarume.
133 Interviews, PT10/2, T11/2, PV53/2, Mhandarume.
134 Interview, PT9/5, Mhandarume.
135 Interview, PT10/5, Mhandarume.
136 Interview, Senior Agritex Extension Officer, Chimanimani, 24 October 1988.
137 DA, Chimanimani to PA, Manicaland, 9 November 1988.
138 Interview, Chief Samuel Mutambara, Guhune, 6 November 1988, and see, for example, Minutes of the Mabvazuwa District Council, Conservation Committee, Chimanimani, 25 April 1984, 18 June 1986, 17 September 1986.
139 Interview, Chief Samuel Mutambara, Guhune, 6 November 1988.
140 Interview, V45/1, Guhune.

141 Interview, C7/2, Guhune.

142 Interview, Chief Samuel Mutambara, Guhune, 6 November 1988 and, for example, interview, PT2/2, Guhune.

143 Interview, Chief Samuel Mutambara, Guhune, 6 November 1988. For a report on chiefs' meetings with President Mugabe and senators, see the *Sunday Mail*, 6 November 1988.

144 Interviews, V45/3, PV43, V44/3, Guhune.

8

The New Politics of an
Unsettled Land

In early 2000, veterans of Zimbabwe's liberation war initiated a wave of occupations of commercial farm land. Their actions heralded a period of escalating political violence, unprecedented economic decline and lawlessness. It suddenly seemed possible to write about politics in Zimbabwe, and specifically about land, without reference to the high modernism or customary projects of previous decades. Analysis shifted to a focus on the partisan violence of veterans, youth militias and security forces, to Zanu(PF)'s manipulations of nationalist history, and to the struggles of civic organisations, trade unions and the political opposition.[1] In a spate of biographies, Mugabe was placed centre stage, and portrayed as a singularly violent tyrant.[2] Zimbabwe seemed to be entering the world described by the political scientists of Africa elsewhere – the 'politics of disorder', the 'politics of the belly'.[3]

But Zimbabwe did not easily fit these models. Violence, corruption and economic collapse were accompanied by a massive redistribution of land; nationalist history – and specifically race and colonialism – played a central role in political discourse. The state did not 'collapse' or 'fail': instead, a closely orchestrated process of remaking the state took place in which land stood centre stage. My focus here is on the shifts in the nature of authority over the land as it was so radically unsettled once again. I leave behind the district studies which have so far informed my analysis, in part simply because it was not possible to carry out the kind of rural fieldwork I had before. I am far more reliant on press, donor and human rights reports. The vibrant, if increasingly embattled, independent press and the state-controlled media offered distinctly different views,[4] but a careful reading of both revealed many first-hand accounts of developments on the ground, and of the political rhetoric that surrounded them.

Land and State-making in the 1990s

In the 1980s, the contradictions between state policy and the popular nationalisms of the liberation war had produced deep divisions within the state and the party, as well as between them. Land redistribution was by no means without benefits – many resettlement schemes did well in terms of the official criteria of poverty alleviation,

productivity and equity, and they were far from negligible in scale.[5] But where resettlement failed was in redressing the demands of rural nationalism, and in providing a
basis for state-building. Interventions in communal area land use and tenure suffered
the same weaknesses. These fed into antagonistic contestations over authority, which
undermined state capacity and political legitimacy. It was thus no surprise that, as the
Zanu(PF) government began to come under threat from political opposition, it
sought to revalue the 'land question' and to seek new means of state-building.

The political discourse around land prior to the 1990 elections took on an aggressive tone that would be maintained throughout the decade. Mugabe proclaimed:
'Never again shall we be slaves in our own country.... There shall never be a "no"
which we shall ever accept again from landowners we approach for land.' The illegit-
imacy of white land ownership, and the duty of Britain as the erstwhile colonial
power to pay for the land, was stressed repeatedly. Amidst this heated rhetoric, the
promulgation of the New National Land Policy in 1990, with its promise of an additional five million hectares for 110,000 families, seemed to mark a renewed
commitment to redistribution.[6] Subsequent constitutional changes and the 1992
Land Acquisition Act were intended to make it easier to compulsorily acquire land,
signalling a new phase in land acquisition strategies after the expiry of the Lancaster
House constitution's restrictions. Provincial land identification committees, with
representatives from Agritex, Zanu(PF), and the Commercial Farmers' Union
(CFU), were established to identify land for acquisition. They worked to a set of
criteria that emphasised productivity and equity, consensus and negotiation.
However, when the lists of farms targeted for acquisition were made public in 1993,
they diverged substantially from those compiled by the committees, apparently
reflecting struggles within the party and state over how and on what grounds
commercial land should be acquired. Two years later, the Zanu(PF)-dominated
National Land Task Force was established, marking an important movement in the
locus of decision-making beyond the reach of ministerial structures.[7]

These shifts would have important consequences in later years, but in the meantime there was little in the way of action. Politicians' radical rhetoric sat
uncomfortably alongside the adoption of a structural adjustment package with its
attendant faith in the market, restrictions on state expenditure and social hardships.
Farms were listed for acquisition only to be de-listed. Ministries concerned with
resettlement received nothing like the funding needed to speed redistribution on the
scale promised by the New National Land Policy, while a renewed emphasis on
productivity meant that it was not the poor but those with resources who were
targeted.[8] In practice, it was not the land hungry but the 'indigenous' elite who
dominated questions of land redistribution. The emphasis on black entry into large-
scale farming was cast as a means of redressing white and foreign domination of the
sector. Sam Moyo has called this 'economic nationalism', and seen its emergence as
linked to the rise of the market ideology of structural adjustment, and to a growing
concern with racial inequality in the economic sphere.[9] Race had not played a major
role in the rhetoric of the 1980s – it had been subsumed under arguments regarding
the economic importance of whites and the need for reconciliation – but in the
second decade of independence, in a context of economic decline and state contraction, the very visible economic clout of whites became a target that politicians and

a frustrated black middle class found it all too easy to hit.[10] According to Moyo, some 400 black farmers, many of whom were closely connected to or members of the ruling elite, leased state land under various programmes in the 1990s; another approximately 350 had acquired commercial farms. 'Resettlement' in the 1990s seemed to focus on the highly visible – if insignificant in terms of its overall impact on the commercial farm sector – accumulation of land by a black elite.[11]

To communal area farmers, Zanu(PF) appeared increasingly corrupt and out of touch, unable and unwilling to meet the demands of its most significant rural constituency. Limited land redistribution sat alongside a continuation of the package of land use planning measures that had so long dominated the state's vision of the communal areas, robust official criticism notwithstanding.[12] The pressures that lay behind the varied practices of 'squatting', and the difficulties of rural state-building, went unaddressed. Declining public investment in services and resettlement, along-side rising unemployment, spiralling costs of living, drought, and the terrible price of the HIV/AIDS pandemic, placed a premium on gaining access to land and other resources: land occupation and resource 'poaching' were essential to people's survival.[13] In this context, 'squatting' took on new characteristics. It more often surfaced within communal areas and state lands, or took the form of illegal gold panning or grass-cutting or poach-grazing. In all these forms, it served to deepen lines of patronage and conflict among councillors, party committees and chiefs, and between central and local government, as they competed for authority over the processes through which people gained access to land.

The cuts in state funding occasioned by structural adjustment, and the long delayed implementation of the Rural District Councils Act, brought other changes for district institutions. In practice, councils were left with expanded powers but declining revenue. As in earlier periods, introducing new taxes and fees was both deeply unpopular and exceptionally difficult to implement.[14] Councils' dependence on donor funds, and so donor priorities, was often accentuated as a result. Donors played a key role in keeping alive land-use planning initiatives that otherwise would have fallen by the wayside through lack of funding and state capacity, and they were central in the promotion of the much vaunted 'Campfire' programme as a means of developing remote communal areas through the exploitation of wildlife. Such inter-ventions deepened disputes over land where they threatened existing land rights and land use practices, in some cases leading to violent evictions in which 'outsiders' were targeted.[15] The parlous state of council finances worsened as the 1990s progressed, and more and more councils fell victim to maladministration. As JoAnn McGregor writes, many councils' legitimacy had 'dwindled to such an extent' that they had come to be 'regarded by the public (and indeed by critical employees and councillors) as corrupt, inefficient and self-serving'.[16]

Councils' weaknesses bolstered the trend towards co-opting customary leaders, as a means of both garnering political support and strengthening and legitimising the local state. As we have seen, chiefs lobbied vociferously for recognition of their authority over land in the 1980s, and they were promised concessions at the time of the 1990 elections. After the elections, they had a series of meetings with politicians and officials. In a speech to chiefs in 1992, Mugabe stressed the importance of 'African-ness'. He condemned the Communal Lands Act for excluding customary

182

leaders from land allocation, and called for them to be granted a greater role in the hierarchy of development institutions.[17] Chiefs were also invoked in the radical rhetoric on land: in 1993, Mugabe suggested they launch a legal claim against the British for compensation for the 'lost lands'.[18] The passage of the Traditional Leaders Act in 1998 marked the culmination of these trends. It granted chiefs, headmen and village heads leadership of development institutions below the council, control over land allocation in communal areas, and a greater role in that one-time bastion of state-directed modernisation, the resettlement areas. Other responsibilities, such as policing, conservation and reporting crime, looked suspiciously like a Rhodesian-era list of chiefs' duties.[19]

The Traditional Leaders Act reflected the increasingly overt ideological shift away from the democratising and modernising efforts of the 1980s. In practice, however, authority over the land remained the subject of heated contestation among a wide range of local and state institutions.[20] Illegal practices flourished. Where land pressure was extreme, membership in communities was defined in increasingly exclusive and at times violent ways in order to prevent settlement by people from other communal areas or those retrenched from formal employment. New arrivals claimed rights to land as citizens of the nation; locals and local authorities defended a far narrower community.[21] The state's ability to control these processes was limited: its authority was undercut in the eyes of both those demanding land, and those seeking to keep people off land they regarded as theirs. Paris Yeros notes 'a deepening breakdown of rural institutions, increased ambiguity of authority in land administration, and the flourishing of "illegal", and costly, arrangements in pursuit of security of tenure – none of which bodes well for citizenship'.[22]

These unresolved struggles posed a formidable challenge to state-building and to Zanu(PF)'s legitimacy – and they were far from the only challenge. In 1996, civil servants went on strike, signalling an alliance with the increasingly confrontational Zimbabwe Congress of Trade Unions (ZCTU), and the emergence of a new political threat from within the professional classes that constituted the state itself. The rise of the trade union movement reflected not least the growing hardships of structural adjustment. Worker activism was paralleled by protests from intellectuals, students, the urban middle classes and, notably, war veterans, all exercised by high-level corruption and abuses of power.[23] Veterans demonstrated violently in 1997, threatening the Zanu(PF) leadership, and widening divisions within it.[24] Mugabe responded by embracing the veterans, acceding to their demands for compensation in late 1997, and thereby ushering in a period of economic chaos and political realignment that heralded a new politics of land.

Shortly after making the concessions to veterans, 1,471 commercial farms were designated for compulsory acquisition, marking a renewal of the struggles within state and party over land policy, and of the populist rhetoric around land, notably from Mugabe himself. Land was one of the few goods that could still be used as a basis for political mobilisation: in the straitened circumstances of the late 1990s, delivering employment, education and health care was a distant dream of the now politically suspect bureaucratic state. However, the hasty and politically charged way in which the listing of farms took place, largely through the Zanu(PF)-dominated structures mooted in 1995, made them vulnerable to technocratic and legal objection from within and without the state.[25] A full 625 farms were 'de-listed' as they did not meet official criteria, while many of the acquisition orders for the remaining farms were successfully challenged in court. The government responded with efforts to mobilise donor support, a strategy that culminated in the high-profile Donor's Conference of September 1998.

The renewed listing of farms created other dynamics too: it had raised expectations as well as suspicions among the land hungry, and it was followed by a spate of commercial farm occupations. These were evocative of the early 1980s in the sense that they received a great deal of media coverage and the attention of prominent politicians. From June to August 1998, occupations spread in central, southern and northern Zimbabwe. In Mashonaland East, people from Svosve occupied four farms in a particularly notable case.[26] They were visited repeatedly by high-ranking politicians and officials, who promised them resettlement. Further occupations followed, involving thousands of people, many of whom received the encouragement of politicians.[27] These movements were dominated by people from communal areas, but also included unemployed workers and war veterans. Most of the occupied farms were white-owned, but state, church and black-owned and leased farms were also targeted. Occupiers justified their actions in terms of their exclusion from resettlement, and their historical claims to land, that is, in terms of restitution and broken nationalist promises.[28]

The official reaction to the occupations reflected continued vacillation within state and government. Mugabe at first defended them, stressing that force should not be used to evict the land hungry, but later reversed his position, warning of stern action. In some places police burnt camps and evicted occupiers. Mugabe was nonetheless happy to use the Svosve occupiers as evidence of land hunger during the September land conference: donors were taken in minivans to speak to them themselves.[29]

Scattered occupations continued in 1999. Moyo notes that there were reasons for waiting: the government seemed to be showing signs of negotiating seriously for land at the Donors' Conference, and of taking action through the Inception Phase Framework Plan of early 1999, under which various resettlement models were to be tried out on one million hectares.[30] Where occupations carried on they at times involved the careful targeting of state land and land leased by the state to Zanu(PF) elites, notably in the Matabeleland Provinces and in Masvingo.[31] Expectations of a renewed commitment to land redistribution clearly ran high.[32] The momentum of occupations was in fact soon to be drastically accelerated, but in such a way as to require a far more radical transformation of authority over the land than so far envisaged.

The 'Third Chimurenga'

The constitutional referendum of February 2000 marked a watershed in Zimbabwean politics, as debate over the proposed constitution developed into a contest between Zanu(PF) and the gathering forces of opposition. Zanu(PF) portrayed the debate as being about ridding Zimbabwe of the colonial legacy of the Lancaster House constitution; a wide range of constituencies, mobilised under the umbrella of the National Constitutional Assembly, saw it primarily as a means of voicing criticisms about post-independence abuses of power and economic hardship. They were concerned to limit the state's, and particularly the president's, power.[33] In a last-minute bid for votes, and under pressure from war veterans, Zanu(PF) tacked onto its draft constitution a clause obliging Britain to pay for land confiscated by the state. The 'No' vote won nonetheless.

The referendum defeat marked the moment when it became clear that the ruling party faced a major electoral challenge in the shape of the Movement for Democratic Change (MDC), formed in late 1999. It forced an immediate and dramatic shift in the strategies of Zanu(PF) in which veterans and the land took centre stage. In a reworked narrative of nationalism, veterans were cast as the heroic liberators of the land from whites seen as unreconstructed racists and a former colonial power which was, twenty years after independence, portrayed more fervently than ever as the obstacle to 'real' decolonisation. Nationalism was exclusively about fighting men and land, about British perfidy and national sovereignty – it was not about democracy or rights, concerns that were recast as part of an alien and imperial agenda.[34] This was the 'Third Chimurenga', a title that invoked an epic lineage of wars against settler rule. In this context, the state's technocratic agenda slipped from view, while parallels to the war years multiplied. Mugabe donned combat fatigues and spoke of enemies and war, veterans occupied farms and revived the liberation war-era meetings called *pungwes*; white farmers reverted to their agric-alert security systems and were once again killed on their land. This was the 'time of *jambanja*', a term popularised in a chart-topping song about extra-marital affairs, and commonly taken to mean a state of disorder and lawlessness.[35]

The land occupations appeared to mark yet another chapter in the long history of 'squatting'. Some have argued that the 'essence' of squatting, from the 1980s to the post-2000 period, 'remained the same'.[36] But there were striking differences, in terms of the leadership and organisation of the occupations, the role of and consequences for the state, and their use in attacking a political opposition. The hierarchy of national to district level veterans' committees, much strengthened through its mobilisation over the claims for and then distribution of compensation, played a central organisational role. Veterans usually initiated occupations. They tended to establish bases on occupied farms, as well as committees responsible for mobilising and keeping registers of occupiers, for fund-raising, and for organising food and security. Veterans assumed the leadership roles, though almost everywhere they made up only a small minority of occupiers, the bulk being drawn from communal and urban areas as well as party youth.[37]

Veteran leaders were also important in publicly defending and justifying the occupations. From the start, they cast them as a response to the rejection of the new constitution, and specifically its clause on land. They explicitly blamed white farmers for the 'No' vote, and portrayed the vote as primarily about blocking land redistribution, not about abuses of power.[38] They used their high-profile position to harangue Zanu(PF) ministers who developed cold feet, and to argue that anyone who opposed Zanu(PF) was by definition opposed to land redistribution.[39] Veteran leaders helped to popularise a political discourse that legitimated the abrogation of the law. Unfavourable judicial decisions were met with threats of 'going to war'; whites and the MDC were cast as 'enemies' who would undo the revolution in the making, and hence as legitimate targets of violence.[40] As Knox Chitiyo writes, 'coercive language framed a coercive reality' – it was 'both cause and effect of violent deeds'.[41]

While veterans were everywhere important, regional variations were significant. The first occupations focused on Masvingo where the provincial veterans' committee led the way, events that were later hailed as the founding moment of the 'Third Chimurenga'.[42] Occupations spread to Mashonaland and Manicaland in the next few weeks, and involved not just veterans but also people from communal areas, chiefs and urban residents.[43] Mashonaland rapidly came to the fore, spurred on by the increasingly prominent and fiery Provincial Governor Border Gezi, and a number of influential veteran leaders, and thereafter this region dominated in terms of numbers of occupations and violence.[44] Matabeleland only later entered the fray. Leading politicians representing the region such as Joseph Msika and Dumiso Dabengwa did not share Gezi's enthusiasm for occupations, and many veterans in Matabeleland proved reluctant to engage in violence in this early period.[45]

A range of state and party actors were also directly involved in the organisation of the occupations.[46] The Central Intelligence Organisation (CIO) and Zanu(PF) Headquarters directed veterans to specific farms, notably those where farmers had contested designations; veterans reported receiving lists of farms to occupy.[47] As the occupations accelerated, the army and CIO engaged in 'negotiations' with the CFU, alongside veteran leaders,[48] and reports of army and CIO involvement in logistical support of the occupations multiplied.[49] The alliance between security agencies, politicians, veterans, and occupiers was certainly formidable, but the occupations were nonetheless unevenly spread and difficult to sustain.[50] There were also signs of division in government over their purpose. Some Ministers, notably Msika and Dabengwa, seemed to think the occupations were no more than symbolic 'demonstrations' that would give way once the state was empowered to act on land reform. They called for them to end as legislation regarding land acquisition was passed in 2000. But their views were heatedly contested from within Zanu(PF), notably by Mugabe, and by veteran leaders.[51]

For an important faction within the ruling party, the land occupations were not simply about making the case for land redistribution – they were also about creating the conditions for a particular kind of political campaign. They were obviously intended to appeal to Zanu(PF)'s most numerous constituency, communal area farmers, but they were also intended to punish constituencies engaged in opposition politics, initially most obviously white farmers and their workers. Farm workers were cast as 'sell-outs' for being too close to their white employers, and both were cast as 'foreign' and hence illegitimate political actors.[52] Zanu(PF) suspicions of the politics of farmers and farm workers were constantly reiterated in the press. Farm workers were subjected to a violent process of 're-education' on some occupied farms, while Mugabe described white farmers as 'our enemies, not just political enemies, but definite enemies in wanting to reverse our revolution and our independence'.[53] As the campaign progressed, those groups categorised as 'enemies', and so beyond the bounds of the nation, rapidly expanded.[54] Veterans, armed with specially allocated 'campaign' funds, alongside Zanu(PF) and the CIO, deployed violence against a broad set of black constituencies identified with the MDC in towns and communal areas throughout the country.[55]

In the 2000 elections, Zanu(PF) tried to make land the central issue, and to convince the electorate that only Zanu(PF) could deliver the land by casting the MDC, white farmers and the British in an unholy imperial alliance. Criticising the occupations was equated with belittling the historical injustice of land alienation, and the real need for land in Zimbabwe's communal areas. The occupations were not, however, just about an unprecedented assault on the unequal distribution of land: they also marked a transformation of the state and political sphere. The combination of Zanu(PF)'s violent electioneering and the land occupations required the state to answer to a new logic. Its authority was to be grounded in political loyalty and patronage, not expert knowledge and bureaucracy, a transformation that set in train a series of struggles that deeply divided the state. The judiciary was attacked and undermined as ruling after ruling was ignored; the police force was politicised and purged of critics; civil servants came under tremendous pressure to support Zanu(PF), and came under violent attack where they did not.[56] At the same time, the ministries charged with agrarian policy were marginalised, in favour of an alliance led by Zanu(PF) and veterans – technocrats were left to lament that their painstaking plans, produced by the 'serious scientific analysis of Zimbabwe's agricultural needs', were 'dead'.[57] The Zanu(PF) leadership had set in motion processes that promised a new politics of land and a remaking of the state.

Fast Track Resettlement

Following Zanu(PF)'s narrow – and highly controversial – win in the parliamentary elections of 2000 the tactics of *jambanja* were intensified. Youth militia were created in 2001, and spread a new reign of terror.[58] By-elections, council elections and the presidential elections of March 2002 were all the focus of intense political violence.[59] As food shortages hit owing to a combination of drought and the land occupations, food was used as a political weapon.[60] War veterans continued to play a central role in the use of partisan violence, in the escalation of occupations, and in the deployment of a radical and intolerant language. The vast expansion in resettlement that took place in this context displaced older forms of authority over the land, and multiplied new claims.

The government's Accelerated Land Reform and Resettlement Implementation Plan, or 'Fast Track' resettlement, initiated a new phase in the land occupations process. Fast Track resettlement eventually encompassed two models: A1, or smallholder farming, to be undertaken on a 'villagised' basis with communal grazing land or within self-contained units, and A2, which was intended for medium and large-scale commercial farming, and aimed at those able to mobilise significant resources. The defining feature of Fast Track resettlement, as with accelerated resettlement in the early 1980s, was its minimal attention to infrastructure and services. Five million hectares were supposed to be settled in all; to begin with, 30,000 families were to be settled 'as soon as possible' on one million hectares.[61] This was already a tall order, but Fast Track resettlement was to expand rapidly.

New targets emerged in response to political pressure from veterans and Zanu(PF), and popular demands for land from a loosely controlled and burgeoning set of constituencies.[62] They were also a response to legal challenges launched by the CFU. In July 2000, the CFU filed a law suit owing to what it described as a 'major resurgence' in occupations and violence, notably in Mashonaland.[63] Veteran leader Chenjerai 'Hitler' Hunzvi responded by attacking white farmers for holding up land reform in the courts, and accusing civil servants of 'conniving with whites' to slow resettlement.[64] Mugabe was angered by the court case; he was also incensed by the CFU's support for strike action by the ZCTU. His response was to announce that he would acquire a much increased total of 3,000 farms.[65] When the CFU returned to the courts in September, Mugabe threatened to prosecute whites for crimes committed in the liberation war.[66] Zanu(PF) placed a two-page newspaper advertisement which accused 'unrepentant and unapologetic Rhodesians' of using the courts to deprive people of their 'heritage'. In a clear rejection of the law's authority, Zanu(PF) urged: 'This land is your land. Don't let them use the courts and the constitution against the masses.'[67]

Legal defeats for the government made no dent in the momentum of the programme. Recourse to the courts was at any rate soon much undermined by the passage of new legislation designed to legalise occupations *post facto*.[68] The failure of its legal defence led to divisions within the CFU, eventually resulting in a split in this once mighty organisation, as it struggled to find a new strategy. Subsequent attempts at a conciliatory approach, in which the CFU offered land and support for resettlement, were equally unsuccessful. By the end of 2001, over 9 million hectares had been gazetted for acquisition according to official figures; that is, the vast majority of 'white' land and nearly double the original goal of five million hectares.[69]

The immense pressure to identify farms and 'beneficiaries' for the greatly expanded Fast Track programme had the effect of giving district and provincial land committees new scope, largely free of the technocratic and legal constraints of earlier years. Committees were theoretically headed by DAs at district level and Provincial Governors at provincial level. Members included veterans, Zanu(PF), chiefs and others. They were explicitly partisan: as Mugabe put it, 'Zanu(PF)'s land acquisition committees' would identify the thousands of farms needed.[70] Provincial Governors emerged as key figures in pressing forward with Fast Track resettlement at provincial level while, at district level, it was Zanu(PF) and veteran leaders, at times in alliance with others such as chiefs, who dominated decision-making. The contrast with the arbiters of access to land for 'squatters' in the 1980s – the Squatter Control Committees – could not have been more stark.

The land committees played a central role in entrenching the politicised state, and in linking access to land and rights to newly elaborated ideas about loyalty and authenticity. Unsurprisingly, the Fast Track programme in Mashonaland immediately proved controversial, with charges from farm workers that they were cast as 'traitors' while all the land was allocated to veterans and occupiers.[71] In Manicaland, veteran leaders of an unofficial 'land committee' reportedly threatened to evict occupiers they accused of voting MDC.[72] In Masvingo, the provincial Zanu(PF) political commissar said MDC supporters 'should be bundled off the land': they should go to the MDC if they wanted land.[73] Charges that only veterans and Zanu(PF) cardholders were given land raised complaints very widely.[74]

The partisan and autonomous character of land committees was particularly stark in Matabeleland where Zanu(PF) had been resoundingly defeated in the 2000 elections, winning just two seats in the region as a whole. These provinces dramatically illustrated the role of the Fast Track land committees in remaking the state. Soon after his appointment in mid-2000, Provincial Governor Obert Mpofu set the tone by publicly announcing that only Zanu(PF) members and veterans qualified for Fast Track land.[75] Veteran leaders and Zanu(PF) stalwarts distrusted virtually all institutions of the state. Civil servants and elected councillors were cast as suspiciously sympathetic to the MDC, as were even certain Zanu(PF) leaders. In Matabeleland South, veterans on the land committee accused civil servants of stalling resettlement due to their MDC sympathies, and literally chased Provincial Administrator Angelous Dube from her offices. Dube was transferred to Harare, and replaced by the Beitbridge DA, a veteran. She eventually left the country.[76] The Gwanda DA also came under attack, as did the provincial Zanu(PF) leadership. Veterans launched protests until they managed to take over key posts in the party and administrative hierarchies.[77] Land committees also spent much of their time, as JoAnn McGregor has shown, shutting down Matabeleland's councils. These were not wholly unpopular moves: as McGregor argues, veterans played on popular grievances over corruption, maladministration and failed development projects, the legacies of the practices of local authorities in the 1990s.[78]

As the Fast Track programme progressed, disputes over land multiplied. The independent press, researchers, and official reports all highlighted a bewildering range of conflicts.[79] In some places, there were clashes between people who had filled in resettlement forms, and those who had earlier occupied land.[80] In Masvingo, villagers from different districts competed for access to particular farms, with both sides claiming precedence based on their history of occupation, or chiefly and ancestral claims.[81] Different groups of veterans clashed over particular pieces of land, such as in Chiredzi.[82] Matabeleland South's provincial land committee was repeatedly defied by occupiers of the Matopos Research Station, leading to a series of violent evictions, and debate over the salience of historical claims to land.[83] In Midlands province, villagers kicked off a farm by veterans alleged that the provincial land committee had 'hijacked' the Fast Track programme such that it only benefited a privileged group of veterans, politicians and business people.[84] In Nkayi, settlers fought over access to property on the farms. One settler alleged that 'most of the prominent people like civil servants and top war vets have been allocated land that includes farmhouses'.[85]

Authority over the land and the kaleidoscope of alliances that shaped access to land was far from stable, a reflection of the long history of contested claims within and between differently defined communities, and with and against the shifting demands of state and party. Policy was regularly made and unmade. For example, shortly after the launch of the Fast Track programme, newly appointed Minister of Home Affairs John Nkomo stated that occupiers would be removed from unlisted farms. He attempted to take action on the farms surrounding Harare, where self-styled commander of farm invasions Joseph Chinotimba held sway.[86] Nkomo's efforts were endorsed by national veteran leader Hunzvi, and police began to burn homes on stands allocated by veterans. Veterans subsequently protested in Harare, denouncing Nkomo, who was hauled in to explain his actions to the Politburo.

Mugabe promptly declared the police to be in the wrong, and people moved back to their demolished sites.[87] In other instances, central ministries clashed with Provincial Governors who acted in alliance with veterans and occupiers, such as in the case of the Minister of the Environment and Tourism's battle to keep occupiers out of the Save Conservancy.[88]

The chaotic and partisan nature of Fast Track laid it open to a wide range of criticism. The MDC and CFU were naturally prominent, if ineffectual, critics of Fast Track. While both endorsed land redistribution, they backed a return to law, and to technocratic planning.[89] Other objections came from the black commercial farmers' union (ICFU), chiefs, the farm workers' union (GAPWUZ), the smallholders' union (ZFU), and women's groups. The ICFU protested that its members' farms had not escaped the attention of land committees and occupiers, and demanded more land for large-scale farming.[90] GAPWUZ repeatedly highlighted discrimination against farm workers, and the immiseration caused by their displacement.[91] Women's groups complained of gender bias in land allocation.[92] The ZFU condemned the lack of support given to those who had been resettled.[93] Settlers faced severe problems in the 2000/01 season due to late settlement on the land, a lack of draught power and inputs, the absence of infrastructure and services, and in some areas drought.[94] In late 2001, a United Nations Development Programme (UNDP) mission found that the vast scale of resettlement posed a threat to national agricultural production and food security, and made the provision of essential services and infrastructure 'impossible' to achieve within a reasonable time frame.[95]

Chiefs had met with Minister of Local Government Ignatius Chombo in early 2001, and publicly backed the government. They said they would demand that white farmers attend their courts to stand trial over the theft of the land, even threatening to take them to the International Court of Justice. But the seemingly whole-hearted support of chiefs was more complicated on the ground where it was not chiefs but veterans, youth militia and party leaders who often held sway. At a meeting with Vice-President Msika chiefs complained that Zanu(PF) and the veterans were out of control. They alleged that civil servants, councillors and chiefs were all being harassed and sidelined. Msika took veterans at the meeting to task: 'If you were disciplined children you were going to consult the chiefs after invading farms.... You are too full of yourselves.... Chiefs and their people fought the war.'[96] In practice, however, Zanu(PF) credentials were necessary to the exercise of authority. Notably during elections, customary leaders were called upon to act in alliance with veterans and Zanu(PF), not the other way around.[97]

None of these objections led to a slowdown in Fast Track resettlement. It was instead pressed forward with ever greater speed, and only the thinnest pretence of planning. Agritex (renamed Arex after its amalgamation with another department) devoted the entirety of its time and resources to Fast Track rather than extension work, but was totally overwhelmed nonetheless.[98] In 2001, teams of 'experts' were hastily recruited from universities, polytechnics, government departments, and even from among school students on their holidays, to aid in implementation.[99] A1 plots were apparently taken up with great speed, and little central supervision, but the 50,000 or so applicants approved for A2 land in late 2001 proved slow to settle the land.[100] In August 2003, the official Utete Report recorded that 7,260 A2 farmers had occupied just over two million (of around four million) hectares, a take-up rate of 66 per cent nationally. They held farms of widely varying size, and were largely drawn from the ranks of urban residents and elites within the party, military, state and rural areas, a wide-ranging constituency that was to become increasingly aggressive in its demands for land. On A1 land, the Report found that 127,192 households, mostly drawn from communal areas, occupied 4.2 million hectares of land, a take-up rate of 97 per cent.[101]

This marked a thoroughgoing transformation of Zimbabwe's commercial farming areas. In the late 1990s, some 4,500 mostly white commercial farmers had lived on the land with over 300,000 farm workers under a system of private tenure. Less than five years later, the number of white farmers actually farming the land had dwindled to under 500, while as many as 200,000 farm workers had lost their jobs, and often with them their homes and access to services.[102] Farm workers had become 'an itinerant, poor and unstable' class, 'almost destitute and constantly drifting'.[103] Their claims to land were especially weak, as compared to the claims of 'new settlers' and 'new farmers', as A1 and A2 farmers were called. The new settlers Lloyd Sachikonye interviewed in 2002 had sought to formalise their authority by establishing Zanu(PF)-linked committees, referred to as the committees of seven, and sometimes including customary leaders or technical, youth and women representatives.[104] Party loyalty was a crucial route to recognition of land claims. A1 settlers also at times sought legitimacy in the eyes of what was left of the technocratic state. A study in Chiredzi showed how veterans had organised settlement in straight lines and pegged lands: 'The recourse to the technical practices and tools and linear spatial ordering of colonial land use planning was a mechanism by which the occupiers sought to become "visible" and gain official recognition.' When Agritex planners arrived they lacked the resources for 'proper' technical planning and so negotiated with the 'plans' of veterans, in the process turning occupied farms into 'resettlement areas'.[105]

Claims to land on A1 farms nonetheless remained insecure. The Utete report catalogued, province by province, the variable effectiveness and composition of settler committees, and the challenges they faced from chiefs, politicians, officials and others. In theory, A1 land was to fall under councils and the provisions of the Traditional Leaders Act, but councils had yet to establish their authority in part because to do so would mean displacing the settlers' own committees or creating 'customary' authorities out of whole cloth among settlers with little shared history.[106] Conflict was common, as was a tendency to keep communal area land as insurance and so as to retain access to services. The situation of A2 settlers was also far from clear. They blamed their insecure tenure for the low rate of settlement on and investment in A2 land.[107] In 2004, draft proposals suggested that A2 farmers would be given long-term leases, conditional on paying rent, farming productively, and meeting a host of other requirements. As Moyo and Sukume write, the unclear conditions under which leases could be cancelled left lessees 'open to abuse by government officials'. A1 settlers had even less by way of legal protection – their offer letters simply stated that the offer of land may be withdrawn at any time, with no obligation to compensate for improvements, as has happened in some instances.[108] The insecurity of tenure alongside the politics of *jambanja* fed criminality on the farms: looting and vandalism of farm property was common, as was tree-cutting, poaching and gold-panning.[109]

Fast Track resettlement was supposedly completed in 2002, but struggles over the land were far from over.[110] White farmers continued to challenge farm acquisitions in the courts, and hundreds of new farms were still being designated long after the 'completion' of Fast Track.[111] It also became apparent that a new dynamic, closely linked to the politicisation of the state and of authority over the land, was underway. Sachikonye describes it as 'a competitive scramble for commercial farms by members of the ruling elite', concentrated in the prime lands of Mashonaland. The 'land grab-bing' of elites provoked veterans into angry protests at Zanu(PF)'s December 2002 congress.[112] In early 2003, the extent of abuses was revealed in an official 'land audit'. It showed, in Brian Raftopoulos and Ian Phimister's words, 'the displacement of resettled people by the party elite; elite struggles over prime land...; the use of "hired thugs" by sections of the Zanu PF leadership to press their demands; and the problem of multiple ownership amongst prominent members of the ruling elite.'[113]

These processes threatened the legitimacy of Fast Track. Mugabe responded by establishing the Utete commission to review Fast Track, and issuing a directive ordering Zanu(PF) leaders to give up excess farms.[114] The Utete Report, released in August 2003, uneasily combined the nationalist discourses of Zanu(PF) and a set of familiar technocratic views about the role of the state and productivity. The International Crisis Group interpreted the Report as 'an effort to limit the internal ZANU-PF spats that had erupted over land benefits, while also trying to serve as a bridge to eventual reconciliation with the international community.'[115] It rapidly became clear, however, that the views that informed the Report did not command political influence. Instead of a focus on providing settlers with the infrastructure, services and secure tenure the Report called for, just a few months after its release the Land Acquisition Amendment Bill was proposed so as to allow the acquisition of previously protected large estates, plantations, forests and conservancies, unleashing another violent scramble for land in which farm workers once again came off worst.[116] In mid-2004 Minister of Lands John Nkomo stated that all land was to become state land, an assertion from which the government appeared to retreat a few days later, leaving further confusion in its wake.[117] Nor did the question of multiple farm ownership go away, despite the concerted efforts of Minister Nkomo, and the establishment of a 'national land inspectorate', drawn largely from members of the security forces and veterans, and dedicated to rooting out multiple farm owners.[118] Struggles over land appeared to be concentrated among the various 'beneficiaries' of reform, thus sidelining white farmers and, in a major humanitarian catastrophe, farm workers, but without establishing a new means by which authority over the land might be consolidated and legitimised.

The economic consequences of the land occupations in combination with drought, international isolation and political conflict were catastrophic. The economy contracted significantly every year from the start of the Third Chimurenga, shrinking by record levels of over 13 per cent in 2002 and 2003.[119] Roughly half of all Zimbabweans were deemed in need of food aid in 2002, and severe food shortages persisted in subsequent years. The manufacturing and mining sectors reported drastic falls in production while agricultural output plummeted, adding to already severe levels of unemployment. Inflation soared out of control, while foreign currency and fuel shortages added to the crisis.[120] Millions of Zimbabweans simply left the country, seeking their fortunes in the wider region or further afield. Amidst an 'uprising' ostensibly designed to address the inequitable distribution of resources of the past, most Zimbabweans, including many who were recipients of land, were left considerably worse off than they had been prior to the Third Chimurenga. As Rob Davies succinctly put it, 'What we are seeing in Zimbabwe at present … is the destruction of the future by the rhetoric of redress for the past.'[121]

Conclusion

Even from a distance, it was clear that the two districts on which this book has focused were transformed by the Third Chimurenga. In Insiza, Chief Vezi Maduna predictably played a central role, but not one in keeping with the rebellious traditions of the Mafu family. Maduna's forbears had allied with the ICU, Voice and finally Zapu. For his allegiance to Zapu, Vezi Maduna had been detained by the Rhodesian regime and persecuted by Zanu(PF). In 2000, however, he sided with Zanu(PF) against the MDC, playing a key role in Zanu(PF)'s violent wresting of the district from the MDC's control in 2002.[122] In Chimanimani, the most high-profile politician in the age of the Third Chimurenga was a white farmer named Roy Bennett. He won the district's parliamentary seat for the MDC in 2000 by a handsome margin, and subsequently found his family and farm workers subjected to a reign of terror, ending in their violent eviction from the district. In 2004, Bennett was sentenced to a year in prison following an altercation in Parliament with a Zanu(PF) Minister who had called his ancestors 'thieves and murderers'.[123]

Maduna and Bennett represented a distinctly different electoral politics to that of previous years; the land too had been transformed. In Insiza, vast swathes of the ranch land that had so long been coveted by communal area farmers had been acquired by mid-2003. People put the land to use by dispatching family members to herd cattle on the ranches, in effect implementing the version of Model D resettlement they had demanded since independence. In Chimanimani, the constraints on land redistribution of the multinational-owned timber, coffee, and other estates limited the scope of Fast Track until the amendments to the Land Acquisition Act of early 2004. Even then, the land looked likely to benefit elites, not smallholders. The Utete Report found that in neither district had communal area 'decongestion' resulted, while conflict over the land among a host of actors remained rife.[124] In both cases the land had come at the price of a violent political polarisation and economic devastation that did not bode well for the realisation of political or economic rights.

Understanding the full implications of the Third Chimurenga will rely on the work of future researchers. Land claims remained deeply contested among small holders and veterans and chiefs and farm workers and political and military elites, and against the continued appeals to law of white farmers. The struggles over property, power and legitimacy deployed a new vocabulary. Land reform was war, the 'Third Chimurenga'. *Jambanja* described a political practice that celebrated lawlessness. Technocratic plans were transmuted into 'Fast Track' reform, and legitimised through patriotic appeals. Occupiers became 'settlers' while whites were reified as 'foreigners' and farm workers as 'aliens'. The new language of authority and land played on, distorted and displaced the long history of appeals to the discourses of custom, technocratic development and nationalism. No one story of land – or of power over the land – easily encompassed this process. Instead, the many strands of Zimbabwean state-making combined anew.

If the partisan politics of land occupations had undercut the technocratic state, its professional and expert bureaucracies, and its claims to ensuring the productivity of the land, the legacies of technocratic planning did not disappear altogether. Settling in lines remained a means of seeking the state's approval in a situation of insecurity much as it had in earlier periods, and the assumptions of high modernism still ran through official reports. Fast Track resettlement was nonetheless a far cry from the tightly administered and planned resettlement schemes of the 1980s. Deploying the tools of technocratic planning was difficult in times of prosperity and state expansion; it was near impossible amidst a politics of partisan violence, patronage and economic collapse. Customary authority had been the shield behind which the embattled Rhodesian state had sought to retreat in the 1960s. For some of the same reasons – threatened political legitimacy, a lack of state capacity, economic contraction – chiefs came to prominence again in the 1990s, and were granted land allocation and governance powers. They were also used to symbolise African authenticity, and so buttress claims to the land against the thievery of white settlers. But though chiefs sought to assert authority over the land, they faced the often incompatible claims of veterans, party leaders and youth. The rhetorical focus on the liberation war emphasised the glories of young fighting men, invoking a time when chiefs were distinctly marginalised.

Before and after independence, the state struggled to control and contain the diverse institutional and ideological influences that mediated power over the land. The neat dichotomies between traditional and modern, between radicals and collaborators could not begin to describe the alliances and ideologies of rural authorities and their interactions with the state. The resilience and adaptability of chieftaincy, the plasticity of custom, the reproduction and manipulation of the ideology and practices of technical development, were central to the making of authority over the land. But perhaps most influential and mutable of all was nationalism. It had served as an ideology of liberation encompassing both the land and rights, as a justification for squatting, as a modernising call to development. In 2000 nationalism was recast in violent and intolerant mode as the foundation of the Third Chimurenga. It was this version of nationalism that – once again – so powerfully unsettled the land and remade the state.

It would, however, be foolhardy to suggest that the Third Chimurenga was poised to succeed as a means of state-building where others had failed. The land remained enmeshed in contestations over authority, over loyalty and belonging. Land claims were simultaneously multiplied and sidelined, tied to the fortunes of a violent nationalism, and hedged against the promise of an alternative politics. Authority over the land remained in the making.

Notes

1 Amidst a fast growing literature, see Hammar, Raftopoulos, and Jensen, 2003; Raftopoulos and Sachikonye, 2001; Raftopoulos and Savage, 2004; Bond and Manyanya, 2003; Ranger, 2004; Rich Dorman, 2003; and special issues of the *Journal of Agrarian Change*, 1, 4, 2001, and *Politique Africaine*, 81, March 2001.
2 Meredith, 2002, and Blair, 2002. The most subtle of the new books on Mugabe is Chan, 2003.
3 See Bayart, 1993; Chabal and Daloz, 1999. Compare to Lodge, 1998, 21, who argues that Anglophone southern Africa's history made it 'exempt from the general conditions of sub-Saharan statehood'.
4 Willems, 2004.
5 See Kinsey, 1999; Cusworth, 2000.
6 On this period, see Alexander, 1991, 604–5.
7 Angus Selby, personal communication, March 2005. Selby's Oxford DPhil thesis, 'Commercial Farmers and the State: Interest Group Politics and Land Reform in Zimbabwe', is due to be completed in 2006. He bases his conclusions regarding the land acquisition process on a detailed analysis of CFU records, as well as interviews with white farmers, ministry officials, and politicians.
8 See Alexander, 1991, 608; Moyo, n.d. [1998].
9 Moyo, 1994; 1995, 7; 2000c, 12.
10 Moyo, 2000c, 23, 33; Raftopoulos, 1996.
11 See Moyo, 2000a, 7. Moyo, 2001, estimates that only ten per cent of commercial land was black-owned in the late 1990s. Also see ICG, 2004, 69.
12 See Land Tenure Commission, 1994.
13 Yeros, 1999; Moyo, 2000b.
14 See Alexander, McGregor and Ranger, 2000, Chapter 10.
15 For recent studies, see Alexander and McGregor, 2000; Hammar, 2001; Hughes, 2001; Dzingirai, 2003.
16 McGregor, 2002, 22.
17 See Alexander, 2001.
18 O'Flaherty, 1998, 537.
19 See Alexander, 2001. On the effects of the Traditional Leaders Act in resettlement areas, see Kinsey, forthcoming.
20 See O' Flaherty, 1998; Andersson, 1999; Moore, 1998.
21 See Nyambara's study, 2001a, of communal area 'squatting' in Gokwe in the 1990s, and Moyo, 1995, Chapter 6.
22 Yeros, 1999, 13; Moyo, n.d. [1998], 8–11.
23 See Raftopolous, 2001b; Yeros, 2000.
24 Kriger, 2001 and 2003; Alexander, McGregor and Ranger, 2000, Chapter 11; Moyo, n.d. [1998], 5.
25 See discussion in Moyo, n.d. [1998], 5, 35; Moyo, 2000c, 25–7.
26 On Svosve, see Yeros, 1999, 13–16. He bases his account on field work by Knight, 1998.
27 See reports in the *Chronicle*, 11 August 1998; *Mirror*, 31 July to 6 August 1998.
28 See Marongwe, 2003, 163–5.
29 Yeros, 1999, 14–15.
30 Moyo, 2001; Moyo and Matondi, 2001.
31 See coverage in the *Financial Gazette*, 9, 25 November 1999; 30 December 1999; *Mirror*, 19 November 1999; Marongwe, 2003, 163.
32 Tens of thousands of people reportedly registered for resettlement in Matabeleland North alone. *Financial Gazette*, 21 October 1999.
33 On the referendum, see Rich Dorman, 2003.
34 See Raftopoulos, 2003, and Worby, 2003.
35 See Chaumba, Scoones and Wolmer, 2003, 540.
36 See Moyo, 2001.
37 Marongwe, 2003; Chaumba, Scoones and Wolmer, 2003. Not all veterans participated in or approved of the occupations. See Alexander and McGregor, 2001; Raftopoulos, 2003; Kriger, 2001.
38 See, for example, war veteran leader Chenjerai Hunzvi's statements in the *Herald*, 1 March 2000.
39 *Financial Gazette*, 13 April 2000; *Herald*, 14 April 2000; BBC Online, 8 May 2000; *New York Times*, 8 May 2000; *Daily News*, 30 May 2000; *Zimbabwe Independent*, 2 June 2000.
40 BBC Online, 16 March 2000, 8 April 2000; *Herald*, 16 March 2000; 20 March 2000; *Mail and Guardian*, 7, 10 April 2000; *Financial Gazette*, 6 April 2000.
41 Chitiyo, 2003, 180.
42 *Herald*, 24 February 2000; 8 August 2002.

43 See Moyo, 2001; *Herald*, 29 February 2000.
44 Three weeks after the start of the occupations, the CFU reported that over 250 of 300 occupied farms were in the Mashonaland provinces. *Financial Gazette*, 9 March 2000. Angus Selby, personal communication, May 2005, notes the central role played by a small number of veteran leaders, in tandem with the police and provincial land committees, in Mashonaland Central.
45 Alexander and McGregor, 2001, 514-20.
46 See discussions in Marongwe, 2003; Sachikonye, 2003, 37-8; Chaumba, Scoones and Wolmer, 2003; Chitiyo, 2003, 180-81, and reports in the independent press, for example, *Zimbabwe Independent*, 26 May 2000.
47 See Alexander and McGregor, 2001.
48 Interview, David Hasluck, Director, CFU, Harare, July 2000; *Financial Gazette*, 16 March 2000.
49 See reports in *Zimbabwe Independent*, 20 April 2000, 28 April 2000, 5 May 2000, 21 May 2000; *New York Times*, 23 April 2000; *Financial Gazette*, 4 May 2000.
50 In mid-April 2000, the CFU, in a bid to convince the courts that it was not unreasonable for the government to remove occupiers, reduced its estimate of the numbers of farms occupied to 500 and the number of occupiers to 6,000-7,000, a far cry from the Attorney General's claim of 60,000 people on 1,000 farms. *Financial Gazette*, 13 April 2000; *New York Times*, 13 April 2000. The figure of 1,000 farms was nonetheless cited repeatedly in the press.
51 In early March, following the gazetting of the previously rejected constitutional clause on land, Dabengwa stated that veterans no longer needed to 'demonstrate', and so should be evicted. He was promptly contradicted by Mugabe and denounced by veteran leaders. See the *Mirror*, 3 March 2000; *Mail and Guardian*, 3 March 2000, *Herald*, 3 March 2000. In mid-April, Msika received the same treatment when he declared that the occupations should stop as the constitutional amendment had been enacted, and hence there was no bar to land reform. See *Mail and Guardian*, 13 April 2000, *Zimbabwe Independent*, 14 April 2000; *Herald*, 14 April 2000; *Financial Gazette*, 13 April 2000. Such exchanges continued in the following months. See *Financial Gazette*, 20 April 2000; *Daily News*, 30 May 2000; *Zimbabwe Independent*, 2 June 2000. Also see discussion in ICG, 2004, Chapter 6.
52 See Rutherford, 2001b, 2001a, 2004.
53 *New York Times*, 18 April 2000. Also see *Financial Gazette*, 23 February 2000, 30 March 2000.
54 See Raftopoulos, 2003, 217.
55 Veteran leader Hunzvi stated that the veteran organisation was given Z\$20 million in early 2000 for campaigning. See *Financial Gazette*, 16 March 2000; *Zimbabwe Independent*, 9 June 2000. On political violence, see Zimbabwe Human Rights NGO Forum, 2001; ICG, 2001; Feltoe, 2001.
56 See McGregor, 2002; Feltoe, 2001; International Bar Association, 2001.
57 *Zimbabwe Independent*, 16 May 2000.
58 See Solidarity Peace Trust, 2003.
59 See Zimbabwe Human Rights NGO Forum, 2002a, 2002b; Zimbabwe Lawyers for Human Rights, 2003.
60 See Zimbabwe Human Rights NGO Forum, 2002c; Crisis in Zimbabwe Coalition, 2002, Annexure 8; ICG, 2002, 2003, 2004.
61 Government of Zimbabwe, 2000.
62 Moyo, 2001; Marongwe, 2003.
63 There were many reports of new occupations and violence. See the *Herald*, 25, 26, 27 July 2000, *Daily News*, 24, 26, 27, 28 July 2000.
64 *New York Times*, 15 July 2000. Also see Hunzvi's comments in the *Daily News*, 7 July 2000; *Zimbabwe Independent*, 7 July 2000, 14 July 2000.
65 See the *New York Times*, 30 July 2000; *Daily News*, 31 July 2000
66 See *Financial Gazette*, 12 October 2000; *Daily News*, 1 November 2000.
67 *Daily News*, 6 November 2000; BBC Online, 21 November 2000.
68 See Madhuku, 2004.
69 UNDP, 2002, 12. Figures need to be taken with a grain of salt: the numbers of farms and area acquired remained unclear several years later. See Moyo and Sukume, 2004, 5, and passim.
70 *Zimbabwe Independent*, 4 August 2000.
71 Rutherford, 2002, and 2001a; *Mirror*, 10 August 2000. Official figures indicated that only 1.7 per cent of resettled households were headed by farm workers in late 2001. UNDP, 2002, 34-7.
72 *Daily News*, 10 October 2000.
73 *Zimbabwe Independent*, 27 April 2001
74 *Mirror*, 10 August 2000; *Zimbabwe Independent*, 11 August 2000; *Daily News*, 22 August 2000.
75 *Daily News*, 8, 10 August 2000, 11 September 2000; *Zimbabwe Independent*, 27 October 2000.
76 *Financial Gazette*, 3 August 2000; *Mirror*, 25 August 2000, 1 September 2000. Dube gave an impassioned

account of her experiences at the Britain Zimbabwe Society Research Day on Zimbabwe Diasporas, Oxford, 14 June 2003, which eloquently underlined the impossible position of professional civil servants in the face of the state's politicisation.

77 *Daily News*, 16 April 2000, *Mirror*, 24 November 2000.
78 McGregor, 2002.
79 See especially Marongwe, 2003, and the many examples recorded in Government of Zimbabwe, 2003.
80 *Daily News*, 6 September 2000.
81 *Daily News*, 21 September 2000, 30 October 2000.
82 *Daily News*, 7 February 2001.
83 *Mirror*, 13 October 2000, *Daily News*, 5 April 2001.
84 *Daily News*, 5 December 2000.
85 *Daily News*, 10 August 2001.
86 *Daily News*, 28 July 2000; *Herald*, 28 July 2000.
87 See coverage in the *Daily News*, 18, 22, 23, 24, 29 August 2000, 19 September 2000, 14 November 2000, *Zimbabwe Independent*, 25 August 2000.
88 See *Daily News*, 11,18, 20 September 2000; 11, 17, 19, 25 October 2000; 19, 21 February 2001; *Zimbabwe Independent*, 15 September 2000.
89 See MDC policy statements on land on the party's official website, www.mdczimbabwe.com.
90 *Daily News*, 15 August 2000; *Mirror*, 4 May 2001; *Daily News*, 23 May 2001.
91 See Sachikonye, 2003, and press reports in *Financial Gazette*, 31 May 2001; *Mail and Guardian*, 8 June 2001; *Zimbabwe Independent*, 8 June 2001.
92 See Farm Community Trust *et al.*, 2001; UNDP, 2002, for these and other concerns.
93 *Zimbabwe Independent*, 1 December 2000; *Zimbabwe Standard*, 3 December 2000; *Financial Gazette*, 12 July 2001.
94 See Sachikonye's analysis, 2003, of the situation on newly settled farms, and press reports, for example, *Zimbabwe Independent*, 1 December 2000; *Zimbabwe Standard*, 3 December 2000; *Daily News*, 5 December 2000; *Mail and Guardian*, 17 January 2001; *Mirror*, 26 January 2001; *Financial Gazette*, 12 July 2001.
95 UNDP, 2002, 21-4, 37. Also see Bond and Manyanya, 2003, 'Afterword'; ICG, 2004, chapters 6 and 7.
96 See Alexander, 2001, 12.
97 See Kinsey, forthcoming, on the Zanu(PF) 'mobilisation' undertaken by some customary leaders.
98 See Moyo and Sukume, 2004, 49-50.
99 See comments from Minister of Local Government Ignatius Chombo in the *Mirror*, 4 May 2001; *Herald*, 1 June 2001, and from Minister of Agriculture Joseph Made in the *Herald*, 27 July 2001; *Chronicle*, 15 August 2001.
100 Minister of Lands Made threatened to withdraw land offers to tardy A2 farmers in mid-2002. *Herald*, 6 August 2002, cited in Sachikonye, 2003, 42.
101 Government of Zimbabwe, 2003, 'Executive Summary of the Main Findings and Recommendations'. Figures are not reliable. See discussion in Moyo and Sukume, 2004.
102 Sachikonye, 2004, 13, cites the figure of 500 farmers based on a CFU report in August 2004.
103 Sachikonye, 2003, 70.
104 Sachikonye, 2003, Chapter 5. A similar transition is recorded by Chaumba, Scoones and Wolmer, 2003.
105 Chaumba, Scoones and Wolmer, 2003, 543-4.
106 Interview, Councillor, Kezi, August 2004.
107 See the Utete Report's province studies, Government of Zimbabwe, 2003.
108 Moyo and Sukume, 2004, 21-22.
109 See Government of Zimbabwe, 2003.
110 Sachikonye, 2003, 17, reports that Fast Track was supposed to be over in August 2002. The ICG, 2004, 106, reports that it was supposed to be completed in early 2003.
111 For ongoing designations, legal cases and compensation claims, see the Justice for Agriculture website, www.justiceforagriculture.com.
112 Sachikonye, 2003, 42. Also see veteran objections in *Mail and Guardian* (online), 8 December 2003.
113 Raftopoulos and Phimister, 2004, 370. Also see ICG, 2004, Chapter 7; Crisis in Zimbabwe Coalition, 2002, Annexure 7.
114 *Herald*, 31 July 2003.
115 ICG, 2004, 109.
116 For example, see reporting on the Charleswood Estate coffee and cattle farm, owned by then MDC MP Roy Bennett, and the horticultural farm Kondozi, both in Manicaland, in the *Zimbabwe Standard*, 18 April 2004, *Tribune*, 29 April 2004; *Zimbabwe Independent*, 9 January 2004. On timber, tea and sugar plantations see, e.g., reporting in the *Zimbabwe Standard*, 24 October 2004, *Zimbabwe Independent*, 13 February 2004.

117 ICG, 2004, 107–8.
118 See, for example, Minister Nkomo's comments in the *Sunday Mirror*, 22 February 2004, 7 November 2004, and *Daily Mirror*, 20 August 2004. A member of the inspectorate told me that the inspectorate, and Nkomo, faced intractable problems in confronting powerful individuals who refused to release land. Interview, member of the national land inspectorate, August 2004. Also see the *Zimbabwe Independent*, 21 May 2004.
119 ICG, 2004, 110.
120 See the discussion of the economy in Raftopoulos and Phimister, 2004, and Moyo, 2003, 9–13.
121 Davies, 2004, 40. See Moyo and Sukume, 2004, for a discussion of the hostile conditions under which A1 and A2 farmers laboured.
122 See Zimbabwe Institute, 2004, Zimbabwe Election Support Network, 2002, and the Zimbabwe Human Rights NGO Forum's monthly political violence reports, available electronically.
123 See Zimbabwe Lawyers for Human Rights, 2004, for an account of the siege of Bennett's farm in Chimanimani, despite a full six court orders ordering the various state organs involved to desist.
124 See discussions of the districts in the Utete Report, Government of Zimbabwe, 2003.

References

A Note on Sources

Archival references in the text are to the National Archives of Zimbabwe (NAZ), Harare, unless otherwise noted. NAZ sources are not cited separately in the bibliography. Many NAZ references are to boxes of papers from the Ministry of Native Affairs and Internal Affairs which had not been filed at the time of research. Citations of official correspondence and reports that do not have an archival reference number are from Ministry of Local Government records kept in Chimanimani and Insiza Districts, listed below. Interviews with officials are listed below, while interviews with Zanu(PF), Zapu, village development committee, and district council leaders as well as with chiefs, headmen and village heads are referred to using a coding system in the text.

Books, Articles and Papers

Agere, Samuel (ed.). 1998. *Zimbabwe Post-Independence Public Administration: Management Policy, Issues and Constraints* (Dakar, Codesria).

Alexander, Jocelyn. 1991. 'The Unsettled Land: The Politics of Land Redistribution in Matabeleland, 1980-1990', *Journal of Southern African Studies*, 17, 4, 581-610.

— 1994. 'State, Peasantry and Resettlement in Zimbabwe', *Review of African Political Economy*, 61, 325-45.

— 1996. 'Things fall apart, the centre *can* hold: Processes of post-war political change in Zimbabwe's rural areas', in Ngwabi Bhebe and Terence Ranger (eds), *Society in Zimbabwe's Liberation War* (Oxford, James Currey).

— 1998. 'Dissident Perspectives on Zimbabwe's Post-Independence War', *Africa*, 68, 2, 151-82.

— 2001. 'Chiefs and the State in Independent Zimbabwe', paper presented to the conference on Chieftaincy in Africa, Oxford, 9 June.

Alexander, Jocelyn and JoAnn McGregor. 2000. 'Wildlife and Politics: Campfire in Zimbabwe', *Development and Change*, 31, 3, 605-27.

— 2001. 'Elections, Land and the Politics of Opposition in Matabeleland', *Journal of Agrarian Change*, 1, 4, 510-33.

Alexander, Jocelyn, JoAnn McGregor, and Terence Ranger. 2000. *Violence and Memory: One Hundred Years in the 'Dark Forests' of Matabeleland* (Oxford, James Currey).

Alexander, Karin. 2004. 'Orphans of the Empire: An Analysis of Elements of White Identity and

References

Ideology Construction in Zimbabwe', in Brian Raftopoulos and Tyrone Savage (eds), *Zimbabwe: Injustice and Political Reconciliation* (Cape Town, Institute for Justice and Reconciliation).

Alvord, E. D. n.d. 'Development of Native Agriculture and Land Tenure in Southern Rhodesia', Rhodes House, Oxford, ms.

Anderson, David, and Richard Grove (eds). 1989. *Conservation in Africa: People, Policies and Practice* (Cambridge, Cambridge University Press).

Andersson, Jens A. 1999. 'The Politics of Land Scarcity: Land Disputes in Save Communal Area, Zimbabwe', *Journal of Southern African Studies*, 25, 4, 553-78.

Arrighi, G. 1967. *The Political Economy of Rhodesia* (The Hague, Mouton and Co.).

— 1970. 'Labour Supplies in Historical Perspective: A Study of the Proletarianization of the African Peasantry in Rhodesia', *Journal of Development Studies*, 6, 3, 197-234.

— 1973. 'The Political Economy of Rhodesia', in G. Arrighi and J. S. Saul, *Essays on the Political Economy of Africa* (New York, Monthly Review Press).

Association of District Councils. 1986. Minutes of the Third Annual Congress [Including appended annexes 1-14 and speeches]. Kariba, 15-17 October.

'Background to Model D Resettlement Schemes in Gwanda District'. 1990. Bulawayo, ms., July.

Banana, Canaan S. (ed.). 1989. *Turmoil and Tenacity: Zimbabwe 1890-1990* (Harare, College Press).

Barber, James. 1967. *Rhodesia: The Road to Rebellion* (London, Oxford University Press).

Batezat, Elinor, Margaret Mwalo and Kate Truscott. 1988. 'Women and Independence: The Heritage and the Struggle', in Colin Stoneman (ed.), *Zimbabwe's Prospects: Issues of Race, Class, State, and Capital in Southern Africa* (London, Macmillan).

Bayart, Jean-François. 1993. *The State in Africa. The Politics of the Belly* (London, Longman).

Beach, D. N. 1974. 'Ndebele Raiders and Shona Power', *Journal of African History*, 15, 4, 633-51.

— 1977. 'The Shona Economy: Branches of Production', in Robin Palmer and Neil Parsons (eds), *The Roots of Rural Poverty in Central and Southern Africa* (London, Heinemann).

— 1980. *The Shona and Zimbabwe, 900-1850* (Gweru, Mambo Press).

— 1986. *War and Politics in Zimbabwe, 1840-1900* (Gweru, Mambo Press).

— 1991. 'The Origins of Moçambique and Zimbabwe: Paiva de Andrada, the *Companhia de Moçambique* and African Diplomacy, 1881-91', Department of History, University of Zimbabwe, ms.

Beinart, William. 1984. 'Soil Erosion, Conservationism and Ideas about Development: A Southern African Exploration, 1900-1960', *Journal of Southern African Studies*, 11, 1, 52-83.

— 1985. 'Agricultural Planning and the Late Colonial Imagination', in J. McCracken (ed.), *Malawi: An Alternative Pattern of Development* (Edinburgh, Centre for African Studies).

— 2000. 'African History and Environmental History', *African Affairs*, 99, 395, 269-302.

Beinart, William and Colin Bundy. 1987. *Hidden Struggles in Rural South Africa* (London, James Currey).

Beinart, William and Saul Dubow (eds). 1995. *Segregation and Apartheid in Twentieth-Century South Africa* (London, Routledge).

Beinart, William and JoAnn McGregor. 2003a. 'Introduction', in William Beinart and JoAnn McGregor (eds), *Social History and African Environments* (Oxford, James Currey).

— (eds). 2003b. *Social History and African Environments* (Oxford, James Currey).

Berman, Bruce. 1990. *Control and Crisis in Colonial Kenya: The Dialect of Domination* (London, James Currey).

Berman, Bruce and John Lonsdale. 1992. *Unhappy Valley. Conflict in Kenya and Africa. Book Two: Violence and Ethnicity* (London, James Currey).

Bernstein, Henry. 2004. '"Changing before our eyes": Agrarian Questions and the Politics of Land in Capitalism Today', *Journal of Agrarian Change*, 4, 1 and 2, 190-225.

Berry, Sara. 1993. *No Condition is Permanent: The Social Dynamics of Agrarian Change in Sub-Saharan Africa* (Madison, University of Wisconsin Press).

— 2001. *Chiefs Know their Boundaries: Essays on Property, Power and the Past in Asante* (Oxford, James Currey).

— 2002. 'Debating the Land Question in Africa', *Comparative Studies in Society and History*, 44, 4, 638-68.

References

Bhebe, Ngwabi. 1978. 'The Ndebele and Mwari before 1893: A Religious Conquest of the Conquerors by the Vanquished', in J. M. Schoffeleers (ed.), *Guardians of the Land* (Gwelo, Mambo Press).
— 1989a. *Benjamin Burombo: African Politics in Zimbabwe 1947-1958* (Harare, College Press).
— 1989b. 'The Nationalist Struggle, 1957-62', in Canaan Banana (ed.), *Turmoil and Tenacity: Zimbabwe 1890-1990* (Harare, College Press).
Bhebe, Ngwabi and Terence Ranger (eds). 1995. *Soldiers in Zimbabwe's Liberation War* (London, James Currey).
— (eds). 1996. *Society in Zimbabwe's Liberation War* (Oxford, James Currey).
Bierschenk, Thomas and Jean-Pierre Olivier de Sardan. 2003. 'Powers in the Village: Rural Benin between Democratisation and Decentralisation', *Africa*, 73, 2, 145-73.
Birmingham, David and Terence Ranger. 1983. 'Settlers and Liberators in the South', in David Birmingham and Phyllis Martin (eds), *History of Central Africa*, Vol. 2 (Harlow, Longman).
Blair, David. 2002. *Degrees in Violence: Robert Mugabe and the Struggle for Power in Zimbabwe* (London, Continuum).
Bond, Patrick and John Manyanya. 2003. *Zimbabwe's Plunge: Exhausted Nationalism, Neo-liberalism and the Search for Social Justice* (Harare, Weaver Press).
Boone, C. 1998. 'State Building in the African Countryside: Structure and Politics at the Grassroots', *Journal of Development Studies*, 34, 4, 1-31.
Bowyer-Bower, T. A. S. and Colin Stoneman (eds). 2000. *Land Reform in Zimbabwe: Constraints and Prospects* (Aldershot, Ashgate).
Bozzoli, Belinda and Peter Delius. 1990. 'Radical History and South African Society', *Radical History Review*, 46-47, 13-45.
Brand, Coenraad. 1991. 'Will Decentralization Enhance Local Participation?', in A. H. J. Helmsing *et al.*, *Limits to Decentralization in Zimbabwe: Essays on the Decentralization of Government and Planning in the 1980s* (The Hague, Institute of Social Studies).
Bratton, Michael. 1978. *Beyond Community Development: The Political Economy of Rural Administration in Zimbabwe* (Gwelo, Mambo Press).
— 1981. 'Development in Zimbabwe: Strategy and Tactics', *Journal of Modern African Studies*, 19, 3, 447-75.
— 1987. 'The Comrades and the Countryside: The Politics of Agricultural Policy in Zimbabwe', *World Politics*, 39, 2, 174-202.
Bulman, M. E. 1973. *The Native Land Husbandry Act of Southern Rhodesia: A Failure in Land Reform* (Salisbury, Tribal Areas of Rhodesia Research Foundation).
Bush, Ray and Lionel Cliffe. 1984. 'Agrarian Policy in Migrant Labour Societies: Reform or Transformation in Zimbabwe', *Review of African Political Economy*, 29, 77-94.
Bush, Ray and Morris Szeftel. 2002. 'Sovereignty, Democracy and Zimbabwe's Tragedy', *Review of African Political Economy*, 19, 5-12.
Cahi, Jackie. 1992. *The Bende Gap People of Nyanga District*, a Report for the Catholic Commission for Justice and Peace in Zimbabwe.
Castro, Alfonso Peter (ed.). 1998. 'Historical Consciousness in Development Planning', special issue of *World Development*, 26, 9, 1695-1784.
Catholic Commission for Justice and Peace/Legal Resources Foundation. 1997. *Breaking the Silence, Building True Peace: A Report on the Disturbances in Matabeleland and the Midlands, 1980-1988* (Harare, CCJP/LRF).
Caute, David. 1982. 'The Politics of Rough Justice', *New Statesman*, London, 16 April.
— 1983. *Under the Skin. The Death of White Rhodesia* (Harmondsworth, Penguin Books).
— 1985. 'Mugabe Brooks No Opposition', *The Nation*, New York, 31 August.
Chabal, P. 1992. *Power in Africa* (London, Macmillan).
Chabal, P. and J-P. Daloz. 1999. *Africa Works: Disorder as Political Instrument* (Oxford, James Currey).
Chan, Stephen. 2003. *Robert Mugabe: A Life of Power and Violence* (London, I. B. Tauris).
Chanock, Martin. 1985. *Law, Custom and Social Order: The Colonial Experience in Malawi and Zambia* (Cambridge, Cambridge University Press).

References

— 1991. 'Paradigms, Policies, and Property: A Review of the Customary Law of Land Tenure', in K. Mann and R. Roberts (eds), *Law in Colonial Africa* (London, James Currey).

Chaumba, Joseph, Ian Scoones and Will Wolmer. 2003. 'From Jambanja to Planning: The Reassertion of Technocracy in Land Reform in South-eastern Zimbabwe?', *Journal of Modern African Studies*, 41, 4, 533-54.

Cheater, Angela. 1990. 'The Ideology of "Communal" Land Tenure in Zimbabwe: Mythogenesis Enacted?', *Africa*, 60, 2, 188-206.

Chimhowu, Admos Osmund. 2002. 'Extending the Grain Basket to the Margins: Spontaneous Land Resettlement and Changing Livelihoods in the Hurungwe District, Zimbabwe', *Journal of Southern African Studies*, 28, 3, 551-73.

Chingono, Mark. 1992. 'Book Reviews', *Africa*, 62, 3, 454-7.

Chitiyo, Knox. 2003. 'Harvest of Tongues: Zimbabwe's "Third Chimurenga" and the Making of an Agrarian Revolution', in Margaret C. Lee and Karen Colvard (eds), *Unfinished Business: The Land Crisis in Southern Africa* (Pretoria, Africa Institute of South Africa).

Cliffe, Lionel. 1986. 'Policy Options for Agrarian Reform: A Technical Appraisal', Report submitted by the FAO for the consideration of the Government of Zimbabwe, February.

— 2000. 'The Politics of Land Reform in Zimbabwe', in T. A. S. Bowyer-Bower and Colin Stoneman (eds), *Land Reform in Zimbabwe: Constraints and Prospects* (Aldershot, Ashgate).

Cliffe, Lionel, Joshua Mpofu and Barry Munslow. 1980. 'Nationalist Politics in Zimbabwe: The 1980 Elections and Beyond', *Review of African Political Economy*, 18, 44-67.

Cobbing, J. R. D. 1976. 'The Ndebele under the Khumalos, 1820-1896', PhD, University of Lancaster.

Colson, Elizabeth. 1971. 'The Impact of the Colonial Period on the Definition of Land Rights', in Victor Turner (ed.), *Colonialism in Africa*, Vol. 3 (Cambridge, Cambridge University Press).

Comaroff, J. L. and J. Comaroff. 1997. *Of Revelation and Revolution: The Dialectics of Modernity on a South African Frontier*, Vol. 2 (Chicago, Chicago University Press).

Cooper, Frederick. 1996. *Decolonization and African Society: The Labour Question in French and British Colonial Africa, 1945-54* (Cambridge, Cambridge University Press).

Cooper, Frederick and Anne Stoler (eds). 1997. *Tensions of Empire: Colonial Cultures in a Bourgeois World* (Berkeley, University of California).

Cousins, Ben. 1987. *A Survey of Current Grazing Schemes in the Communal Lands* (Harare, Centre for Applied Social Science).

— 1990. 'Property and Power in Zimbabwe's Communal Lands', Paper presented to the Land Policy in Zimbabwe After 'Lancaster' Conference, University of Zimbabwe, 13-15 February.

Cousins, Ben, Dan Weiner and Nick Amin. 1992. 'Social Differentiation in the Communal Lands', *Review of African Political Economy*, 53, 5-24.

Crisis in Zimbabwe Coalition. 2002. 'Zimbabwe Report', Harare, 20 June.

Crummey, Donald. 1986. 'Introduction', in Donald Crummey (ed.), *Banditry, Rebellion and Social Protest in Africa* (London, James Currey).

Cusworth, John. 2000. 'A Review of the UK ODA Evaluation of the Land Resettlement Programme in 1988 and the Land Appraisal Mission of 1996', in T. A. S. Bowyer-Bower and Colin Stoneman (eds), *Land Reform in Zimbabwe: Constraints and Prospects* (Aldershot, Ashgate).

Davies, Rob. 2004. 'Memories of Underdevelopment: A Personal Interpretation of Zimbabwe's Economic Decline', in Brian Raftopoulos and Tyrone Savage (eds), *Zimbabwe: Injustice and Political Reconciliation* (Cape Town, Institute for Justice and Reconciliation).

De Valk, Peter. 1986. 'An Analysis of Planning Policy in Zimbabwe'. Workshop on the Planning System in Zimbabwe, Department of Rural Development, University of Zimbabwe, Harare, 4-7 February.

De Valk, Peter and K. Wekwete. n.d. [c. 1985]. 'District Councils in Zimbabwe: Possibilities and Constraints. A Profile of their Operation as Planning Units', ms.

Dopcke, Wolfgang. 1990. 'Chiefs and the State in Colonial Zimbabwe: Some Preliminary Thoughts', St. Antony's College, Oxford, ms.

— 1991. 'The Chiefs and the State in Zimbabwe – Collection of Ideas', St. Antony's College, Oxford, ms.

Drinkwater, Michael. 1987. 'Loans and Manure: the Dilemma of Access', Working Paper, Department of Agriculture and Extension, University of Zimbabwe.

— 1989. 'Technical Development and Peasant Impoverishment: Land Use Policy in Zimbabwe's Midlands Province', *Journal of Southern African Studies*, 15, 2, 287-305.

— 1991. *The State and Agrarian Change in Zimbabwe's Communal Areas* (Houndsmills, Macmillan).

Dubow, Saul. 1989. *Racial Segregation and the Origins of Apartheid in South Africa, 1919-36* (London, Macmillan).

— 2000. 'Introduction', in Saul Dubow (ed.), *Science and Society in Southern Africa* (Manchester, Manchester University Press).

Duggan, W. 1980. 'The Native Land Husbandry Act of 1951 and the Rural African Middle Class of Southern Rhodesia', *African Affairs*, 79, 315, 227-39.

Dusing, Sandra. 2002. *Traditional Leadership and Democratisation in Southern Africa: A Comparative Study of Botswana, Namibia, and South Africa* (Munster, Lit Verlag).

Dzingirai, Vupenyu. 2003. '"Campfire is not for Ndebele Migrants": The Impact of Excluding Outsiders from CAMPFIRE in the Zambezi Valley, Zimbabwe', *Journal of Southern African Studies*, 29, 2, 445-60.

Eiselen, W. 1959. 'Harmonious Multi-community Development', reprint of *Optima*, March.

Englund, Harri. 2002. 'Introduction: The Culture of Chameleon Politics', in Harri Englund (ed.), *A Democracy of Chameleons: Politics and Culture in the New Malawi* (Stockholm, Nordiska Afrikainstitutet).

Escobar, Arturo. 1995. *Encountering Development: The Making and Unmaking of the Third World* (Princeton, Princeton University Press).

Falk Moore, Sally. 1986. *Social Facts and Fabrications: Customary Law on Kilimanjaro, 1880-1980* (Cambridge, Cambridge University Press).

— 1996. 'Post-Socialist Micro-Politics: Kilimanjaro, 1993', *Africa*, 66, 4, 587-605.

Farm Community Trust Zimbabwe, Women and Land Lobby Group and Friedrich Naumann Foundation. 2001. 'Summarised Report on the One-Day Workshop to Review the Land Reform Programme in Zimbabwe', Harare International Conference Centre, 10 May.

Feierman, Steven. 1990. *Peasant Intellectuals: Anthropology and History in Tanzania* (Madison, University of Wisconsin Press).

Feltoe, G. 2001. 'The Onslaught Against Democracy and the Rule of Law in Zimbabwe', ms, Harare.

Ferguson, James. 1990. *The Anti-Politics Machine: 'Development', Depoliticization and Bureaucratic Power in Lesotho* (Cambridge, Cambridge University Press).

Fields, Karen. 1997 [1985]. *Revival and Rebellion in Colonial Central Africa* (Portsmouth, NH, Heinemann).

Fisiy, C. 1995. 'Chieftaincy in the Modern State: An Institution at the Crossroads of Democratic Change', *Paideuma*, 41, 49-62.

Floyd, B. N. 1959. 'Changing Patterns of Land Use in Southern Rhodesia', Vols 1-3, PhD thesis, Syracuse University.

— 1961. *Changing Patterns of Land Use in Southern Rhodesia* (Lusaka, Rhodes-Livingstone Institute).

Gaidzanwa, N. R. B. 1981. 'Promised Land: Towards a Land Policy for Zimbabwe', MSt Thesis, The Hague, Institute of Social Studies.

Garbett, G. K. 1963. 'The Land Husbandry Act of Southern Rhodesia', in D. Biebuyck (ed.), *African Agrarian Systems* (Oxford, Oxford University Press).

Gasper, Des. 1988. 'Rural Growth Points and Rural Industries in Zimbabwe: Ideologies and Policies', *Development and Change*, 19, 3, 425-66.

— 1990. 'What Happened to The Land Question in Zimbabwe? Rural Reform in the 1980s', Paper for presentation to EADI General Conference, Oslo, 27-30 June.

— 1991. 'Decentralization of planning and administration in Zimbabwe. International perspectives and 1980s experiences', in A. H. J. Helmsing *et al.*, *Limits to Decentralization in Zimbabwe: Essays on the Decentralization of Government and Planning in the 1980s* (The Hague, Institute of Social Studies).

Geschiere, Peter. 1993. 'Chiefs and Colonial Rule in Cameroon: Inventing Chieftaincy, French and British Style', *Africa*, 63, 2, 151-75.

Glassman, J. 1995. *Feasts and Riot: Revelry, Rebellion and Popular Consciousness on the Swahili Coast, 1856-1888* (London, James Currey).

Gluckman, Max. 1949. 'The Village Headman in British Central Africa: Introduction', *Africa*, 19, 2, 89-94.

Gonese, F. T. [Assistant Director, Department of Rural Development]. 1988. 'A Framework for Communal Land Reorganisation in Zimbabwe', Paper presented to the Seminar on Communal Lands Reorganisation, Harare, 4-5 August.

Gray, R. 1960. *The Two Nations: Aspects of the Development of Race Relations in the Rhodesias and Nyasaland* (London, Oxford University Press).

Hagberg, S. 1998. *Between Peace and Justice: Dispute Settlement between Karaboro Agriculturalists and Fulbe Agro-Pastoralists in Burkina Faso* (Uppsala, Uppsala University).

Hammar, Amanda. 2001. '"The Day of Burning": Eviction and Reinvention in the Margins of Northwest Zimbabwe', *Journal of Agrarian Change*, 1, 4, 550-74.

Hammar, Amanda, Brian Raftopoulos and Stig Jensen (eds). 2003. *Zimbabwe's Unfinished Business: Rethinking Land, State and Nation in the Context of Crisis* (Harare, Weaver Press).

Helle-Valle, Jo. 2002. 'Seen from Below: Conceptions of Politics and the State in a Botswana Village', *Africa*, 72, 2, 179-202.

Helmsing, A. H. J. 1991. 'Rural local government finance. Past trends and future options', in A. H. J. Helmsing *et al.*, *Limits to Decentralization in Zimbabwe: Essays on the Decentralization of Government and Planning in the 1980s* (The Hague, Institute of Social Sciences).

Helmsing, A. H. J *et al.* 1991. *Limits to Decentralization in Zimbabwe: Essays on the Decentralization of Government and Planning in the 1980s* (The Hague, Institute of Social Studies).

Herbst, Jeffrey. 1990. *State Politics in Zimbabwe* (Harare, University of Zimbabwe Press).

Holleman, J. F. 1969. *Chief, Council and Commissioner* (London, Oxford University Press).

Hoogeven, J. G. M. and Bill H. Kinsey. 2001. 'Land Reform, Growth and Equity: Emerging Evidence from Zimbabwe's Resettlement Programme – A Sequel', *Journal of Southern African Studies*, 27, 1, 127-36.

'How Zapu cadre tried to cut SA's Dukwe link'. 1990. *Parade*, September.

Howman, Roger. 1963. *African Local Government in British East and Central Africa, 1951-1953*, re-issued in the Reprint Series of the University of South Africa, Vol. 2, No. 4 (Pretoria).

— 1966. 'Chieftainship', *NADA*, 9, 3, 10-14.

— 1967. 'Changing Social Structure and Land Tenure', *First Rhodesian Scientific Congress*.

Hughes, David. 1999. 'Refugees and Squatters: Immigration and the Politics of Territory on the Zimbabwe–Mozambique Border', *Journal of Southern African Studies*, 25, 4, 533-52.

— 2001. 'Rezoned for Business: How Eco-Tourism Unlocked Black Farmland in Eastern Zimbabwe', *Journal of Agrarian Change*, 1, 4, 575-99.

Hughes, A. J. B. 1956. *Kin, Caste and Nation Among the Rhodesian Ndebele*, Rhodes-Livingstone Papers, No. 23 (Manchester, Manchester University Press).

— 1974. *Development in Rhodesian Tribal Trust Lands: An Overview* (Salisbury, Tribal Areas of Rhodesia Research Foundation).

Hyden, Goran. 1983. *No Shortcuts to Progress: African Development Management in Perspective* (London, Heinemann).

Iliffe, John. 1990. *Famine in Zimbabwe, 1890-1960* (Gweru, Mambo Press).

International Bar Association. 2001. 'Report of Zimbabwe Mission 2001', London, IBA, April.

International Crisis Group [ICG]. 2001. 'Zimbabwe in Crisis: Finding a Way Forward', Africa Report No. 32, Harare and Brussels, ICG, 13 July.

— 2002. 'Zimbabwe: The Politics of National Liberation and International Division', Africa Report No. 52, Harare and Brussels, ICG, 17 October.

— 2003. 'Zimbabwe: Danger and Opportunity', Africa Report No. 60, Harare and Brussels, ICG, 10 March.

— 2004. *Blood and Soil: Land, Politics and Conflict Prevention in Zimbabwe and South Africa* (Brussels, ICG).

Isaacman, Allen. 1990. 'Peasants and Rural Social Protest in Africa', *African Studies Review*, 33, 2, 1-120.

— 1996. *Cotton is the Mother of Poverty: Peasants, Work and Rural Struggle in Colonial Mozambique* (London, James Currey).

Jackson, J. C. and P. Collier. 1988. 'Incomes, Poverty and Food Security in the Communal Lands of Zimbabwe', RUP Occasional Paper No. 11 (Harare, Department of Rural and Urban Planning, University of Zimbabwe).

Jeater, Diana. 1993. *Marriage, Perversion and Power: The Construction of Moral Discourse in Southern Rhodesia, 1894-1930* (Oxford, Oxford University Press).

— 2002. '"I am willing to pay for the damage done": Parallel Systems of Criminal Law in White-occupied Southern Rhodesia, 1896-1923', paper presented to the conference on Crime in Eastern Africa: Past and Present Perspectives, 8-11 July, Naivasha, Kenya.

Johnson, David. 1992. 'Settler Farmers and Coerced African Labour in Southern Rhodesia, 1936-1946', *Journal of African History*, 33, 1, 111-28.

Johnson, R. W. M. 1964. 'Introduction', *Rhodes Livingstone Institute Journal*, 36, 1-6.

Jordan, J. D. 1964. 'Zimutu Reserve: A Land-Use Appreciation', *Rhodes Livingstone Institute Journal*, 36, 59-81.

Kaarsholm, Preben and Deborah James. 2000. 'Popular Culture and Democracy in some Southern Contexts: An Introduction', *Journal of Southern African Studies*, 26, 2, 189-208.

Kay, G. 1980. 'Towards a Population Policy for Zimbabwe-Rhodesia', *African Affairs*, 79, 314, 95-114.

Kazembe, Joyce. 1986. 'The Women Issue', in Ibbo Mandaza (ed.), *Zimbabwe: The Political Economy of Transition 1980-1986* (Dakar, Codesria).

Keigwin, H. S. 1923. 'Native Development', *NADA*, 1, 1, 10-17.

Khadani, Xavier M. 1986. 'The Economy: Issues, Problems and Prospects', in Ibbo Mandaza (ed.), *Zimbabwe: The Political Economy of Transition 1980-1986* (Dakar, Codesria).

Kinsey, B. H. 1982. 'Forever Gained: Resettlement and Land Policy in the Context of National Development in Zimbabwe', *Africa*, 52, 3, 92-113.

— 1983. 'Emerging Policy Issues in Zimbabwe's Land Resettlement Programmes', *Development Policy Review*, 1, 2, 163-96.

— 1999. 'Land Reform, Growth and Equity: Emerging Evidence from Zimbabwe's Resettlement Programme', *Journal of Southern African Studies*, 25, 2, 173-96.

— forthcoming. 'Fractionating Local Leadership: Created Authority and Management of State Land in Zimbabwe', in S. Evers, M. Spierenburg and H. Wels (eds), *Competing Jurisdictions: Settling Land Claims in Africa* (Leiden, Brill Academic Publishers).

Knight, R. 1998. 'Zimbabwe's Land Invasions: An Investigation into the Grassroots Politics of Land Redistribution and Resettlement', ms.

Kriger, Norma. 1992. *Zimbabwe's Guerrilla War. Peasant Voices* (Cambridge, Cambridge University Press).

— 1995. 'The Politics of Creating National Heroes: The Search for Political Legitimacy and National Identity', in Ngwabi Bhebe and Terence Ranger (eds), *Soldiers in Zimbabwe's Liberation War* (London, James Currey).

— 2001. 'Les veterans et le parti au pouvoir: Une cooperation conflictuelle dans le longue duree', *Politique Africaine*, 81, March, 80-100.

— 2003. *Guerrilla Veterans in Post-War Zimbabwe: Symbolic and Violent Politics, 1980-1987* (Cambridge, Cambridge University Press).

— 2005. 'ZANU(PF) Strategies in General Elections, 1980-2000: Discourse and Coercion', *African Affairs*, 104, 414, 1-34.

Ladley, Andrew. 1985. 'Courts and Authority: A Study of a Shona Village Court in Rural Zimbabwe',

205

PhD, University of London.

— 1990. 'Just Spirits? Chiefs, Tradition, Status and Contract in the Customary Law Courts of Zimbabwe', ms.

Lan, David. 1985. *Guns and Rain: Guerrillas and Spirit Mediums in Zimbabwe* (Harare, Zimbabwe Publishing House).

Lawyers' Committee for Human Rights. 1986. *Zimbabwe: Wages of War. A Report on Human Rights* (New York, LCHR).

Lee, M. E. 1974. 'Politics and Pressure Groups in Southern Rhodesia, 1898-1923', PhD thesis, University of London.

Lee, Margaret and Karen Colvard (eds). 2003. *Unfinished Business: The Land Crisis in Southern Africa* (Pretoria, Africa Institute for South Africa).

Lewis, J. 2000. *Empire State-building: War and Welfare in Kenya, 1925-52* (Oxford, James Currey).

Lodge, Tom. 1998. 'The Southern African Post-Colonial State', *Commonwealth and Comparative Politics*, 36, 1, 20-47.

Lonsdale, John. 1986. 'Political Accountability in African History', in Patrick Chabal (ed.), *Political Domination in Africa: Reflections on the Limits of Power* (Cambridge, Cambridge University Press).

— 1992. 'The Moral Economy of Mau Mau: Wealth, Poverty and Civic Virtue in Kikuyu Political Thought', in Bruce Berman and John Lonsdale, *Unhappy Valley: Conflict in Kenya and Africa. Book Two: Violence and Ethnicity* (London, James Currey).

Lonsdale, John and Bruce Berman. 1979. 'Coping with the Contradictions: The Development of the Colonial State in Kenya, 1895-1914', *Journal of African History*, 20, 4, 487-505.

Low, D. A. and John Lonsdale. 1976. 'Introduction: Towards the New Order, 1945-1963', in D. A. Low and A. Smith (eds), *History of East Africa*, Vol. 3 (Oxford, Oxford University Press).

Mackenzie, A. F. D. 2000. 'Contested Ground: Colonial Narratives and the Kenyan Enviroment, 1920-1945', *Journal of Southern African Studies*, 26, 4, 679-718.

Madhuku, Lovemore. 2004. 'Law, Politics and the Land Reform Process in Zimbabwe', in Medicine Masiiwa (ed.), *Post-independence Land Reform in Zimbabwe: Controversies and Impact on the Economy* (Harare, Friedrich Ebert Stfitung and Institute of Development Studies).

Maier, Karl. 1989. 'Zimbabwe grapples with the law of the land', *Independent*, London, 28 October.

Makumbe, John. 1991. 'The 1990 Zimbabwe Elections: Implications for Democracy', in Ibbo Mandaza and Lloyd Sachikonye (eds), *The One Party State and Democracy: The Zimbabwe Debate* (Harare, SAPES).

Mamdani, Mahmood. 1996. *Citizen and Subject: Contemporary Africa and the Legacy of Late Colonialism* (London, James Currey).

Mandaza, Ibbo. 1986a. 'Introduction: The Political Economy of Transition', in Ibbo Mandaza, (ed.), *Zimbabwe: The Political Economy of Transition 1980-1986* (Dakar, Codesria).

— 1986b. 'The State and Politics in the Post-White Settler Colonial Situation', in Ibbo Mandaza (ed.), *Zimbabwe: The Political Economy of Transition 1980-1986* (Dakar, Codesria).

— (ed.). 1986c. *Zimbabwe: The Political Economy of Transition 1980-1986* (Dakar, Codesria).

Mandaza, Ibbo and Lloyd Sachikonye (eds). 1991. *The One Party State and Democracy: The Zimbabwe Debate* (Harare, SAPES).

Manicom, L. 1992. 'Ruling Relations: Rethinking State and Gender in South African History', *Journal of African History*, 33, 3, 441-65.

Mann, Kristin and Richard Roberts (eds). 1991. *Law in Colonial Africa* (London, James Currey).

Manor, James (ed.). 1991. *Rethinking Third World Politics* (London, Longman).

Marks, Shula and Richard Rathbone (eds). 1982. *Industrialisation and Social Change in South Africa* (London, Longman).

Marongwe, Nelson. 2002. *Conflicts over Land and Other Natural Resources in Zimbabwe* (Harare, ZERO).

— 2003. 'Farm Occupations and Occupiers in the New Politics of Land in Zimbabwe', in Amanda Hammar, Brian Raftopoulos and Stig Jensen (eds), *Zimbabwe's Unfinished Business: Rethinking Land, State and Nation in the Context of Crisis* (Harare, Weaver Press).

References

Martin, David and Phyllis Johnson. 1981. *The Struggle for Zimbabwe. The Chimurenga War* (Harare, Zimbabwe Publishing House).

Masiiwa, Medicine (ed.). 2004. *Post-independence Land Reform in Zimbabwe: Controversies and Impact on the Economy* (Harare, Friedrich Ebert Stfitung and Institute of Development Studies).

Maxwell, David. 1999. *Christians and Chiefs in Zimbabwe: The Social History of the Hwesa People, c. 1870s-1990s* (Edinburgh, Edinburgh University Press).

Mbelesi, M. and P. Ngobese. 1990. 'The Impact of the Model "D" Project on Cattle Owners in Ward 8 of Gwaranyemba Communal Lands, Gwanda District', ADA Research Seminar, Harare, 12-13 July.

McGregor, JoAnn. 1991. 'Woodland Resources: Ecology, Policy and Ideology. An Historical Case Study of Woodland Use in Shurugwi Communal Area, Zimbabwe', DPhil thesis, Loughborough University.

— 1995. 'Conservation, Control and Ecological Change: The Politics and Ecology of Colonial Conservation in Shurugwi, Zimbabwe', *Environment and History*, 1, 3, 257-80.

— 2002. 'The Politics of Disruption: War Veterans and the Local State in Zimbabwe', *African Affairs*, 101, 402, 9-37.

Meredith, Martin. 2002. *Mugabe: Power and Plunder in Zimbabwe* (Oxford, Public Affairs).

Mlambo, Alois. 2003. 'The Social Costs of the Zimbabwe Crisis Since 2000', in Margaret C. Lee and Karen Colvard (eds), *Unfinished Business: The Land Crisis in Southern Africa* (Pretoria, African Institute of South Africa).

Mnangagwa, Emmerson D. 1989. 'Post-independence Zimbabwe (1980-87)', in Canaan Banana (ed.), *Turmoil and Tenacity: Zimbabwe 1890-1990* (Harare, College Press).

Moore, David. 1991. 'The Ideological Formation of the Zimbabwean Ruling Class', *Journal of Southern African Studies*, 17, 3, 472-95.

— 1995. 'The Zimbabwe People's Army: Strategic Innovation or More of the Same?', in Terence Ranger and Ngwabi Bhebe (eds), *Soldiers in Zimbabwe's Liberation War* (London, James Currey).

— 2001. 'Is the Land the Economy and the Economy the Land? Primitive Accumulation in Zimbabwe', *Journal of Contemporary African Studies*, 19, 2, 253-66.

— 2004. 'Marxism and Marxist Intellectuals in Schizophrenic Zimbabwe: How Many Rights for Zimbabwe's Left? A Comment', *Historical Materialism*, 12, 4, 405-25.

Moore, Donald S. 1998. 'Clear Waters and Muddied Histories: Environmental History and the Politics of Community in Zimbabwe's Eastern Highlands', *Journal of Southern African Studies*, 24, 2, 377-404.

Mosley, Paul. 1983. *The Settler Economies: Studies in the Economic History of Kenya and Southern Rhodesia 1900-1963* (Cambridge, Cambridge University Press).

Moyana, Henry. 1984. *The Political Economy of Land in Zimbabwe* (Gweru, Mambo Press).

Moyo, Jonathon. 1991. 'The Dialectics of National Unity and Democracy in Zimbabwe', in Ibbo Mandaza and Lloyd Sachikonye (eds), *The One Party State and Democracy: The Zimbabwe Debate* (Harare, SAPES).

Moyo, Sam. 1986. 'The Land Question', in Ibbo Mandaza (ed.), *Zimbabwe: The Political Economy of Transition 1980-1986* (Dakar, Codesria).

— 1990. 'The Zimbabweanisation of Southern Africa's Agrarian Question: Lessons or Domino Stratagems?', Zimbabwe Institute of Development Studies, Harare, ms.

— 1991. 'The Role of Agriculture in Zimbabwe: Some Initial Findings', Zimbabwe Institute of Development Studies Seminar on Zimbabwe's ESAP, Kadoma, 18-21 November.

— 1994. *Economic Nationalism and Land Reform in Zimbabwe*, occasional paper series no. 7 (Harare, SAPES Books).

— 1995. *The Land Question in Zimbabwe* (Harare, SAPES Books).

— n.d. [1998]. 'The Land Acquisition Process in Zimbabwe (1997/8)', Harare, UNDP.

— 2000a. 'The Interaction of Market and Compulsory land Acquisition Processes with Social Action in Zimbabwe's Land Reform', paper presented to SARIPS of the SAPES Trust Annual

References

Colloquium on Regional Integration: Past, Present and Future, Harare, 24–27 September.

— 2000b. *Land Reform under Structural Adjustment in Zimbabwe: Land Use Changes in the Mashonaland Provinces* (Uppsala, Nordiska Afrikainstitutet).

— 2000c. 'The Political Economy of Land Acquisition and Redistribution in Zimbabwe, 1990–1999', *Journal of Southern African Studies*, 26, 1, 5–28.

— 2001. 'The Land Occupation Movement and Democratisation in Zimbabwe: Contradictions of Neoliberalism', *Millenium. Journal of International Studies*, 30, 2, 311–30.

— 2003. 'Land Redistribution: Allocation and Beneficiaries', Harare, African Institute for Agrarian Studies, June.

Moyo, Sam and Chris Sukume. 2004. *Agricultural Sector and Agrarian Development Strategy*, final draft report, Harare, African Institute for Agrarian Studies, 2 June.

Moyo, Sam *et al.* 1989. 'Medium and Long Term Prospects for Economic Development and Employment in Zimbabwe: Agriculture', Harare, Zimbabwe Institute of Development Studies.

Moyo, Sam and Prosper Matondi. 2001. 'Conflict Dimensions of Zimbabwe's Land Reform Process', ms, Harare, May.

Moyo, Sam and Tor Skalnes. 1990. 'Zimbabwe's Land Reform and Development Strategy: State Autonomy, Class Bias and Economic Rationality', Zimbabwe Institute of Development Studies, Research Papers, Harare.

Moyo, Sam and Paris Yeros. Forthcoming. 'Land Occupations and Land Reform in Zimbabwe: Towards the National Democratic Revolution', in Sam Moyo and Paris Yeros (eds), *Reclaiming the Land: The Resurgence of Rural Movements in Africa, Asia, and Latin America* (London, Zed Books).

Mugabe, Robert Gabriel. n.d. 'Inside the Third Chimurenga', ms.

— 1983. *Our War of Liberation: Speeches, Articles, Interviews, 1976–1979* (Gweru, Mambo Press).

Mukamuri, B. B. 1995. 'Local Environmental Conservation Strategies: Karanga Religion, Politics and Environmental Control', *Environment and History*, 1, 3, 297–312.

Mumbengegwi, Clever. 1986. 'Continuity and Change in Agricultural Policy', in Ibbo Mandaza (ed.), *Zimbabwe: The Political Economy of Transition 1980–1986* (Dakar, Codesria).

Munro, William. 1995. 'Building the Post-Colonial State: Villagization and Resource Management in Zimbabwe', *Politics and Society*, 23, 1, 107–40.

— 1998. *The Moral Economy of the State: Conservation, Community Development, and State Making in Zimbabwe* (Athens, University of Ohio Press).

Murapa, Rukudzo. 1984. 'Race and the Public Service in Zimbabwe, 1890–1983', in Michael Schatzberg (ed.), *The Political Economy of Zimbabwe* (New York, Praeger).

— 1986. 'Rural and District Administrative Reform in Zimbabwe', Bordeaux, Centre d'Etude d'Afrique Noire.

Murray, D. J. 1970. *The Governmental System in Southern Rhodesia* (Oxford, Clarendon Press).

Mutizwa-Mangiza, Naison. 1991. 'Decentralization and Local Government Administration. An Analysis of Structural and Planning Problems at the Rural District Level', in A. H. J. Helmsing *et al.*, *Limits to Decentralization in Zimbabwe: Essays on the Decentralization of Government and Planning in the 1980s* (The Hague, Institute of Social Sciences).

Ncube, Welshman. 1989. 'The Post-unity Period: Developments, Benefits and Problems', in Canaan Banana (ed.), *Turmoil and Tenacity: Zimbabwe 1890–1990* (Harare, College Press).

— 1991. 'Constitutionalism, Democracy and Political Practice in Zimbabwe', in Ibbo Mandaza and Lloyd Sachikonye (eds), *The One Party State and Democracy: The Zimbabwe Debate* (Harare, SAPES).

Nkala, Collett. 1988. 'Surrender! Rebels take the chance to come in from the cold', *Parade*, July.

— 1989. 'Peace returns – but militia are now jobless', *Parade*, April.

Nobbs, Eric A. 1927. 'The Native Cattle of Southern Rhodesia', *South African Journal of Science*, 24, 328–42.

Ntabeni, Faith. 1986. 'Land Deprivation: The Root of Underdevelopment in Mzingwane District, 1930-1960', MA thesis, University of Zimbabwe.

Nyambara, Pius S. 2001a. 'The Closing Frontier: Agrarian Change, Immigrants and the "Squatter Menace" in Gokwe, 1980-1990s', *Journal of Agrarian Change*, 1, 4, 534–49.

— 2001b. 'Immigrants, "Traditional" Leaders and the Rhodesian State: The Power of "Communal" Land Tenure and the Politics of Land Acquisition in Gokwe, Zimbabwe, 1963-1979', *Journal of Southern African Studies*, 27, 4, 771-92.

O'Flaherty, Michael. 1998. 'Communal Tenure in Zimbabwe: Divergent Models of Collective Land Holding in the Communal Lands', *Africa*, 68, 4, 537-57.

Oomen, B. 2000. '"We must now go back to our history": Retraditionalisation in a Northern Province Chieftaincy', *African Studies*, 59, 1, 71-96.

Palmer, Robin. 1977a. 'The Agricultural History of Rhodesia', in Robin Palmer and Neil Parsons (eds), *The Roots of Rural Poverty in Central and Southern Africa* (London, Heinemann).

— 1977b. *Land and Racial Domination in Rhodesia* (London, Heinemann, 1977).

— 1990. 'Land Reform in Zimbabwe, 1980-1990', *African Affairs*, 89, 355, 163-81.

Palmer, Robin and Neil Parsons (eds). 1977. *The Roots of Rural Poverty in Central and Southern Africa* (London, Heinemann).

Passmore, Gloria. 1972. *The National Policy of Community Development in Rhodesia* (Salisbury, University of Rhodesia).

— n.d. 'Editor's Introduction', in Gloria Passmore (ed.), *H. R. G. Howman on Provincialisation in Rhodesia, 1968-1969*, Cambridge African Occasional papers, 4.

Phimister, Ian. 1986. 'Discourse and the discipline of historical context: Conservationism and ideas about development in Southern Rhodesia, 1930-1950', *Journal of Southern African Studies*, 12, 2, 263-75.

— 1988a. 'The Combined and Contradictory Inheritance of the Struggle against Colonialism', in Colin Stoneman (ed.), *Zimbabwe's Prospects: Issues of Race, Class, State, and Capital in Southern Africa* (London, Macmillan).

— 1988b. *An Economic and Social History of Zimbabwe, 1890-1948: Capital Accumulation and Class Struggle* (London, Longman).

— 1993. 'Rethinking the Reserves: Southern Rhodesia's Land Husbandry Act Reviewed', *Journal of Southern African Studies*, 19, 2, 225-39.

Potts, Deborah and Chris Mutambirwa. 1990. 'Rural-Urban Linkages in Contemporary Harare: Why Migrants Need Their Land', *Journal of Southern African Studies*, 16, 4, 677-98.

Prescott, J. R. V. 1961. 'Overpopulation and Overstocking in the Native Areas of Matabeleland', *Geographical Journal*, 127, 2, 212-25.

Raeburn, Michael. 1978. *Black Fire. Narratives from Zimbabwean Guerrillas* (Harare, Zimbabwe Publishing House).

Raftopoulos, Brian. 1996. *Race and Nationalism in a Post-colonial State* (Harare, SAPES Books).

— 1999. 'Problematising Nationalism in Zimbabwe: A Historiographical Review', *Zambezia*, 26, 2, 115-34.

— 2000. 'Constitutionalism and Opposition in Zimbabwe', paper delivered to the African Studies Seminar, Oxford, June.

— 2001a. 'De l'emancipation du mouvement syndical a l'affirmation du MDC', *Politique Africaine*, 81, March, 26-50.

— 2001b. 'The Labour Movement and the Emergence of Opposition Politics in Zimbabwe', in Brian Raftopoulos and Lloyd Sachikonye (eds), *Striking Back: The Labour Movement and the Post-Colonial State in Zimbabwe 1980-2000* (Harare, Weaver Press).

— 2002. 'Briefing: Zimbabwe's 2002 Presidential Elections', *African Affairs*, 101, 404, 413-26.

— 2003. 'The State in Crisis: Authoritarian Nationalism, Selective Citizenship and Distortions of Democracy in Zimbabwe', in Amanda Hammar, Brian Raftopoulos and Stig Jensen (eds), *Zimbabwe's Unfinished Business: Rethinking Land, State and Nation in the Context of Crisis* (Harare, Weaver Press).

— 2004. 'Nation, Race and History in Zimbabwean Politics', in Brian Raftopoulos and Tyrone Savage (eds), *Zimbabwe: Injustice and Political Reconciliation* (Cape Town, Institute for Justice and Reconciliation).

Raftopoulos, Brian and Ian Phimister. 2004. 'Zimbabwe Now: Challenging the Political Economy of Crisis and Coercion', *Historical Materialism*, 12, 4, 355-82.

References

Raftopoulos, Brian and Lloyd Sachikonye (eds). 2001. *Striking Back: The Labour Movement and the Post-colonial State in Zimbabwe 1980-2000* (Harare, Weaver Press).

Ranger, Terence. 1970. *The African Voice in Southern Rhodesia* (London, Heinemann).

— 1978. 'Growing from the Roots: Reflections on Peasant Research in Central and Southern Africa', *Journal of Southern African Studies*, 5, 1, 99-133.

— 1979. *Revolt in Southern Rhodesia, 1896-7* (London, Heinemann).

— 1982a. 'Survival, Revival and Disaster: Shona Traditional Elites Under Colonialism', Round Table on Elites and Colonialism, Paris, July.

— 1982b. 'Tradition and Travesty: Chiefs and the Administration in Makoni District, Zimbabwe, 1960-1980', *Africa*, 52, 3, 20-41.

— 1983. 'The Invention of Tradition in Colonial Africa', in E. Hobsbawm and T. Ranger (eds), *The Invention of Tradition* (Cambridge, Cambridge University Press).

— 1985a. *The Invention of Tribalism in Zimbabwe* (Gweru, Mambo Press).

— 1985b. *Peasant Consciousness and Guerrilla War in Zimbabwe* (Harare, Zimbabwe Publishing House).

— 1988. 'The Communal Areas of Zimbabwe', Symposium on Land Reform in African Agrarian Systems, University of Illinois, Urbana-Champaign, 10-12 April 1988.

— 1989. 'Matabeleland Since the Amnesty', *African Affairs*, 351, 88, 161-73.

— 1990a. 'The One-Party State Debate and Resettlement Policy in Zimbabwe', London, Britain Zimbabwe Society, ms.

— 1990b. 'The Sequence of Opposition in (and from) Filabusi', St. Antony's College, Oxford, notes.

— 1991. 'Religion and Witchcraft in Everyday Life in Contemporary Zimbabwe', in Preben Kaarsholm (ed.), *Cultural Struggle and Development in Southern Africa* (London, James Currey).

— 1993. 'The Invention of Tradition Revisited: The Case of Colonial Africa', in T. Ranger and O. Vaughan (eds), *Legitimacy and the State in Twentieth Century Africa* (Houndsmills, Macmillan).

— 1999. *Voices from the Rocks: Nature, Culture and History in the Matopos Hills of Zimbabwe* (Oxford, James Currey).

— 2001. 'Democracy and Traditional Political Structures in Zimbabwe, 1890-1999', in Ngwabi Bhebe and Terence Ranger (eds), *The Historical Dimensions of Democracy and Human Rights in Zimbabwe. Volume One: Pre-colonial and Colonial Legacies* (Harare, University of Zimbabwe Press).

— 2002a. 'The Zimbabwean Presidential Elections: A Personal Experience', *Zimbabwe Review*, Britain Zimbabwe Society, 02/2, May.

— 2002b. 'Zimbabwe's "cultural revolution"', Oxford, ms.

— 2004. 'Nationalist Historiography, Patriotic History and the History of the Nation: The Struggle over the Past in Zimbabwe', *Journal of Southern African Studies*, 30, 2, 215-34.

Ranger, Terence and Mark Ncube. 1996. 'Religion in the Guerrilla War: The Case of Southern Matabeleland', in Ngwabi Bhebe and Terence Ranger (eds), *Society in Zimbabwe's Liberation War* (Oxford, James Currey).

Rathbone, Richard. 2000. *Nkrumah and the Chiefs: The Politics of Chieftaincy in Ghana, 1951-60* (Oxford, James Currey).

Reeler, Tony. 2003. 'The Role of Militia Groups in Maintaining Zanu PF's Political Power', March.

Rennie, J. K. 1973. 'Christianity, Colonialism and the Origins of Nationalism Among the Ndau of Southern Rhodesia, 1890-1935', PhD, Northwestern University.

— 1978. 'White Farmers, Black Tenants and Landlord Legislation: Southern Rhodesia, 1890-1930', *Journal of Southern African Studies*, 5, 1, 86-98.

Reynolds, N. and P. Ivy. 1984. *Proposals for a National Land Use Programme* (Harare, Agritex).

Reynolds, Pamela. 1990. 'Children of Tribulation: The Need to Heal and the Means to Heal War Trauma', *Africa*, 60, 1, 1-38.

Rhodesian Front. 1974. *Provincialization*, Mimeo.

Rich Dorman, Sara. 2001. 'Inclusion and Exclusion: NGOs and Politics in Zimbabwe', DPhil thesis, Oxford.

— 2002. '"Rocking the Boat?": Church NGOs and Democratization in Zimbabwe', *African Affairs*, 101, 402, 75-92.

— 2003. 'NGOs and the Constitutional Debate in Zimbabwe: From Inclusion to Exclusion', *Journal of Southern African Studies*, 29, 4, 845-64.

Riddell, Roger. 1979. 'Prospects for Land Reform in Zimbabwe', *Rural Africana*, 4-5, 17-32.

— 1988. *Industrialisation in Sub-Saharan Africa. Phase One: Country Case Study – Zimbabwe* (London, Overseas Development Institute).

Robins, Steven. 1994. 'Contesting the Social Geography of State Power: A Case Study of Land-Use Planning in Matabeleland, Zimbabwe', *Social Dynamics*, 20, 2, 119-37.

— 1998. 'Breaking out of the Straitjacket of Tradition: The Politics and Rhetoric of "Development" in Zimbabwe', *World Development*, 26, 9, 1677-94.

Roe, Emery. 1995. 'More than the Politics of Decentralization: Local Government Reform, District Development and Public Administration in Zimbabwe', *World Development*, 23, 5, 833-43.

Rutherford, Blair. 2001a. 'Commercial Farm Workers and the Politics of (Dis)placement in Zimbabwe: Colonialism, Liberation and Democracy', *Journal of Agrarian Change*, 1, 4, 626-51.

— 2001b. *Working on the Margins: Black Workers, White Farmers in Postcolonial Zimbabwe* (London, Zed Books).

— 2002. 'Zimbabwe: The Politics of Land and the Political Landscape', *Green Left Weekly*, 487, 10 April.

— 2004. 'Desired Publics, Domestic Government and Entangled Fears: On the Anthropology of Civil Society, Farm Workers and White Farmers in Zimbabwe', *Cultural Anthropology*, 19, 4, 122-53.

Sachikonye, Lloyd M. 1986. 'State, Capital and Trade Unions', in Ibbo Mandaza (ed.), *Zimbabwe: The Political Economy of Transition 1980-1986* (Dakar, Codesria).

— 2002. 'Whither Zimbabwe? Crisis and Democratisation', *Review of African Political Economy*, 91, 13-20.

— 2003. 'The Situation of Commercial Farm Workers after Land Reform in Zimbabwe', Report prepared for the Farm Community Trust of Zimbabwe, May.

— 2004. 'The Promised Land: From Expropriation to Reconciliation and *Jambanja*', in Brian Raftopoulos and Tyrone Savage (eds), *Zimbabwe: Injustice and Political Reconciliation* (Cape Town, Institute for Justice and Reconciliation).

Samasuwo, Nhamo. 2003. 'Food Production and War Supplies: Rhodesia's Beef Industry during the Second World War, 1939-1945', *Journal of Southern African Studies*, 29, 2, 487-502.

Sandford, S. 1982. *Livestock in the Communal Areas of Zimbabwe* (London, Overseas Development Institute).

Schmidt, Elizabeth. 1990. 'Negotiated Spaces and Contested Terrain: Men, Women, and the Law in Colonial Zimbabwe, 1890-1939', *Journal of Southern African Studies*, 16, 4, 622-48.

— 1992. *Peasants, Traders and Wives: Shona Women in the History of Zimbabwe, 1870-1939* (London, James Currey).

Scoones, Ian. 1990. 'Livestock Populations and the Household Economy: A Case Study from Southern Zimbabwe', PhD thesis, University of London.

Scoones, Ian and Ken Wilson. 1988. 'Households, Lineage Groups and Ecological Dynamics: Issues for Livestock Research and Development in Zimbabwe's Communal Areas', in B. Cousins, C. Jackson and Ian Scoones (eds), *Socio-Economic Dimensions of Livestock Production in the Communal Lands of Zimbabwe* (Harare, Centre for Applied Social Studies).

Scott, James C. 1976. *The Moral Economy of the Peasant* (New Haven, Yale University Press).

— 1985. *Weapons of the Weak* (New Haven, Yale University Press).

— 1998. *Seeing Like a State: How Certain Schemes to Improve the Human Condition have Failed* (New Haven, Yale University Press).

Sibanda, Sipho [ORAP], Reverend Osborne Mpofu [Methodist Church] and Moses Dlamini [ORAP]. 1986. 'The Political Economy of Drought in Matabeleland South: An Analysis of the Extent and Effects of Drought, Immediate Remedial Measures and Long Term Alternatives', Report prepared for Oxfam, Bulawayo, April.

Sinclair, Shirley. 1971. *The Story of Melsetter* (Salisbury, M. O. Collins).

References

Sithole, Ndabaningi. 1970. *Obed Mutezo: The Mudzimu Christian Nationalist* (London, Oxford University Press).

Smith, Randal. 1992a. "'There and Back Again": The Integration of Unofficial Courts in Southern Rhodesia', SOAS, African History Seminar, 29 April.

— 1992b. "'Traditional Leaders" and Native Commissioners', SOAS, London, ms.

Solidarity Peace Trust. 2003. 'National Youth Training Service: "Shaping youths in a truly Zimbabwean manner". An overview of youth militia training and activities in Zimbabwe, October 2000–August 2003', 5 September.

Spierenburg, Marja. 2004. *Strangers, Spirits and Land Reforms: Conflicts about Land in Dande, Northern Zimbabwe* (Leiden, Brill).

Steele, M. C. 1972. 'The Foundations of a "Native" Policy in Southern Rhodesia, 1923-33', PhD, Simon Fraser University.

Stoneman, Colin. 1988a. 'The Economy: Recognising the Reality', in Colin Stoneman (ed.), *Zimbabwe's Prospects: Issues of Race, Class, State, and Capital in Southern Africa* (London, Macmillan).

— (ed.). 1988b. *Zimbabwe's Prospects: Issues of Race, Class, State, and Capital in Southern Africa* (London, Macmillan).

Stoneman, Colin and Lionel Cliffe. 1989. *Zimbabwe: Politics, Economics and Society* (London, Pinter Publishers).

Summers, C. 2002. *Colonial Lessons: Africans' Education in Southern Rhodesia, 1918-1940* (Oxford, James Currey).

Sylvester, Christine. 1985. 'Continuity and Discontinuity in Zimbabwe's Development History', *African Studies Review*, 28, 1, 19-44.

— 1986. 'Zimbabwe's 1985 Elections: A Search for National Mythology', *Journal of Modern African Studies*, 24, 1, 229-55.

Suzuki, Yuka and Eric Worby (eds). 2001. *Zimbabwe: The Politics of Crisis and the Crisis of Politics* (New Haven, Yale Center for International and Area Studies).

Thomas, Stephen J. 1991. *The Legacy of Dualism and Decision-Making: The Prospects for Local Institutional Development in 'Campfire'* (Harare, University of Zimbabwe, Centre for Applied Social Sciences).

Thornycroft, Peta. 1989a. 'Massive Investment in Eastern Border Co-operatives', *Parade*, February, 6.

— 1989b. 'Resettlement Blunders Leave Co-op Homeless, Christmas in the Cold for Evicted Co-operators', *Parade*, February, 7-8.

Tshuma, Lawrence. 1997. *A Matter of (In)justice: Law, State and the Agrarian Question in Zimbabwe* (Harare, SAPES Books).

'Tribal Psychology and Tribal Structure'. 1966. *NADA*, 9, 3, 15-27.

UNDP. 2002. *Zimbabwe. Land Reform and Resettlement: Assessment and Suggested Framework for the Future*, Interim Mission Report (New York, UNDP).

Vail, Leroy (ed.). 1989a. *The Creation of Tribalism in Southern Africa* (London, James Currey).

— 1989b. 'Introduction', in Leroy Vail (ed.), *The Creation of Tribalism in Southern Africa* (London, James Currey).

Van Onselen, Charles. 1973. 'The Role of Collaborators in the Rhodesian Mining Industry, 1900-1935', *African Affairs*, 72, 289, 401-18.

— 1980. *Chibaro. African Mine Labour in Southern Rhodesia, 1900-1933* (Johannesburg, Ravan Press).

Van Rouveroy van Nieuwaal, E. A. B. (ed.). 1987. 'Chieftaincy and the State in Africa', special issue of the *Journal of Legal Pluralism*, 25, 6.

Van Rouveroy van Nieuwaal, E. A. B. and Rijk van Dijk (eds). 1999. *African Chieftaincy in a New Socio-Political Landscape* (Hamburg, Lit Verlag).

Weiner, Daniel. 1988. 'Land and Agricultural Development', in Colin Stoneman (ed.), *Zimbabwe's Prospects: Issues of Race, Class, State, and Capital in Southern Africa* (London, Macmillan).

— 1989. 'Agricultural Restructuring in Zimbabwe and South Africa', *Development and Change*, 20, 3, 401-28.

References

Weiner, Daniel *et al.* 1985. 'Land use and agricultural productivity in Zimbabwe', *Journal of Modern African Studies*, 23, 2, 251-85.

Weinmann, H. 1974. *Agricultural Research and Development in Southern Rhodesia Under the Rule of the British South Africa Company 1890-1923*, Department of Agriculture, Occasional Paper No. 4 (Salisbury, University of Rhodesia).

— 1975. *Agricultural Research and Development in Southern Rhodesia 1924-1950* (Salisbury, University of Rhodesia).

Weinrich, A. K. H. 1964. 'The social background of agriculture in Chilimanzi Reserve', *Rhodes-Livingstone Institute Journal*, 36, 7-39.

— 1971. *Chiefs and Councils in Rhodesia: Transition from Patriarchal to Bureaucratic Power* (London, Heinemann).

— 1975. *African Farmers in Rhodesia* (London, Oxford University Press).

— 1977. 'Strategic Resettlement in Rhodesia', *Journal of Southern African Studies*, 3, 3, 207-29.

Weitzer, Ronald. 1984. 'In Search of Regime Security: Zimbabwe Since Independence', *Journal of Modern African Studies*, 22, 4, 529-57.

Wekwete, K. 1991. 'Decentralized Planning in Zimbabwe. A Review of Provincial, Urban and District-level Development Planning', in A. H. J. Helmsing *et al.*, *Limits to Decentralization in Zimbabwe: Essays on the Decentralization of Government and Planning in the 1980s* (The Hague, Institute of Social Sciences).

Wekwete, K. and A. H. J. Helmsing. 1986. 'Financing District Councils: Local Taxes and Central Allocations', Third Annual Congress of the Association of District Councils, Kariba, 15-17 October.

Werbner, Richard. 1991. *Tears of the Dead: The Social Biography of an African Family* (London, Edinburgh University Press).

— 1998. 'Smoke from the Barrel of a Gun: Postwars of the Dead, Memory and Reinscription in Zimbabwe', in Richard Werbner (ed.), *Memory and the Postcolony* (London, Zed Books).

Werbner, Richard and Terence Ranger (eds). 1996. *Postcolonial Identities in Africa* (London, Zed Books).

White, Luise. 2003. *The Assassination of Herbert Chitepo: Texts and Politics in Zimbabwe* (Bloomington, Indiana University Press).

Whitsun Foundation. 1978. *A Strategy for Rural Development*. Data Bank No. 2, The Peasant Sector, Salisbury.

— 1983. *Land Reform in Zimbabwe* (Harare).

Willems, Wendy. 2004. 'Peasant Demonstrators, Violent Invaders: Representations of Land in the Zimbabwean Press', *World Development*, 32, 10, 1767-83.

Williams, Gavin. 1982. 'Equity, Growth and the State', *Africa*, 52, 3, 114-20.

Wilson, Ken B. 1986. 'History, Ecology and Conservation in Southern Zimbabwe', Oxford, ms.

— 1987a. 'Constraints to Development: Peasant Views from Mazvihwa, Zvishavane', Oxford, ms.

— 1987b. 'Research on Trees in the Mazvihwa and Surrounding Areas', ENDA-Zimbabwe, Harare, ms.

— 1989. 'Trees in Fields in Southern Zimbabwe', *Journal of Southern African Studies*, 15, 2, 369-83.

— 1990. 'Ecological Dynamics and Human Welfare: A Case Study of Population, Health and Nutrition in Southern Zimbabwe', PhD, University College London.

— 1992. 'The impact of drought and structural adjustment on household livelihood and welfare in the Mazvihwa Communal Area of Zvishavane District of Southern Zimbabwe', Refugee Studies Programme and Oxfam, Oxford, September.

— n.d. 'Access to Arable Land', Oxford, ms.

Wolmer, William and Ian Scoones. 2000. 'The Science of "Civilized" Agriculture: The Mixed Farming Discourse in Zimbabwe', *African Affairs*, 99, 397, 575-600.

Wood, Brian. 1988. 'Trade Union Organisation and the Working Class', in Colin Stoneman (ed.), *Zimbabwe's Prospects: Issues of Race, Class, State, and Capital in Southern Africa* (London, Macmillan).

213

References

Worby, Eric. 1994. 'Maps, Names and Ethnic Games: The Iconography and Epistemology of Colonial Power in Northwestern Zimbabwe', *Journal of Southern African Studies*, 20, 3, 371-92.

— 1995. 'What does Agrarian Wage Labour Signify? Cotton, Commodotisation, and Social Form in Gokwe, Zimbabwe', *Journal of Peasant Studies*, 23, 1, 1-29.

— 1998. 'Tyranny, Parody and Ethnic Polarity: Ritual Engagements with the State in Northwestern Zimbabwe', *Journal of Southern African Studies*, 24, 3, 561-78.

— 2000. '"Discipline without Oppression": Sequence, Timing and Marginality in Southern Rhodesia's Post-War Development Regime', *Journal of African History*, 41, 1, 101-25.

— (ed.). 2001a. 'The New Agrarian Politics in Zimbabwe', special issue of the *Journal of Agrarian Change*, 1, 4.

— 2001b. 'A Redivided Land? New Agrarian Conflicts and Questions in Zimbabwe', *Journal of Agrarian Change*, 1, 4, 475-509.

— 2003. 'The End of Modernity in Zimbabwe? Passages from Development to Sovereignty', in Amanda Hammar, Brian Raftopoulos, and Stig Jensen (eds), *Zimbabwe's Unfinished Business: Rethinking Land, State and Nation in the Context of Crisis* (Harare, Weaver Press).

World Bank. 1985. *Zimbabwe: Land Sector Study*, Report No. 5878-ZIM.

— 1991. *Zimbabwe: Agriculture Sector Memorandum.* Volume 2, Main Report, Report No. 9429-ZIM.

Yeros, Paris. 1999. 'Peasant Struggles for Land and Security in Zimbabwe: A Global Moral Economy at the Close of the Twentieth Century', ms.

— 2000. 'Labour Struggles for Alternative Economics in Zimbabwe: Trade Union Nationalism and Internationalism in a Global Era', ms.

— 2002a. 'The Political Economy of Civilisation: Peasant-Workers in Zimbabwe and the Neo-colonial World', PhD thesis, LSE, London.

— 2002b. 'Zimbabwe and the Dilemmas of the Left', *Historical Materialism*, 10, 2, 3-15.

Young, Tom. 2003. 'Introduction', in Tom Young (ed.), *Readings in African Politics* (Oxford, James Currey).

Yudelman, Montague. 1964. *Africans on the Land* (Cambridge, Mass., Harvard University Press).

Zanu(PF), Department of the Commissariat and Culture. n.d. [1985]. *Zimbabwe at Five Years of Independence: Achievements, Problems and Prospects* (Harare, Mardon Printers).

Zimbabwe Institute. 2004. 'Playing with Fire'. Johannesburg, March.

Zimbabwe Election Support Network. 2002. 'Preliminary Summary of Insiza By-Election', 31 October.

Zimbabwe Human Rights NGO Forum. 2001. 'Politically Motivated Violence in Zimbabwe, 2000-2001. A report on the Campaign of Political Repression Conducted by the Zimbabwean Government under the Guise of Carrying out Land Reform', Harare, July.

— 2002a. 'Are they Accountable? Examining Alleged Violators and their Violations Pre and Post the Presidential Election, March 2002', Harare, December.

— 2002b. 'Political Violence Report: September 2002', Harare, 9 October.

—. 2002c. 'Vote ZANU(PF) or Starve', Harare.

Zimbabwe Lawyers for Human Rights. 2003. 'Press Release on Local Government Elections', Harare, 22 July.

— 2004. 'Chaos in Parliament of Zimbabwe. MP Momentarily Detained', Harare, 18 May.

Government of Zimbabwe Sources

Agricultural and Rural Development Authority. 1985. *Communal Area Development Report No. 13, South Matabeleland, Glassblock Communal Area Baseline Survey* (Harare, ARDA).

Agritex. 1988. 'The Communal Area Reorganisation Program: Agritex Approach', Discussion paper, Harare, July.

— n.d. [1988]. 'The Sidzibe Ward 5 Plan Report', Filabusi.

Central Statistical Office. various dates. *Grain Marketing Board Annual Report*.
— various dates. *Cotton Marketing Board Annual Reports*.
Chimanimani District Development Committee. n.d. [1986]. *Chimanimani District Five Year Development Plan*.
Department of Rural Development. 1983. 'Progress Report on the Intensive and Accelerated Resettlement Programme', Harare.
— 1987. 'Action Plan: Hurungwe District Squatter Committee', 28 January.
Department of Rural Development, Ministry of Local Government, Rural and Urban Development in collaboration with the FAO of the UN. 1987. 'Report on the National Symposium on Agrarian Reform in Zimbabwe' [Nyanga Symposium], Nyanga, 19-23 October.
— 1988. 'Summary Report of the Seminar on Agrarian Reform and Communal Land Reorganisation' [Harare Agrarian Reform Seminar], Harare, 4-5 August.
Government of Zimbabwe. 1981a. *Growth with Equity: An Economic Policy Statement* (Harare, Government Printer).
— 1981b. *Report of the Commission of Inquiry into Incomes, Prices and Conditions of Service* [Riddell Commission], Chairman R. Riddell.
— 1982a. *District Council Handbook*, Vol. I, Administrative (Harare, Government Printer).
— 1982b. *Report of the Commission of Inquiry into the Agricultural Industry* [Chavanduka Commission], Chairman Professor G. L. Chavanduka.
— 1982c. *Transitional National Development Plan: 1982/83-1984/85*, Vol. 1 (Harare, Amalgamated Press).
— 1986. *First Five-Year National Development Plan: 1986-1990*, Vol. 1 (Harare, Government Printer).
— 1988. *First Five-Year National Development Plan: 1986-1990*, Vol. 2 (Harare, Government Printer).
— 1989. *Report of the Commission of Inquiry into the Distribution of Motor Vehicles* [Sandura Commission], Chairman Justice Sandura (Harare, Government Printer).
— 1998. *Land Reform and Resettlement Programme Phase II. A Policy Framework* (Harare, June).
— 2000. *Accelerated Land Reform and Resettlement Implementation Plan: 'Fast Track'* (Harare).
— 2003. *Report of the Presidential Land Review Committee on the Implementation of the Fast Track Land Reform Programme, 2000-2002* [Utete Report], Chairman Charles M. B. Utete (Harare).
Land Tenure Commission. 1994. *Report of the Commission of Inquiry into Appropriate Agricultural Land Tenure Systems*, vol. 1 (Harare, Government Printers).
Manicaland Provincial Development Committee. 1985. *Manicaland Provincial Development Plan*, Vol. 1, draft study, prepared on behalf of the Manicaland Provincial Council, September.
Mashonaland West Provincial Development Committee, Council, and Squatter Control Committee. n.d. [1987]. 'Mashonaland West Squatter Problem: Towards Effective Action', Compiled by F. H. Munyira, Provincial Administrator and Chairman, Provincial Squatter Control Committee.
Matabeleland South Provincial Development Committee. 1985. *Matabeleland South Provincial Development Plan, 1985/86-1989/90* (Bulawayo).
— 1988. *Matabeleland South Provincial Annual Development Plan, 1988/89* (Bulawayo, May).
— 1989. *Matabeleland South Provincial Annual Development Plan, 1989/90* (Bulawayo, January).
Ministry of Economic Planning and Development. 1981. *Zimbabwe Conference on Reconstruction and Development (ZIMCORD): Report on Conference Proceedings* (Salisbury, Government Printer).
Ministry of Information, Posts and Telecommunications. n.d. *Provincial Governorship of Zimbabwe* (Harare, Government Printer).
Ministry of Lands, Resettlement and Rural Development. 1981. *Intensive Resettlement: Policies and Procedures* (Harare, Government Printer).
— 1985. *Communal Lands Development Plan: A 15-Year Development Strategy*, first draft (Harare).
Ministry of Local Government and Town Planning. 1985. *1984 Delineation of Village and Ward*

Development Committee Areas in District Council Areas of Zimbabwe (Harare, Government Printer).

Ministry of Local Government, Rural and Urban Development. 1985. Circular No. 10, Addendum A, circulated to District Councils.

— 1986. 'Policy: Allocation of Land within Communal Lands', Circular Minute 1/1986 to District Councils.

— 1987a. 'District and Rural Councils: Committee Officers Training Report', February–March.

— 1987b. 'Resettlement Progress Report as at August 31, 1987', Harare.

Government of (Southern) Rhodesia Sources

Central Statistical Office. 1962. *Sample Survey of African Agriculture* (Salisbury, Government Printer).

Government of Rhodesia. 1971. *Report of the Secretary for Internal Affairs for the year 1970* (Salisbury, Government Printer).

— 1973. *Report of the Secretary for Internal Affairs for the year 1972* (Salisbury, Government Printer).

— 1974. *Report of the Secretary for Internal Affairs for the year 1973* (Salisbury, Government Printer).

— 1979. *Integrated Plan for Rural Development* (Salisbury, Ministry of Finance).

Government of Southern Rhodesia. 1925. *Report of the Land Commission* [Morris Carter Commission], Chairman W. Morris Carter.

— 1944. *Report of the Native Production and Trade Commission* [Godlonton Commission], Chairman W.A. Godlonton.

— 1955. *What the Native Land Husbandry Act Means to the Rural African and to Southern Rhodesia* (Salisbury, Government Printer).

— 1959. *Annual Report of the Director for Native Agriculture for the Year 1958*, R. M. Davies (March).

— 1960. *Second Report of the Select Committee on Resettlement of Natives* [Quinton Report], (Salisbury, Government Printer).

— 1961a. *Report of the Commission Appointed to Inquire into and Report on the Administrative and Judicial Functions in the Native Affairs and District Courts Departments* [Robinson Commission], Chairman Sir Victor Robinson (Salisbury, Government Printer).

— 1961b. *Report of the Mangwende Reserve Commission of Inquiry* [Mangwende Commission], Chairman J. S. Brown (Salisbury, Government Printer).

— 1962a. *First Report of the Commission of Inquiry into the Organisation of the Southern Rhodesia Public Services* [Paterson Commission], Chairman T. T. Paterson (Salisbury, Government Printer).

— 1962b. *Report of the Advisory Committee on the Economic Development of Southern Rhodesia with particular reference to the Role of African Agriculture* [Phillips Commission], Chairman John Phillips (Salisbury, Government Printer).

— 1962c. *Report of the Secretary for Native Affairs and Chief Native Commissioner for the Year 1961* (Salisbury, Government Printer).

— 1962d. *African Local Government in British East and Central Africa. A Report by R. H. Howman. Southern Rhodesia 1951-1953.*

— 1964. *Report of the Secretary for Native Affairs and Chief Native Commissioner for the year 1963* (Salisbury, Government Printer).

Ministry of Internal Affairs. 1963a. Delineation Report, Mapenga Community: Chief Ndube, Glassblock TTL, B. N. Gaunt, District Commissioner, and A. D. Elliot, Delineation Team, 9 December.

— 1963b. Delineation Report, Ndube Community: Chief Ndube, Glassblock TTL, Filabusi District, A. D. Elliot, Delineation team, 15 December.

— 1963c. Delineation Report, Sibasa Community: Chief Sibasa, Insiza TTL, Filabusi District, A. D. Elliot, Delineation Team, 13 September.

— 1963d. Delineation Report, Velapi Community: Chief Maduna, Godhlwayo TTL, Filabusi District, A. D. Elliot, Delineation Team, 24 December.

— 1964a. Delineation Report, Bafana Community: Chief Maduna, Godhlwayo TTL, Filabusi District, A. D. Elliot, Delineation Team, 7 January.

— 1964b. Delineation Report, Godhlwayo NPA Community, Filabusi District, B. N. Gaunt, District Commissioner, and A. D. Elliot, Delineation Team, 9 January.

— 1964c. Delineation Report, Gwatemba Community: Gwatemba NPA, Filabusi District, B. N. Gaunt, District Commissioner, and A. D. Elliot, Delineation Team, 9 January.

— 1964d. Delineation Report, Maduna Chieftaincy: Godhlwayo TTL, Insiza District, B. N. Gaunt, District Commissioner, and A. D. Elliot, Delineation Officer, 11 January.

— 1964e. Delineation Report, Ngomondo Community: Chief Maduna, Godhlwayo TTL, Filabusi District, A. D. Elliot, Delineation Team, 8 January.

— 1964f. Delineation Report, Nhlogotshane Community: Chief Maduna, Godhlwayo TTL, Filabusi District, A. D. Elliot, 27 August.

— 1965a. Delineation Report, Chikukwa Chiefdom: Martin Forest Estate, National Land, Melsetter District, C. J. K. Latham, November.

— 1965b. Delineation Report, Dzingiri Community: Chief Muushu, Ngorima TTL, Melsetter District, November.

— 1965c. Delineation Report, Guriyanga Community: Chief Muushu, Muushu TTL, Melsetter District, C. J. K. Latham, November.

— 1965d. Delineation Report, Mutambara Chiefdom: Mutambara TTL, Melsetter District, C. J. K. Latham, November.

— 1965e. Delineation Report, Muushu Chiefdom: Muushu and Ngorima TTL, Melsetter District, November 1965.

— 1965f. Delineation Report, Ndima Chiefdom: Ndima TTL, Melsetter District, C. J. K. Latham, November 1965.

— 1965g. Delineation Report, Ngorima Chiefdom: Ngorima TTL, Melsetter District, C. J. K. Latham, November 1965.

— 1965h. Delineation Report, Tribal Trust Lands in Melsetter District: General Report, C. J. K. Latham, Senior Delineation Officer, November.

Chimanimani District Records

Ministry of Local Government, Correspondence Files.

Ministry of Local Government, PER 5 and PER 4 Chiefs' and Headmen's Files.

Minutes of District Resettlement Meetings, Chimanimani, 11 November 1987.

Minutes of the Manicaland Provincial Council of Chiefs, Mutare, 5 January 1989.

Minutes of the Mabvazuwa District Council and Sub-committee for Conservation, Chimanimani, 1980s.

Minutes of a Meeting at the District Commissioner's Conference Hall, Melsetter, 27 February 1981.

Minutes of Meetings for the Formation of a District Council in Melsetter, Melsetter, various dates in 1980.

Minutes of Provincial District Administrators' Meetings, Mutare, 7 August 1987; Chimanimani, 30 October 1987.

Minutes of the (Provincial) Meeting with the Deputy Minister of Lands, Resettlement and Rural Development at the Office of the Under Secretary (Development), Mutare, 1 October 1981.

Minutes of Special Meetings of the Mabvazuwa District Council and Party Representatives, Chimanimani, 9 April 1986; 18 May 1986.

Minutes of the Squatter Control Committee, Chimanimani, 21 April 1988, 2 August 1988, 30 September 1988.

Insiza District Records

Agritex. n.d. [1988]. 'The Sidzibe Ward 5 Plan Report'.

Chiefs' and Headmen's Meetings, Filabusi, 6 June 1964 to 20 January 1978.

Insiza District Conference, Filabusi Minutes, 6 October 1965 to 6 August 1976.

Insiza District Squatter Control Committee. 1988. 'Squatters' Return', July.

Mberengwa Rural Council. 1987. List of Lessees, 10 September.

Ministry of Local Government, Correspondence Files.

Ministry of Local Government, PER 5 and PER 4 Chiefs' and Headmen's Files.

Minutes of the Insiza District Council, Filabusi, 1980s.

Minutes of the Insiza District Development Committee and Sub-committees, Filabusi, 1980s.

Minutes of the Insiza Reserve and Glassblock and Panasequa Native Occupation Areas Native Council [Insiza Council], Filabusi, 5 August 1948 to 21 March 1950.

Minutes of the Insiza Reserve, Godhlwayo and Glassblock Native Council [Godhlwayo Council], Filabusi, 22 October 1953 to 20 February 1964.

Minutes of the Provincial Governor's Meeting with the Insiza District Council and Representatives of Government Departments, Filabusi, 29 March 1984.

Minutes of the Zhulube Council, Filabusi, 13 August 1969 to 13 February 1979.

Interviews with Officials

Acting District Administrator, Insiza District. Filabusi, 18, 19 August 1988; 1, 26 September 1988; 14 April 1989, 10 August 1990.

Administrative Officer, Chimanimani District. Chimanimani, 16 November 1988, 15 March 1989.

Agritex Irrigation Manager and Agritex Extension Workers, Nyanyadzi Irrigation Scheme, Chimanimani District, Nyanyadzi, 21 November 1988.

Agritex Extension Officers, Chimanimani District, Chimanimani, 24, 25, 28 October 1988, 1, 22 November 1988.

Agritex Extension Officer, Insiza District, Sibasa, 22 August 1988.

Assistant Director (Technical), Agritex, Harare, 21 September 1988.

Assistant Resettlement Officer, Chimanimani District, Shinja Resettlement Scheme, 26 October 1988.

Chairman, Nsiza Rural Council, Bulawayo, 11 October 1988.

Chairman, Mabvazuwa District Council, Mhandarume, October 1988.

Chief Planning Officer, Agritex, Harare, 6 April 1989.

Chief Samuel Mutumbara, Chimanimani District, Guhune, 6, 10 November 1988.

Chief Vezi Maduna, Insiza District, Avoca, 14 April 1989.

Commanding Officer, 12th Infantry Battalion, Chimanimani District, Mutambara, 26 October 1988.

Cooperative Development Officer, Ministry of Cooperative Development and Women's Affairs, Chimanimani District, Chimanimani, 26 October 1988.

Councillor, Mberengwa Rural Council and Matabeleland South Provincial Council, 4 October 1988, 13 April 1989, 10 August 1990 and others.

Deputy Secretary, Rural and District Councils, Ministry of Local Government, Rural and Urban Development, Harare, 7 September 1988.

Deputy Director in Charge of Regional Planning, Department of Physical Planning, Harare, 6 September 1988.

Director, Department of Rural Development, Harare, 5 September 1988.

Director, Department of Physical Planning, Harare, 4 August 1988.

District Administrator, Chimanimani District, Chimanimani, 21 November 1988.

District Administrator, Insiza District, Filabusi, 18 July 1991.

District Administrator, Matobo District, Kezi, 19 July 1991.

References

District Agritex Extension Officer, Chimanimani District, Chimanimani, 4, 22 November 1988.

District Agritex Extension Officer, Insiza District, Filabusi, 18 August 1988, 28 September 1988.

District Development Fund Officer, Insiza District, Filabusi, 4 October 1988.

Executive Officer for Administration, Insiza District Council, Filabusi, 15 August 1988, 27 September 1988.

Executive Officer for Administration, Mabvazuwa District Council, Chimanimani, 1, 2 November 1988.

Forestry Commission Manager, Chimanimani District, Cashel, 26 October 1988; Chimanimani, 3 November 1988.

Forestry Commission Research Officer, Harare, 7 August 1990.

Kwirire Cooperative Chairman, Nyahodi Valley, Nyahodi, 18 November 1988.

Local Government Promotion Officers, Chimanimani District, Chimanimani, 24, 25, 31 October 1988, 21 November 1988, 15 March 1989.

Local Government Promotion Officers, Insiza District, Filabusi, 18, 30 August 1988, 3, 4, 5, 7 October 1988, 13 April 1989.

Magistrate, Chimanimani District, Chimanimani, 3 November 1988.

Officer in Charge, Zimbabwe Republic Police, Insiza District, Filabusi, 14 April 1989, 10 August 1990.

Provincial Administrator, Manicaland, Mutare, 24 November 1988.

Provincial Administrator, Matabeleland South, Gwanda, 23 August 1988.

Provincial Agritex Extension Officer, Matabeleland South, Bulawayo, 10 October 1988.

Provincial Planning Officer, Agritex, Bulawayo, 10 October 1988.

Provincial Planning Officer, Department of Rural Development, Manicaland, Mutare, 24 November 1988.

Provincial Planning Officer, Department of Physical Planning, Matabeleland South, Bulawayo, 20, 22 July 1988, 29 September 1988, 29 December 1988, 8 August 1990.

Provincial Promotion and Training Officer, Matabeleland South, Gwanda, 23 August 1988.

Resettlement Officer, Insiza District, Filabusi, 7 October 1988.

Secretary, Chimanimani Rural Council, Chimanimani, 3 November 1988.

Senior Administrative Officer, Chimanimani District, Chimanimani, 20, 24 October 1988, 14 March 1989.

Senior Administrative Officer, Insiza District, Filabusi, 12 April 1989.

Senior Agricultural Extension Officer, Chimanimani District, Chimanimani, 24 October 1988.

Social Services Officer, Department of Social Services, Chimanimani District, Chimanimani, 21 October 1988.

Social Services Officers, Department of Social Services, Insiza District, Filabusi, 28 September 1988.

UNDP Technical Adviser, Department of Rural Development, Harare, 22 March 1989.

Newspapers and Magazines

African Daily News
African Weekly
Bantu Mirror
Chronicle
Daily News
Financial Gazette
Guardian (London)
Harvester
Herald
Horizon

Mail and Guardian (South Africa)
Manica Post
Mirror
Moto
New York Times
Parade
Rhodesia Herald
Sunday Mail
Zimbabwe Independent
Zimbabwe Standard

Also cited are press reviews in *Zimbabwe Project News Bulletin* and Terence Ranger, *Review of the Press*, Britain Zimbabwe Society, various dates.

Index